Endorsements

"Joyce Gerrish is a true pioneer, having started he⬚⬚⬚⬚⬚ forty years ago. I highly recommend *Secrets of Wisdom*. The wisdom she⬚⬚⬚⬚⬚⬚ enrich your life physically, emotionally, mentally, and Spiritually."

Dr. Georgianna Donadio

Founder of National Institute of Whole Health

Author of Best Selling Book, *Changing Behavior*

"Joyce writes wonderful spiritual messages. She is a spiritual teacher whose writings guide the seeker to attain knowledge and wisdom that can lead to a more fulfilling and harmonious life."

Dee Patterson

Publisher and Editor in Chief of Odyssey: Body, Mind, Spirit

"I feel that *Secrets of Wisdom* is a substantial contribution to Spiritual literature. I was intrigued by the idea of each chapter being devoted to enhancing within oneself one of the transformative Divine Qualities such as Forgiveness or Empowerment. Spending some quality time with each chapter is already benefiting me. I also appreciate Joyce's kind, supportive, insightful writing style. It speaks to the heart as well as to one's whole mind/body/Spirit Self. The book is very clear and easy to read--there is no abstruseness about it. I highly recommend it."

Dr. Lynda Wells CNS, LND

"The first three letters of Joyce's name are 'joy.' How appropriate for a messenger of Divine Qualities. And make no mistake--and be aware as you read her words--that Joyce is a Great messenger! She is a messenger in every sense of the meaning of the word messenger."

William Evans, M.D.

"Your soul songs really speak to my heart. They are so beautiful."

Mary Ann Ballard.

"I've been enjoying listening to your soul songs. It is wonderful to hear your voice's beautiful resonances and the uplifting healing energy that shines through!"

Henry Lepler, Musician and Healing Sound Guide (See Resources Page)

"Joyce is very wise, and she is a wonderful artist, musician, and healer. She has helped me tremendously with her healing gifts. *Secrets of Wisdom* is an excellent resource for people in search of inner peace and Spiritual growth. Joyce has been a gift in my life and I'm so thankful."

J.C.

"From reading *Secrets of Wisdom* I have gained insight about issues from my past, and I have learned information and gained inspiration that will guide me Spiritually while traveling my life path. Thank you."

Billie Jo Free

"I felt much "lighter" after our session. You're an Angel! You have helped me immensely over the past twenty plus years of my life. Time flies!"

Linda J.Berry

Secrets
of
Wisdom

Secrets of Wisdom
Awaken To The Miracle Of You

Joyce C. Gerrish

Editor Sybil

Proofreader Judy Conley

BALBOA.
PRESS

A DIVISION OF HAY HOUSE

Balboa Press books may be ordered through booksellers or by contacting:

Balboa Press
A Division of Hay House
1663 Liberty Drive
Bloomington, IN 47403
www.balboapress.com
1 (877) 407-4847

ISBN: 978-1-4525-2262-3(sc)
ISBN: 978-1-4525-2263-0 (e)

Printed in the United States of America.

Balboa Press rev. date: 12/17/2014

Table of Contents

Dedication

I dedicate this book
in great gratitude and joyful service
to the Divine.

Disclaimers

The information in this book is not in any way intended as medical advice, but rather what has been helpful for the author and her clients and students or for the other people who contributed writings for sections of the book. Be sure to consult your health care practitioner before making any significant changes in nutrition, exercise, or for medical or serious psychological issues. Always consult your health practitioner before discontinuing or changing any prescription medications.

Neither Joyce Gerrish nor anyone who contributed to this book can be held responsible for anyone's choice of the appropriateness of any specific health practice or other practice for any specific person. Great care has been taken to choose practices that are generally very helpful for almost all people, yet everyone is somewhat unique. As stated, consult your health care practitioner before trying something that is new or different for you. Make any changes slowly and gently.

The ideas presented in the main text of this book reflect the opinions, insights, and experiences of the author, Joyce Gerrish. The ideas presented by the people who so kindly contributed personal sharings for this book reflect their own opinions, insights, and experiences--and may or may not be the same as Joyce's viewpoints. Some differences of opinion are natural, because we are all unique individuals.

It is important to know that when an individual begins to eat a healthier diet or experiences any natural healing technique (such as reflexology), the body is likely to release some stored toxins. It is the body's natural way of cleansing itself when it has an opportunity. At such a time it is desirable to drink some extra water to help wash out any toxins that may be releasing.* After healing practices a person may possibly feel a little more tired than usual for a few hours or a couple days - - depending on the degree of toxin release. This is one reason that it is good to make any changes gradually and not all at once. A person may also feel some old emotions come up when experiencing a healing release. As described in the book -- these old emotions are only coming up very briefly in order to be understood, healed, and released. This gradual releasing of old toxins or old repressed emotions can, over time, allow one to feel better physically, emotionally, mentally, and Spiritually.

It is not my intention to scare you, but to reassure you that it is possible after you experience a really deep healing that your body may temporarily feel as though it is a little sick. That feeling is probably from a release of toxins. Wait at least twenty four hours, increase your water intake, and it may well be completely gone, and you may feel better than ever after having released those toxins. That can be true after nutritional cleansing or after therapeutic bodywork.

Each and every individual must always accept full responsibility for their own well-being.

*It is very valuable to drink plenty of water at all times (at least eight cups a day).

Preface

Dear Reader,

Have you ever asked yourself "Who am I--really?" or "What is the true purpose of my being here on Earth?" Join me for this fascinating multi-media adventure of self discovery! Explore the secrets of wisdom. Open to the miracle of who you truly are.

Please take time to delve into all the aspects of this book in order to receive the full experience of immersing yourself in the *Secrets of Wisdom, Awaken to the Miracle of You*. Listen to, or sing along with, the audios of my Soul Songs: there is one for each chapter. Be uplifted with the guided meditations. Those audios can be listened to free on the accompanying website SecretsofWisdom.net. Enjoy my original art designs found with each chapter. If you are reading the printed version of this book, or if your e-reader device doesn't show color--PLEASE experience the designs in full glowing color on the website. Many people say that the full color experience is really special. Some of the finest designs are only on the website.

Read, and be inspired by, the wisdom and invaluable insights found in the chapters. Be moved by the heart warming sharings from numerous people, as they have walked their path of opening ever more fully to the miracle of their being. Delve deeply into the "Questions for Reflection and Discussion." Do some of the action suggestions as they encourage you into valuable interesting experiences. Allow your vision to grow. Consider joining with friends as a support group to explore this journey! In the study and application of these Divine Qualities you will find priceless insights for every life question or challenge. It is food for a life time of inspired study, prayer, meditation, and action.

Believe in yourself! Awaken to the miracle of you! The truth of who you truly are can shine forth more radiantly every day. Allow Divine Love to surround and bless you. You are the only YOU! You are a unique soul with special qualities to share with the world around you. You are needed. Spread your wings and fly!

Peace and Blessings,

Joyce

Acknowledgments

I thank the Divine for inspiring and sustaining this project.

I give huge appreciation to Sybil who edited this book and to Judy Conley who was proofreader. Sybil also is the excellent web-master for the accompanying website, SecretsofWisdom.net.

I give huge appreciation to the people who graced this book with their sharings from their life experiences and wisdom.

For encouragement and insights I thank my sisters Ann Hemdahl-Owen and Karen Coit. Likewise I thank Dr. Lynda J. Wells, William Evans, M.D., Linda Lee, Lynne Coachran, and Sarah Levy.

I thank Kenny Marine for his magnanimous support in teaching me how to record my own audios of my songs and meditations. He also polished the recordings and brought them into finished form.

I thank the myriad of students and clients who have walked some part of their life path with me. You are awesome precious souls.

I thank my friends who warm my heart with our shared joys and life journeys. I pray for the highest blessings for all of you.

I extend profound appreciation to those who read this book and find it helpful. You complete the cycle of reciprocity in this creative endeavor. You were in my heart every moment of the writing and creation of this book.

I pray that Divine Peace, Joy, Illumination, and all the Divine Qualities be with all of you, always.

Two Women Celebrate New Adventure
Original art by Joyce J.C. Gerrish

Chapter One

THE ADVENTURE OF THE SECRETS OF WISDOM BEGINS

Awaken To The Miracle Of You

Enjoy listening to, or singing along with, this peaceful soul song I've composed and sung about opening to the miracle of your being, "*Look Deep In Your Heart.*" Consider it a prayer in song. I invite you to visit SecretsOfWisdom.net where you can listen to the audio soul song and simultaneously gaze at the full color design "Two Women Celebrate New Adventure."

We All Have Magnificent Potential Beyond Our Dreams

The Divine spark is within each of us. We have magnificent potential beyond our dreams. It is time to wake up to who we truly are. We can all be magnificent together. There is nothing to fear. We are embraced in God's love.

The purpose of this book is to step by step in very practical ways help you enhance your positive strengths and joy of life--and support you to move closer to your goals. How can you do this? Believe in yourself! Read and practice applying the techniques and information that inspire you in this book and other excellent sources. Choose a dream worthy of your highest good. Know that you are not alone. Seek out the company of good people so you can encourage each other in beneficial ways. Know that your prayers and higher consciousness can access the support and resources of the Divine. Put your faith in God.

What Is My Purpose? Why Am I Here On Earth?

We live in extraordinary times. Life on planet Earth is changing and transforming in many ways. As we each lift our heart and soul we have the opportunity to become more than we have thought possible. Within all this change, challenge, and opportunity--many people are wondering, "Why am I here on Earth? What is my purpose?" More and more of us are having intuitive and Spiritual experiences and subtle mystical longings in our hearts. We are all here on Earth together to create something wonderful--the potential is unlimited. Each of us has special qualities that are needed. Destiny is calling us. Together with God we can create miracles in our own lives and help lift those around us. It is possible!

We may have often heard that we use only a small part of our brain potential, and that we have capacities far more advanced than we imagine. The truth is that the brain is like a small physical receiving station for the human consciousness which is immensely vast in its capability. In the Bible it says that humans are created in the image of God. Our consciousness has the capacity to attune to truly magnificent Divine sources of inspiration and awareness. We have wondrous capacities far in advance of the most amazing computer. It might take practice to learn how to activate some of these abilities. Others we already use and enjoy all the time--and perhaps take for granted.

Our Spiritual Connection Can Help Hold Us Steady

There are many interpenetrating levels of our consciousness. Even while we are busy with everyday life responsibilities, with practice we can also simultaneously be conscious on intuitive and Spiritual levels. We are each a physical human being, and at the same time our Higher Self (the higher levels of our consciousness) is one with the Divine. That Spiritual connection can hold us steady when things don't seem to be going as we may wish. We can keep an uplifted focus, rather than allowing our mind and emotions to be pulled down into depression, anger, fear, or worry. In this way we can make wiser choices for a better life.

To enhance our ability to draw on our higher awareness, it's very important to learn how to focus and quiet our mind so that it can become like a clear quiet pool in which we can see the peaceful reflection of the sky. That is perhaps why so many of us like to sit by a placid lake in order to help still our minds. When we keep distractions and busy sounds going on around us all the time, it's hard to hear the "music of the heavenly spheres." We have a choice. Even short periods of quiet time at intervals throughout the day can help us to stay in touch with the truth of our being.

The Divine Qualities are deeply needed in fuller expression on planet Earth today. It's of great benefit that we lift our consciousness and pray that the magnificent Divine Qualities of God bless us, our loved ones, and the whole planet. The Bible says, "Ask and you shall receive." Being open to receive and knowing that we are worthy to receive are a crucial part of receiving.

The adventure of this book is learning how to ever more fully enhance and activate these qualities within yourself. Each chapter focuses on one of these superb qualities and guides you by the hand in stepping more fully into it. Each Divine Quality reveals powerful wisdom when understood at deeper levels.

What is the difference between these Divine Qualities and more typical mainstream perceptions of these words? The meaning of some of these words such as love and power is often distorted in current usage, so this book seeks to help restore them to their more true purer meaning. There is a Spiritual energy that supports each of these Divine Qualities. They are all expressions of the Divine. Seventeen are included in this book, and there are many more. These powerful transformative qualities and some ways they can help us are explored in this book.

◆ **Joy**. Helps you live with a light heart. Encourages you to engage more frequently in the activities that give you true joy.

◆ **Love**. Helps nurture you emotionally, and helps you be nurturing for others. Helps deepen the love and caring you share with others.

◆ **Forgiveness**. Supports you to forgive others--and to forgive yourself. Helps you release the past so you can move forward more freely and creatively in the present.

◆ **Clarity**. Helps you clear your mind for more effective living, and helps clarify your life focus and purpose. This chapter contains excellent techniques to assist you to live and do your work more efficiently and with less stress.

◆ **Purpose**. Helps you to move ahead in your life goals, dreams, and soul purpose.

◆ **Peace**. Helps you find peace, or deepen your peace. Helps enhance your peace with others and support world peace.

◆ **Power**. Helps you have enhanced courage, perseverance, and power. Power is good as long as it is used for the good of all. We can all be powerful together.

◆ **Devotion**. Helps you to find inspiration and comfort in Spiritual Devotion. Helps you share devoted loving service for others--and realize the heartwarming joy that comes with assisting others in need.

◆ **Illumination**. Supports your Spiritual growth through enhancing your connection to your Higher Consciousness and the Divine. Learn numerous approaches for beginning to meditate or deepening your meditation practices. Learn about auras and chakras--and practical uncomplicated ways to energize and illumine them.

◆ **Healing**. Helps you support healing for yourself and for others. Learn "hands on" beginning Hand and Foot Reflexology (which is related to Acupressure) and Zone Energy Healing. Learn very important realistic ways to improve your health through nutrition and natural foods.

◆ **Wisdom**. Aids you at times of making decisions (large and small), and in distilling wisdom from your life experiences. Learn ways to increase your intuition.

◆ **Harmony**. Aids you to stabilize and harmonize your life, and supports harmony in the midst of chaos. Promotes harmony with all aspects of creation through ecological living.

◆ **Freedom**. Helps you enhance your freedom to be who you truly are and choose to be.

◆ **Transformation**. Supports you to move forward in becoming your ever more confident true magnificent self.

◆ **Grace**. Supports you in drawing on Spiritual support when challenges seem heavy. This chapter describes Spiritual realms and metaphysical realities.

◆ **Abundance**. Enhances your well-being within the material world. Helps support the well-being of all people and all creation through living lightly on the land.

◆ **Truth**. Aids you to discern the truth of a situation, and to be aware what is deception or illusion. Helps you walk a clearer path through life's challenges and opportunities. Learn timeless metaphysical and mystical truths.

In the study and application of these Divine Qualities you'll find insights and answers for every question. It's food for a lifetime of inspired study, prayer, meditation, and action. Explore and understand the secrets of wisdom! Are you ready? Take it at your own pace. If you wish, find one or more friends to join you for this life-enhancing journey. Get together, telephone, or communicate online at regular intervals to share the adventure and support and encouragement.

You choose the order in which you wish to immerse yourself in each Quality and its chapter unit. Each chapter is created as an experiential multifaceted awakening "seminar" or "workshop." This is not a book to speed read. Stop and think now and then as you read. Immerse yourself in the unique offerings included with each chapter: inspired ideas, audio soul song for that special quality, audio meditation with affirmations, real life sharings of how each quality has blessed the lives of numerous people just like you, questions to think about and discuss, "how to" action suggestions for enhancing the quality in your life, and inspirational art. Let your heart and mind soar! Enjoy, explore, and really experience the different offerings of each chapter and allow them to reveal their secrets to you!

Each Chapter Unit With its Special Divine Quality Includes:

Audio Inspirational Soul Song

Each chapter has an audio inspirational soul song that I composed to help you feel deep connection to that marvelous quality and its energy. The soul songs can be listened to free through the SecretsofWisdom.net. They were created as a form of prayer and meditation in music and sound. As you listen or sing, allow yourself to float in them like in a flowing stream and allow them to carry you peacefully. Each song is intended as a healing uplifting experience. Harmonious gentle sound can have a very beneficial effect for one's consciousness and body, particularly when one focuses on it with openness to receiving a healing uplifting experience.

Audio Guided Meditations

On the website there are audio meditations for you to listen to. There is a twelve minute "Meditation To Enhance Your Experience of the Divine Qualities." It can help you open your awareness to the wonderful inspiration and support that's possible with each specific quality. The meditation starts with a brief guided relaxation. It then guides you through soothing breath awareness, color visualization, and special affirmations that are different for each quality. For those who choose not to access this meditation in audio form, there is a complete transcribed version included in each chapter. I would encourage you to enjoy this twelve minute meditation often (audio or transcribed version).

I have also included, on the same website, a special 17-minute audio "Guided Relaxation and Healing Visualization Meditation." It will help guide you into a place of peaceful relaxation. For people who may be fairly new to meditation, this would be a particularly good meditation to start with for the first several times you sit down to meditate - - or as often as you wish.

There is also included on the website an audio "Meditation to Enhance Spiritual Awakening and Illumination." It is thirty-four minutes long. I feel that you will find it Spiritually uplifting and consciousness expanding. I suggest that you enjoy this meditation at least once or twice a week, alternating with the others.

Meditation is a powerful way to expand and open your consciousness to new, wonderful, helpful ways of life enrichment. Prayer is also powerful and effective. Each of these qualities that is focused on in this book is very sacred, and has its own unique special healing energy and contribution for your life.

Please pause here and listen to the 17-minute "Guided Relaxation and Healing Meditation." You can listen to it free at <u>SecretsofWisdom.net</u>.

Real Life Sharings

There are real life sharings in each chapter about how that quality has enriched different people's lives in very tangible ways. These will warm your heart. What special memories come to your mind from your life experiences regarding some of these qualities? I encourage you to tell them to some of your close friends and family. Gently ask them to tell you some of their life stories regarding the quality on which you are focusing. This can create memorable moments of sharing. Distilling the wisdom from your life is one of the sacred purposes of your soul being in a physical body.

Questions For Reflection And Discussion

There are questions at the end of each chapter to inspire and stimulate your thinking and feeling. Let your heart pour out and express itself. Don't hold back. I encourage you to do journal writing, drawing, or express your feelings in other creative ways such as dancing. These methods can help bring your thoughts, insights and intuitions more clearly into focus in your mind and heart. For journal writing, you may wish to choose a notebook especially for that purpose and always keep it in the same place so you'll be able to find it easily.

Action Suggestions To Support You Into Your Next Step

There are action suggestions for supporting you as you take the next step of beginning to put into motion in your life some of what you may hold dear in your heart and soul. You may have been yearning quite a while for certain possibilities that would be helpful in your life. There are perhaps intriguing ideas toward which you may have felt a longing now and then. Choose one small (or large) step, and one step can organically lead to another life-affirming step. It's your life! Step into it, adjust it, and transform it as you feel drawn from within your heart and soul.

Inspirational Designs

Within each chapter, there are two inspirational art works that I created to help inspire you. Sometimes images can speak to your soul even more powerfully than words. Colors and shapes and images are a universal language all of their own. As an artist, I have immersed myself deeply in the study of the psychological, healing, and Spiritual effect of colors, geometric shapes, and archetypal images. The brilliant twentieth century psychologist Carl Jung was a great mentor to me in those respects. In ancient Egypt the application of the tremendous power of geometric shapes was carried to an extremely high art, as in the design of the pyramids. Buddhist monks have traditionally created beautiful designs within a circle. These are called mandalas and are intended to be gazed at during meditation. Mandalas are very centering and calming for the consciousness. Many of the designs in this book are mandalas. As you listen to or sing the soul song for each quality, you may wish to gaze at the accompanying design. Full color versions of one design for each chapter are available to enjoy looking at on the website along with the audios. This will provide you a fuller experience of these designs than the black and white versions available in some forms of this book.

Inspired Text

The text section of each chapter was inspired during prayers and deep meditations in oneness with the Divine. I have a great deal of education, experience, and awareness in the areas addressed in this book. In addition to that, a significant part of these chapters came from areas of intuitive knowing that exist beyond knowledge.

We are living in an amazing time when life on earth is changing at an incredibly rapid pace. I feel that there is less of a veil between the physical world and the Spiritual realms than previously. This is a wonderful gift to humanity. Divine Spirit has always been radiating blessings to help uplift and illumine every human on planet Earth, and I feel that this is increased even more so now. Each quality described in this book has its own unique important contributions for us. In the following chapters, I will go much further in exploring how we can work with, embrace, and embody these beautiful qualities. Each is a Divine gift.

Printable Charts and Tables

Many of the charts and tables from this book can be printed, free of charge, from the website accompanying this book. This is for your convenience when studying and using those charts. I sincerely hope that you will use the charts and practice the natural healing techniques often to enhance your well-being and that of your loved ones.

Special Note Concerning Your Aura and the Power Of Your Mind, Body, Spirit Connection.

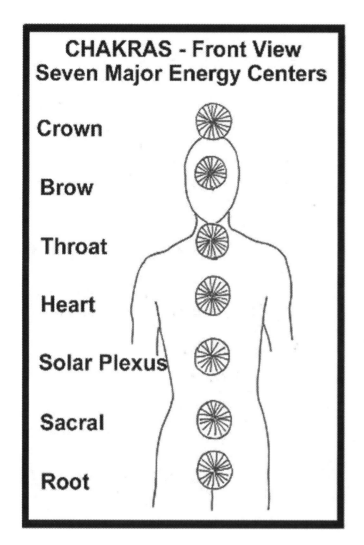

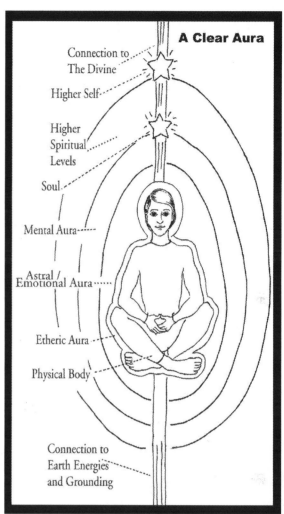

Before venturing further into the fascinating exploration of how these magnificent qualities can enhance one's life, I want to share a few important understandings. All people, animals, plants, minerals, and the earth itself have an energy field/aura within and around them. The human aura has a number of levels or aspects including: etheric (which is the energy equivalent of the physical body), astral/emotional, mental, and the progressively more Spiritual levels of the consciousness. Each of these different levels of one's energy field/ aura fills one's physical body and extends beyond the body. There are chakras that are special energy centers within the aura. There are seven major chakras which are located along the spine, and there are many additional chakras. If used regularly, the meditations accompanying this book and the natural healing techniques presented here can help clear and illumine one's aura and chakras and enhance one's energy and life.

As humans, our amazing aura/energy field performs a powerful role in our life. It has a strong direct reciprocal connection with the well-being of all aspects of our body and consciousness. This relationship is like a circle. Within this reciprocal circle, our body, emotions, mind, and Spirit have a powerful effect on our aura. Likewise, our aura/energy field has a powerful effect on our mind, emotions, Spirituality, physical health, and total life. This is the well-known Mind-Body-Spirit Connection.

In a sense, our aura energy field functions as a filter as to how we experience our world. Our thoughts and emotions are recorded in our aura somewhat like music is recorded by an electronic recording device. Positive uplifted thoughts and emotions and inspiring Spiritual experiences help keep our aura clear and open to our highest good and effective joyful living. Angry or depressed or worried feelings and thoughts can build up static and blockages in our aura which can make it harder for us to relate well with the people and world around us. An aura with static and blockages is like dark clouds hiding the sunlight on a cloudy day. The sun is there shining above the dark clouds, but it is difficult for a person to be aware of it in that situation. Hence it is important to keep our aura clear.

Let's make conscious choices to support our Mind-Body-Spirit Connection. We shall explore this further in the chapters ahead.

Angel With Stars
Original art by Joyce J.C. Gerrish

Chapter Two

LET JOY LIGHTEN YOUR DAY
Enhancing Divine Joy In Your Life

Music is a true joy to me. I have composed a soul song to express the essence of Joy "*I Am Joy.*" You may wish to visit the website SecretsofWisdom.net where you can listen to this audio soul song, and at the same time gaze at the full color design "Butterfly and Lilies Rejoice."

I Lift To The Sky and I Am Joy!

Joy is a state of mind, not a reaction to an event. We can choose to be joyful. We don't need something to cause us to feel joy, it can come from within. Pure joy is a Divine gift straight from God. Our true nature is joyful. What can weigh us down is the sense of separation from the truth of our being. Many people believe that to feel cheerful they need to hear or see something funny. They wait for a person or something else to connect them to joy. It is sad to give away or outgrow our natural joy. We are not dependent on anyone else to give it to us. It is part of our innate being. Joy naturally bubbles up from our oneness within the Divine. The Divine is joyful. Joy is one of the Divine Qualities. May we never lose access to this very precious part of ourselves and our oneness with the Divine! It makes everything else feel worthwhile.

Sometimes a person works very hard to advance in his or her profession. Year after year the person pushes and succeeds in accomplishing goal after goal. Then one day the realization comes that joy has been lost somewhere along the way. Through all of the struggle to accomplish, something hardened inside. Joy is a precious flower that needs peace and regular nurturing to thrive within one's being. Sheer willpower can achieve certain goals, but it can stamp out the beauty and joy of it all. People thrive on joy and need it to maintain balance and true connection within this three dimensional world.

Remember How Spontaneous Joy Felt as a Child!

Do you remember as a child running and jumping just for fun? There didn't have to be a reason. It was just fun to be alive. As a child I spent as much time as possible playing happily and carefree outside with neighborhood children in our yards or at a nearby park. Even now, get me near a full size swing set and you'll find me happily swinging to my heart's content. We played all kinds of make-believe games, front yard simple ball games, coloring, bicycling, climbing trees, and playing with pets. We explored the world of grasshoppers, butterflies, crayfish, dandelions, and wild flowers. Seeing the sun shining and breathing fresh air can be intoxicating all in themselves without any further stimulants.

Many of us are so out of touch with our natural joy of life that we turn to multiple stimulants just to get going in the morning and to keep us going throughout the day. Each effort to jack ourselves up in those artificial ways pulls us further off center and out of touch with the spontaneous place of joy within our being. If we just take at least five minutes for a brisk walk, stretching and breathing deeply periodically during the day when we feel a need to be revived-- we may find that we no longer need those stimulants.

We Are Each Like a Song With Our Own Rhythm and Melody and Lyrics

We each have a unique and natural pace at which we feel most vibrantly alive. We each express ourselves in our own special way. This needs to be respected and honored. As said, we are each like a song. If we try to sing someone else's song, we are likely to feel out of touch with who we are and with our natural delight. Joy is not something we can force or put on a schedule. Its very essence is freedom to be ourselves.

Many of us work very hard to make ends meet financially and to keep up with seemingly endless responsibilities. There may seldom seem to be time to satisfy yearnings in our heart. After a while in this mode, something can harden in the inner psyche, and we may feel that what we yearn for isn't meant to be. We may just try to keep a stiff upper lip and get on with responsibilities no matter what. If that sounds familiar, would you like some relief?

Try This Experience In The Joy of Simple Pleasures

Here is an experience you can try. It is important to do this over a period of time, not just once. A few times a week give yourself the gift of an hour for discovery. Make a date with yourself and put it in your calendar if necessary. (If an hour seems too much, try half an hour.) Give yourself permission to do whatever nurturing activity seems to well up from your inner being seeking expression. Let it be something you don't normally allow yourself to do very often. It may be to take a walk in a park on a nice day. It may be to just get down on the floor and have fun playing with your child or pet. It may be to relax and lie in a lounge chair in the backyard and watch the clouds roll by. Or perhaps it is to take out an arts and craft project you started and continue it, or maybe even finish it. Let this be something that feels like a gift from you to your inner child.

With practice, this experiment can become a treasured part of our week, whether it is half an hour three times a week or an hour or two on the weekend. What is important is that it brings us simple harmless pleasure and brings a spontaneous smile to our face. For the purposes of this experiment in spontaneous joy, it is important that it not require anything that we put in our mouth to cause the pleasure effect. Let's just let it be our own being that supplies the endorphins to stimulate the feeling of joy. The whole idea is that we remember how to feel like a spontaneous child again and give ourselves permission to enjoy it now and then. A large percentage of people find they are fairly out of touch with their inner child. For each of us the process of connecting more fully with that inner child will probably be a little different.

Let's All Choose to Be Joyful and Light-hearted

My inner child really loves to play when I give myself a chance. I guess one of my biggest sources of joy is playing my guitar and singing. For me, time disappears with music. Something else my inner child loves is taking walks and just feasting my senses by looking at every little bird and bush and feeling the sunshine or breeze.

What simple pleasures give you joy? Maybe it is hiking in nature, playing tennis, dreaming up creative ideas with your family photos, or making a fun woodworking project. Those simple enjoyments are important for your emotional, physical, mental, and Spiritual well-being. Please remember to give yourself permission to indulge in simple pleasures.

What's the Difference Between Joy and Entertainment

Now let's think about what joy isn't. Joy and entertainment are somewhat different. Entertainment has its place in our life, for sure. It helps distract us from worries and responsibilities, and it helps us laugh or be impressed with something outside ourselves. For a little while, it helps us forget about ourselves and our lives. It may feel like a relief to be in a different "world" for a while.

Some people, though, try to live their life vicariously through the entertainers. There are people who treasure the celebrities as protection against feeling empty inside. That is one reason why celebrities are such big business. At some level the observer can pretend to be doing something exciting along with the performer. This can be helpful to inspire us and spur us on, as with singing and dancing. The important thing is to recognize the wondrous possibilities of YOU. Don't lose yourself by being absorbed with the life events of entertainers. The bottom line is to remember that you have a goldmine of wholesome capacities and creativity within yourself. These are talents and gifts that are yours to express. The expressing and sharing of these can make the world a better place for everyone.

True Joy Is Being Your Own Unique Expressive Self! Trust Yourself

Creativity can only thrive and blossom into its true nature by giving it opportunity to express itself. Let your true nature come out into the light of day at frequent intervals. Have the courage to be your unique expressive self. That is the true source of joy, which is very different than entertainment. With entertainment you are treading water, with creativity you are swimming. Believe in yourself and your journey of self-discovery. It is in the development of your own potentials that you can truly feel elation.

Don't let anyone's teasing cause you to close the door to your inner gifts. You don't need to compare how you do something with how other people do it, and you don't need to worry about other people making comparisons. This isn't about comparison. As you pursue something you love to do, your skills will develop. If anyone discourages you from your journey of creative self-expression, keep in mind that person may feel threatened by your courage, and may want you to only do what he or she does and not have your own interests. It is possible to periodically take turns trying out each other's joys together. Sometimes it is possible for you and a family member or significant other to each follow your own joy simultaneously nearby each other. You don't always have to do the same things at the same time in order to enjoy the company of each other. Life is a precious journey. Have fun on the way. I hope that these thoughts have encouraged you to believe in yourself and to open more fully to your inner treasure of spontaneous joy. Don't allow the judgment of society to stop you from being yourself. If something gives you joy, that is what matters.

Let's Support Each Other's Joyful Creativity

A fun way for friends to support each other's joyful creativity is with having a "creative sharing." Each person is welcome to share something with the group--if they wish. It could be: a short five minute story, a joke, a song played on a musical instrument, a painting recently completed, a magic trick, a dance step, anything! This is a marvelous way to share in a meaningful manner and have a really good time. I've enjoyed that with friends often. People on national television singing or dancing competitions often seem to feel that they have failed if they don't win at the national level, even though they may have tremendous talent. I feel that the important thing is to enjoy one's talents and skills wherever one is. There are so many ways to enjoy sharing them locally in churches, schools, community centers, cafes, celebrations, and gatherings of all kinds. We don't need to be in competition, let's support each other!

I have fond memories of my mother dancing happily around the living room to music from the radio. Who would try to dampen that spontaneous joy? It got me dancing, too. Let's go for it! Let's allow our hearts to sing! True innocent spontaneous joy is food for the soul. It supports our joy of life "joie de vie." Let's each nourish our soul!

Real Life Sharings Of The Uplifting Power Of Divine Joy

A Return To Joy
~ by Sybil

Everyone has something that they loved to do as a child, the doing of which made them feel great joy and happiness. I have a friend who says her greatest joy as a child was running barefoot on a warm spring day through freshly plowed fields. As an adult, living in the city far from the farm, she forgot all about that simple childhood pleasure. For years, she had an unidentified longing, as if something were missing. But as her life was full and busy she did not know what could possibly be missing.

One day, while driving through a farming area, she saw a freshly plowed field and yelled at her friend "STOP! There, under the shade tree. STOP!" The car had barely come to a full stop before she had her shoes off and was out the door. To the astonishment of her friend, she ran into the freshly plowed dirt and just buried her feet in. Then, completely oblivious to his presence and the expensive suit she wore, she was running and dancing and flinging her hands toward the sky. She stopped every few steps to bury her toes into the warm dirt. The friend could see she was in ecstasy. He wondered how this could possibly be the same woman who only a few minutes before was complaining about intense pain in her legs.

When she returned to the car, she was dirty, disheveled, starry-eyed and looked very much like a happily tired child. "That was FUN!" she sighed as she fell into the seat, a huge smile on her face. He had never seen her so disheveled, nor had he ever seen her look so happy; her whole being sparkled. The woman who had previously been complaining of pain seemed to have vanished before his eyes.

After that, she would choose a warm sunny day and go driving through the country side during spring plowing and spend an afternoon playing in the dirt--barefoot, in some farmer's freshly plowed field. She said that just one day could sustain her for a whole year. When she felt that unnamed longing, she only had to remember the afternoon in the warm sunshine with her feet in the sun-warmed dirt, and joy would bubble up from somewhere deep inside, bringing a smile to her face. Her inner child was joyful, and the pain in her body seemed to disappear for a while.

The Power of Joy
~ by Elsa Lichman, Waltham, Massachusetts

Years ago, I was struggling through a lengthy period of pain, following back surgery. I went unsuccessfully from one famous pain center to another. In the cold wintery northeast, I was living in a fast-track society; life spun around me as I rested. I was on medical leave from work. Taking a leap of faith, I found the shortest direct flight to the Caribbean--to the island of Antigua. I sent my bird to my Mom. I kissed my family, friends, and neighbors goodbye and traveled to the unknown.

The first few days were rocky; I felt lost and alone. But soon I was walking in the healing balmy air, swimming, and reaching out to the new culture around me. A musician invited me to his group's Valentine's Day gig. He taught me rhythms by tapping out beats on a plastic audio tape cover with a pen. And so began my love affair with the arts, the kids, the music, the people, and the colors.

I photographed and painted, learned batik and portraiture, wrote, and studied percussion. My two-week visit extended to six months. I became part of the community as it geared up for Carnival. I went to outdoor concerts, passionately waving my arms to the beats. I was invited to play a variety of instruments with steel bands. The culmination of my trip coincided with the rich experience of the festival.

Just before leaving my new second home, I was given an unexpected and priceless gift. A musician friend said that early on, they had given me a nickname, but feared telling me what it was. When I discovered that it was "Rhythm," I promptly had it printed on the back of my tee shirt--which I proudly wore home. (See Resources Page)

A Child Shares What Gives Her Joy
~ by Lillian

I love to spin and dance around. When I go to the spring carnival, I love to jump in the inflated bouncing house. I love all kinds of games. In school I like my art class best of all. We do fun projects. In my homeroom, I like the math games.

Lillian's mother added, "She is so full of joy every day. She teaches me lots about being in the moment. When I take time out from my job, computer work, or house work and spend some uninterrupted time with her -- the reward is pure joy. She is a wonderful blessing and joy to me."

The Joy of a Birdfeeder and Fish Tank
~ by K.C.

My favorite bird to watch is at my bird feeder right now. He is a downy woodpecker. He is at my window looking in. He is so wonderful, I love him--and there are about a dozen cardinals. There haven't been quite so many cardinals here very often. There are other birds that are here all the time, too. There is a wren that is charming, I adore him; and there are chickadees. They are lovely birds. They are here often. The bird feeders are by my kitchen window where I cook, eat, wash dishes, read, and talk on the telephone. They are delightful. I put my new fish tank here, so I can watch them, too. The fresh snow outside is beautiful. All this gives me much joy!

Accessing Divine Joy Through Our Oneness With God
~ by William Evans, M.D.

Joy is a Divine characteristic of God. We are created by God in his image. Therefore, joy is one of the natural qualities or characteristics deep within each of us. When we fully recognize our oneness with God and our Higher Self, we very naturally experience the inner quality of Divine Joy, and indeed all the Divine Qualities of God existing in Oneness. To really experience this true joy, we only have need of removing the obstacles we have placed between ourselves and the inner Reality of this experience. Our Spiritual path ideally helps us to move through and heal those obstacles which limit our experience of joy.

When we align our mind and vibrations to the Divine deep within, we will experience joy as a natural consequence of our true essence as created by God. While personally delving deeply into the highest expressions of Spiritual Truth I could find to study and align with, I have more times than I could possibly say been literally thrilled and joyous from experiencing the reality of these Truths in every fiber of my being. This experience is available to everyone.

The Joy of a New Shared Venture
~by Anonymous

My wife and I have found something new that we are both enjoying a lot. She talked me into trying it at first, now I'm the first one ready and eager to go. It's the community theater in our town. Neither of us is really into the idea of acting, at least not anytime soon. It's just fun to be around it all as a volunteer. I help construct the sets and get involved in painting the backdrops. I'm learning all kinds of things. I like being involved in creating the illusion of a scene--and on such a big scale. Susan is helping with the props and the costumes. She has created some dynamite original costumes. I'm proud of her. I think this is bringing us closer together in some ways, and we're making new friends. We usually go once a week, except on the weekend of performances when we go more often. Little did I know that I'd ever be into the theater this way!

I'm A Naturally Joyous Person
~ by Kesha M. Shahid

I'm a naturally joyous person. I love to laugh and live life joyfully as I believe the Creator intended us all to do. So it is my nature to be joyous. I come from a large family. My paternal great-grandmother had five children and my grandmother had seven children. Growing up, I spent a lot of time at my great-grandmother's home, which was always filled with family members and very good memories of love and joy. Most of us are rarely able to get together now, because we are so spread out geographically. When we are able to get together it brings me great joy, and it is as if we just left each other the day before. Like my great-grandmother and mother, I also have five children. My children, of course, bring me much joy. Being with them, listening to them interact with each other, and seeing them learn and grow is so delightful!

Another thing that brings me great joy is traveling. I love to travel, see different places, taste the food, and interact with people. I was recently blessed with the opportunity to finally go to the Mother Land for the first time. I first arrived in Morocco, and the next day was in Accra, Ghana. I found out that Ghana is the only country in Africa that has never had a civil war. I suppose that is one of the reasons why the people there were so genuine, loving, helpful and friendly. Staying at a hotel where I could hear the tides of the Atlantic Ocean all night long was so peaceful, rejuvenating, and reviving. I had the pleasure and experience of visiting and staying in a village which was very soothing, carefree and relaxing... away from the hustle and bustle of the city. The energy there was pure and the air and rain water very clean and refreshing. I truly loved and enjoyed my two week stay there, which was too short a time. I can't wait to go back again to work on plans of opening a Holistic Health and Well-being Center, and working on a Tropical Rivers Community Project. The most important thing that sustains me and brings me the greatest joy of all is Divine Love which comes in many forms and is also found in all of the things I listed above. Healthy, functional, unconditional love. I wholeheartedly know that "Where two or more are gathered in the Creator's name, S/He is there," and "No man is an island." So in being with the man I love, I feel free, light--the ultimate joy. This type of joy sounds like birds singing in the morning, smells like roses, tastes like my great-grandmother Bettye's homemade German chocolate cake (in which she always used fresh coconut), looks like the sun shining, and feels like me lying in the grass looking up at the clouds drifting by in the sky as the cool breeze blows through my toes! Beautiful! (See Resources Page)

Man Feels Joy in Nature
Original art by Joyce J.C. Gerrish

WORKBOOK: Enrichment Experiences For Enhancing Joy In Your Life

Enjoy the adventure of exploring these enrichment experiences on your own, or gather a few friends to share the journey with you. Be inspired by the audio meditation and soul song for this chapter. Reflect on some of the stimulating ideas and questions. Perhaps share with friends and/or family some of your heartfelt insights and formative experiences.

Questions For Reflection and Discussion

Reflection, discussion, journal writing, expressing your feelings in drawings or other creative ways can all be very valuable to help you delve into these questions in truly meaningful and relevant ways. Before focusing on the questions, you may wish to meditate with the twelve minute audio or transcribed meditation--and/or listen to the soul song "I Am Joy."

1. Make a list of some of the things that you enjoyed doing as a child. These may include: playing with a pet, playing games, riding your bike, swinging, swimming, going for walks, drawing, or painting. Whatever comes to your mind, jot it down. Have fun remembering your childhood pleasures. (Please don't include T.V. or electronics at this time.)

2. What gives you true joy as an adult? When was the last time that you truly felt spontaneous joy that wasn't dependent on an outside stimulus such as a funny T.V. show? Perhaps the joy was inspired by walking outside on a beautiful day. Perhaps the joy was inspired by something that you created such as a craft, or by spending relaxed pleasant time with a friend. Write down whatever comes to your mind that really gives you joy.

3. Create a separate place on your page (see Question 2 above) to write sources of joy from entertainment. Entertainment is good and can be wonderfully helpful to lift the mood, but it is different from spontaneous joy from within one's own life experience. Enjoy them both for their special gifts.

4. Look at your list of what gives you true joy (not including entertainment at the moment). Which have you enjoyed regularly recently, and which have you perhaps not given yourself the opportunity to enjoy for quite a while? ---Months? ---Years? ---Since you were a child? How do you feel about life when you are engaged in doing something that gives you true spontaneous joy? How does that perhaps differ from how you feel about your life when you haven't given yourself the time or opportunity to engage in that treasured activity? It is very important to be aware of that difference.

Action Suggestions For Enhancing Joy In Your Life

1. Choose one of these joyful experiences from the treasure chest of your heart that you would like to reactivate or increase in your life (see Journal Writing Suggestions 1 and 2 above). Plan when and how you would like to enjoy it. It might be in small ways to start. Maybe take a friend or child to enjoy walking in a nearby park or by a river. Sign up for some classes in dance exercise or painting. Open yourself up to something you have loved to do, but perhaps have let slide.

2. Find a support group or start a little group of people who love to do something that you love to do. This might be bird watching, playing the ukulele, or walking in a park. It might be playing card games, or knitting, or storytelling. The sky is the limit. Find some friends or new acquaintances with whom you can share joy on a regular basis such as once a month or more often.

3. Experiment with finding the joyful side of whatever is going on all day. This can seem like a difficult thing to do, but it can really happen. When we wake up in the morning, we can make a decision to find the joy, as much as possible, in whatever we do that day. This is sometimes called "walking on the sunny side of the street." If you have a lot of errands or appointments or clients to see, focus on something interesting or special about each person with whom you come in contact. Find something to share a chuckle about. Tell the person a cheerful little incident, and they may tell you something amusing or fascinating. Be alive to life in the moment, and allow it to be joyful. It beats being sad, right? Why not!

4. As you get ready for bed at night, bring to your mind some of the little things that brought you joy throughout the day. Let them bring a smile to your lips. This may help you sleep more peacefully.

Audio: "Meditation to Enhance Your Experience of the Divine Qualities," with Special Focus on Joy

Pray to the Divine to bless your meditation and enhance Divine Joy in your life. With this audio you'll be guided to sense yourself immersed in the wonderful uplifting feeling of joy. Choose one or more of the following affirmations (or something similar) that feels particularly helpful to you. Before transferring to the website to listen to the meditation, write down on a small piece of paper the affirmation(s) you choose and the helpful color peach. Later place the affirmation(s) where you'll see it daily and be reminded to affirm it for a minute or two several times a day.

◆ I am joyful and light-hearted.

◆ I have a naturally cheerful outlook on life.

◆ I find joy in the simple rhythms of life.

◆ I am blessed with Divine Joy and I radiate it out to everyone I meet.

Helpful color to visualize when meditating on Divine Joy: Peach.

I encourage you to enjoy this meditation when you wish to enhance Joy in your life. Connect to SecretsofWisdom.net to listen to the twelve-minute audio "Meditation to Enhance Your Experience of the Divine Qualities."

(Also, see "Transcribed Version of Meditation to Enhance Your Experience of Divine Joy" at the end of this chapter.)

Uplifting Audio Soul Song: *"I Am Joy"*
Composed and sung by Joyce

Consider it a prayer in song for enhancing Divine Joy within you. As you chant it or listen to it, feel yourself relax and allow it to help bring you into a lighthearted, uplifted feeling of peaceful joy.

I whirl like the wind and I am joy.

I flow like the brook and I am joy.

I lift to the sky and I am joy.

Yes, I am joy.

Oh, I am joy. Yes, I am joy.

You can listen to the audio *"I Am Joy"* at SecretsofWisdom.net.

Transcribed Version of Meditation To Enhance Your Experience of Divine Joy

If possible, listen to some relaxing nonverbal music. Say a short prayer calling on the Divine to bless your meditation and enhance joy in your life.

Visualize yourself in a ball of light to help strengthen your energy field.

Become aware of and follow your breath as it gently flows in and out your nose at its own relaxed pace.

Imagine yourself as a tree sending powerful roots deep into the earth to help you feel grounded and prevent possibly feeling spacey.

Then as you breathe in your nose, imagine you are breathing the strength of the earth up into your body. Repeat several times.

Listen to the relaxing music as you focus on gently breathing in and out your nose.

Visualize the color peach like a beautiful glowing peach colored sunrise filling the sky.

As you breathe in your nose, imagine that you are breathing glowing peach light into your whole being.

Silently pray to the Divine that your life be uplifted and blessed with Divine Joy.

Next breathe in your nose and out your mouth for about a minute VERY GENTLY.

Now, very gently breathe in your mouth and out your nose for about a minute.

Then extra gently breathe in and out your mouth for a minute or so.

Now return to breathing in and out your nose.

As you breathe in your nose, imagine you are breathing in peach color into your whole being.

As you breathe out your nose, periodically say one or more of the following or similar affirmations silently.

◆ I am joyful and light-hearted.

◆ I have a naturally cheerful outlook on life.

◆ I find joy in the simple rhythms of life.

◆ I am blessed with Divine Joy and I radiate it out to everyone I meet.

Continue in that manner for a few minutes or as long as you wish.

Conclude by thanking the Divine.

Then once again send down roots for grounding.

I encourage you to enjoy this meditation to enhance joy in your life. Write down the affirmation(s) you choose and place it where you'll see it several times a day and be reminded to affirm it for a minute or two.

Man and Woman Feeling Inspired Love
Original art by Joyce J.C. Gerrish

Chapter Three

LOVE NOURISHES AND HEALS

Enhancing Divine Love In Your Life

Enjoy listening to or singing along with this peaceful soul song I've composed and sung: "*I Am Love.*" Consider it a prayer in song. Connect to the <u>SecretsofWisdom.net</u> website where you can listen to the audio "*I Am Love*" and gaze at the accompanying full color design "Butterfly and Roses Symbolizing Love."

What is Love? Let's Explore the Unfathomable Mystery of Divine Love

Love is many things to many people. How can we all possibly agree? Love is colored by the person expressing it, and by the person receiving it. There is pure love, there is totally selfish love, and there is every gradation in between. The kind of love that is truly a blessing to receive is Divine Love. Divine Love pours from the higher levels of consciousness and from a pure heart. Anger doesn't thrive in this sphere, nor does jealousy or selfishness. The higher Spiritual levels of our consciousness are immersed in peace. It's not self-seeking at the expense of others. It embraces harmony and compassion for oneself and for all beings. In this realm all is well.

As soon as we start trying to control those around us to behave as we desire, sweet gentleness is distorted. The only person we can truly control is ourself. This does not mean that Divine Love is weak. It is powerful. It has the power and clarity to stand steady when all around may be reeling in confusion and fury and are hurling threats of retaliation if the object of love doesn't do as instructed. (Note: The care of children is, of course, a special case requiring wise guidance and sufficient control for the child's own good.)

Pure Love Holds the Beloved in the Heart of Hearts and Reflects Back True Wholeness to Help Inspire the Beloved to Be All that He or She Can Be

It is the fragrant aroma of gentle caring that draws others into the sphere of one who shares Divine Love. This pure love holds the beloved in the heart of hearts–the sacred space of perfect vision of the true wholeness of one's being. Divine Love sees the perfection of a person's highest potential and reflects that back to the loved one as a mirror of remembrance. When loved by such a one, whether as a friend or family member or lover–it can encourage one to be true to one's inner higher vision. It is a great gift to be held in this manner. It is a constant reminder to be worthy of the trust. It tends to help lift the recipient to be all that he or she can be.

When individuals constantly complain to each other about every little thing and degrade one another with negative talk, it drags both people down. Sometimes a person thinks that it is helpful to point out another's faults. This seldom is received well. It sometimes even causes the person receiving the comments to dig in deeper with the behavior that irritated the other person in the first place. Constructive evaluation of something specific can periodically be helpful when requested, but even that needs to be done with gentle consideration.

Know That You Have a Source of Divine Love in Your Heart That is Always There For You

Look within for your source of comfort, courage, and love to share with others. Find your source within the Spiritual center of your being. Be a fountain of nurturing love for yourself and your needs first--and then let that healing gentle love flow out to all who share your life. This love gives people a relaxed safe uplifted feeling in body, emotions, mind, and Spirit. If we are trying to draw from other people the love that we need to sustain us, we may sometimes come up empty when the people around us are feeling depleted. Where can we find our source of Divine Love? We can find it in the sweetness of communing with the peaceful essence within our own heart and soul, and our connection to the Creator. If meditating in this way feels difficult, try finding a group which seems to embody gentle nurturing love. Let that group support you in finding in your heart your own connection to the Divine source of love. Also, enjoy the audio "Meditation to Enhance Your Experience of the Divine Qualities" (with focus on Divine Love), which accompanies this chapter.

As We Allow Divine Love to Flow Through Us to Others, We Are Helping to Heal All Life Around Us

All aspects of creation are held in manifestation through Divine Love. Without the cohesive power of Divine Love, the rhythms of creation could not hold true. Pure love is of the Creator's essence. All is held in the Creator's embrace. When we allow Divine Love to express through our being, we are placing ourselves in harmony with the rhythms of the cosmos. This is not intended to sound grandiose, but rather to portray the unfathomable mystery of true love and its power.

As we each open our heart to express pure unselfish love we become a conduit of God's work on planet Earth. We are God's hands and feet and heart in physical manifestation. What greater calling can there be? It doesn't matter what our job description may be according to an employer or family member, our true work can be healing all life around us simply by holding pure Divine Love in our heart. This doesn't necessarily mean that we constantly talk about love or hug a whole lot of people-- though both of those can be good. The crucial thing is to be acting and thinking and feeling from a loving place of honoring the highest good of all. As more and more people are holding this profound consciousness, a planetary network is created to help sustain the struggling souls who haven't yet found that sacred place of healing in their hearts.

Love Is the Cohesiveness That Draws People Together

Divine Love heals not only the person or persons with whom we share it, but also ourselves. Love heals. Love is the cohesiveness that draws people together. Divine Love is the cohesive energy that holds our cells together to form organs within our body. The energy of Divine Love inspires the cells within an organ or body system to cooperate and function for the highest good of the total organism. Chronic anger, stress, frustration, or related emotions can set the stage for possible disease. Those emotions can become so repressed that we are barely conscious of them. But they can still be exerting their undermining influence anyway. When we have feelings of anger or frustration or sadness, we need to find constructive wholesome ways to express them so they don't become chronic and eat us up inside. It isn't healthy to completely hold feelings inside. We can heal this and restore loving harmony within our being.

Journal writing about our feelings can be helpful. Talking to a trusted friend, counselor, or religious professional can help. Calmly and rationally talking with other people involved in an upsetting situation may help to negotiate a better solution. A daily relaxed walk is balancing and stabilizing. Meditation, prayer, yoga, tai chi or something similar can be very beneficial. We can pray to be immersed in gentle warm loving feelings for other people, ourselves, and life in general. A kind loving heart is a gift from God and our Higher Self--and it is a blessing to share with others. It is a precious gift indeed. Approaching life through the heart of compassion and gentle love can help heal us emotionally and physically. Pure love grows through sharing it. Let's send out pure love and share it. It will circle around and return to us increased many-fold--sometimes from the least expected sources.

What Is Important to You in a Romantic Relationship?

Romantic love is passionate and can be very good, but it has numerous other elements within it other than Divine Love. Romantic love comes in as many different forms as there are people in love. Each individual synthesizes within his or her being a unique blend of characteristics that express as romantic love. One person may have a great deal of undemanding adoration for the beloved. This person wants to please the other and do things that are helpful for the beloved. His or her requests tend to be reasonable and the love tends to be ongoing and stable. This love is not withdrawn every time the other person does something of which the loving person disapproves. It is not a demand for general obedience. It is an extension of tender feelings and caring within reasonable mutual agreements. Adoration can grow into mutual shared devoted love and a very beautiful relationship. This type of love can also exist between friends and family members.

Another kind of love is demanding love. Here the tables are turned from that just described. The person who extends demanding "love" is focused primarily within his or her own feelings. The person "loved" exists mainly as an externalization of the demanding person's wants and demands. The energy of demanding love is often harsh and angry. It frequently inspires fear or anxiety in the receiver. There is often concern of not sufficiently pleasing the demanding one. It isn't a balanced relationship. Everything centers on the moods of the person who is being demanding. Demanding love can turn to near (or actual) hate sometimes. This is only love in name, not in reality. It is helpful to avoid this kind of person when possible.

Clear Agreements Can Be Very Helpful Between Partners in a Loving Relationship--How Has That Worked for You?

Obviously there needs to be a certain amount of responsibility within a loving relationship of any type. Every loving relationship is based on an agreement of some sort. This agreement will vary tremendously according to the type of relationship it is. Let's look at couples. Some couples may agree to split responsibilities within a relationship. In this case it is a form of respect between the two people to uphold the agreements. If both people in a two-person agreement are faithful in their responsibilities, things can run fairly smoothly. This was the case for a very long time in a lot of marriages. It was tradition that the man would have certain jobs to take care of in the family, and the woman would have others. To some extent they could pretty much count on each other to live up to their word. This worked fairly well for many families.

Things are very different today for couples living together in a romantic relationship. Roles are not at all clear-cut anymore. Many decisions need to be made as to who is responsible for what. It is important to bring to mind that most women are now working a job in addition to any child care and home upkeep. This significantly affects fair sharing of the load of responsibilities in the home in order to avoid possible physical and emotional drain and burnout. Eating most of the meals out really isn't a healthy solution. You can read more about healthy solutions in the chapter "Walking the Path to Wellness." Also relevant to this discussion is that traditional roles are sometimes stifling to both women and men. Not all women want to fulfill the typical feminine roles in a relationship, and not all men wish to fulfill the typical masculine roles. Additionally, many couples today are not heterosexual. Same sex relationships bring up inevitable decisions as to who would like to meet which needs within a relationship or home. The important issue is that realistic agreement needs to occur as to what is expected of each other.

Tremendous honesty is necessary here if the loving relationship will thrive. If there is honesty and good intention, there is a good chance for the two people to be happy. Another crucial piece of the agreement in order for it to succeed is trust. An agreement between two people in a romantic relationship needs to be a sacred trust. Honesty, good intention, and trust will go a long way toward allowing romantic love to last and thrive. Without these, it is anything but love--it becomes control and struggle.

What About Sexual Faithfulness in a Romantic Relationship?

I feel that Divine Love doesn't give either person in a romantic relationship license to be unfaithful to the other. That can, of course, cause great heartbreak emotionally. Also, when a person is unfaithful to his or her sexual partner and has an affair elsewhere, this can put the original partner in possible serious danger of sexually transmitted disease. Many people don't realize when they are carrying a sexually transmitted disease and it can be transferred around to others without anyone knowing it at the time. This can be an extremely serious health risk. Some men are unable or unwilling to use a condom, and thereby increase the risk of sexually transmitted disease being transmitted through casual sex.

When one is sharing Divine Love, the peace and happiness and health of the beloved are of immense importance. The sacredness of the relationship will not be broken just for fascination elsewhere. If change to the relationship is necessary because of insurmountable differences, deep searching is needed and possibly therapeutic support. Separation with love may sometimes seem to be necessary. If so, the relationship can possibly continue in a supportive caring way in a different form.

Films and Media Often Portray Sexual Unfaithfulness as Exciting--What About the Heartbreak and Broken Families?

Why is this discussion of Divine Love focusing so much on the importance of making and keeping agreements within romantic love? It is because the perception of romantic love has too often lost its sacred core and sense of responsibility. This is one reason that so many children are growing up in single parent homes. Responsibility to agreements needs to be equal with romance in order to form a true love in which Divine Love can thrive. Irresponsible love is idealized in media, and leads to much unnecessary confusion, disappointment and pain.

From where will the leadership come for healing romantic love back into alignment with Divine Love? This is a huge moral need today, particularly for younger people. Attitudes are to a high degree drawn from mass media, and people in mass media too often have little sense of responsibility for the long term welfare of their audience. Thankfully there are exceptions. Many people in society at large are floundering and looking to drugs or alcohol or overeating to camouflage their feelings of unease or confusion. Good role models are seriously needed wherever possible.

Trust, Respect, and Good Intention Can Create a Safe Space In Which True Love Can Thrive--We All Need That, Right?

Love is not just a feeling, or passion, or excitement in the presence of the beloved--it is a trust and respect and the intention to treat each other very well and live up to agreements. This can create the safe space in which true love can thrive, whether it is romantic love or an agreement between any two people.

The form that the agreements might take would vary greatly depending on the needs of the two people and their life style. If they are living together or plan to live together, the agreements might include (among other things) decisions as to: feelings about children and their care; how money is handled; feelings about sex; religion; the sharing of home responsibilities (house cleaning, grocery shopping, cooking, washing dishes, laundry, yard care, car care, etc.); and what is or isn't expected of each other regarding sharing each other's strong special interests. This can make for very helpful valuable discussions which can deepen and enhance understanding and clarity in a relationship.

Divine Love is Ideally Active in Our Lives All the Time--A Person Filled With Divine Love Radiates Peace and Goodwill! Pure Love is Contagious!

Let's return and look deeper at what Divine Love is and how it can enhance our lives. A person feeling Divine Love is interested primarily in the welfare of other people, not mainly what others will do for oneself. This is a huge difference of which it is crucial to be keenly aware. A person trying to get something from others will often give an appearance of being very ingratiating. This can be charming and at the same time deceptive. There is usually a sense, however subtle, that something is a little off.

On the other hand, a person filled with Divine Love radiates peace and well-being. To the extent that one is operating from Divine Love, that individual is focused on supporting others to follow their heart's call. They listen to others carefully, absorb the deeper meaning, and respond in a real way. If there is an agreement between two people, with Divine Love that is honored and fulfilled quietly and reasonably without undue fuss.

Divine Love is ideally in operation at all times in one's life. It is not something to be saved for only those to whom one is close. Divine Love overflows the banks of one's life. It is generous. As said, it is not looking mainly for return. When one is filled with Divine Love, the act of loving is its own reward. There is a joy in seeing others happy or content. Just to smile at someone and see them smile back can be uplifting for both. Don't underestimate the power of small blessings, they can add up. Divine Love is contagious. People sense its authenticity. Others can bask in the warmth of Divine Love. They may want to emulate it in order to enhance this wonderful feeling in their own life. It can become like a hunger to experience more and more of this ambrosia. It is free and there are no downsides. It creates only good. What more can one ask?

We Can Embody Power and Pure Love at the Same Time

As we grow in Divine Love, it is important to maintain our boundaries at the same time. Being a fountain of Divine Love for others does not mean that we allow others to trample on us. When some people experience the sweetness of a person radiating Divine Love, they may get the idea that here is someone they can manipulate and of whom they can take advantage. That is far from the truth and should be firmly avoided. A Spiritually mature person should ideally embody not only Divine Love, but also Divine Wisdom. Unless we have made an agreement with someone, we are not responsible to follow their directions or allow them to control us. Bossy people sometimes feel that a gentle loving person is an open invitation to be pushed around. This is not true. Spiritual people are powerful people and stand their ground. Being a person filled with and radiating Divine Love has nothing to do with being weak or unduly pliable.

Divine Love draws or attracts others to cooperate in mutual agreement. It is a healing energy. Divine Power is an outward radiating energy. Divine Power holds a vision and manifests action toward the vision through firm persistence and persuasiveness. The two can balance each other within one person. The two have sometimes been considered opposites, but it is very important that they be understood to be mutually complimentary within one individual. Separating Divine Love and Divine Power into separate individuals within a relationship can be harmful to the development and highest good of each individual. The primarily loving individual may feel dependent on the partner to forge a path ahead in life. She or he doesn't want to offend anyone or appear to be in competition with others, so there may be a hesitation to take necessary risks. Change can feel intimidating. With Divine Love, sometimes we are so content with loving whatever is around us, that evolving into something more may have little appeal. Life never stands still, it is always evolving. If we are to grow and thrive, we need to keep opening to our own flowering potential. This is where the balance of Divine Love and Divine Power comes in. Divine power gives us the courage and confidence to follow our dream and vision confidently without fear or hesitation. This is a powerful combination.

At one time in past periods of history, it may have seemed that a person couldn't handle embodying too many Divine Qualities at a time. It may have seemed best for an individual to focus on one major character quality in a lifetime. That may have served humanity well in the past, but we are now in a different stage of human development. We are ready for more complex roles in life. It isn't necessarily an easy transition. It may seem stressful to be truly powerful and truly loving at the same time. Once it is understood as normal and nothing to fear, then it will manifest for more and more people effortlessly.

Heart centered loving people have great need for the capacities possible through embracing power in their life. It is hard to emphasize this sufficiently. Heart centered loving people must believe in themselves and in their crucial role in healing humanity and our global community at this time. Divine Love is the great healing energy, and Divine Power is its rightful partner--not its adversary. They need to go hand in hand in each individual to truly move forward the highest good for all.

How About the Balance of Power and Pure Love in Businesses and Commerce?

With this alignment of love and power, more businesses will have increased conscience and higher morals. Business people will realize ever more fully that success is only possible when it serves the highest good of all people. It will be clear that getting ahead of the competition at the expense of the true welfare of the employees or the customers doesn't work. The Spiritual law of cause and effect will always circle around and bring back to them what they do unto others or what they cause. It is just a matter of when. With Divine Love at the center of power, then commercially prepared foods will first and foremost be supportive of health. There would be no desire (on the part of some businesses) to fool the public into thinking that what is being offered in a food product is going to sustain health when it won't. A truly open heart couldn't bear to put profit above compassion and caring for the highest good of all. Sometimes businesses may not really understand the total effect of their product on their customer's lives, but they truly need to give very deep consideration to this. They need to consider how a realistic sized serving a customer eats will fit into his/her total day's intake of sodium, calories, fat, and other nutrients (and also consider food coloring, preservatives, and other additives). Great appreciation is extended to those commercial food processing companies that ARE truly putting the health of the customers first.

Love Yourself and Know That You Are Truly Worthy of Human Love and Divine Love

As more and more people are holding this profound consciousness of Divine Love, a planetary network is gradually being created to help sustain the struggling souls who haven't yet found that Sacred place of healing in their heart. Love yourself and know that you are truly worthy of human love and Divine Love. Frequently affirm silently or out loud, "I love myself, I believe in myself. I love you, God. I am Divinely loved. I am Divinely worthy." Believe in Divine Love. Pray for and invoke it. It is inexhaustible and it comes directly from the Divine.

Divine Love is always available at any time if we allow ourselves to open to it. It can help transform our lives into enhanced steady peace and joy. May we learn to feel it independently of another person. It's a very real feeling that wells up in the heart. Let's feel ourselves overflowing with Divine Love, and share the overflow with people around us. This ability to experience Divine Love makes it possible for us to share it with other people at a much deeper and more real level. May we allow Divine Love to bless us, and help each of us to open ever more fully to the true magnificence of our being. Blessings!

Real Life Sharings Of the Healing Power Of Divine Love

A Devoted Family Man Looks At Love
~ by Kenny Marine

My wife and I have been married for sixteen years; we've known each other for twenty four years. I can't imagine being without her. I've loved her most of my life. I was "in love" with her first, before I really loved her. I never really let her know that until after we both graduated from high school. That led to us getting married and having children. It is hard to explain, but both of our children are a continuation of our love together. We didn't plan on having children as quickly as we did, but it has worked out well. Whenever I see them, I see a reflection of her. She is the other half of me. If anything ever happened to her--I would maybe date somebody else, but I would never marry again. There could never be that connection ever again.

My Mom was very loving. She inspired strong moral values in me. This ring on my finger really means something. Some of my friends get engaged after six months. I knew my wife a long time before I ever got married. I can't imagine going through this crazy thing called life without my wife. She is my conscience. She is the angel on my shoulder saying don't do that--or that's O.K.

My love for my kids is the same way. I can't imagine my life being what it is without my kids. My son is fourteen and my daughter is soon to be twelve, and they are great kids. They are very loving kids because we have passed on to them to be that way. Every once in a while I have to give a little "reset" to remind one of them to "think about more than just you, it's about everybody here." Among my children and my wife and my Mom, whenever we are on the phone--the last thing we say to each other is "I love you." There's never a lack of love, that's for sure. (See Resources Page)

A Case History Of Healing Love Through Couples Counseling
~ by Joyce

A couple comes to my mind that seemed to love each other very much--but sort of quibbled a lot. We'll call them Carl and Stacy. The first session when I did couple's counseling with them, their words were tumbling all over each other. One would speak and the other would often speak at the same time. They were both busy speaking, but who was listening? They seemed to be disconnected from hearing each other. I sensed strong caring, but there seemed to be "weariness" on both sides as to whether they would ever be understood. They both struck me as highly sensitive people with intense feelings. They had a lot in common such as a strong religious faith, and a network of close friends. She had numerous allergies, which he sometimes didn't want to hear about. Yet his health required a gluten free diet that took a lot of special effort on the part of Stacy to prepare. It was clear to me that my job was to get them to slow down and stop talking long enough to listen to each other.

We started each session with a short guided relaxation listening to soothing music. We each simply focused on our breath as it flowed naturally in and out. Then I encouraged each of them, one at a time, to say three things they appreciate about the other. The peaceful music, guided relaxation, and sharing appreciation helped create a nurturing supportive space. Then I had them take turns speaking for four minutes without being interrupted. In this approach the speaker is to talk about his or her own feelings about life and what is going on within--and not about the other person at all. The partner simply listens attentively.

True listening is a profound experience. The Sufi culture in Middle Eastern countries has "wisdom stories." These stories are said to have nine levels of meaning. In true listening the intent is to deeply absorb the subtle nuances of some of the layers of what another person is communicating to you. In usual conversation, a large percentage of people are focusing on what they want to say ncxt--rather than on the complexity of what the person with whom they are conversing is sharing.

When one listens with an open heart and mind, various of these layers of meaning can be understood. One layer may be the surface words, another layer may be the tone of the voice and the posture. Another layer may be what the person is saying "between the lines." Another layer may be the emotions you sense within your partner. Another layer may be how you sense your partner is responding as you really listen in a caring way.

After the first person speaks, then the second person has the precious opportunity to speak uninterrupted for four minutes while the other listens with full attention. This can go back and forth a few times during a session. I call this "heart centered deep listening," and it can work miracles. Carl and Stacy began to listen to each other rather than talking over each other. There was some interrupting, but they did pretty well. Their "assignment" between sessions was to practice their "heart centered deep listening" each evening, if only for one round of four minutes speaking for each--preceded by the relaxation and the sharing of appreciation.

After a few sessions along this line of "heart centered deep listening," they came in for their fourth couple's counseling session with an increased sense of gentleness and patience between the two of them. I didn't need to be the referee any more. There was a warm respectful tone in their voices. They looked at each other with smiling eyes and listened with real attention when each other spoke. We all felt that they were ready to take it from there on their own. They promised to keep practicing their "heart centered deep listening" skills. About six months later they let me know that they were doing well. They were enjoying exploring vegetarian cooking together and were having fun taking ballroom dance classes as a couple.

Bridging Love With My Father
~ by David

This is about when my Dad became sick. I drove him the day that he went to the oncologist. When I went with him into the exam room, I noticed a newspaper clipping describing that the doctor my father was seeing was starting an acupuncture practice. That sort of fit with new things I was learning about alternative healing. The doctor came in and pretty much said that he couldn't do anything to help Dad. The results showed that the cancer had advanced to a point that there was nothing that he could provide. He could do some very aggressive things that might possibly extend my father's living just a little bit longer, but it was essentially not a good approach because it would lower his quality of life to go through these really harsh things. Back in the car I said to Dad that I would try to find out about something that could help him feel better. So I talked to several people and I found out about Reiki Energy Healing Therapy. Shortly afterward I took a beginning Reiki Course. A person doing Reiki Therapy allows Spiritual healing life energy to flow through him to the receiver. Reiki means universal life energy in the Japanese language. The very first time that I gave Dad a Reiki treatment (for about an hour) he said, "I don't know what you did, but the pain is gone."

I spent a lot of time with him in the following months doing Reiki for him. This created a new bond for Dad and me that wasn't there before. He was a quiet person who didn't like to touch or hug other people. He was a farmer who worked by himself through most his life.

Reiki usually involves lightly touching the recipient (who is fully clothed). This was a completely new way for us to have a relationship with each other. It was a transformation for both him and for me. The numerous times I did the Reiki for him were gentle healing experiences for both of us. My dog often came in to sit by him and Dad patted her. I played quiet soothing music. Every time I worked with him he said it eased the pain.

Before long he began to decline physically as the doctor predicted, but the Reiki did ease the pain and help him feel better. Mom and I stayed by his bed when it seemed that he might soon be passing on. I felt his presence Spiritually comforting us. When I went out to the backyard on the night that he transitioned to the Spirit world, the moon was shining brightly and there were little clouds to both sides of the moon that looked to me like angel wings. I felt very close to Dad through this period, and I felt his love more than ever before.

Note from Joyce: Reiki Energy Healing enhances the aura of a person, animal, plant, or anything else--though usually it is utilized for people. For those who are somewhat new to Reiki (pronounced Ray-Key) I'll mention a few important pieces of information. Reiki and other forms of healing energy therapy are more and more widely recognized by mainstream America as very beneficial. Large numbers of nurses have been trained in Reiki and use it to help their patients. Nurses can receive Continuing Education Credits by taking training in Reiki Energy Therapy. There are a tremendous number of Reiki Therapists around the United States and the world. Reiki normally involves the therapist lightly touching the recipient. Through prayer and focused intention, the therapist is able to act as a conduit of universal life energy to support the enhanced health and healing and general well-being of the recipient. There is some relation between Reiki and "laying on of hands" as practiced by some traditional churches.

Sharing Love Within Friendship

~ by Anonymous

I'm single and quite content with my life. I enjoy gardening here in southern California, and I delight in photographing the flowers and vegetables that I grow. I also enjoy photographing wild flowers when I'm out with my hiking club. I'm a dental hygienist with a busy dental office, so I interact with a lot of people. I basically like my job. The office staff says I'm good at calming nervous patients. I got divorced over ten years ago. He got involved with a woman from his company. At first I thought I wanted to get married again right away, but now that's not on my mind.

My hiking club is important to me: we often go on outings together on weekends. There are some awesome people in the group. We have fun. I have a really close friend in the hiking club who shares my enjoyment of reading. When we walk together, we talk at length about the books we are reading. Every book I read is like a new window on life to me. My Spirit can soar with some of these authors. She feels the same way. She's like my "Soul Sister." My biological family almost all live on the east coast--and here I am out on the west coast. Since I'm not married, don't have children, and my family are far away--holidays used to be sort of a challenge. Since I've found my "Soul Sister" I'm fine. Her friendship means the world to me. We understand each other. I love her. She is like family to me.

True Love
~ by K.C.

True love is unconditional, unselfish, permanent, ego-less, painless, understanding, accepting, beautiful. These things I have learned. I'm still working on some of them. Some are easy, some are hard--maybe that's why I'm still here. (Written by a busy grandmother of five.)

Finding My Son After 26 Years
~ by Linda Cassidy Lee, Louisville, Kentucky

I was blessed with Divine Love when I found my son, Rusty, in 1996 through NBC Studios in New York City. I had responded to a telephone number I saw going across the screen when I was watching Oprah. I believe it was for USA People Search. They must have called NBC and told them they had a "live one," meaning I was an emotional crier. I was invited to go on a T.V. show that doesn't exist anymore that brought people together with lost loved ones. I was reunited with my son right on stage twenty-six years after having given him up for adoption. I had lived for years with the grief of having to give up my son. Not a day went by that I did not think of Rusty, wondering if he was loved and happy. I had given Rusty up for adoption in California because I come from a devoted Catholic family in Kentucky and I did not want them to know that I had gotten pregnant out of wedlock. I had wonderful parents who adopted me at the age of five through their Divine Love.

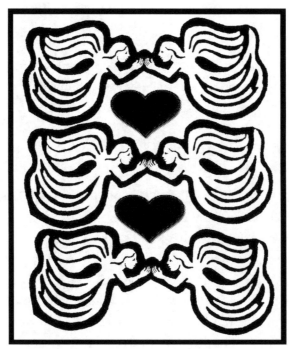

Angels Share Divine Love
Original Art by Joyce J.C. Gerrish

WORKBOOK: Enrichment Experiences For Enhancing Divine Love In Your Life

Enjoy the adventure of exploring these enrichment experiences on your own, or gather a few friends to share the journey with you. Be inspired by the audio meditation and soul song for this chapter. Reflect on some of the stimulating ideas and questions.

Questions For Reflection And Discussion

Reflection, discussion, journal writing, expressing your feelings in drawings or other creative ways can all be very valuable to help you delve into these questions in truly meaningful and relevant ways. Before focusing on the questions, you may wish to meditate with the twelve minute audio or transcribed meditation --and/or listen to the soul song "I Am Love."

1. What kind of love am I expressing in my relationships? Are there times when I share Divine Love? Are there times when I seem to be expressing controlling or demanding love? How do I feel about that?

2. How do I love myself? Am I patient and kind to myself? Do I encourage myself, or do I sometimes keep berating myself? Do I have loving gentle feelings for myself? If not, how can I be more loving in this way?

3. What is my blend of Divine Love and Divine Power? Am I able to be loving and yet powerful at the same time? In what situations do I succeed in that, and in what situations do I want to enhance that?

4. (For those who have children in their life) What is my optimum blend of controlling love and Divine Love with children? How can I nurture their free spirit and soul growth, and at the same time protect and guide them adequately?

Action Suggestions For Enhancing Divine Love In Your Life

1. Choose some aspect of your life that is important to you. Decide on how you might enhance it through being even more heart centered than usual. Try it. Beam out compassionate caring and love from your heart center. Your awareness of beaming out love will naturally affect how you speak, how you act, and your facial expression. There is also an energy of Divine Love that people will sense and respond to unconsciously (or consciously). Do people react to you somewhat differently when you are sending out the feeling of love? Do you enjoy it? Would you like to practice being even more heart centered in other aspects of your life, too?

2. Practice being truly loving and yet truly powerful at the same time. Is there a situation in your life where you would like to apply that? Practice in your mind how you would act and what you would say. As an example, imagine that at your job (or volunteer position) you and a co-worker are responsible for an assignment together. You sense that the other person isn't really doing a fair share of the work. Is there anything like that going on in your life now? How would you be heart centered and kind--yet at the same time be clear spoken regarding fairness in the situation? Sometimes it can be helpful to first express your goodwill, respect, and friendship. Then get the other person to talk to you about how they see the situation and the responsibilities that each of you are carrying and fulfilling. While you are talking, practice beaming out love from your heart center. Sometimes talking together in a relaxed way about the specifics of the division of shared responsibilities can bring greater clarity and cooperation. In a kind but firm manner perhaps say in what manner you feel the situation would be a bit more balanced. Try beaming out love to that person whenever you think of them and when you see them. The person will feel it subconsciously, if not consciously. Try doing that in some aspect of your life. After you have worked at it some, ask yourself the following questions. "How did it go? Was it helpful? How did I feel about it? How did the other person or persons seem to react?"

3. Choose an aspect of your life where agreements with another person could help enhance the relationship and avoid some of the pitfalls. This could be with a family member, friend, co-worker, significant other, or someone else. Invite the other person to sit down and plan some agreements with you. Be sure that you both feel positive about the agreements, and that you are both "on board." It is important that the agreements are fair to both of you. This is a situation where combining Divine Love and Divine Power may be important.

Audio: "Meditation to Enhance Your Experience of The Divine Qualities," with Focus on Divine Love

Pray to the Divine to bless your meditation and enhance Divine Love in your life. Choose one or more of the following affirmations (or something similar) that feels particularly helpful to you for affirming during the meditation. Write down the affirmation(s) you choose and place it where you'll see it daily and be reminded to affirm it for a minute or two several times a day.

◆ I love myself, I believe in myself.

◆ I am Divinely loved, Divinely worthy.

◆ Divine Love fills my being, and radiates out to all those around me.

◆ My love for others is kind, fair, and nurturing.

Helpful color to visualize when meditating on Divine Love: Pink or Green

I encourage you to enjoy this meditation when you wish to support Love in your life. Connect to website to listen to the twelve-minute audio "Meditation to Enhance Your Experience of the Divine Qualities," focused on Love.

(See transcribed version of this meditation at the end of this chapter.)

Uplifting Audio Soul Song: *"I Am Love"*

Original music composed and sung by Joyce.

Consider it a prayer in song for enhancing warm, nurturing Divine Love within yourself and your life. The words are:

I am love,

I am love.

(In many melodic variations)

As you sing or listen to this song, just feel yourself beginning to melt into the experience of Divine Love. Close your eyes and really sense it helping to bring you into a warm feeling of peaceful love. I invite you to the website where you can listen to *"I Am Love."*

Transcribed Version of Meditation to Enhance Your Experience of Divine Love

If possible, listen to some relaxing nonverbal music. Say a short prayer calling on the Divine to bless your meditation and to enhance Divine Love in your life.

Visualize yourself in a ball of light to help strengthen your energy field.

Become aware of and follow your breath as it gently flows in and out your nose at its own relaxed pace.

Imagine yourself as a tree sending powerful roots deep into the earth to help you feel grounded and prevent possibly feeling spacey.

Then as you breathe in your nose, imagine you are breathing the strength of the earth up into your body. Repeat several times.

Listen to the relaxing music as you focus on gently breathing in and out your nose.

Visualize the color of pink or green.

As you breathe in your nose, imagine that you are breathing glowing pink light or green light into your whole being.

Silently pray to the Divine that your life be nurtured and blessed with Divine Love.

Next breathe in your nose and out your mouth for about a minute VERY GENTLY.

Now, very gently breathe in your mouth and out your nose for about a minute.

Then extra gently breathe in and out your mouth for a minute or so.

Now return to breathing in and out your nose.

As you breathe in your nose, imagine you are breathing in pink or green color into your whole being.

As you breathe out your nose, periodically say one or two of the following (or similar) affirmations silently.

◆ I love myself, I believe in myself.

◆ I am Divinely loved, Divinely worthy.

◆ Divine Love fills my being, and radiates out to all those around me.

◆ My love for others is kind, fair, and nurturing.

Continue in that manner for a few minutes or as long as you wish.

Conclude by thanking the Divine. Then once again send down roots for grounding.

I encourage you to enjoy this meditation when you wish to enhance Divine Love in your life. Write down the affirmation(s) you choose and place it where you'll see it several times a day and be reminded to affirm it for a minute or two.

Peace.

Four Women Join Hands in Forgiveness
Original Art by Joyce J. C. Gerrish

Chapter Four

HEALING YOUR HEART WITH FORGIVENESS
Enhancing Divine Forgiveness In Your Life

Enjoy listening to or sing along with this soul song about Divine Forgiveness "I *Am Forgiving.*" I invite you to visit the website SecretsofWisdom.net where you can listen to it and also enjoy looking at the accompanying full color design "Mother and Child Share Forgiveness."

Forgiveness Can Help Free You to Move Ahead in Your Life

Forgiveness is love in action. Forgiveness is power. Forgiveness is understanding or accepting another person's weaknesses and loving them anyway, even if it occasionally needs to be tough love. Forgiveness is seeing, understanding and accepting your own weaknesses and loving yourself anyway. Forgiveness includes the wisdom of not allowing others to take advantage of you. Forgiveness is the path to your own peace and well-being. Forgiveness has been greatly misunderstood throughout much of history. In this chapter, we take a look at forgiveness from many perspectives. We will look at how it can help transform your life and how it can help you embody your radiant visions.

Ideally we experience each moment as a Divine gift to be savored for all its beauty and potential. I believe that is the intention of the Creator. Each moment is like a blank artist's canvas on which we can paint luminous images. As we lift our consciousness Spiritually we can receive intuitions to help us step ahead on our life path.

This can be an adventure beyond belief. There needn't be anything holding us back from manifesting the life of our dreams. But many of us do allow some things to hold us to the past such as emotional hurts, trauma, or anger. Being bound to the past acts like cement holding us somewhat inert and static.

To Truly Thrive We Need to Be Fully Present in the NOW

In order to grow and blossom we need to be fully focused in the present. Imagine a long passageway in which there are windows. Some of the windows look out on scenes from the past of our life. Some of the windows look out at people who were important to us in the past. Through those windows we can see events that happened to us back then that involved the people surrounding us. Even though the events happened long ago, those memories can bring up feelings of sadness or happiness. Looking through some of the windows gives us joy, while looking through others may cast us into regret or despair or anger. When we continue to dwell at length on those feelings we are being pulled into the past. There is one window that looks out at the present moment. The one window that looks out at the present moment is the only one that invites and enables us to be vitally alive and creative in the NOW. That is the one window where we need to ideally stay focused if we choose to thrive. The other windows, those that look into the past, can lead to melancholy or day-dreaming.

We Can Learn and Grow From Old Mistakes and Move On

Seeking to understand the past can be useful in order to avoid repeating past mistakes. We can learn from the past. Once we learn the lessons from the past--then it is crucial to bless it, thank it, and release it with love. If we are willing, we can continue actively growing and evolving creatively for as long as we are in a physical body. That is the intention of life.

Many people start fairly early to live in the past, while others live in the future focusing on their wishes for times ahead. All those windows to the past and to the future are closed tight and impenetrable. We can gaze for a few moments and reflect, but in a real sense we are left a passive bystander. The window to the present moment, however, is like a glass door that opens easily so we can enter for dynamic participation. This is the window where life is calling to us. This is the window where life is welcoming us. This is the window where we are needed and have an important role to play.

Ways to Help Heal Our Past Into Greater Peace

How can we heal our past into greater peace so that we can stay more fully focused on living in the present? Forgiveness is a major key. Each of us may hold some regret in our heart and wish that we had done something better. No matter how well we performed in a past situation, it is always possible to wish that we had done even better or had handled a situation in a different manner. It is important to understand that we do the best we can in our own way in each moment. Once that moment is passed, we cannot change it. We can, though, change the way we perceive it. We also can change how we relate in the present to any people that were involved in that situation in the past. This is true whether they are still an active part of our life, or whether we and the other person are not in touch any more, or if the person is deceased. This is empowerment in the present. (In this regard, we can also change how we currently relate to other people in a situation that is somewhat similar to the situation from the past we wish to heal.)

If there is a hurt or angry place in your heart toward someone, try writing a letter to the person. With pen and paper, really tell that person how you feel. Be honest with your feelings. The act of writing the letter from your heart is therapeutic. You don't need to mail or give the letter to the person unless you choose to. After writing a letter (or several letters) to him or her, and after reflecting on the contents of this chapter and its audios--you may feel increased clarity on the relationship. If you are still in contact you may wish to talk to the person. Create an opening for possible peaceful communication. The opening can be as simple as "How are you? I wanted to say hello and wish you well." If you don't know how to reach the person or if he or she is deceased, writing the letters can be powerful and healing anyway. Let those old feelings come up a little at a time so they can be healed and released. They are only coming up briefly for that purpose--to let go. Give the old painful feelings to God-- give them to the Light. To support your forgiveness and letting go, try the helpful "Exercise of the Healing Garden Pool" at the close of the chapter.

Past events can run before the screen of our awareness almost like a video or movie. Sometimes we may have a memory that seems to go on and on vividly in our mind, or a scene may repeat over and over. It can have a tendency to keep running and holding our attention. Sometimes it may feel really intense or occasionally a little overwhelming. To the extent that we allow these memory video clips to hold our awareness--that is the extent to which we have less clarity to devote to actively living in the present. Through forgiveness we can let go of repeatedly running these old video clips. Sometimes forgiveness doesn't need to be long and drawn out, it can possibly be as simple as silently saying, "I give this old memory to the light. I did the best I could at the time. I thank it for helping me learn and grow through this experience." Often it is more a sense of attitude than anything else. It is a willingness to let go of and give the pain to the Divine. In a sense, all life can become a meditation on staying fully present in the moment.

Sometimes Forgiveness Can Mean that We Agree to Respectfully Disagree

Give thought to what was learned through the experience that needs healing. Sometimes it is a matter of one or possibly both people being a little more patient with the other. Is it possible that one or maybe both people needed to give a little more caring attention to the other in some way? There are times when trauma is caused by our perceiving a situation differently than another person or group perceives it. Maybe neither person nor group was all right or all wrong; but rather it could be that a difference of opinion caused the severe pain. In a case like that, some relief and healing can be gained from seeking to grasp the perspective of the other. It is helpful to understand the situation from the viewpoint of the other person. With everything in our heart and soul we may not agree, but sometimes we have no choice but to make some room for the very different opinions of others who occupy an important place in our life. Divine Love and compassion can sometimes help soften the sharp grating edges between people of very different mindsets. It can sometimes be a matter of respectfully agreeing to disagree.

Forgiveness Doesn't Mean That We Have to Re-Expose Ourselves to Danger or Abuse

There are times when a true and terrible wrong has been done--as in the case of having been physically abused, serious emotional abuse, child abuse, murder of a loved one, or other tragedies. Then it is not a matter of perceived offense, it is a real offense. This pain can be profound and truly needs the support of emotional therapy, if possible, to gradually bring some healing to it. Eventually, once wisdom is somehow drawn from it, however that seems possible--then to whatever extent we can, we need to give the pain to God so it doesn't eat us up inside. It is possible to pray that the abusive person's soul is lifted and healed--but that the person stays far away. It is possible to forgive someone and pray for their highest good as a way to free ourselves from being tied to them by the "cord" of our own anger or fear. Forgiveness doesn't mean that we have to re-expose ourselves to danger or abuse.

Forgiving Fate for the Loss of a Loved One

Let's look at forgiveness in regard to loved ones who died a natural death from illness or old age, or who died in an accident. It is natural to deeply miss a loved one who has died. Sometimes it is important to forgive fate for taking away the dear one. Perhaps there was some unfinished emotional business between us and the deceased. As profoundly sad as it is, we gradually need to grieve the loss and eventually move on. It is important and good to have precious memories which we treasure and to which we return periodically. That is honoring the person and the special moments in the past that helped to create who we are today.

Loved ones who are no longer with us in a physical body surely continue to hold a special place in our hearts. It can be comforting to have a photograph in the home as a reminder. It may be natural to create a ritual in honor of the loved one who has passed on. Such a ritual often consists of periodically visiting a place that person loved and saying a prayer for them--and allowing the love that was shared to fill our hearts. Occasionally they may visit us in a very special dream or when our consciousness is unusually uplifted. We may intuitively know that the loved one's soul briefly visited to extend well wishes or a message. It is possible to treasure these memories and feelings and yet not have them anchor us in the past. For us to have the possibility of living our amazing life to the fullest, it is extremely important to stay fully focused in the present.

If we are focused in memories it is like we are looking at the clouds in the sky rather than the vast luminous sky. Take a moment, and imagine that you are gazing at the beautiful radiant blue sky on a clear day. What an uplifting sight! The clear sky is extraordinarily lovely. Our memories could be compared to clouds in the sky of our consciousness. The more often we visit them and allow them to build up, the bigger they get. If we give too much attention to dwelling in old memories, those clouds can fill the sky. This is like a cloudy day when all we see are the clouds; the extraordinary reality of the vast blue luminous sky and glowing sun are hidden. The potential within each moment is unlimited if we stay totally present to the inherent opportunities within it. May we rejoice in the everyday miracles presenting themselves to us minute-by-minute--the feel of the breeze on our cheek, the incredible beauty of flowers courageously reaching for the sun, an opportunity to share our experience in some way in our community to help meet a need, the heartwarming smile of a friend, or sharing enriching thoughts and ideas. It is worth being totally present in the moment in order to savor and respond fully to these and so much more. Talents and skills can keep growing and developing as we pursue them actively and apply them in ways that are helpful for ourselves and those around us. It is all a great adventure for which it is worth staying totally focused and alert.

It's Valuable to Understand Why a Trauma Happened

How can we forgive and let go of old traumas so that they don't weigh us down and divert our attention and energy from the present? As said earlier, it is an inner orientation and decision to totally embrace the ongoing panorama of life as it presents itself to us in all of its glory and challenges. This isn't to say that it is easy to stay fully awake. We might prefer to not be aware of some things. But that isn't how we grow. We grow by pondering on the deeper meaning of all that we experience and see, and by distilling from it valuable insights and understanding to enhance life now. It is impossible to long for the past or to be bored when we are totally connected in the present.

If possible, it is valuable to understand why a trauma happened. Frequently an abusive person was abused as a child him or herself, and that is the behavior they know (or knew). Soldiers who have experienced combat duty have profound experiences of violence that can unfortunately haunt them and sometimes unintentionally carry over as some abusive behavior in their personal life. Sometimes people learned abusive behavior as a youth or as a young adult through peer pressure regarding alcohol, drugs, or violent behavior. They were perhaps trying to somehow achieve a misplaced sense of importance or a form of emotional release in that way. Therapeutic support and healing are needed in all these situations.

Helpful Group Support for Healing and Forgiving

It is well known that there are free therapeutic Twelve Step Programs to support people dealing with a wide range of issues. Forgiveness is a significant part of the Twelve Step programs. You may be very aware that there are valuable groups for not only alcohol, but for issues of overeating, narcotics, gambling, debt, and excessive shopping. There are Al-Anon groups for family members, and there are teen support groups. These and other similar groups and individual therapy can be deeply helpful for some people for healing and forgiving themselves and others. Healing and forgiveness are a noble and important journey that can require courage. The reward is the priceless treasure of mended relationships and renewed heart centered openness to the joy of life and its profound possibilities.

There are those who feel that everything happens for a reason. I personally feel that is often true, but not always. Childhood abuse is tragic and all too common. The child is not in a position to do much of anything about it except to endure it somehow. Those sufferings can continue to weigh heavily on an individual as she or he gets older. My article "We Can Heal Childhood Wounds From Abuse" can be accessed through the website that accompanies this book. It may be very helpful for some people.

Forgiveness in Relation to Reincarnation

If there seems to be no apparent reason for a situation of abuse, it can possibly be a carry-over from a previous reincarnation when the individuals knew each other before. That does not in any way excuse the abusive behavior in this lifetime, but it may give some understanding why those souls were drawn together.

A high percentage of people in the world believe in reincarnation: Hindus, some Buddhists, many Christians around the world, and various other religions and groups in the United States and elsewhere. Let's discuss the theory of reincarnation for a moment to help shed light on forgiveness in relation to past lives. A soul incarnates in a physical body to learn the Divine wisdoms. Each incarnation of a soul is a different personality and tends to look different, though there may be some similarity of interests and inclinations. Members of a soul group may weave in and out of each other's lives from incarnation to incarnation. We perform different roles for each other at different times--sometimes as married partners, sometimes as business partners, sometimes as soldiers fighting for different countries and meeting in battle. It can be a very complex interweaving from life to life. This interweaving can keep occurring from life to life to help bring balance between any two or more souls. Where there has been abuse or violence, it needs to be somehow brought into balance and healed. We learn through all that happens to us. Even if we unfortunately die from an experience, as a soul we learn through it and it wasn't totally wasted--as difficult and painful as that may be to imagine.

Life on physical plane Earth is a laboratory of learning for each of us as a soul. Terrible things that happen can sometimes be borne and comprehended more readily if seen from the long range vision of the soul. Each lifetime is like a day in the life of the soul. Some days are more how we would wish them than others; some lifetimes are more how we would wish them than others. In some ways, we may grow more through challenging lifetimes than through easy lifetimes. None of this makes painful experiences easier, yet it can give some perspective as to the many layers of it all. It may be helpful to know that there can be another chance in another incarnation. Past life therapy can be helpful for situations related to a past life. Many people, including myself, can do past life readings for people to aid deep soul level forgiveness and healing.

Pause, Think, Meditate, and Pray for Understanding

If a situation is from a past life or from our present life, the important thing is to understand the situation as well as possible. Did we learn anything from the interaction? The learning may be something to help us and the other person understand each other better in the future. On the other hand the learning derived from it may be the awareness of how to keep a distance from that person in the future and protect ourselves better to whatever extent possible. Even in the case of deciding to keep a distance from a person, forgiveness is an important piece of the process. Anger at a person can create a cord of energy which draws a person back to us until it is dissolved and resolved.

Forgiveness is a vast subject. A few aspects of it have been touched on here that will hopefully stimulate your awareness. Other aspects of forgiveness have been and will continue to be discussed in my writings in this book and in other collections. In summary, if you have had a difficult or traumatic situation with a person or group--step back and meditate on it or pray to understand it. Ask yourself -- what are the dynamics of the situation? What are the underlying reasons that you acted the way you did and feel the way you do, and what do you sense are the underlying reasons that the other person or persons felt and acted the way they did?

Taking time to understand is a huge step. Talking with a trusted friend or counselor may be helpful to reach greater clarity. Pray for enhanced understanding, courage, and love. Don't respond in haste if it is a current issue. If it is a past issue, be gentle with yourself yet persistent in working it through. What is the wisdom inherent in the situation for you? Wisdom is the pearl in the oyster shell. The oyster formed that precious pearl because there was the irritating trauma of a grain of sand within the oyster's shell home. We also can derive a pearl of wisdom when we are faced with trauma. Study the situation and ask yourself the following questions. "Which of the Divine Qualities of God do I need to apply here? (Peace, Love, Forgiveness, Wisdom, Clarity, Harmony, Healing, or one of the others.) What do I need to learn in this situation?" That will help put you on the right track.

Keep the Wisdom, Let Go of the Pain

Forgiveness does not mean being weak. It does mean being fair. Sometimes what we learn from a situation is to protect ourselves better in the future. Other times we may learn that we need to be more compassionate and loving in a similar situation in the future. Keep the wisdom and let go of the pain. Give the trauma to God. "To for-give" means "to give forth" the pain to God. Don't let that trauma of anger or resentment burn and hurt you inside. Extract the wisdom-- and give the pain, sadness, or anger to God. Release with love. Keep the pearl of wisdom from the situation and act from that. Forgiveness is a choice.

The important thing to remember is that everything we experience in the "school house of planet Earth" is potentially a learning experience. Everything we experience is an opportunity to grow Spiritually. Nothing is wasted if we stay awake to the moment in all its potential. True reality is in the Spiritual dimensions. The Spiritual realms are more real than the physical world in which we dwell as a soul in a physical body. Planet Earth is the "school house" where we can learn to embody the Divine Qualities of God. Every situation is an opportunity to practice applying one or more of the Divine Qualities. That is what is truly of great significance in every interaction. Reflect and ask yourself the following: "How can I be true to the highest Divine in this moment? How can I enact one or more of the Divine Qualities?"

If one doesn't somehow work through to forgiveness for the issues that come up in one's life, it can sadly lead to gradually somewhat shutting down the heart. Then one may miss out on much of the wondrous joyful opportunities that may come one's way to share love and goodwill and to contribute to all life around. Everyone has a special purpose for being here on earth and needs to keep the heart open in order to embody and share that precious gift.

Let's Remember to Forgive and Love Ourselves

I can't emphasize sufficiently the great importance of loving and forgiving ourselves. We learn through trial and error to a large extent. This inevitably involves making some large and small mistakes. Making a certain number of mistakes is simply a part of being alive. We can't beat ourselves up about every little thing that we may think that we didn't do just right. We need to love and encourage ourselves! What we may think was just terrible, others may have barely noticed or may have already forgotten about. In every situation seek to understand the underlying dynamics of why it happened. What is the wisdom to be gleaned from the situation? If one or more other people were involved, and if it seems appropriate--talk with them and see if some reasonable understanding can be reached to restore harmony.

Almost every time I lead a guided meditation, I include focusing in the heart chakra in the center of one's chest and saying encouraging and loving affirmations to oneself. "I love myself, I'm a good person. I do the best I can in my own way." Keep the wisdom from what may sometimes feel like a mistake, and let go of the pain. Give the pain to God to be dissolved in the Light. Act from the wisdom and move on to welcome each new day with an open heart!

Real Life Sharings Related To Forgiveness

Brother Broke My Baby Buggy--Forgiveness Healed Chronic Pain
~ by S.W. T.

Over the years, I have been working on forgiveness and keeping a forgiveness journal. I thought I had pretty much worked through any and all old issues with my immediate family, except with the brother just younger than me. As an adult, I remember that in any of our conversations I always felt an underlying frustration bordering on anger toward him. I could not figure out what it was. I just pushed it away.

One night a few months ago, I was looking through a magazine when I saw a picture of a little girl pushing an old-fashioned baby doll pram. I thought, "I had one just like that when I was little. I wonder what ever happened to it?" Then I had a flash back to when I was nearly three.

My brother is twenty-one months younger than me. When he was a baby, my greatest pleasure was to drag him off the bed, put him into my baby doll buggy and push him around the house. I loved it because it made him giggle. When he was six months old, mom started telling me, "Sister, he is too big for your buggy. He will break it. Don't put him in it anymore." But because it gave both of us so much pleasure, I didn't listen. One day, I put him in and was pushing when the bottom ripped out and he fell through. It scared both of us. He started screaming because he was hurt and/or scared. I was screaming at him because he broke my buggy. I was also scared that he may be hurt. My childhood vision faded at the point where I saw Mom run into the room to see what all the ruckus was about.

In the moment of that memory, I was so very angry at my brother, I probably would have punched him if he had walked into the room. I was that little girl standing looking at her screaming baby brother sitting on the floor in the middle of the broken baby buggy. I was so very, unbelievably angry and scared. My heart was racing and I could feel my blood pressure rising, I had the feeling that I just needed to scream; I could feel my face flushing with anger. I was REALLY angry. I was blaming him for something he was not at all responsible for. Of course, I also realized that I was really angry at myself for not listening to Mommy. Now my buggy was ruined and baby was hurt and Mommy was gonna be mad. It took a lot of "I forgive you, I forgive me," breathing out anger and breathing in peace, to let that anger go. Until that moment, I had forgotten all about that incident. Funny how little things can trigger something we so desperately need to heal.

After having done the forgiveness work on that incident, the next time I saw my brother, I talked to him as if I truly loved him and there was no underlying anger or upset below the "niceness." I genuinely loved him and was really happy to see him. In addition to healing that emotional angst toward my brother, a pain that had bothered me in my right shoulder for as long as I could remember was gone. Instantly in the moment of true forgiveness--that chronic, nagging pain was gone. Poof! Gone. Forgiving my brother for breaking my baby buggy healed a chronic physical pain that has not come back.

Now, when I think of the incident, I do so with laughter. Because really, if there had been a video camera there, I'm sure the whole incident could have made it to America's Funniest Home Videos or gone viral on YouTube!

THAT is the power of true forgiveness--emotional, mental, and quite often, physical healing. The ultimate result of forgiveness is inner peace, which I am becoming--one forgiveness at a time.

The Grace Of Forgiveness
~ by Judy

I tossed and turned in the wee hours of the morning, my mind replaying the decision that a person in my life made that adversely affected many areas of my life in a long-term way. Although it had been over two years, I still carried a lot of resentment and anger toward this person. Honestly, my negative feelings toward this person were holding me hostage.

For not the first time, I called out to God for help. I called maybe more sincerely this time-- perhaps because I was finally more open to receive help. I sat up, flipped on the light, and gazed at a stack of books at my bedside. I picked up one, flipped through it, and quickly came upon a chapter on forgiveness. An exercise for forgiveness was given. This exercise suggested visualizing the person you are having problems with, and saying that "I (your name) forgive and release you (the other person)" and ask that all things between both of you be finished. Then, still visualizing the person, ask that the Christ or Higher Self of that person forgive and release you and that all things between you and that person be finished. If the person doesn't want to forgive, the Christ or the Higher Self of that person would want to. This exercise immediately began to free me in the early hours of the morning, and I fell into a contented sleep. I had to repeat this exercise a few times afterward, but the quality of Divine Forgiveness truly freed and healed me.

Forgiveness Can Help Set Your Soul Free

~ by Luna

My friend's name is Natalie and she will forever have a magical, vibrant place in my heart. Natalie drove to see me one autumn weekend from the small town where we grew up together. I helped her to pick out clothes and she helped me with my make-up. She and I went out for the evening. We danced, giggled, and talked almost exclusively about boys. In the wee hours of the following morning, Natalie and I had a petty quarrel. We had been friends since 6th grade and I don't remember us ever having an argument. Eventually, we got back to my apartment and Natalie stated that she was going to drive home early. She was upset and so was I. I didn't get to give her a hug or tell her how much I love her. Natalie didn't make it home.

In the years following Natalie's death, I went through extremely challenging times. I lost myself for a while--and almost forever. I want to share this story with you, because forgiveness helped to set my soul free.

It's now been five years and it is Christmas time. I suddenly feel the strong inclination to walk out on my back deck. I take in the quiet sunset and breathe the crisp air as I gaze out at the trees. I feel clear, still, and open. I close my eyes to say a prayer of gratitude. I hold a special prayer for Natalie. I send her love from my heart and tell her I miss her ever so dearly. I tell her that I feel her forgiveness and love. I open my eyes and see a small misty orb of light floating through the sunbeams and I know that she is here with me.

I'd like to share some of what has been helpful to me on this healing journey:

◆ Yoga--lots and LOTS of yoga.
◆ Find a Spiritual guide who resonates with your Spirit. (Joyce is my Spiritual guide.)
◆ Surround yourself with loving family and friends who make you giggle.
◆ Eat local and/or organic whole foods. When you have time, prepare the food yourself.
◆ Walk out in nature, be with animals.
◆ Listen to uplifting music.
◆ Pray to the Universe.

Forgiving And Receiving Love

~ Anonymous

At the time, I had been a social worker for Child Protection Service for two years. Coming up was the first case at which I had to testify and advocate to "terminate parental rights." The anxiety, the tremendous agitation within me just at the thought of "terminating a parent's rights to their child" was overwhelming to me. I could not understand this extreme upset within me. I could not understand the revulsion within me to have to sever a parent from their child--even though I fully understood the utter irresponsibility of this parent. The precipitating factors for a termination are neglect/abuse of a child as a result of longstanding drug or alcohol or mental health issues. Why was I so upset?

There was something within me in great agitation concerning the rules of state law demanding a parent's rights must be terminated after a given period of no improvement, so that the child can be adopted and have other parents. It was as if I was unconvinced of the "rightness" of terminating a biological parent's right--neglectful or abusive or irresponsible as the parent may have been.

I did a "Spiritual Healing" session with Joyce. The hour unfolded incredibly. She said to visualize that I was in a beautiful serene place in nature. A wooded field is what I selected. I was guided to imagine a lovely healing pool in my special place in nature. She said to visualize my father on the other side of the healing pool. I felt his presence with us. Joyce asked, "What do you want to say to him?" As soon as that question was posed, I was certain of what I wanted to say. I said to my father, "I know you did the best you could. You loved us the best you could. You had such pain inflicted upon you as a child, being deserted by your father when you were twelve years old. Your mother taught you to hate your father. You felt such pain and rejection, and then you covered it up and denied it all your life. Yet it made you angry, you were always a hair's breath away from explosive anger and upset. We never knew when it would burst out of you. You would yell, rant, and sometimes you hit us. It was always supposedly our fault when it happened. You would yell mercilessly at our Mom. I came to accept that this is 'just how life is.' And day by day, week by week, year by year--my clearest memory is your daily mantra to us, "show me respect."

That was it! I had 'absorbed' the concept that a parent could be any way they wanted. They could inflict any rage, fear, upset, or smack--and yet demand respect. I had absorbed the concept that parents had the right to be abusive. I absorbed the attitude that a child must simply endure and submit--that was the role of a child.

A miraculous healing occurred and that old feeling began to dissolve that night with my new perspective. But wondrously, this realization did something else-- it transformed my heart toward my father. My heart saw more deeply than ever before the depth of his pain. I saw his lifetime of pain that caused his uncontrollable displays of anger.

I became aware of an unexpected genuine feeling of love for my father. And then I told him, "I forgive you, I know you did the best you could." And then another thing happened that had not happened to me before. I sensed my father's love for me. I felt love flow between us; acceptance flowed between us. It was strong and totally new. I felt his presence.

My unconscious had walked free from an imprisoning concept. All agitation ceased within me. Following this experience I felt absolutely released and free. I could do my job of terminating an abusive/neglectful parent's rights over the victim child. A new understanding had dawned, and with it paradoxically came deep forgiveness for my father and an exchange of love.

Two Horses in Circle of Understanding
Original art by Joyce J.C. Gerrish

WORKBOOK: Enrichment Experiences For Enhancing Forgiveness In Your Life

Enjoy the adventure of exploring these enrichment experiences on your own--or gather a few friends to share the journey with you. Be inspired by the audio meditation and soul song for this chapter. Reflect on some of the stimulating ideas, questions and suggestions.

Questions For Reflection And Discussion

Reflection, discussion, journal writing, expressing your feelings in drawings or other creative ways can all be very valuable to help you delve into these questions in truly meaningful and relevant ways. Before focusing on the questions, you may wish to meditate with the twelve minute audio or transcribed meditation--and/or listen to the soul song "I Am Forgiving."

Bring to your mind a situation for which you would like to enhance healing and forgiveness. Feel the situation in your heart as you move through the following suggestions. (Afterwards, you may wish to apply the same experiences to another situation in your life that would benefit with healing support.)

1. What are the dynamics of the situation? What are the underlying reasons that you acted the way you did, and feel the way you do? What are the underlying reasons that the other person or persons seem to feel the way they do, and have acted the way they have? Taking time to understand is a huge step. (Talking with a trusted friend or a counselor can sometimes be helpful in addition to work that you do on your own.)

2. Try writing a letter to the individual or individuals with whom you have (now or in the past) a disagreement or disharmony. You don't need to mail the letter, unless you wish to. The forgiveness

is for your healing as much as for finding harmony with the other person(s). It is possible that the other person may have forgotten or may barely remember the incident. Just writing the letter can be very helpful and therapeutic for you.

3. What do you need to learn in this situation that will help put you on the right track for the miracle of greater healing? What is the wisdom that it would be helpful for you to understand and glean from this situation in order to help you be even wiser and stronger and happier?

4. How can you stay more fully present in each moment and let go of the past and this situation more fully?

5. In addition to Divine Forgiveness, which of the other Divine Qualities would it be helpful to keep in your heart to deepen your healing? (Divine Peace, Divine Wisdom, Divine Love, Divine Harmony, or one of the others?)

6. Sometimes you may be somewhat hard on yourself. Is it possible that you feel ready to forgive yourself for something that you may have been beating yourself up about? Sometimes finding forgiveness with yourself is as important as finding forgiveness with someone else. Once again, the important thing is to keep the wisdom from the situation, and let go of the trauma.

Action Suggestions and Experiences To Enhance Forgiveness In Your Life

Choose an event in your life to which you would like to bring some healing with another person. The following are guided experiences you can repeat as often as you wish to help bring healing for different emotional wounds. As preparation, you may wish to listen to the audio "Meditation to Enhance Your Experience of the Divine Qualities," with focus on Forgiveness; or the Soul Song Audio for Forgiveness.

1. Healing Mandala Experience

Is there something in your life that seems to hang as a shadow in your consciousness? Maybe there are numerous events or periods of your life to which you would like to bring greater harmony. Embrace them with love and peace. They are a part of you and need healing and forgiveness. Forgiveness doesn't necessarily mean that you will even see that person or persons again, though that could be helpful. The crucial thing is to truly love free that hurt place in your heart and being. Use colored markers, colored pencils, or whatever you have available. Take a piece of white paper and draw a circle on it almost as large as the paper allows. You can use a plate or bowl upside down on the paper as a guide to draw the circle.

Inside the circle express your feelings about a memory or situation in your life that needs the support of healing. It can be expressed as simple stylized people, shapes, flowers, animal forms--or simply as an outpouring of colors. Don't worry about being artistic. Use lots of color to fill in areas of your creation. Colors express our feelings as powerfully as images. Allow it to be a therapeutic outpouring. When you have expressed your feelings to some extent, pause for the moment and LOVE your creation and yourself.

In any empty spaces inside the circle and in the corners outside the circle draw things that express gentleness and love to you. These could be hearts, rainbows, shining sun, stars, butterflies, birds or other symbols. Love is healing. You are creating a healing mandala which is a design in a circle of wholeness. When you are ready, pray over what you have created. Forgiveness doesn't mean that it is O.K. what happened, but that you are ready to release the heaviness from your heart and give it to the Divine. Forgiveness occurs in stages. One of the most important stages is loving yourself and forgiving yourself anything you may hold against yourself. From there you can let love be your guide and sense what else is possible.

Note: When a person has been abused or wronged, often on a subconscious level one ironically feels guilty as though believing that one must have been the cause of the abuse or wrong. This sense that oneself must be bad can be very strong after having been abused by someone else. Particularly a child doesn't know why else she/he would have been abused except for having been bad. So it is important to love and forgive oneself. At the same time it is important to be open to the possibility that there may have been two sides to the situation, particularly when neither of the individuals involved were children. The following "Exercise of the Healing Garden Pool" can be helpful for better understanding the dynamics on both sides.

2. Guided Visualization of the Healing Garden Pool To Support Forgiveness

This exercise can be helpful for enhancing understanding with another person when there is, or has been, disagreement or disharmony. It can also be helpful for healing past trauma with a person with whom you are out of touch, or when the other person is deceased.

Lift your consciousness with the Forgiveness Soul Song and/or Forgiveness Meditation first. Then, if convenient, turn on relaxing non-verbal instrumental music to create a peaceful background during the following meditation.

Imagine yourself walking down a lovely garden path with your guardian angel on a peaceful warm day.

The earth is soft beneath your feet and the sun feels warm on your cheeks.

You feel safe and serene.

You find a very special area of the garden that has a small circular reflecting pool.

Beautiful radiant flowers gracefully drape over the natural stones encircling the pool.

Sense the feeling of deep harmony.

There is a lovely rose quartz bench on one side of the healing pool.

A luminous angel sweetly invites you to sit and relax there, and you do.

Your guardian angel is now on one side of you, and a healing angel is nearby.

You feel loved and attended to.

On the other side of the pool across from you is another rose quartz bench with a lovely healing angel.

In a moment you will invite someone to sit on that other bench.

When you are ready, invite a person with whom you wish to enhance peace, understanding, and forgiveness.

Visualize that person sitting there with a lovely kindly healing angel by his or her side.

Speaking silently or aloud, what would you like to say to that person?

What do you feel that person would like to say to you?

Filled with the peace of the healing pool, the angels, and the Divine--what do you wish to say to that person?

Filled with the peace of the healing pool, the angels, and the Divine--what might that person say to you?

Do you feel ready to say some words of forgiveness?

Take it at your own pace. It is up to you.

What words of forgiveness do you feel that they might be inspired to say to you?

Feel peace enhanced between you.

Visualize the other person leaving with their healing angel.

Continue for awhile breathing in violet light while you listen to peaceful music.

As you breathe out, you may wish to affirm,

◆ I am blessed with Divine Forgiveness.

◆ I forgive and my heart is at peace.

In closing, it might be good to listen to the Forgiveness Soul Song audio or read some passages from your favorite inspirational book.

Blessings to you.

Note: It takes personal inner strength to forgive. Keep in mind, that with some people it is still important for you to set healthy boundaries to enhance the reality that future interactions will be appropriate.

3. Meet With or Telephone the Person with Whom You Would Like to Enhance Forgiveness, if it Feels Helpful

If it is appropriate for your situation, telephone or meet with the other person. It doesn't need to be a long conversation or meeting at first. If you don't live together, chose a meeting place that feels comfortable for you both. Be sure to listen carefully to what each other says. Sometimes it is helpful to agree that you speak one at a time while the other listens for three minutes. After one person has spoken for three minutes, then the other person speaks for three minutes while the first speaker listens, and back and forth. It is helpful to start and close your time together with each person saying something kind to the other. Blessings and peace to you both.

Audio: "Meditation To Enhance Your Experience Of The Divine Qualities," with focus On Divine Forgiveness

Pray to the Divine to bless your meditation and enhance Divine Forgiveness in your life. With this audio you'll be guided to sense yourself immersed in this profound feeling of Divine Forgiveness. Choose one or more of the following affirmations (or something similar) that feels particularly helpful to you for affirming during the meditation. Before transferring to the website to listen to the meditation, write down the forgiveness affirmation(s) you choose and the helpful color violet. Later, place the affirmation(s) where you'll see it often and be reminded to affirm it for a minute or two several times a day.

◆ I forgive myself my mistakes. I learn and grow from them, and move on.

◆ When I consider another person's point of view--it helps me find understanding, common ground, and forgiveness.

◆ Profound love can grow and flourish between forgiving hearts.

◆ As I forgive others, it frees me from being weighed down by my old emotional hurts.

◆ I know that sometimes tough love and distance are necessary when someone has abused me.

Helpful color to visualize when meditating on forgiveness: Violet

I encourage you to meditate with this audio when you wish to help support forgiveness in your life. Connect to the website where you can listen to the twelve-minute audio "Meditation to Enhance Your Experience of the Divine Qualities." I encourage you to do something nurturing for yourself after this meditation, such as taking a nice walk or soaking in a hot tub.

(Also, see transcribed version of this meditation at the end of this chapter.)

Uplifting Audio Soul Song: *"I Am Forgiving"*

Original composition sung by Joyce

Consider it a prayer in song for enhancing forgiveness within yourself. The words are:

I am forgiving all shadows from my past.

I am releasing.

I free my soul to fly.

Ah o-ou, Ah o-ou, Ah o-ou, Ah o-ou.

As you sing, just feel yourself beginning to let go of old trauma or hurt or anger. Let yourself feel peacefully immersed and flow with it. Close your eyes and really sense the song helping to bring you release and healing. You can access the audio at SecretsofWisdom.net.

Transcribed Version of Meditation to Enhance Your Experience of Forgiveness

If possible, listen to some relaxing nonverbal music. Say a short prayer calling on the Divine to bless your meditation and enhance forgiveness in your life.

Visualize yourself in a ball of light to help strengthen your energy field.

Become aware of and follow your breath as it gently flows in and out your nose at its own relaxed pace.

Imagine yourself as a tree sending powerful roots deep into the earth to help you feel grounded and prevent possibly feeling spacey.

Then as you breathe in through your nose, imagine you are breathing the strength of the earth up into your body.

Repeat several times.

Listen to the relaxing music as you focus on gently breathing in and out your nose.

Visualize the color violet like a lovely violet colored flower or an amethyst crystal.

As you breathe in through your nose, imagine that you are breathing glowing violet light into your whole being.

Silently pray to the Divine that your life be uplifted and blessed with Divine Forgiveness.

Next breathe in your nose and out your mouth for about a minute VERY GENTLY.

Now, very gently breathe in your mouth and out your nose for about a minute.

Then extra gently breathe in and out your mouth for a minute or so.

Now return to breathing in and out your nose.

As you breathe in your nose, imagine you are breathing in violet color into your whole being.

As you breathe out your nose, periodically say one or more of the following (or similar) affirmations silently.

◆ I forgive myself my mistakes. I learn and grow from them, and move on.

◆ When I consider another person's point of view--it helps me find understanding, common ground, and forgiveness.

◆ I find that profound love can grow and flourish between forgiving hearts.

◆ As I forgive others, it frees me from being weighed down by my old emotional hurts.

◆ I know that sometimes tough love and distance are necessary when someone has abused me.

After you have focused on an affirmation for a while, then simply breathe in light -- and as you breathe out, feel yourself letting go of any lingering heavy feelings that are ready to release. After any release, be sure to breathe in Divine Peace and Divine Love until you feel well centered again. Conclude by thanking the Divine for the enhanced peace and forgiveness. Send down roots again to help you feel well grounded.

Meditate on Divine Forgiveness as often as you wish to enhance healing, peace, and forgiveness in your life. I encourage you to do something nurturing for yourself after this meditation, such as taking a walk or soaking in a warm tub or listening to harmonious music. Write the affirmation(s) you choose and place it where you'll see it several times a day and be reminded to affirm it for a minute or two.

Peace.

Woman With Leaves
Original Art by Joyce J.C. Gerrish

Chapter Five

TRUE CLARITY SUPPORTS BRILLIANCE
Enhancing Divine Clarity in Your Life

Enjoy listening to or singing along with this peaceful soul song I've composed and sung about Divine Clarity: "*Clear Mind*." I invite you to SecretsofWisdom.net where you can listen to the audio "*Clear Mind*," and see the full color design "Woman Holding Cat Feels Peace and Clarity."

Who Me? Multi-task?

Life is complicated. Many of us have multiple responsibilities, interests, and concerns that pull us in various directions. Often we are trying to do numerous things at the same time. This is, of course, called multi-tasking. If there isn't more time in the day to help fit in all that we feel we've got to do, then many of us start layering our responsibilities one on top of another simultaneously so we can fit in more. Sometimes this works better than other times. Certainly we can walk our dog, get in our own exercise, and at the same time talk to a friend who may have joined us for the walk. We can listen to music, radio, or T.V. and at the same time do something that doesn't require serious thinking--such as house cleaning, cooking a familiar dish, or painting a wall.

Some things we can do at the same time without seriously interfering with how well we do them. Other responsibilities or activities may not combine so well. What about having T.V. or verbal radio on while trying to do something that requires close focused thinking such as studying or doing mentally exacting work? Many of us find it difficult to think deeply when the attention of the mind is divided. Driving a car and listening to a radio or audio player has been working well for decades, but driving a car and talking on a mobile phone isn't really considered safe. Apparently this is because our mind feels drawn out of the car toward a friend we are talking with who is elsewhere.

Once when I was talking on a mobile phone while driving, the friend I was talking with told me something startling. I lessened my clear driving focus for only an instant, but had to slam on the car brakes to avoid running a stop sign. Since then I don't talk on a mobile phone while driving.

Dividing attention between driving a car and texting or reading is definitely dangerous. One time I was walking down a quiet street and I saw an acquaintance drive by while reading from a notebook. She was not looking at the road directly--probably she saw it somewhat with peripheral vision. I felt serious concern for her. Tragically, within a month I was attending a memorial service for her. Apparently her car had crashed with a huge truck. Her significant other and young daughter and son were heartbroken.

What about doing business or socializing on the phone while sitting at the dinner table with family members or a friend? Why miss out on fully tasting the food and enjoying the people who are actually there? A client once told me of having been asked by his girlfriend to drive her to an event an hour and a half away. The whole way there and most of the way back the girlfriend texted or talked on her mobile phone to other people. He said that he felt progressively more and more hurt, and then somewhat irritated, and finally just began to wonder "why bother hanging out with her?" Over the months after that they went through a gradual process of drifting apart. He felt that when they were together she was only partly there. It's apparent that multi-tasking interferes to at least some degree with being fully present.

Stress and Other Ways Clarity Gets Obscured

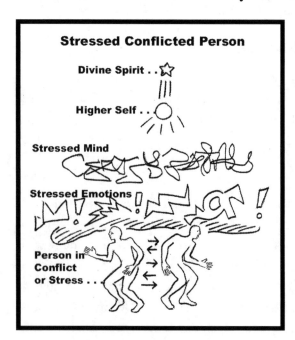

We constantly have choices as to how to use our time. Time is a very precious commodity. Many of us seem to find that we have more and more demands on our time. How we use our time is an investment. When we feel we don't have enough time to get everything done that we think we should, it's easy to feel overwhelmed. When we feel overwhelmed, it can sometimes be hard to focus clearly on anything. Part of us is perhaps worried about how we're going to get all these other things done. We may be concerned about what is going to happen if we don't get them completed on time. This can set up a real stress circle in our mind.

It has been scientifically proven that during stress a person's frontal lobes of the brain which are the seat of the intellect are much less active than usual. The more primitive back areas of the brain tend to be more active when a person is feeling anxious; hence, clear thinking is difficult. It appears wisest to not make important decisions when under stress, or at least not until after pausing to center and relax. As the old time honored truism says, "Take time to sleep on an important decision." The mental focus to do work requiring close clear attention is also impaired during stress. In such a situation it would be helpful to take a few moments to stretch, walk for a few minutes, and focus on your breathing until feeling more centered and relaxed.

For Some People, Clarity of Awareness Can Seem Too Painful

How to keep our consciousness clear is an art. For many people it is a lost art. In order to strive for clear consciousness, we need to first believe that there is value in it. Many people don't want clarity. Their desire may actually be to drown out any clarity of awareness. It's true, there are endless things to worry about such as: money, job issues, health, sex, violence, environmental pollution, or "do I look good enough?" There is no shortage of things to worry about. I have only listed a few. Vast numbers of people choose to do whatever possible to drown out clarity. Clarity of awareness can seem too painful.

The ways to obscure our clarity are well known. Alcohol is a popular method, and abuse of prescription and nonprescription drugs is certainly another. Overeating is a familiar way to attempt to deaden one's feelings and awareness. Remember for a moment how you perhaps felt after a large Thanksgiving meal--perhaps bloated and sleepy--not alert. For many people it hurts too much to be aware of life in a clear way. Listening to constant media and electronic devices can also be a diversion from being fully present to life in the moment.

If one tries hard enough to obscure clarity, one's consciousness and aura energy field can eventually become congested with stuck static energy. This can make it much more difficult to access one's higher levels of consciousness and the Divine. This can unfortunately become a downward spiral. The more depressed one feels, sometimes the more one may close down to the very sources of renewal so greatly needed. Sad!

Ways to Enhance Clarity--It's Worth It!

Ideally life energies are constantly flowing freely throughout one's aura. This is an ongoing process of renewal through accessing universal life energies and the Divine. These higher energies and impressions are extremely important because they help one to feel more connected to a sense of meaning in life. It is helpful for a person to stay connected to higher Spiritual awareness through meditation, prayer, inspirational pursuits, or something else that is uplifting in a wholesome way.

Group support can be helpful for regularly opening up to renewing energies and to the Divine. You may already be part of such a group. Many people feel they find that support in a church, temple, or synagogue. Some people prefer finding their Spiritual support by coming together with a group for meditation, tai chi, yoga, or something similar. That can be good, too. While many consider it valuable to have group support and a leader, some people may prefer being on their own. It can be fulfilling to set aside time at home for individual renewal experiences such as meditation, prayer, inspirational reading, uplifting music, or other peaceful Spiritual practices. These various options can help people stay in touch with the reality of the Spiritual dimensions and to periodically open their consciousness to receive renewal and enhanced clarity.

Clarity Is Like a Brightly Shining Diamond

Clarity is perhaps an under rated virtue. Being more fully aware of what is going on within and around one may seem to be ordinary to some. Truly, it is anything but ordinary. Once I asked the members of a class to each share in a few words what they were particularly focusing on enhancing in their life at that time. One woman said that for her it was clarity. I've always remembered the alert relaxed intelligent clear shiny look on her face. Clarity is like a brightly shining diamond. Everything is illumined and can be understood and integrated more optimally when the clarity of Divine light shines around and within one. This can help one make clear decisions and respond to situations more wisely. It may be tempting sometimes to just do what others are doing or what someone famous and admired is doing. But that may not actually be the wisest course of action for oneself. Clarity is needed in order to cut through the maze of potential choices. Making the effort to stay clear is definitely worth it.

How can a traveler get to the desired destination if not paying attention to road signs or a GPS system? In the "journey of life" road signs and GPS systems could be said to symbolize crystal clear awareness, good old fashioned common sense, and your intuition guiding you on the most optimum route to your goals and your highest good. We need quiet time for meditation, independent thinking, alert observation, and evaluation in order to enhance clarity. It is prudent to not take things on face value. Think it through. Without clarity-- much time and effort may be wasted in life detours and dead ends leading to disappointment and heartbreak. We all probably have stories to tell about that. Who needs it? Let's promise ourselves to stay in touch with our inner GPS system and fully embrace the miracle of our "journey of life!"

The Art of Clear Focus Supports Success

Look around yourself right now for a few moments and take in as many details as possible of the room or place where you are. Visually examine all the details. It can be a lot to absorb at once. Your consciousness learns how to make choices as to where to focus attention, since you can't pay attention to everything at once. This is particularly true in a very busy place such as a crowded street. If you try to be aware of everything at once, it may become a sort of blur. An important role of consciousness is to choose the aspect of what is going on around you that is most crucial--and let that be your focal point. This capacity is of extreme importance, and mastering it is one of the secrets of successful living. This is the ability to focus your awareness with total clarity on the issue with which you are dealing at the moment. Anything extraneous to the important issue at hand sort of ceases to exist to your consciousness for that period of time. Those who are exceedingly successful in any walk of life or profession are likely to have this capacity well-developed.

A Person With Really Clear Focus Can Accomplishment More in a Shorter Time With Less Stress! Now That Sounds Good!

Consciousness can become like a laser beam and powerful understanding can be grasped in that way. A person with this super clarity of focused consciousness can accomplish in a short period of time what someone with an unfocused mind might take a much longer period of time to accomplish.

Do you know someone who has an impressive ability to concentrate? Maybe you have this gift. A person who has developed this capacity can read very quickly and comprehend on a deep level. When able to focus so fully on a client in need, a counselor can grasp more readily the issues and how to help. Finishing a work assignment on time for a deadline can be greatly facilitated through intense focus. The precise work of a surgeon requires absolutely steady focus of consciousness. An artist in the act of creation becomes totally absorbed in the creative process to the extent that nothing else exists. This is a path that allows genius to express itself.

When one is totally absorbed in what one is seeking to accomplish, then this can open a channel to higher levels of consciousness. This clarity of awareness can allow crucial creative insights for extraordinary possibilities. Really think about that, it is extremely important. Many people allow their consciousness to be so scattered that they don't give themselves a chance to have profound insights and the joy of truly creative ideas.

The Incredible Cat with Laser-Like Focus

One time I was leaving a friend's house. My friend had left earlier before we had completed a project, so I was letting myself out of the house on my own. Her cat was across the street on a neighbor's porch. I didn't know if she wanted her cat inside while she was gone or outside. I decided instantly to close the door and leave the cat outside until my friend got home. All I needed to do was to step out the door and close it. The cat apparently had FULL CLEAR INTENTION that he would enter the house. His eyes focused on me with laser intensity. His body and legs bounded like a panther in the wilds with unbelievable speed. It was absolutely incredible. That cat defied all laws of physics by springing off the distant porch, hurdling across the street, vaulting along the front walkway, leaping up the cobble stone stairs, and whizzing through the door and into the house before I could just step out and close the door. It was like time stood still a moment. Wow! That was an amazing demonstration of what is possible with utterly clear focus and intention. He did the (near) impossible, as far as I was concerned. The cat appeared to have never doubted himself for a moment. That is perhaps a valuable lesson for all of us. I've never ceased to be impressed with that demonstration of the power of focus and clear intention.

Learning Concentration Skills Supports More Powerful Mental Focus--and is the Beginning of Meditation

How can one develop and enhance that laser-like clarity of consciousness and intention? In order to achieve that clear mind focus, one first needs to learn to truly relax the physical body and calm the emotions. Those are very valuable skills. To move in this direction, it is important to give oneself some quality quiet nurturing time on a regular basis: fifteen minutes a day of deep relaxation and meditation is a start if one is not already doing so. Setting aside this quiet time may seem selfish compared to the demands of job, home upkeep responsibilities, family needs, and apparent social and community obligations. One's life can sometimes feel so jam packed that not even fifteen minutes seems possible. The truth is that work output can actually increase when one feels more relaxed, refreshed, balanced, and clear.

I encourage you to choose a regular time each day for your relaxation/concentration/meditation practice. You may wish to listen to the twelve minute audio "Meditation to Enhance Your Experience of the Divine Qualities" (with focus on Clarity). It can be accessed at the website that accompanies this book: SecretsofWisdom.net. There is also a transcribed version of the same meditation at the end of this chapter. Another choice would be the seventeen minute audio "Guided Relaxation and Healing Visualization Meditation" (which accompanies Chapter 1) available at the same website. With both of these meditations, the focus is on being aware of your breath flowing in and out. Don't try to breathe extra deeply or hold your breath, just be gently aware of it. If your mind wanders just gently bring it back to your breath. Another option is to simply be aware of your breath flowing in and out as you listen to nonverbal relaxing music. It can be helpful to either close your eyes or focus your gaze on one thing such as a flower or a candle. Imagine sending roots deep into the ground and visualize yourself in a ball of light. For one minute hold your hands together in prayer position at your waist, then allow them to rest in your lap. Let go of any worries or thoughts for the time being. You can practice those skills off and on during the day for a few minutes whenever you may feel stressed or your mind feels scattered. That will hopefully help you feel more clear and refreshed when you return to what you were doing previously.

When you feel ready for the next step you may wish to listen to the thirty-four minute audio "Meditation to Enhance Spiritual Awakening and Illumination" at the same website that accompanies this book. That audio helps activate the chakras and begins to move into a more advanced form of meditation.

Inspired Insights and Solutions Can Be Accessed During Meditation

Inspired ideas can be accessed in quiet clear moments of meditation or contemplation. Those inspired ideas can cut right through perplexing problems and create a pathway of solutions for clear sailing ahead. We may wonder, "Why didn't I think of that before?" Inspired creative solutions can come through to us when we take time to truly relax and center on a regular basis. The reason is that those inspirations exist on a higher more subtle level of consciousness than the daily busy mind set of the typical everyday rushed life style.

When we step out of the house on a cloudy day, everything may seem a little dreary and depressing. But as previously mentioned, the sun is always shining above the clouds. If we have a cloud of worry and static blocked energies around us, all we need to do is to raise our consciousness above the level of these stuck energies. Through the peace of meditation we can re-experience the shining sunny clarity of our true connection to our Spiritual Divine energy source. This energy can flow in and gradually dissolve the static and help sustain us in serene clarity.

Insights on Breaking the Cycle of Distraction to Find Greater Clarity

1. **Recognize you can't know and do everything.** It is humanly impossible to be in the know of everything all the time. Give up as much as possible the things you already consider a waste of your time trying to do or keep track of--and then perhaps consider dropping a little more if you still feel over extended.

2. **Give yourself regular short breaks to stand and stretch**. Become aware of your breath for a while and breathe more deeply. Perhaps take a short walk down the hall and get a drink of water. Become aware of your thoughts and behavior as to how long you can concentrate well and when you need at least a short break. If you are feeling stressed and are having difficulty focusing on your work or something else that you need to do, try taking a brisk walk for five minutes or more.

3. **Prioritize.** If everything has the same weight, you won't be able to control your time and what you do with it. Learn to prioritize and focus. What responsibilities are absolutely crucial to be accomplished today or soon? What matters to you most, what do you enjoy? What can perhaps wait a while, perhaps be delegated to someone else, or just released?

4. **Do one thing at a time.** Focus on the quality of your work instead of quantity.

5. **Slow down.** Allow yourself enough time to get things done or to be somewhere. Enjoy the process or the trip. Do everything deliberately and calmly. Multitasking and rushing produce mediocre

results that reflect the scattered effort and focus put into the actions. When everything you read is skimmed, scanned, or glanced at--you don't gain real in-depth knowledge.

6. **You have a lot to contribute**, and distractions take away from what you can offer the world. What would happen if you don't check Twitter or Facebook for a couple of days? With e-mails perhaps just check the subject line of e-mails and the sender--that can perhaps clarify which are important to read.

7. **Become more present**. Being fully immersed in the present moment keeps you focused and distractions just fade away. Give undivided alert, yet relaxed, attention to everything you do. Set your intention to do the best you can on a specific task.

8. **Surrender and allow**. Dealing with challenges is never easy. When challenges and problems pop up, a lot of people tend to slip into old habits and become stressed and panic. When things don't work out well or we don't get the results we expect, we often tend to get frustrated and sometimes eventually give up. This attitude does not help. If things don't work out, pause and think about how to try a somewhat different approach. We can allow ourselves to be human and make mistakes now and then. It is part of the journey. Let's stay as calm and positive as possible and nurture ourselves along the way.

Real Life Sharings Of Enhancing Clarity In One's Life

Job Success through Prioritizing and Setting Limits (It was a Stretch!)
~ by Joyce

I innocently accepted a full time job as Activity Director of a nursing home with ninety residents. I had no assistants for the first year. This was years ago just before I became deeply involved as a holistic therapist. The needs at the nursing home were massive beyond belief. How in the world was I to create meaningful experiences for ninety infirm people, about 20% of whom were bedridden? Every morning and every afternoon I walked around to greet and personally invite each person who was able to walk or to roll in a wheelchair to come join us for an activity in the central large room. The nursing home was in a modest sized New England town that really supported and got involved with it in impressive ways. I was immediately deeply drawn into coordinating with large numbers of the town clubs and civic groups, churches, town leaders, volunteers, the library, entertainers, and more. The annual fund raising fair was in my lap, and it had always been (and was expected to be) an extravaganza. PRIORITIZING WAS THE ONLY WAY TO SURVIVE, AND I KNEW IT. IT WASN'T POSSIBLE TO DO ALL THAT WAS PRESENTING ITSELF TO BE DONE.

The paperwork and supplies had been left in shambles by the last Activity Director who had apparently not prioritized and had left within six months, a frazzled lady. The directors of the other departments were eyeing me to see how much of their work they could transfer to me, such as cutting everyone's fingernails and toenails and running general errands for the residents. Yikes!! I quickly learned how to say an emphatic **NO** as a necessary survival technique. To make a long story short I got very efficient at prioritizing. My #1 task every morning was to select the group of things that were most crucial and possible to get done that day. Then I reassigned the remainder of the list to other days on the weekly calendar, or to the monthly calendar, or to the "MAYBE NEVER LIST." I made my peace with that "maybe never list;" not everything could possibly get done.

I came to love those folks and indeed the whole town--as so many of its residents poured into the nursing home at regular intervals. During those years I learned how to lead lively sing-a-longs with my guitar, lead church services, facilitate meaningful interactive discussions for big groups, put on enjoyable parties, guide all kinds of games and crafts, and many other types of programs. It was actually fun! Prioritizing was the saving grace!

A Close Call Inspires Clarity
~ by Lynne

When I was thirty five all seemed well in my life, a husband and two daughters and a cozy home in a pleasant area. I drifted in a soft cocoon of emotional comfort until one morning in the mirror I noticed a black mole raised on a red pillow of skin. Red and black, rouge et noir. When the mole was removed and biopsied, it was a malignant melanoma, potentially a virulent, rapidly developing cancer. When it was removed along with some lymph nodes, it was diagnosed as stage one and caught before metastasizing. Close call! Suddenly I had a pressing need for my life's goal, meaning, and clarity. This need for clarity and life focus led me to enter a graduate program in speech pathology as well as other life changes. I have now had twenty years as a working speech therapist, and am still cancer free. I realize that the life threatening illness brought me clarity--a clarity of life focus. That was an enormous gift!

Walking Through Life's Myriad Patterns
~ by Joyce

Patterns form, I see the patterns form one at a time,

and rejoice at each one's presence.

Each exists for a season or for a moment's breath,

and is the right pattern to bring understanding

and energy to that day's task.

I welcome the arrival of today's new pattern,

and will maintain peace at its departure.

No pattern can persist forever,

and when the dissolution comes, it is for a purpose.

I choose to always walk through life's myriad patterns

in faith, clarity, courage, and joy.

Finding Clarity: We Choose the "Story" That Guides Us
~ by Ashley Barnes, Sellersburg, Indiana

Most people, at some point in their lives, are abused by another. Physical, sexual, emotional, or all three--we all have our "stories." The problem lies in the fact that many of us, then, never stop abusing ourselves. We carry on that abuse, long after the initial trauma was over. We remind ourselves how ugly we are, how our feelings don't matter, and how we are not worthy of love. We keep ourselves locked in our "story" and then wonder why we can't escape, and how to break up the blocks. Awareness is the key.

We have so many choices in life and sadly we often focus on the ones that don't mean that much: what clothes to wear, what to make for dinner, what products to buy. We have so many trivial choices that we're numbed by them--overwhelmed. What we often don't realize is that we have the power to make bigger choices in life. We can make choices about the kind of life we want to have, the blocks that stand in our way, the "story" in which we reside. Often it seems as if these choices are made for us, by fate perhaps, or unkind others. But our "story" is told only by us. When we give up our personal power over a "story" we don't want, we create our own failures. Others may influence our lives, but we control the "story" that guides us. (See Resources Page)

Eye Opening Experiences
~ by Joyce

An important memory is of a friend asking me who wrote the European history text book I was studying during college for an exam. I didn't have the book with me at that moment and had no idea who the author was. I thought it was a curious question. "Why is the author so important?" I asked. I had naively taken text books for granted as being unquestionably accurate, and I sort of vaguely thought that all text books on a subject more or less agreed. Since then, I've been extremely aware that every book, piece of printed material, and news broadcast is tremendously colored by the person writing or speaking (or the person paying them). I learned a lot in college, but I'm not sure if I had yet really started thinking independently for myself. I spent a summer working in Paris, France and traveling third-class trains around Europe with a friend--and learned that the whole world doesn't revolve around the United States or the English language. There are many ways to live and do things. All the fascinating unusual people and experiences of that summer were eye opening at the time. It helped launch me into a much greater level of independence of thought and expanded clarity.

Woman With Bird Symbolizing Clear Uplifted Thoughts
Original Art by Joyce J.C. Gerrish

WORKBOOK: Enrichment Experiences For Enhancing Clarity In Your Life

Enjoy the adventure of exploring these enrichment experiences on your own--or gather a few friends to share the journey with you. Be inspired by the audio meditation and soul song for this chapter. Reflect on some of the stimulating ideas and questions.

Questions For Reflection And Discussion, And Action Suggestions

Reflection, discussion, journal writing, expressing your feelings in drawings or other creative ways can all be very valuable to help you delve into these questions in truly meaningful and relevant ways. Before focusing on the questions and action suggestions, you may wish to meditate with the twelve minute audio or transcribed meditation--and/or listen to the soul song "Clear Mind."

Planning Your Days For Clarity--What Are Your Priorities?

Create a schedule plan for each day. It can be simple, but it should include the things that you need to do. First write all the events and responsibilities that you feel need to be dealt with today. Perhaps on the weekend write a longer range plan of events and responsibilities that need to be dealt with this week. Do the same for this month. This gives you a frame of reference for the demands on your time. Learning how to create a schedule plan that works for your lifestyle is a very important skill for successful healthy happy living.

PRIORITIZE. Depending on the intensity of your responsibilities, you may need to be sparing in your time allocations. What is absolutely necessary for your health and personal life? **Write that in first**. What is your exercise routine? Write in a daily thirty minute walk or whatever you do to take care of yourself in that way. What do you do for your peace? Do you meditate for a while regularly or something else that supports your peace? Do you relax and read a book or listen to music for a while in the evening? Write that in. Do you have absolutely essential family or other responsibilities, such as preparing dinner or the need to drive someone somewhere? Write those in. Write in your approximate meal times and your needed bed time.

Now examine the remaining things that require your time today. Do you have regular work hours, do you have irregular work hours, are you self-employed, are you a homemaker and child care provider, or other? You know your special life rhythms. First write in responsibilities or plans that must happen today. Block in the time if it is an event or responsibility with a fixed time. Now examine what time you have left. Look at your week schedule. Using a Weekly Planner calendar and a Monthly Planner calendar can be helpful for that. Write your longer range responsibilities and plans in pencil on your weekly schedule and your monthly schedule. Be as realistic as possible in the amount of time things will take. The further ahead you are looking, the more general you can be. Do your plans and responsibilities seem to fit in comfortably into your weekly plan and monthly plan?

Maybe your life is very regular and you tend to do more or less the same things every week, such as attending certain groups or events at the same time each week, or you do similar family or social events each week on specific days and times. Then planning your life becomes easier. Most of us, though, have all kinds of unusual or unexpected events and responsibilities that come up fairly regularly. How does one fit those in without interfering with your health, peace, and emotional needs?

Sometimes it becomes necessary to delegate or remove something from what you consider necessary. There is a limit to what a person can do without jeopardizing one's health. Sometimes we try to do it all until we don't feel as well and our work suffers. We do have options if we stay clearly focused. Prioritize is an extremely important word. To be able to prioritize is a true art. It benefits us all to learn how to do it well. What is absolutely essential in your typical day and week? What is valuable but not absolutely essential? What is something that you have been doing for a while and has gotten to be a habit--but now and then you think that maybe you don't feel such a strong commitment to it anymore? That is a good candidate to let go of. Time is too precious to do anything mainly out of habit.

Look through your list of events and responsibilities and see what you are ready to let go of. Some things are worthy, but we can't do everything. Take the plunge if you feel your life is over-scheduled. Decide what you are ready to let go of. This can be a sensitive but important decision. Maybe your significant other does a certain activity with you regularly and would be hurt if you quit. That would take some careful discussions and diplomacy. Sometimes creating some free time in your life is extremely important for staying in touch with yourself, and maintaining your health and clarity and peace of mind. It is an investment.

Note from Joyce: Revisit "Insights on Breaking the Cycles of Distraction to Find Greater Clarity" earlier in the chapter. It has numerous valuable suggestions for reflection and discussion - - and action suggestions.

Audio: "Meditation To Enhance Your Experience Of The Divine Qualities," with focus on Clarity

Pray to the Divine to bless your meditation and enhance Divine Clarity in your life. Choose one or more of the following affirmations (or something similar) that feels particularly helpful to you for affirming during the meditation. Before transferring to the website to listen to the meditation, write the affirmation(s) you choose and the helpful color aqua. Later, place the affirmation where you'll see it daily and be reminded to affirm it for a minute or two several times a day.

- ◆ My growing clarity supports my brilliance.
- ◆ My clear awareness enhances my creative insights.
- ◆ My ability to focus and concentrate well is a secret for my successful living.
- ◆ As I prioritize my plans for each day, I am more efficient and effective.

Helpful color to visualize when meditating on Clarity: Aqua.

Connect to SecretsofWisdom.net where you can listen to the twelve-minute audio "Meditation to Enhance Your Experience of the Divine Qualities," with Focus on Clarity. I encourage you to enjoy this meditation anytime you wish to enhance Clarity in your life.

(Also see transcribed version of this meditation at the end of this chapter.)

Uplifting Audio Soul Song: *"Clear Mind"*

Composed and sung by Joyce

Consider it a prayer in song for enhancing Divine Clarity within yourself. The words are:
Clear mind like the clear sky,
Clear mind like the clear sky.
My mind reflects the peaceful vast sky.
I gaze into the clear blue sky,
I feel the heavens fill my mind.
Ou-u-u-u. Ah-h-h-h.

As you sing, or listen to the Soul Song, just feel yourself letting go of distractions and relaxing into the experience of Divine Clarity. Close your eyes and really sense it helping to bring you into a calm feeling of alert clarity. You may wish to visit SecretsofWisdom.net where you can listen to *"Clear Mind,"* while viewing the full color design: "Woman Holding Cat Feels Peace and Clarity."

Transcribed Version of Meditation to Enhance Your Experience of Divine Clarity

If possible, listen to some relaxing nonverbal music. Say a short prayer calling on the Divine to bless your meditation and enhance Divine Clarity in your life.

Visualize yourself in a ball of light to help strengthen your energy field.

Become aware of and follow your breath as it gently flows in and out your nose at its own relaxed pace.

Throughout this meditation you don't need to breathe extra deeply or hold your breath extra-long.

Just be aware of your breath as it flows gently in and out.

Send down roots deep into the earth to help yourself feel grounded and prevent possibly feeling spacey.

Imagine yourself as a tree sending powerful roots deep into the earth from the base of your feet or the base of your spine.

Then as you breathe in your nose, imagine you are breathing the strength of the earth up into your body.

For a few minutes listen to the relaxing music.

As you breathe in through your nose, imagine you are breathing in light into your being.

Next visualize the color aqua--like the sparkling sea on a clear day.

As you breathe in your nose, imagine that you are breathing glowing aqua light into your whole being.

As you breathe out, silently pray for Divine Clarity to help uplift and bless your life.

Next breathe in through your nose and out your mouth for a little while.

Now, gently breathe in through your mouth and out your nose for a few minutes.

Then very gently breathe in and out your mouth.

Now return to breathing in and out your nose.

As you breathe in through your nose, imagine you are breathing in aqua into your whole being.

As you breathe out through your nose periodically silently say one or two of the following or similar affirmations.

◆ My growing clarity supports my brilliance.

◆ My clear awareness enhances my creative insights.

◆ My ability to focus and concentrate well is a secret for my successful living.

◆ As I prioritize my plans for each day, I am more efficient and effective.

◆ Continue in that manner for a few minutes or as long as you wish.

Conclude by thanking the Divine, and then once again send down roots for grounding.

Enjoy this meditation when you wish to help enhance Divine Clarity in your life. Write down the affirmation(s) you choose and place where you'll see it often and be reminded to affirm it for a minute or two.

Man And Woman Inspired By Purpose
Original Art by Joyce J.C. Gerrish

Chapter Six

FOLLOW YOUR HEART AND SOUL
Enhancing Divine Purpose in Your Life

Enjoy listening to or sing along with this peaceful soul song I've composed and sung: "I Open My Heart." Consider it a prayer in song. Please go to SecretsOfWisom.net where you can listen to the audio "I Open My Heart" and see the full color version of design "Man and Woman Inspired by Purpose."

Deep In Our Hearts We'll Find the Next Step of Our Soul Purpose

We're each born with a soul mission which we chose as a soul before we were born. Our soul mission is what our soul, with the help of the Divine, chose to focus on developing in this life. Our purpose is intended to be something that we will truly enjoy pursuing. The range of different possible soul missions is as varied as there are different people. Probably no two are exactly the same. The marvelous thing is that the more we delve into the depths and majesty of our own heart and passion and soul, it brings us into the next step of our true mission. Life develops a whole new level of adventure and meaning as we walk and explore this path. Each person's soul purpose is crucial to the new more wonderful possibilities which I believe are unfolding on planet Earth for all of us. We each have an important part to contribute to the whole. Never under estimate anyone.

We are all needed each in our own unique way. It may be the special way that we help people feel confident and to not give up. Our calling may be in any field of human endeavor. All aspects of life greatly need the services of wise Spiritually-awakened people with far-sighted vision and heart. We're all needed, and the time is now to step even more fully into our true calling--whatever it may be.

We Are Each a Magnificent Being Created by God

Let's hold the vision that we all together lift our hearts and minds to help create a better life for everyone. Let's envision that the time of abuse, selfishness, and violence can be risen above and left behind permanently. It is truly possible, we just need to each do our part and believe with all our heart in the power of good and God.

Too long have many of us been held down by lack of belief in our higher capabilities and true power. We are each a magnificent being created by God. We have tremendous ability to co-create a more glowing reality for ourselves and our planet. It is time for all humanity to wake up to the next step of the possible dream and bring it into realization. We can all do it together. No one is acting alone. It is so important to remember that. We are all the human family, and are daughters and sons of God. There is support. May we each dedicate ourselves to expanded commitment to actualizing a dream we hold in our heart that is beneficial to some aspect of humanity and our planet. As we do so, we will be drawn to other people pursuing a similar vision. That is the way of the universe. Like attracts like through resonance. We each hold a piece of the puzzle. Someone else may complement our skills and experience, and he or she may supply another piece of the puzzle. As we join together with others, our combined energy attracts even more opportunities and resources.

Connect to that Serene Inner Sacred Place of Renewal, Insights, and Higher Potentials

Regularly spend some quiet peaceful time away from the stressful rush. Allow your mind to relax and lift upwards to meditate, pray, or contemplate. In this way you can access a serene inner sacred place of renewal and higher awareness. This is a priceless resource for accessing insights and intuitions as to how to proceed to actualize your vision. You don't need to understand every step of the process. It can grow organically. Other people may be able to fill in holes for you along the way. Start by taking a step, and the clearer road map will before long reveal itself.

Believe in yourself. Trust your gut feeling, trust your heart. The thing to be cautious of is mental chatter of self-put-down. It is too easy to let some old limiting thoughts or "carry over" from past discouragements move in and pull you down. Some people have a "mental loop" in their brains that repeats over and over "it will never work" or "I can't pull it off." Those are called thought forms. Who needs them? Keep in mind that who you are today is not who you were in the past. If you sense such thoughts crossing you mind, just breathe in light and silently affirm a positive affirmation such as "I believe in myself. I am capable and worthy of my highest good."

You Can Re-create Yourself Anew as You Follow Your Star

You can re-create yourself anew free of limitations of the past! This is true. It's a matter of how you focus your awareness. When your consciousness is uplifted, you are connected to your higher potentials. It is valuable to keep in mind that following your heart and soul may not always seem to be a straight forward path. It may take some twists and turns which can be part of the learning process. It may even seem to pause sometimes as you perhaps realign in some way. The important thing is to keep following your star and not lose heart. Keep believing in yourself and your vision.

An important key to true meditation and to higher intuition is to lift your consciousness above the dense lower emotional confusion of the mass mind. As you open to the path to which you are truly being called within your heart and soul, then the needed information will manifest in some form. Profound concepts may flood into your mind while meditating, walking quietly, showering, or watching the sun set behind the trees. The way will show itself. Knock on the door, and be prepared to recognize an unexpected opportunity. Sometimes even an apparent disappointment can be a gift in disguise. It may assist you to open to options or possibilities that you had not previously considered. These may be even more valuable than the exact outcome you had expected.

Intuition Can Help Us Make a Significant Contribution to the World

Spiritual intuition has inspired many people throughout history and prerecorded history to significant creative contributions. This is how some outstanding composers wrote their music. They became aware of it or "heard it" in the Spiritual levels of consciousness, and then they downloaded it into their physical brain and onto paper (or to their musical instruments). Some scientific inventions come to the scientist through a dream or inner knowing. Artists often have a strong Spiritual vision before even starting their creation. Healers frequently know exactly what is needed for someone's highest good through connecting to higher Spiritual levels of insight. This is intuitional awareness, and it is a totally normal human capacity. Many have just forgotten that this is each person's birthright. Intuition and higher Spiritual clarity are of tremendous value to help one move forward on this wonderful adventure of following one's life path.

There are new career paths manifesting on Earth right now. There are types of callings emerging that have never before existed. I'm mentioning this because we or someone we know may feel a profound urge to study and learn about something that seems totally impractical and irrelevant to mainstream life. It may be that skill will become extremely valuable and in demand in surprising ways in the not too distant future. New technologies and possibilities are evolving every day. We tend to think of a life purpose as being something that will support us in a solid way throughout our life. The world may not yet know that it needs our unique set of gifts or insights. But maybe it does! It's good to trust our hearts. In the meanwhile, though, we need to cover our financial bases. Maybe we can pursue our dreams in our spare time as a hobby for now. Even spending a few hours a week following our passion can be deeply rewarding. If we want to invest more time than that, it can be helpful to live simply and lightly if we're pursuing a life mission that many might consider alternative to the mainstream. I've been following an alternative life style most of my life, and it feels natural for me. Money may come to be perceived somewhat differently in the future, too, with plans such as Time Bank and bartering.

Professions and Jobs are Reinventing Themselves. Watch for Trends

In times of transition like now, professions are reinventing themselves somewhat. What has always been a mainstream job such as a restaurant chef is now going in increasingly varied directions. One chef may feel that his role is to educate people nutritionally about truly healthy food. The menus may be packed full of nutritional information about the delicious yet totally healthy food served there. This is the chef as an educator. He may serve a lot of vegetarian and raw dishes and specialize in organically and locally grown salads and foods. Another chef may feel a passionate longing to help families feel closer again. He may design his restaurant to have very homey sections, and serve home-style cooking in large serving bowls at the table for a family or group. He may specialize in foods children will like, yet that are healthy at the same time. Another chef may have a service where people can come and cook family meals in a special kitchen under his expert instruction. He would have the fresh vegetables and other ingredients all ready and waiting for the participants so they can prepare them quickly into delicious meals for several evenings. This way the customer knows exactly what is going into the food and can adjust for preferences, special health needs, and possible allergies. When the customer gets the food home, one or two of the meals could possibly be frozen for upcoming days. People are looking for new ways of doing things.

Ideas May Spontaneously Occur to You for Practical Ways to Make Money Doing What You Love

If there is something that you long to pursue but seems impractical, it may be worthwhile to take some training anyway. Career fields are morphing and evolving. When you start delving into your passion, practical ways to apply it to make money may spontaneously occur to you. Just don't let your mind be rigid. Increasingly more and more people will be self-employed rather than working a 9:00 to 5:00 job for someone else. Many people are self-employed and also work a part-time job elsewhere. Business people that own or manage companies are doing all they can to cut down on employees in order to save money on salaries. This is a matter of survival. Machines and technology are replacing many jobs. Obvious examples are customers at grocery stores checking out their own purchases and at factories a whole assembly line being controlled by computers and robots. I feel that will be happening more and more everywhere. Additionally, of course, many jobs are shipped to other countries where salaries are lower.

What does this mean for people looking for employment? One needs to be creative in one's approach to earning a living. It isn't as cut and dried as in the past when our grandfathers accepted a job right after completing school, and worked at that job until they retired at around sixty-five years of age. Maybe they got promotions periodically or maybe they didn't, either way they tended to stay put. There was a certain security to it that way, but it also wasn't always highly stimulating intellectually or creatively. Now, in order to even hope to keep a job, one needs to prove oneself indispensable. Nothing is guaranteed at all! Employment could be terminated at any time that the employer figures out a quicker or cheaper way to handle a particular employee's responsibilities. There tends to be limited loyalty to the employees. Jobs don't tend to last as long as in the past. It is too often a frenzy of survival for the supervisors and the workers.

Is There a Slow Down Button on This Merry-go-round of Stress?

What is the effect of all this intensity on people's psyche? Not too many people are going to sleep on the job. Most people by necessity are wide awake and giving all they can to the work. Both sides of the paycheck know that hard work and ingenuity are the only way to really succeed. But it tends to be stressful. The nervous system is highly charged up. People are actively thinking and problem solving more than ever. The brain isn't simply cycling in loops of habitual thoughts and reactions as much as in the past. People are multitasking more than ever. The brain isn't really designed for multitasking, but it is being forced to learn how to cope with it. This is how humanity gradually evolves as a species.

We are forced to adapt in order to deal with new conditions and realities. Our brain will gradually be more comfortable and adept at performing more than one task or responsibility at a time. That doesn't make it comfortable or easy on our nervous system now. It is taking its toll. In order to counteract the stress from our work and from our personal life, many of us are finding that we must take definite steps to de-stress on a regular basis.

It used to be that people could let go of any stress on the way home from work. Perhaps they walked home for several miles through tree-lined streets and past a few meadows. When they got home maybe they took a nap before dinner or sat on the porch and rocked for a while and waved to neighbors. They let any tension drop away and they relaxed. Renewal was simple and natural.

These days many people take on overtime when their employer cuts down on the number of staff to save money or doesn't replace an employee who leaves or is transferred. Other people take on an extra part-time job in order to supplement their budget to cover the bills. Trying to squeeze in extra work in that way takes its toll. So people need help letting go of stress. Sitting down in an easy chair and watching the news is not necessarily relaxing. It may just remind one of another whole set of problems. Meditation, taking a relaxing walk, yoga, tai chi, and other renewing practices are becoming recognized as literal life savers. Taking time to unwind is no longer simply a nice idea. People need something on a regular basis to help them center, calm the nervous system, relax the muscles, and recharge. It is a necessity for emotional and physical health.

Discovering the Lifestyle that Really Supports Our Emotional and Physical Well-being

It may perhaps sometimes feel like a challenge to consciously create our life path and mold it in the direction that we sense evolving within our heart space--but it is an exhilarating opportunity! It truly requires that we stay fully alert. It requires that we deeply know who we are and what we want to accomplish in this life. What do we want to contribute to our fellow humanity? We might think of our life as a theater production that we are creating. What is the message that we want to express with our real-life theater? The other people in our lives are our fellow actors and actresses. Something important is being conveyed in this theater, and we are the ones in charge of our life presentation. Let's ask ourselves, what is our vision?

There is a broad array of ways to be of service and make money independently, if that is desired. It can be very helpful to take a career training course with a proven track record in the area of your specialty. This doesn't need to be a college degree, unless that is what you want to do. Maybe you already have the training, and just need the confidence. A life coach or an enthusiastic self-employed friend could be helpful. Building a business online is, of course, growing by leaps and bounds. Journal write about your possible ideas. If it seems like a good idea for you, start somewhere and build it with love, creativity, and enthusiastic work. Networking with other people in the same or similar field is very helpful. Share insights and tips. It is an adventure that is never boring.

In pursuing your career calling, it is important to decide how much money you need for your life style. Some people may require more money because of their life situations and who they support. Other people may feel more able to be adventuresome and to flow with what evolves as they follow their passions. How much money you need to make depends on how much money you feel is crucial for financial stability. For some people this is more than for others, depending on various factors as mentioned previously.

If you are already in a job or life situation that feels just right for your life path, congratulations! It doesn't matter whether or not it seems prestigious to the world. If you know that you are contributing from your heart and helping the world in a way that is important to you, that is what counts. Go for it. If you feel that the job or work that you are doing now is not allowing you to feel fulfilled, then it may be time to begin to explore your options. It is clearly crucial to not leave yourself without a financial safety net. We don't want to completely walk out of one door until another door is open.

Maybe There is Room in Your Current Job for Increased Creative Innovation

My suggestion is to really look around in your current position if you are employed, and sense what you might be able to create right there. Maybe your job has lots of room for creativity; on the other hand maybe it doesn't seem to have much flexibility. At one time I had a part-time job where my main focus was leading arts and crafts, singing, and drama with people who had developmental disabilities and mental retardation. It was sometimes stressful work, but it was really rewarding--and it was flexible. There is a huge need to bring loving services and care to these people. I started a singing group and we sang our hearts out. Before long we were going out to share sing-a-longs at other centers for people with developmental disabilities. This was exceedingly heartwarming and joyful. We became a real singing traveling troop, going all over the city twice a week sharing sing-a-longs and joy. Those sing-a-longs were a wonderful way for these folks to get out and around, meet new people, and know that they counted. Those years are a chapter in my life that I hold dear. I haven't heard of many people doing just that, but the agency fully supported it. It took a vision, some confidence, hard work, and a willingness to pour love into it. It was done within a fairly conventional job with a salary--but it was uniquely my creation.

Something different that I did to stabilize my life financially while I pursued my evolving life dreams was to buy a hundred-year-old, three floor Victorian house. It had been converted into four apartments by the previous owners. The whole building cost no more than a moderate size single family house, yet it created a financial backup for me to follow my life purpose more freely. Living in my own apartment building has worked well. I live in one apartment, and the rent from the tenants helps pay a big part of the mortgage, property tax, building insurance, utilities, and repairs. I get free rent, while the equity of the building exists as savings. Providing excellent, reasonably priced rental housing can be a heartwarming and valuable life path in and of itself.

I hope that these various ideas have given you some helpful insights into enhancing or creating a career path which can serve as a vehicle for your soul mission service, for your personal life development, and for your joy. It is so marvelous when these can all be knit together in a unified whole. Stay alert. Keep up-to-date on things that really interest you. You may hear of someone creating a service or small business with skills and interests similar to yours. If one person does it successfully, it may be that you could, too.

It's important to not expect a new small business or service to be an overnight financial success. It tends to be gradual. When you're self-employed, it is often necessary to work harder or longer hours than someone with a more conventional job, but this is often more than offset by the passion you have for the work. It becomes a labor of love, where the margin between work and play is blurred. The work can feel like something you want to do just because you enjoy doing it. The important thing is to keep your sense of life purpose alive and strong. Without that, life can feel somewhat flat and dull. Hold the direction of the ship of your life aimed toward your soul vision. If you need a non-related job in order to pay your bills, see if you can adapt it in some way to relate to your special interests. Keep in mind that it's possible to pursue one's unique interests after work. A homemaker can perhaps start a part-time business in the home. Be the captain of your ship. Follow your dreams. Blessings to you.

Real Life Sharings About Discovering Life Purpose

I Learned Early The Importance Of Sharing And Helping Others
~ by Dr. Renee Campbell

When I think about purpose, it brings to mind why a person is put here on earth. Through the years and during my personal and professional life, I have heard individuals say they don't know what their purpose in life is. This has always been astonishing to me because I already knew at an early age what my purpose was.

I grew up in rural Western Kentucky in a town called Adairville. Adairville had a population of about 1500 people at that time. My Mother and Father both worked a lot so I spent a significant amount of time with my Grandmother. I was two years old when I met her. She was the typical Grandmother of that time with a rounded shape, brown skin, and gray hair. My Grandmother taught me a lot of things by her actions and her words. Miss Lottie, as everyone called her, was a staunch church-going woman who called herself a religious fanatic. As a little girl of five years old, one of the things that I always saw her do was help other people in the community. I remember her letting the girls and boys whose parents weren't attentive come to her house and stay with her during the day. Sometimes the other children were hungry and she would feed them. Little girl's hair wouldn't be combed, and Miss Lottie would comb their hair. Then I learned to comb their hair. Combing their hair and making sure they looked neat was just seen as the right thing to do. My Grandmother had "fish fries" and "weenie roasts," and she would give people food even if they didn't have the money to make a purchase.

As a little girl, I learned that my purpose in life was to help others. My purpose was defined more as I got older. As a teenager, I helped my peers who were struggling with life issues. The fact that my Grandmother was always giving didn't mean that our family had a lot. It just meant that we felt it was important to share and help others. I also watched my Mother fix other people's hair. She would straighten it with a straightening comb and I watched her do a "good job," so I learned that my purpose was to always do a good job and make sure that people were satisfied with what I did. I watched my Mother cook the best meals and sometimes cook for others. A good job was always the goal. I also learned about my purpose through other people helping me. I knew how it felt to be helped, so I wanted others to experience that same feeling.

As I said, we didn't have much at all--many times I didn't have the clothes that I wanted to wear, was hungry, and had a low self-image. There were wonderful teachers and professors who believed in me and were profoundly helpful in encouraging me to move forward on my journey through high school, college, and graduate school. People who came into my life were caring, non-judgmental and supportive. They mentored me up close and from afar about my purpose and that I had important things to say.

My life experiences made my purpose clear to me. I have always known that my purpose is to reach out and help others, assist people to see their full potential, and to point out to people the value of having a vision and faith. This includes allowing people to hear my story as a sign that overcoming obstacles to success is possible--and to speak and advocate for those who are discriminated against, to speak for those who don't often have a voice. I feel it is important to pass on a legacy for my children, grandchildren, and for generations to come. I know that my purpose is a global purpose, and I am supposed to positively affect everyone's life that I touch. From an early age my purpose has always been vivid and evident to me.

Post script: Renee is president/C.E.O. of a major community services organization in Louisville, Kentucky. At the moment of this writing, she is in New York City as a delegate to the United Nations Summit on Women and Girls and Domestic Violence. (See Resources Page)

I Love To Write And Produce Plays For Children
~ by Lisa Essenpreis

I've always loved children's stories and children's theater. It's really creative. The stories are simple and honest. I find them uplifting. I think that is what moves me. I like what I write to have some depth to it and maybe show something that children can learn from--and be inspired by. I've done children's theater as an actress, and I've had the opportunity to see how an audience responds. I love to see light come into the children's faces. I love to see the joy that it brings them, and how they respond to the music. Children are an honest and spontaneous audience. It is heartwarming. I think it's important to introduce children to live theater. It is a wonderful experience. I'd hate to see it die out.

I was very influenced by theater at a young age when I was in school. Participating in theater gives children confidence and the ability to express themselves creatively. When performing together in a play, children work together as a team. It can help draw out a child who is shy.

Putting on a play is fulfilling, and it makes the hard work worthwhile. When I've completed a production, I have a great sense of peace. I know I have done what I feel I am here on Earth to do. Anytime anyone actualizes himself or herself--and does what he or she feels to be here on Earth to do, it encourages all of us to do what we are here to do. We are all one.

Since I have my regular job, I do this on the side. My dream is to eventually be able to earn my living just doing my theater work. I also am writing children's stories. I've recorded one of my stories to create a book on tape. I'm going to market it online. I've started a play about the rain forest. That is something I want to finish and get out to the world. Through it I'm teaching something important that is going on in the world--about protecting the environment. I'd like to get those kinds of messages to children. (See Resources Page)

Spiritual Warrior
~ by Ashley Barnes

Just when I thought the time

of grand pronouncements was over,

that I would no longer find myself

in strange churches or quiet moments

receiving holy messages,

God speaks when you least expect it,

a burning bush for everyday life.

Like Hildegard, I am called to be a Spiritual Warrior

to use my creativity to wake up the world.

The white hot fire of Spirit is inside me.

Time to summon my moral outrage

to reclaim the Divine Feminine

and march forth to stake my claim in this world,

make a difference, elicit perhaps only the slightest change,

in a person, a community, a country, or a universe.

(See Resources Page)

Finding One's Life Purpose
~ by Paul Graber

I firmly believe that each and every human being is created for a specific purpose. I know that I was born to study and teach martial arts. I knew this was my purpose the very first time I helped another person with a disability do something he or she could not do before. There was something magical in seeing the spark of accomplishment in that person's eyes. I knew instantly that I would never tire of that feeling. I consider myself very lucky. Many of us have no idea what our true purpose in life is. Our society has created a multi-billion dollar industry that promises to help you find it. That is the problem. Everyone is looking outside themselves for something that can only be found by looking within. Too often we allow the noise of our ultra-modern world to drown out our inner voice. It is this voice that connects us to the Universe and each other. This voice which should be our loudest guide is barely a whisper in most. Doubt and fear can silence it completely.

To find one's true purpose, be still and listen. Hear the Universe. Hear the World. Soon you will hear a call that you know can only be answered by you. As you move to answer that call, the Universe will act in harmony with you, as it does with all that moves in accordance with the Universal design. Happiness and fulfillment will be the natural reward for a life well lived. (See Resources Page)

My Journey To Butterfly Wellness
~ by Kimberly D. Withrow

I often gazed upon the mysterious image in the mirror. My curiosity kept me intrigued by her presence. Who is she and what is her purpose? Those were the questions that I pondered upon on a regular basis. I suffered silently as I journeyed through this life of uncertainty. I had no esteem, no opinion, and no voice. I felt as though I was merely taking up space, null and void of any purpose or destiny. Walking aimlessly is not only unfruitful, but it's dangerous. It's a dangerous thing not to know who you are, where you're going and why you were created.

It's a lonely world for those who have lost themselves. Some have lost themselves in the identity of others. Some have catered to the needs of others and placed themselves on the back burner. As a result they run to-and-fro seeking answers from those that don't have a true understanding of the question. The question is "Who am I?" Many translate the answer to fit who they want and need you to be. Their answers soothe the pain, but only temporarily. You see, I ran around that mountain of despair and confusion several times. And it always led me to my knees and basking in the Divine Presence of God, my creator.

The Divine Power of God is my only source of truth. He created me and He knows me better than I know myself. He has placed gifts and talents within me that have been hidden behind doubt and fear. He created me with Divine purpose and destiny, but only He had the power to reveal it to me. My eyes have been opened by His Divine wisdom.

I have been awakened, encouraged, empowered and loved, all by the Divine Power of God. He has brought healing to my confused mind. My life is symbolic of the transformation of the caterpillar into the butterfly. Even though the caterpillar endures a season of discomfort, she emerges with beautifully colored wings that are prepared to embrace the world. She expands her wings and sails into the heavenly skies, giving thanks and praise to her Creator. And so it is with me.

I open my arms with sincere gratitude. I thank God for answering the baffling question, "Who am I?" And with deep compassion, He answered me in a still small voice, "You are mine." Now the void has been filled. I know who I am, I belong to God. By His Divine Power I am able to declare with confidence that I am a child of the Most High God and by His Divine Power I have been made whole.

The magnificence of my journey has birthed a passion within me to assist others in finding the answer that holds the key to their destiny. As a result of that passion, The Butterfly Wellness Program was established. Our wellness program is based on total healing. We believe that the Spirit, mind, and body must be in complete harmony in order to experience complete wholeness. For that reason--Spiritual growth and encouragement, fitness, nutrition, and emotional healing are addressed. Our vision is to bless and inspire others to be all that God has created them to be. (See Resources Page)

My Growing Sense of Purpose as an Artist at Twenty-Nine
~ by Joyce

When I was about twenty-nine years old and recently divorced, I was working a job that had little relevance to my sense of who I was and what I loved to do. Sometimes each day seemed like a drag of watching the clock go around until 5:00 p.m. I had many strong interests, which perhaps complicated matters as far as deciding which direction to go. At the time, my primary passion was to be an artist and to paint. Finally, I just couldn't hold it down any longer, so I decided to live my dreams.

Prior to that decision, I tended to have a strong sense of needing to have plenty of money to ensure an excellent car, a large upscale apartment, really attractive clothes in the latest styles, and the resources to ski in Colorado when I chose. It just seemed the way to do it. At that point I decided that there is another way to do it, and I dove in. First I calculated how much money I absolutely needed to cover my most basic needs. I decided where I could cut expenses and live more simply. I couldn't believe that I was actually seriously considering this life changing step. I would work part-time and also hopefully sell paintings. My plan was that as I sold more paintings, I could put in fewer hours at my part-time job. With a lot of pencil pushing, eventually my income column and my expenses column began to balance. Could I really do it? Yes! Yes!

I moved from the outskirts of Boston to the center of the city in an area very alive with the arts. I shared an inexpensive apartment with a delightful woman. I sold my car because in the city center I could easily walk to my group art studio, my part-time job, to the park and the Charles River, to the grocery store, to friends' apartments, and to the subway. I shed expenses like water off my back. My sense of elation was growing. I happily wore denim and simple tops. A friend was stunned when I gave away some beautiful clothes--she was frustrated because they didn't happen to be her size.

I didn't want to be weighed down with too many objects. I was living lightly and loving it! My sense of what was beautiful was evolving--the simpler and more natural the better. It turned out that I did sell paintings. I came through this transformation experience a changed person, with my heart and eyes wide open. Life was dynamic and really alive with possibilities now. I didn't know just where it would lead, but I felt confident and very awake. Little did I know how many amazing experiences my life ahead held for me, or how one mind-opening opportunity would lead to the next. Little did I know that the various things I loved to do would eventually come together organically in synchronistic ways. I knew that life is meant for living with all your heart and Soul and I was doing my best to do just that.

I want to say that for those people who can pursue their dreams within a well-paid job, that is fantastic and ideal! Go for it. Since I love to do some things that are not always practical, I have learned to combine practical pursuits with less practical pursuits, so they can sort of balance each other. In today's tight economy it is very important to not leave a job unless one is really clear how one's expenses will be covered. Sometimes one can transform a job from within, or one can pursue evolving interests on weekends and after work.

Angel Inspires Woman to Awaken to Her Life Purpose
Original Art by Joyce J.C. Gerrish

WORKBOOK: Enrichment Experiences for Enhancing Purpose in Your Life

Enjoy the adventure of exploring these enrichment experiences on your own--or gather a few friends to share the journey with you. Be inspired by the audio meditation and soul song for this chapter. Reflect on some of the stimulating ideas and questions.

Questions For Reflection And Discussion

Reflection, discussion, journal writing, expressing your feelings in drawings or other creative ways can all be very valuable to help you delve into these questions in truly meaningful and relevant ways. Before focusing on the questions, you may wish to meditate with the twelve minute audio or transcribed meditation--and/or listen to the soul song "I Open My Heart." The following questions may help you more fully understand your life journey and sense the next step of your life purpose.

1. What inspirations and aspirations arise in your heart and mind as you listen to the meditation audio and soul song? Life purpose is an ongoing process in everyone's life. It isn't static. I encourage you to write about your inspirations and aspirations for your next step at this time. At this point just allow your feelings and thoughts to flow freely without feeling a need to be specific (unless that comes spontaneously). You may be a little surprised at some of your insights! Feel free!

2. Write about your plans for the coming year in your life--what would you like to bring to fruition? Allow your heart and imagination to be free, bold, and confident. The world needs people with a vision and sense of purpose. Look around you in your community and town. What would set your heart aflame to help manifest? Help start or join a support group of friends/acquaintances

concerning an issue that is very important in your life? Help organize a community talent show to raise money for a local urgent need. Start or contribute to community flower gardens? Volunteer for a committee in local community government to support something you really care about? Develop a new aspect of your business? How would you like to see your coming year develop?

3. What is your five year plan? Remember a time in your life when you felt a sense of destiny or "knowingness of being in harmony with the flow of life" and truly needed in your own special way. We each are created with a unique "gift" to share with the world around us. We can sense that calling to us as yearning in our heart. What do you sense as your contribution in life at this time? What is the next unfolding step of your life purpose? Help organize an after school center for young people to have interesting enrichment opportunities? Start a small business that will serve a real need in your town? Run for a local government office? What is your perhaps longer range plan?

Action Suggestions To Enhance Purpose In Your Life

1. Choose one part of your plans for the coming year (see Journal Writing suggestion #2). Bring it clearly into your awareness. How would you like to move toward that in a very practical way? Who would it be helpful to talk to? Make a list of some things you plan to do to bring it into action. What place or places would it be helpful to visit? What would you like to read about (research) online or in books or elsewhere to support this?

2. Call or contact someone who can be helpful in moving you forward to your next step. Follow up until you reach them, someone they recommend, or someone else who can give you helpful information regarding it. Let it be a fun adventure of meeting new people or deepening your association with people currently in your life. Enjoy learning new things and opening your life to new possibilities.

3. Find out if you can volunteer, participate, assist in some way, or simply observe at a location related to your special interest (part of your plan for the coming year or years). If this isn't possible at one place, check out another. Enjoy the adventure. People appreciate a motivated learner, and some are very happy to help and encourage you along your way.

4. Is there a class or course that is important to take at this point? If you feel that some type of formal training would be important, check that out. It could be as simple as a weekend workshop, or a series of a few classes at an adult education center, or maybe it would be an actual training program of a longer commitment. Online courses are available, too. Find what seems valuable to you at this time. Life can be a stimulating journey of ongoing discovery and possibilities.

5. Follow your dream step by step. Don't let anything discourage you. Find a mentor or life coach, if that feels important. Have fun!

Audio: "Meditation To Enhance Your Experience of The Divine Qualities," Focusing on Divine Purpose

Pray to the Divine to bless your meditation and enhance Divine Purpose in your life. This audio will help enhance your experience of opening to life possibilities. Choose one or more of the following affirmations (or something similar) that feels particularly helpful for you to affirm during the meditation. Before transferring to the website to listen to the meditation, write down the affirmation(s) you choose and the color peach. Later, place it where you'll see it daily and be reminded to affirm it for a minute or two several times a day.

◆ When I pray or mediate, I feel blessed and in touch with my heart and soul.

◆ Deep in my heart--one step at a time--I feel a growing sense of the next step of my life purpose.

◆ I am needed on Earth in my own unique way.

◆ I open to my vision of what I would like to contribute to my fellow humanity and the planet.

◆ I have the confidence, wisdom, and courage to pursue my dreams in a way for my highest good.

Helpful color to visualize when meditating on Divine Purpose: Peach.

I encourage you to enjoy this meditation when you wish to support and enhance opening ever more fully to your life purpose. Connect to the website to listen to the twelve-minute "Meditation to Enhance Your Experience of the Divine Qualities" with focus on Purpose.

(Also, see transcribed version of this meditation at end of this chapter.)

Uplifting Audio Soul Song: *"I Open My Heart"*

Composed and sung by Joyce

Consider it a prayer in song for enhancing the feeling of opening ever more fully to life and its wondrous possibilities. The words to the soul song are:

I open my heart to love those around me.

I open my eyes to see the good.

I open my mouth to speak kind words.

I open my arms to life.

I open my arms to life.

I open, I open. I open, I open.

As you chant it or listen to it, feel free and open. Allow inspiration to flow. Connect to <u>Secretsof Wisdom.net</u> where you can listen to *"I Open My Heart."*

Transcribed Version of the Meditation to Enhance Your Experience of Divine Purpose

If possible, listen to some relaxing nonverbal music. Say a short prayer calling on the Divine to bless your meditation and enhance your experience of Divine Purpose.

Visualize yourself in a ball of light to help strengthen your energy field.

Become aware of and follow your breath as it gently flows in and out your nose at its own relaxed pace.

Throughout this meditation you don't need to breathe extra-deeply or hold your breath extra-long.

Just be aware of your breath as it flows gently in and out.

Imagine yourself as a tree sending powerful roots deep into the earth from the base of your feet or the base of your spine to help you feel more grounded and prevent possibly feeling spacey.

Then as you breathe in through your nose, imagine you are breathing the strength of the earth up into your body.

Repeat several times.

Listen to the relaxing music as you focus on gently breathing in and out through your nose.

Visualize the color peach like a beautiful sunrise spread across the sky.

As you breathe in through your nose, imagine that you are breathing glowing peach colored light into your whole being.

Silently pray to the Divine that your life vision be clarified and enhanced with Divine Purpose.

Next, breathe in your nose and out your mouth very gently for about a minute.

Now, breathe in your mouth and out your nose very gently for about a minute.

Now, breathe in and out your mouth very very gently for about a minute.

Now return to breathing in and out your nose.

As you breathe in through your nose, imagine you are breathing peach color into your whole being.

As you breathe out your nose, periodically silently say one or two of the following (or similar) affirmations:

◆ When I pray or meditate, I feel blessed and in touch with my heart and soul.

◆ Deep in my heart--one step at a time--I feel a growing sense of the next step of my life purpose.

◆ I am needed on planet Earth in my own unique way.

◆ I open to my vision of what I would like to contribute to my fellow humanity and the planet.

◆ I have the confidence, wisdom, and courage to pursue my dreams in a way for my highest good.

Continue in that manner for a few minutes or as long as you wish.

Conclude by thanking the Divine for the blessings.

Then once again send down roots for grounding.

I encourage you to enjoy this meditation when you wish to enhance Divine Purpose in your life. Write down the affirmation(s) you choose and place it where you'll see it several times a day and be reminded to affirm it for a minute or two.

Blessings on your path.

Woman Feels Peace With All That Is
Original design by Joyce J.C. Gerrish

Chapter Seven

CHOOSE PEACE, GLORIOUS PEACE
Enhancing Divine Peace in Your Life

Enjoy listening to, or sing along with, this serene soul song about Divine Peace "Golden Peace." Connect to SecretsofWisdom.net where you can listen to *"Golden Peace"* while gazing at the full color design "Dove of Peace."

Our Ancestors Found Inner Peace Through Harmony With Nature

Peace is a rare feeling these days for many people. There seem to be countless things that can interfere with one's feeling of real inner peace. Actually, deep inner peace is one's true nature. Somehow that has gotten lost for many, though. A lot of folks yearn to once again embrace their true natural peace. This chapter will be exploring inner personal peace as well as peace between individuals and groups.

In the past people lived more in harmony with nature and the seasons. There were natural cycles to life. Each day had its rhythm and flow. One awoke with the sunrise and the rooster crowing. For most people the day consisted of growing crops, raising some animals, and preparing simple food from the crops grown. It was very clear what needed doing and how to do it. People worked hard, but they set their own pace. Sometimes they would sing while they did their chores--other times they would stop and listen to the birds sing. They would pause and pat their dog that probably followed them around. It was a human natural pace of life. One talked to friends when meeting on the road, at the market, or at church--but there weren't constant phone calls or digital communications. Events moved more slowly. There was time to think and reflect. Breathing was deep and steady. Food was natural. People listened to their bodies. Sleep came easily after a long day's work, and the deep sleep could truly bring restoration. Their nervous system thrived living in harmony with Mother Nature.

Today's Stress Is Hard on Us Physically, Emotionally, and Mentally

Today's pace of life is very different. Most people are separated from a truly natural environment and life style. Time is of the essence, and every minute seems to need to be accounted for. Lots of folks have schedules that keep them going at a rapid stressful pace often well into the night. The economy leaves many uncertain as to what to expect. Simply paying the bills can be a huge burden.

Many jobs don't pay enough to cover an individual's or a family's basic expenses, so frequently a second job is required. Maybe there is a large mortgage to pay off or massive student loan payments. Two adults within a household very frequently need to both hold down full time jobs, if they can land them. Lovingly taking care of children, being attentive to a significant other, housework, grocery shopping, cooking, lawn care, helping out relatives in need, and being responsible to one's community can be exhausting after working all day. Life today seems to be conducive to serious stress for many.

When we have a crisis, our nervous system is frequently thrust into overdrive. The adrenal glands secrete extra adrenalin into the body to prepare us to try to meet the challenge of the emergency. This is the sympathetic aspect of our nervous system going into action. When we are able to calm down again this is the parasympathetic aspect of our nervous system bringing our body back into balance. (Note: The sympathetic and parasympathetic are two aspects of the autonomic nervous system. The autonomic nervous system is involuntary which means we don't control it directly - - as compared to the voluntary nervous system with which we consciously move our body parts.) If we get intensely worried about challenges, deeply concerned about other people's problems, and overly wrapped up in world issues--the sympathetic nervous system takes over and we may feel stressed and tense. If this happens repeatedly, this can become chronic. This partially shuts down our digestive system to the extent that we can't digest food well. It makes our nerves hyper-alert and on edge to the extent that we can't relax or sleep well. Anybody recognize this? The heart pumps harder and eventually this can stress the cardiovascular system. Who needs all that? Our nervous system doesn't have to be in permanent readiness for mega emergencies!

We have a choice. We can observe life around us calmly without allowing ourselves to get pulled off center by it all. This can allow us to stay clearer, be able to make wiser decisions, act more efficiently, and sleep better at night. Sounds good, right? It is possible. It's helpful to pray and put the problem or emergency in God's hands. We can focus on our steady smooth breathing and remember to be a calm observer of the situation. This doesn't make us less helpful and loving. It actually can enable us to live our own life more effectively and have increased strength and emotional reserves to be there in a more valuable way for our loved ones. I know a woman who once was anxiously rushing around trying to help an injured family member and then she fell and broke her own wrist. At that point she wasn't able to help at all. Too often a helper may just keep pushing him or herself to the point of serious chronic exhaustion and depletion. It's crucial to not wait until "someday challenges are over" before taking good care of ourself. We need that nurturing self-support all along the way. Periodic challenges are perhaps just a natural part of the life cycle.

How Can We Lower This Stress? Oh, The Soothing Balm of Peace

How can we maintain peace in the midst of sometimes high odds against it? This is a very important question. Remember that peace is our true nature; it isn't something remote and foreign to our being. Peace is "normal," chronic stress is abnormal. Peace is the state in which the human body is designed to function well. How can we move out of stress and re-balance into greater peace? As previously mentioned, to relax more fully we can focus our awareness in our breath and allow our breathing to slow down and become steadier for a while. Stretching our body can feel wonderful. We can rotate our shoulders and other joints gently to help release possible tension there. Periodically throughout the day taking a mini break to do what I just described can be extremely valuable. Taking a relaxed walk each day can also do wonders to enhance our tranquility. Even a short walk a few times during a busy day can be helpful. The steady rhythm of the steps is calming for the body, and helps release muscles possibly frozen tight in knots here and there. I once worked two and a half miles from work. Parking was limited at the work site and the subway was very crowded (like sardines) at rush hour going home. So I rode the subway in and walked home. I felt relaxed and peaceful by the time I got home. Another option is to drive or ride public transportation part way and walk part way.

It is good to reduce caffeine, sugar, and artificial chemicals which can work havoc on our nerves. We can eat simple yet delicious fresh healthy meals and snacks to give ourselves solid steady energy. Caffeine and sugar can jerk our energy levels way up high for a little while--and then before long cause our energy to crash way down. That can then cause us to crave more caffeine or sugar. It can be a vicious cycle. I cured myself from that cycle many years ago by eating a good protein food when I felt a need for an energy lift. This protein food might be ten or fewer raw, unsalted (or low salt) almonds, or a glass of milk, or a tablespoon of unsweetened nut butter on a cracker or two. Drinking plenty of pure water or herbal tea is also refreshing and renewing.

Let's remember to love ourselves and silently tell our body that it is O.K. to relax. A rest during the day or after work, even ten minutes if time is limited, can help us unwind. Meditation can be a very effective way to enhance peace. There are many wonderful approaches to meditation. You may find it helpful to listen to my audio "Meditation to Enhance Your Experience of the Divine Qualities," with Focus on Peace. Perhaps consider joining a yoga or tai chi class. We need to remember to take good care of ourselves and not willfully override our true needs for a balanced healthy life style.

"What Does Peace Feel Like, I've Forgotten?"

~A Case History

This is a sharing of an actual person beginning to rediscover peace when it has felt lost. Rhonda (not her real name) came into my office our first session visibly upset. She said that she just couldn't keep going the way she was. The stress was really getting to her and making it hard to concentrate at work or to enjoy her life. She couldn't sleep well at night and woke up exhausted in the morning. She said, "What does peace feel like? I've forgotten." Her work load at the office had increased heavily when a co-worker had been transferred and not replaced. It meant overtime work and skipping lunch sometimes. Her mother was in the midst of treatment for a serious medical condition, and Rhonda was really worried. She said her mother was being as brave as could be expected, but was getting weaker and needed a lot of help. The doctor apparently felt the treatment was proceeding reasonably well. Rhonda said that she tried to be as strong and supportive for her mother as she could, but inwardly she was quite concerned. Rhonda had been grabbing take-out food fairly often to save time--she was having indigestion and gas.

I said to Rhonda, "It is crucial for you to take good care of yourself in the midst of these challenges. You can't be there for your mother or your boss or the other people in your life who depend on you if you don't take care of yourself. Your health and strength could suffer. You count and are very important, too!" We did a guided deep relaxation together to help Rhonda begin unwinding a little. Some tears rolled down her cheeks. She said that she hadn't felt that calm in far too long.

We then talked about the importance of healthy home cooked food to help support her nervous system and sustain her health. I said to her, "Eating most fast food on the run is like NOT putting in your car's gasoline tank what your car needs to keep running well." Rhonda laughed and said, "What? I wouldn't dream of doing that to my car!!" She looked a little more serious and said, "But maybe, just maybe, I might put things in myself that won't help keep me running well." I responded, "That's the way it is with a lot of people. Sadly, the very high salt, fat levels and sweeteners take a heavy toll on your health and nerves." We talked about easy quick healthy ways to prepare delicious meals with fresh whole foods. We talked about easy-to-fix big salads and how they could be enjoyed with quality cheese and 100% whole wheat bread. Simple crock pot ideas felt possible to her. Some chopped pieces of vegetables, potatoes, and meat can simmer all day in a crockpot and be ready when you get home. Rhonda said, "I feel hopeful--no complicated recipes, just simple good food to help my stomach feel better."

I encouraged Rhonda to invest at least thirty minutes a day to taking care of herself. Walk for at least twenty minutes, and do a relaxation meditation for at least ten minutes. Rhonda felt encouraged to have some tools and some supportive structure to help her re-balance. She said that she knew with all her heart that she needed to make a few changes for her peace and health.

She came back in a week and said she did her self-care most days, and felt it made a difference. She said that she felt hopeful for the first time in a while. The twenty-minute walk was a relief for her stiff muscles, and her body seemed to really thank her. She enjoyed seeing the squirrels scamper and the birds flying. Meditating and relaxing with the twelve-minute meditation on the website helped her quiet her racing mind. She said that her mind still wandered sometimes, but she was able to bring it back and not judge herself. Sometimes she felt really peaceful and was encouraged. She was doing better with nourishing her body. She knew it would need to be a gradual transition, but she already had less heartburn and indigestion. She said that the short breaks off and on through the day to stretch and do some relaxing breathing were helping, too.

The Acupressure Technique for Emotional Peace, and How it Helped Rhonda

At the second session, I then guided Rhonda through a simple form of acupressure that is helpful for calming the emotions. This technique involves light fingertip tapping on certain locations on the head, hands, and upper torso. This can easily be done for oneself or for someone else. I taught Ronda how to do it for herself so she could do it at home to enhance her peace. All the points can be gently tapped in about four minutes.

It is helpful to repeat the cycle several times. Halfway through each cycle and between cycles, it is good to consciously breathe in peace and breathe out stress. It can give some relief for worry and tension. Acupressure is related to acupuncture except that fingertip pressure or tapping is used instead of very tiny thin needles as in acupuncture. Tapping on the acupressure points was a real surprise for Rhonda. She felt that it actually made some kind of shift for her. Even though she didn't totally understand why yet--it seemed to help. The people of Asia have been benefiting from acupressure for thousands of years. Rhonda agreed it was worth trying since there are no side effects.

She found benefit through the various approaches described above. She was sleeping a lot better most nights and feeling more peaceful during the day. The sleeping pills were collecting dust on the shelf. Note: To learn how to do acupressure for the emotions, see information on "Emotional Freedom Technique" on the Resources Page. (End of case history)

Peace With Others Through Cooperation and Compassionate Understanding

Peace is a choice. Because there is so much chaos in our world, maintaining peace requires an active choice. Peace with others is the result of cooperation and active compassionate love. This involves being compassionate with oneself and one's true well-balanced needs, as well as compassionate and understanding and cooperative with others. Some people may think of cooperation and compassionate active love as weak qualities pursued by fragile people who aren't strong enough to be powerful on their own. In truth, peaceful cooperation and compassionate active love are two of the most powerful capacities to which people can aspire. One person on his or her own is like an atom needing to integrate into a molecule. It is as the units arrange themselves into cooperative groups that greater good can be accomplished. What holds people together in a group or holds atoms together in a molecule is love and peace. We aren't talking about sentimental love or dreamy-eyed peace, but rather about cohesive love and cooperative peace. This is powerful and it is a choice.

Peace is desperately needed in today's fragmented world. Every individual needs inner peace and the planet as a whole needs peace. Without peace every effort is at risk of being futile, and people risk giving up inside. Some people feel that struggling is noble as long as it is for a worthy cause. Yet there are times when we need to let go of the struggle and "wage peace." When we come into a group with good faith to make a decision that affects the good of the whole, the focus needs to be on finding the common denominator-- not on just trying to get the other side to do it our way. Does this sound as though it might be helpful for some politicians?

Consensus Decision Making is Extremely Valuable for Maintaining Peace

Consensus decision making is the essence of peace within a group. With consensus decision making, everyone's needs are addressed as well as possible. Each person won't get everything he or she wants, but will probably get a good part of it. With time, individuals may begin to feel that how they had seen the situation originally wasn't as desirable as the way the group consensus decision eventually evolved. Consensus is the way of survival. It is important at this time in human history that everyone move above the strictly personal perspective to view the group needs and find a common denominator.

Consensus is not always a highly popular idea. It is easy to understand why. At the most basic level everyone wants his or her own way. One approach to this need to have one's own way in life and still thrive as a group is for each person to have a private/sacred space of his or her own. This private/sacred space is just for oneself to control. Even having an area of one's life on which no one else can trample can be very important for one's psyche. The type of group being considering here could be a family, a business, a church, a neighborhood, a city, a state, nation, or the planet Earth. In other words, consensus decision making helps just about any kind of group. If anyone is left totally powerless and unhappy, there will never be peace because there will always be those who are desperately trying to get their needs met and to be heard. I belonged to a very active community group for fourteen years in which most decisions for the activities and welfare of the community were made by consensus of the group. It took a lot of discussion and sharing of ideas, but for many matters it did work quite well in the long run.

Power has to be somewhat evenly distributed to achieve peace. Too often a leader thinks that totalitarianism can achieve the best results because the decision can be made quickly by one person. Then the idea, of course, is that it is just up to the other people to get busy and do the work as demanded. It might appear that this is an efficient approach, but the factor that is not taken into account by such thinking is that people work harder and more creatively when they feel (and know) that they contributed to the decision making. Most people start to balk when they feel ignored and taken for granted. Many people start shutting down, and they begin contributing the bare minimum to the cause. This doesn't build group spirit and enthusiasm.

Let's look more closely at the relationship between consensus decision making and peace. Peace within a group occurs when all participants are O.K. with the tenants of the sustaining agreements. Then the group members can enjoy going about the work or activity that brings the group together. If some members are not content, there will be grumblings and lack of peace. You might think to yourself that decisions and goals within a group could be set by someone in charge--and those individuals who don't agree could just leave. This is often the case, but it isn't ideal. The reason this isn't ideal is because another point of disagreement will surely come up again very shortly. Hence, the population of the group will keep changing, or some people will be left feeling powerless and unhappy. It is crucial to slow down and listen to each other even if it seems less efficient. In the long run it works out better. A little listening on all levels goes a long way.

Creating Peace Within the Parts of Oneself

Within oneself this same idea is important. A human is one person, but there are many parts of the self. In order to feel peaceful, a person needs to achieve harmony within these parts. Listening to all parts of the whole is just as important within one individual as within a group of individuals. There is a part of a person that wants to sleep and rest. There is a part that wants to go outside and walk or enjoy a sport. There is a part that probably wants to hug and have physical closeness and warmth. There is a part that wants to create something attractive or interesting, and a part that yearns for Spiritual connection. And as you well know, there are other parts. Inner peace is achieved through allowing these different aspects of a person to have an opportunity to express appropriately. If any strong need gets ignored, it will likely stir up unrest or trauma.

One may be thinking that there are parts of the self that may be better off not expressed. This may be true. This is where sublimation can help. Sublimation is not repression which involves simply burying and trying to ignore something traumatic or frustrating. With sublimation a person finds a constructive way to express those emotions harmlessly. A person may feel serious anger at someone else. Maybe the other person is not willing or is not available for talking together and hopefully working it out. Then one needs to let that anger express itself harmlessly somehow. If it is ignored it will turn into stress inside. One can talk with a trusted friend or a counselor about the angry feelings. One can pound a pillow. One might express the feelings through music, dance, or painting. The important thing is to not just let them build up inside until they explode in some manner--perhaps at the wrong person and in an inappropriate situation.

Striving for integration within ourselves is very important. Sometimes we may feel a strong conflict about two options. If this conflict is left unaddressed it can lead to civil war within ourselves and total lack of inner peace. Probably we have all experienced powerful conflict at various times. It isn't a pleasant feeling. The important thing is to know that conflict is normal and natural. The crucial thing is to work with it actively and not allow it to fester unattended.

If internal conflict builds up too much it can actually cause a serious personality disturbance over time. As said, it is very valuable to allow the feelings to express harmlessly and begin to release before the trauma gets to that point. Give some kind of wholesome recognition and outlet for expressing the conflicted feelings. This is true whether seeking peace within oneself or within a group. Sometimes a bridge can be found between the seemingly irreconcilable parts of oneself or a group. Within an individual this may be a bridge between one's inner passionate interest (or fury or something else) and one's inner self judgment.

Honoring Each Other's Honest Self Expression

Maybe it is another person that is influencing the conflicted person into thinking that something loved is totally unacceptable. This can be very sad. It can be seen when parents or school counselors push a young person into a line of work or profession against the individual's true wishes. It can sort of break a person's spirit. This kind of pressure can also come from a spouse, significant other, or peers. We all have a right to honor what we love as long as it doesn't hurt someone else or break a law. There is so much room for personal differences if we can respect each other's individuality and not try to hoist our preferences on others. A good motto is: "I respect and love you for who you are in your own unique way as long as you are not harming others. I may not always agree with you, but I honor your right to develop peacefully unimpeded." Of course, if someone is injuring himself or another or breaking a law, that is different.

In the past there have been serious strait-jackets put on people to conform to the majority opinions. Many individuals have struggled to suppress strong creative beautiful parts of themselves in order to fit in with their society. This can cause severe lack of inner peace through strangulation of the true self. We come back to the same principle for maintaining peace. We all need communication, respect, and recognition of our right to express ourselves in our own unique way. This is what can enrich our societies and groups and can enrich ourselves. May we find peace within and without through cooperation, seeking the highest good for all, and through active compassion. In today's complicated world, peace is an accomplishment and a goal that we need to intentionally cultivate.

To Maintain Peace Requires Steady Consciousness Holding the Vision

God's creation is not static; it doesn't just stay the same. It is always building up or disintegrating. To hold anything in manifestation, including peace, requires steady consciousness holding the vision. To maintain the physical body, people need to keep periodically eating, drinking, breathing, bathing, and eliminating. The body itself is extremely busy maintaining all the body systems and organs. It is an intricate balance of creation, change, and renewal. Even what may appear to stay the same is constantly reinventing and reintegrating itself. This is the nature of reality. It doesn't allow anything or anyone to just be. That would invite disintegration. That is how it is with peace. In today's stressful world we need to believe in peace and create conditions for peace. To have peace within and/or without we need to walk the path of peace.

I encourage you to meditate and relax with the audio meditations on the website--or meditate on your own. A good meditation to enhance inner peace is to visualize the color gold. As you breathe in, imagine that you are breathing the color gold into your whole body. As you breathe out, affirm "I am blessed with Divine Peace" or another appropriate affirmation. Giving yourself a chance to center using some of the suggestions in this chapter or other relaxation approaches on a regular daily basis (even for short periods of time) can truly help enhance your inner peace. Mental focus may feel clearer and more uplifted, emotions and worry may feel soothed, digestion and sleep may improve. It may feel like a whole new lease on life through peace. May peace bless your life today and each day. May peace bless all of us and our whole planet.

Real Life Sharings of Ways To Enhance Peace Within Oneself and With The World Around

Staying Centered in my Heart Helps Me Feel Peaceful

~ by Lisa Wilbanks

Staying in touch with my breath helps me stay focused in my body instead of being up in my head all the time. When I am in my heart, everything is O.K.--I don't judge things so much. Whatever I happen to feel is O.K. Otherwise, when I'm in my head, I may be trying to not experience things that are normal to experience. That's pushing against life and not flowing with it. When I breathe and get more into my loving heart space, then it is O.K. what is happening in my life--because it's not good or bad, it just is. We can't really know if something is good or bad until hindsight. It might be the best thing that ever happened. Who knows? Especially if you are a real feeler, like I am. When I am focused in my heart, I can sort of flow with life instead of backing away. I try to practice that. Singing, playing the keyboard or drums, and taking walks in nature also help me feel peaceful. I love to sit and look at nature. Being very present in the moment is calming.

Finding Peace In God

~ by Niki Nichols

What is peace? Peace is for me a deep realization that I am O.K. and that my life is O.K. Does that mean that I am in a bubble, and nothing challenging is happening? No, that isn't it. It is a deep confidence and trust. That trust is in God. It is in life. The way I got this was a long, long journey. Now whatever happens, Iv make God my source. For example--perhaps your husband has walked out on you, or you lost your job, maybe you're mad at your girlfriend, or your kids are being terrible, or you got a bad diagnosis. In reaction your stomach just goes to the floor. With all of those things, invite God into the situation. It is O.K. to have a bad reaction to something at first. You may not remember immediately. But as soon as you remember, pray and ask God to show you what to do. Know that God is your source for everything. It may take a while, but eventually you'll come to know that your source for everything is God. This is a God Path. It is an invitation to God to enlarge your life. It is a prayer. The more you make God your source, the more peace you have. It gets rooted within you. God is within you. The Holy Spirit is within you. The Holy Spirit to me is the deepest intuitiveness within me. One time I was with a co-worker who was very angry at me for no reason. I prayed to God and I was filled with love for her. I got up and hugged her without knowing why. She cried and apologized. She was upset and worried that she might lose her job.

Don't be afraid to journal your feelings. You'll get a lot of answers. Tell God your feelings. He already knows anyway. If there is a problem in your life, that is a good time to pray and turn it over to God and to the Holy Spirit. Holy Spirit may show you a place in your life or within yourself that needs a little bit of tweaking to restore peace. From that can come peace and gratefulness. Have confidence in God. Have confidence in the Holy Spirit in you. Have confidence in your prayers. Know that you can handle whatever comes up because you know that you can go to God. This is really working for me. My last three years have been extraordinary. Invite God to be your Source.

How a Pet Can Enhance Our Peace
~ by Ann

Raven is a very special friend. We communicate with body language, sounds, and gestures. She is a standard poodle and very wise. My husband chose her as a puppy because she climbed up to his ear and whispered and licked his face. He was enamored. He didn't even complain when she wet on him during the long drive home. They were constantly together for three years until he died two years ago. That was a time of confusion. I felt very alone. Gradually with healing, I realized Raven was there for me. Our relationship is very different, of course--but she always is very happy to see me when I return home and attentive when she senses I am lonely or just open for pats and loves. Raven is protective and I feel completely safe with her presence. She is joyous with company. We enjoy playing games outside and talking walks. I really appreciate her companionship when I garden. She listens carefully, never judges and is very loving. I am blessed with many friends, and especially with my very special friend, Raven. (See Resources Page)

A Creative Way to Support World Peace
~ by Fleming

After 9-11 my husband and I were in a state of imbalance. The drums of war were heard faintly and then in earnest. Our anxiety and faith led us to design our Thanksgiving greeting card that year with peace in mind. That first year we made a pin of our peace design and sold them to food co-ops around the country, donating the money to Oxfam International and the American Friends Service Committee. Both organizations work for peace and social justice throughout the world. We were trying anything to keep the vision of peace alive. Peace has remained a theme of our holiday greeting cards since then, and several new pins were made. Since the beginning, friends and family have passed out pins at gatherings, peace rallies, May Day, Earth Day, and all celebrations. We have sent out 10,000 pins to the world. Knowing Joyce has brought me great peace. Her Spiritual guidance brings the Divine into view--such peace and love. (The "Floral Peace Symbol" above is one of Fleming's lovely Peace designs.)

My Experience in the Peace Corp

~ Anonymous

I was inspired to join the Peace Corps in the 1990s because I wanted to be able to draw on an experience with people from a very different culture for the rest of my life in terms of compassion for people in other situations. The Peace Corps provided that for me. How much a Peace Corps volunteer can help the people in the country where he or she is assigned is complicated. I was in a small village in Mali, Africa. They had very little infrastructure, but their needs were fairly well met locally. There was a clean pipe for water in the village, where I got my drinking water along with everyone else. They made their homes from mud bricks formed in molds and dried in the sun. The roofs were thatched. These homes met the people's needs better than more western style metal roofs that were very hot and were noisy when it rained. They grew their food. There were issues that needed some improvement such as malaria, cholera, and educational levels. I spent my first year there learning the language, getting to know the people and the village, and figuring out a project. It was a growing experience for me. I enjoyed my time there. I miss it sometimes even now years later. I learned respect for the Muslim religion. I'm not afraid of Islam as other people might be who haven't lived in a culture that adheres to it. It is a good idea to spread understanding of people in other cultures.

Two Lions Symbolizing the Dynamics of Peace and Power
Original art by Joyce J.C. Gerrish

WORKBOOK: Enrichment Experiences For Enhancing Peace In Your Life

Enjoy the adventure of exploring these enrichment experiences on your own--or gather a few friends to share the journey with you. Be inspired by the audio meditation and soul song for this chapter. Reflect on some of the stimulating ideas and questions.

Questions For Reflection And Discussion

Reflection, discussion, journal writing, expressing your feelings in drawings or other creative ways can all be very valuable to help you delve into these questions in truly meaningful and relevant ways. Before focusing on the questions, you may wish to meditate with the twelve minute audio or transcribed meditation--and/or listen to the soul song "Golden Peace."

1. What helps you feel at peace? Why is inner peace important to you in your life? How can you expand and support peace in your life? Would you like to carve out more time in your life to do these?

2. How does inner peace improve the quality of your relationships and your life in general? Are you a somewhat different person when you are peaceful than when you are stressed?

3. How does inner peace improve the quality of your work? When you are feeling peaceful--do you find that you can concentrate and think better? Are you more accurate? Are you more effective? Do you have more energy to do your work? Do you experience more joy in doing your work? Do you get along better with your co-workers? Does maintaining inner peace perhaps have payoffs for you that are valuable to keep clearly in mind?

Action Suggestions For Enhancing Peace In Your Life

1. For the week ahead, every hour pause a moment and simply be aware of your breathing for two minutes. If possible stand and stretch for those moments. Yawn or sigh a couple times to help release stress. Do this at the beginning of each hour that you are awake. If you miss the beginning of the hour, do it when you think of it--such as at 1:12 pm. or 1:21 pm. instead of 1:00 pm. See if you can find a family member or friend who also wishes to try it. At the end of each day, if possible, check in to encourage and support each other. Knowing that you are going to be checking in with each other can help you stay on track with enhancing your life in this way. Feel free to vary the peace enhancing techniques that you use hourly.

2. Give yourself the gift of a special time each day for your "inner sanctuary of peace," even if it is only five minutes a day. You may already have this built into your life in some way. If so, good for you--continue. This "inner sanctuary of peace" time may be in the form of meditation or prayer. It may be taking a peaceful walk. It may be taking a fifteen minute nap. Maybe it is listening to peaceful music. Whatever it is, the important thing is that this "inner sanctuary of peace" time helps you feel peaceful and renewed. The length of time you need depends on how long it takes for you to feel refreshed and at peace. Invest in your well-being and peace of mind, it will pay you dividends.

3. To enhance your inner peace, try prioritizing your reactions to events around you. Decide what you can react to and what you need to sort of ignore for now. It is possible you might wear yourself out and shatter your inner peace by overreacting to things happening around you and in the world. There are certainly endless events around you and in the world that you may have good reason to get upset about, but it doesn't help you to get thrown off-center. It can pull you down and make it harder for you to respond effectively and take care of yourself and your loved ones. It may seem paradoxical, but the more problems that may manifest in your life--the more crucial it is for you to stay as centered and as calm as possible. Your judgment and your energy reserves are curtailed by reacting in high stress. When challenges loom, that is the time to draw on your peace enhancing practices--not to skip them. You need them even more. Choose the most pressing challenges to focus on now, and allow others to wait a little while until you can handle them better. If you wish, create three columns on a piece of paper. Label one "Immediate challenges." Label another "challenges that can wait a little while." Label another column "challenges which I have to leave to others and to God." Prioritizing can help you let go of some issues and put some on the back burner. Then you can focus more effectively on what truly needs your attention, and on doing it more calmly and optimally.

Audio: "Meditation To Enhance Your Experience Of The Divine Qualities," with special focus on Peace

Pray to the Divine to bless your meditation and enhance Divine Peace in your life. With this audio you'll be guided to sense yourself immersed in the serene well-being of peace. Choose one or more of the following affirmations (or something similar) that feels particularly helpful to you for affirming during the meditation. Before transferring to the website to listen to the meditation, write down on a small piece of paper the peace affirmation(s) you choose and the helpful color gold. Later, place the affirmation(s) where you'll see it daily and be reminded to affirm it for a minute or two several times a day.

◆ I find peace in oneness with God.

◆ I find peace through meditation, prayer, and other inspirational sources.

◆ My peace is enhanced by living in harmony with nature.

◆ My peace is enhanced through love and cooperation with others.

◆ I allow each person to be his or her own unique self.

◆ I listen to the needs of my body for rest, relaxation and exercise.

Helpful color to visualize when meditating on Peace: Gold

Enjoy this peace meditation when you wish to help enhance peace in your life. Connect to the website to listen to the twelve-minute audio "Meditation to Enhance Your Experience of the Divine Qualities," with focus on Peace.

(See transcribed version of this meditation at the end of this chapter.)

Uplifting Audio Soul Song: *"Golden Peace"*

~ By Joyce

Consider it a prayer in song for enhancing Peace within yourself and your life. The words are:

Lift my Soul higher,

Golden peace soothes me, soothes me.

Oh, Divine, Dear Divine. Ou – u. Ah – h.

As you sing or listen, feel yourself relax into the experience of Peace. Close your eyes and really sense it helping to bring you into a warm, uplifted feeling of peace. Connect to SecretsofWisdom.net to listen to *"Golden Peace."*

Transcribed version Of Meditation To Enhance Divine Peace

If possible, listen to some relaxing nonverbal music. Say a short prayer calling on the Divine to bless your meditation and enhance Divine Peace in your life.

Visualize yourself in a ball of light to help strengthen your energy field.

Become aware of and follow your breath as it gently flows in and out at its own pace.

Imagine yourself as a large tree sending powerful roots deep into the earth to help you feel grounded and prevent feeling spacey.

As you breathe in your nose, imagine you are breathing up the strength of the earth into your body. For a few minutes listen to the relaxing music.

As you breathe in your nose imagine you are breathing in light into your being.

Next visualize GOLD light.

Periodically as you breathe in through your nose, imagine that you are breathing gold light into your whole being.

Silently pray to the Divine that your life be uplifted and blessed with Divine Peace.

Next breathe in through your nose and out your mouth for about a minute VERY GENTLY.

Now, very gently breathe in your mouth and out your nose for about a minute.

Then extra gently breathe in and out your mouth for a minute or so.

Now return to breathing in and out your nose.

As you breathe in through your nose, imagine you are breathing in gold light into your whole being.

As you breathe out your nose, periodically silently say one or more of the following affirmations (or something similar).

◆ I find peace in oneness with God.

◆ I find peace through meditation, prayer, and other inspirational sources.

◆ My peace is enhanced by living in harmony with nature.

◆ My peace in enhanced by listening to the needs of my body for rest, relaxation and exercise.

◆ My peace is enhanced through love and cooperation with others.

◆ I allow each person to be his or her own unique self.

Pray for support in helping you to make room for peace in your life.

Continue in that manner for a few minutes or as long as you wish.

Conclude by thanking the Divine and sending down roots to Mother Earth for stability and grounding.

I encourage you to enjoy this meditation when you wish to enhance Divine Peace in your life. Write the affirmation(s) you choose and place where you'll see it several times a day and be reminded to affirm it for a minute or two.

Peace.

Leopard Expresses Power For Good
Original art by Joyce J.C. Gerrish

Chapter Eight

WE CAN ALL BE POWERFUL TOGETHER

Enhancing Divine Power In Your Life

Enjoy listening to, or sing along with, this uplifting soul song I've composed and sung. Connect to SecretsofWisdom.net to hear "*True Power is to Stand in the Light.*" There on the website you can also gaze at the full color design, "Blue Leopard Expresses Power for Good."

We All Have Incredible Potential Power

We should never be afraid of being powerful. It's very important for every one of us! It's the abuse of power that is harmful. We all have incredible potential power within our beings. Sometimes we may forget this in the midst of everyday life and challenges. Life around us may from time to time feel a little overwhelming, and we may feel less than powerful. Valid claiming of personal power is crucial for all of us. There are many ways to experience power, and different people have varied ideas of what power really is. Even within any one person there are usually overlapping different kinds of power. Ideally these different types of power can support each other in the best sense. As an example, a teacher with a powerful intellect can more readily reach students if he or she also has a strong emotional presence that is warm and colorful rather than dry. An excellent athlete's physical power can be enhanced by strong mental power in order to come up with winning game strategies. Let's explore types of power in order to understand more fully what they may mean in our lives.

Some people think of power mainly as physical strength. They may be wondering who is physically stronger than whom--or who can win in a sport or fight! This is physical strength power. There are times when this can be very important, but this is a limited perception of power. The physical body is a magnificent creation. Its potential is wondrous. People explore this potential with running, football, tennis, gymnastics, weight lifting, dance, physically demanding jobs, hiking, mountain climbing, and with all the myriad other forms of sports and physical activities. This is mostly all good. The physical body thrives on being physically active. The important thing to remember regarding physical power is humility. The responsibility and sacred trust of physically powerful people is to help protect those around them. Those who study the martial arts know this deeply. It is desirable for all of us to be physically active. Physical power definitely has its place as an extremely important form of power, but it is only one kind of power and not the greatest.

Physical Strength, Emotional Charisma, and Mental Brilliance Are Ways to Express Our Personal Power - - and Spiritual Power Helps Us Use All Our Powers Wisely.

The emotions can also be a source of power in our lives. Some people experience their lives mainly through their emotions. Their emotions may take them on a roller coaster of feelings all day long--day after day. Emotions can seem like powerful storms or like exciting fireworks to people who consider their emotions as their source of power. Some people may try to control the people around them by pulling on their emotions. That is not a positive use of the emotions. Emotions are good when they are kept in balance and are used with consideration. Emotions used positively can add color, warmth, and charisma to our interactions with people and ongoing life. People can more readily access their higher consciousness and know the wisest course of action at any given time when their emotions are calm and balanced. Emotional equilibrium supports the development of Spiritual power.

The mind when keen and clear can work with significant ideas and be a source of power. Strong well-constructed thoughts can build useful projects and plans. Powerful ideas can bring groups of people together to do valuable work for the good of many, or for less glorious purposes. Intellectual ideas held clearly in the mind can have a powerful effect in the world for sure. Politicians can mobilize great power through a combination of insightful ideas and emotional appeal. Business people use focused ideas and savvy to offer services and products--and if successful they accumulate profits. Then the money amassed becomes its own form of power. Authors and public speakers juggle concepts and theories to influence large numbers of people through the mass media of T.V., books, magazines, and on-line. Teachers tirelessly seek to motivate their students' minds. Mental power can be used in the service of the greater good of all people, or a busy overactive brain can be attracted to limited self-focused concepts and possibilities. We can quiet our busy brain and allow higher Spiritual inspiration to uplift our mind. This can help us to think outside limited conventional approaches. Valuable innovative ideas then have a chance to flower. This is mental power and it can be vast indeed, but it is not the greatest form of power.

We Can All Be Spiritually Powerful. Spiritual Power Helps Us Move Forward On Our Soul Path.

A greater form of power is Spiritual power, and we can all claim our Spiritual power--every one of us. Spiritual power is being the master of our own nature. It is taking the next step of developing our potentials in harmony with the Divine Qualities--and utilizing them generously to benefit our fellow men, women, and the planet. Spiritual power is latent within everyone, and can grow rapidly as we commune with the Divine in meditation or prayer. May we feel love in our hearts and pray to be immersed in the bliss of Divine Oneness. May we set aside at least one quiet time each day when we can relax physically, still the busy brain, steady the perhaps fluctuating emotions, and meditate or pray peacefully. In this quiet uplifted time, we can begin to feel immersed within a wondrous sense of peace and communion with the higher levels of our consciousness and the Divine. At the Spiritual levels we can all be powerful together. Spiritual power is collective power for the highest good of all. Spiritual power supports our strength and courage and wisdom to move forward on our soul path and to accomplish great good.

I feel that God wants each of us to be powerful. Throughout history intuitive people have accessed profound insights and valuable information during higher meditation, dreams, or quiet contemplation. These may be ideas for inventions, composing music, writing, healing, art, and for all fields of endeavor. May we welcome into our lives the reality of the boundless potential of human creativity and ingenuity as we lift our consciousness into oneness with the Divine.

In The Bible, Genesis 1:27 Says That Human Beings Are Created In The Image Of God. That Is Incredibly Powerful

We are not unworthy beings struggling to survive. We are beloved souls created by God with extraordinary potential. With prayer and meditation we can access wondrous Spiritual gifts. We should never doubt ourselves. May we allow the Light of God to shine in and magnify the seeds of our consciousness. Let us water these seeds with our love and, and allow the petals of the flower of our consciousness to open luxuriously in the warmth of Divine Light.

We mostly exist as potential. It is important to not think that what we've got going now is all that we are. A vast majority of people labor under that illusion. We are tremendously more than what society might lead us to think. We are each a marvelous being with vast potential. This potential can be developed with steady patience and perseverance. Every step of the way can be exhilarating. It is crucial that we not doubt ourselves for a minute. Life is about steadily discovering the truth of our being. What might distract us from our true power more than anything else is believing that we have none. We are powerful! We are created by God and we have the capacity to draw on the blessings of the Divine Qualities of God. That is what this book is about. This doesn't mean that we own these Divine Qualities and their capacities--and no one else can access them. We are simply allowing them to flow through us, bless us, and manifest in our lives. They can enrich the lives of everybody else, too. We can all be powerful together and create a bountiful benevolent world.

The basic approach for invoking and accessing the Divine qualities, such as Divine Power, into our life is presented in the meditations accompanying this book. It is important to find quiet time each day to still the mind, emotions, and body. Someone may say, "I just can't meditate. My mind wonders all over the place!" We've been programmed by current culture and media to believe that we can't thrive without constant distraction of cell phones, computer games, social media, and the latest music. These build up the illusion that there isn't anything significant going on within us if all this barrage of input ceased--which is very far from the truth. The glories of Divine potentials exist at a subtle level of consciousness. These are as powerful as the roaring ocean when we develop our skills of opening to them. They will most likely remain hidden to those who tune their consciousness mainly to the mass mind and the latest popular fads. The sacred treasures of higher potentials reveal themselves freely to those who approach with quiet respect, clarity, purity, and patience.

There is a conduit of powerful energy that opens up from one's crown center at the top of the head and gradually accesses up toward the higher Spiritual levels of consciousness which come down to meet it. This is one's connection to higher realities. It is one's lifeline to expressing brilliance and profound capacities. This pathway to God Consciousness is a superhighway that cuts right through the chatter of the mass mind and limited thinking and self-doubt. It is a direct access route to the powers of one's Higher Self and God.

Note: See Charts concerning the accessing of the higher levels of one's consciousness in chapter five "True Clarity Supports Brilliance" and chapter ten "Activating the Energies of Your Aura."

True Power Really Means Developing Our Own Full Potentials, Not Comparing Ourselves To Anyone Else. We Can All Be Powerful Together

Divine Power is different from power as understood by the world at large. Most people think of power as the ability to control or lead others, as the capacity to get others to do what we want them to do, and as the right to take what we want. Privilege for a few is not the true meaning to power. Power really means developing our full potential. Please think about this true meaning of power. It doesn't involve a comparison to anyone else. It is not about trying to be more powerful than someone else--which may involve being a bully or a tyrant. Being powerful means having developed our latent capabilities in our own unique way. No two souls are exactly the same. Each is unique. Our soul potential means the seeds inherent within us waiting to be actualized. These are our true treasures--these latent gifts.

In the Bible is the Parable of the Talents. To the soul that develops and uses his gifts--more are given. To the soul that does not develop and use his gifts--even what he has may be taken away. This means that as a person actively develops his inner capacities, then his consciousness and energy field/aura become more potent and energized. An energized and powerful person then attracts even more opportunities into his life. Like attracts like. A person who sits idly by without using his gifts becomes lazy and passive. Because he is allowing life to slip through his fingers, people don't pay too much attention to him. Opportunities don't seem to come his way because he isn't radiating energy and ideas and interacting actively. Passivity doesn't attract, it deflates. Passivity is defaulting from developing potentials and is not powerful.

True Power is Not About Controlling Others or Feeling Privileged. Stewardship is the Responsibility of Power.

I feel that God wants us to rejoice in being all that we inherently are. A flower is powerful when it blooms forth in all its radiant beauty. Some might think that a flower is a strange symbol for power because it appears delicate. But flowers are incredibly powerful in the dedicated way in which they unfurl their full potential and beauty. The beauty of the flowers attracts to them bees and other helpful insects to spread their pollen and make it possible for them to multiply. The message here is to sense in our hearts what are our unique gifts and passionate interests--and then dedicate ourselves to developing those. May we use our unique capacities for the welfare of the world around us. Surely that's a worthy recipe for true power. We can draw to ourselves others with similar dreams, visions, and skills. We can also draw to ourselves those whose gifts can complement ours. This weaves a powerful fabric of wholeness and cooperation--people working together to create something that has great meaning for everyone. Now that is power for the good! If it isn't possible to follow your passionate interests during working hours, perhaps they can be pursued to some degree during non-working hours. (See Chapter Six "Follow Your Heart and Soul.")

People who try to control those around them for selfish purposes are creating a rigid situation. When a person coerces others, it creates resentment. This is no beautiful flower that attracts others for mutual benefit. Selfish attempts to force others into submission create a very weak situation. There is no real loyalty. Other people are likely to attack rather than mutually support. Control is just an illusion of power and it leaves the would-be tyrant feeling very empty inside.

Now is the Time for a New Definition and Perception of Power. Let's Look at Political and Economic Power

What is your feeling about power? Do you view power as the capacity to serve as a catalyst to create good through dynamic positive interaction? Unfortunately too many see power as a race for who can control the most resources--even if it burdens others. Now is the time on planet Earth for a new definition and perception of power!

George Washington was the first president of the United States. When some influential people wanted to make him king, he said "No." He stood firm on sharing and not controlling power. There would be duly elected presidents, not a king. He was a wise leader.

Let me share with you a positive vision of true power. In a land espousing true power, each person would know that his or her voice and work matter. That is the vision on which the United States constitution was based. It is a noble vision, but not an easy one to truly put into practice. Large numbers of people get under represented and aren't truly included in the economic benefits of society. There are always the haves and have nots. The "haves" tend to feel justified that they work harder or "smarter," and hence deserve more rewards. There is a very valuable perspective that the brightest people with the most skills and resources have a responsibility to look out after the less fortunate. This is the role of a person of true power, to be a good steward for the welfare of all. Being a powerful person does not give one license to take advantage of others, it gives one responsibility to help look out for the welfare of others. This is the leap of consciousness that I feel needs to occur at this time in our planetary history. Powerful Spiritual energies are available to support this renewal of human consciousness.

People are waking up to the fact that excellent hard-working people are being squeezed out from a fair chance for a rewarding productive life. It is really a matter of a fair distribution of resources and opportunities. How can we help support this realignment? We can hold the vision that everyone deserves a fair piece of the economic pie. We can know that we are powerful and our voices matter. That is what democracy is all about. May we know that each person is a sacred "child" of God, and is to be honored. Some sort of reasonable range of salary between the highest paid and the lowest paid people working in the same corporation is logical. We all have similar basic human needs. I feel that these should be honored.

Our Amazingly Powerful Human Consciousness Has Capacities Beyond Most People's Wildest Imagination

Science fiction films and T.V. shows don't begin to do justice to the human potential. What they often show is mostly the sad abuse of power which inevitably eventually leads to self-destruction. The truth of power is that it is intended only for the good of all. Any attempt at the abuse of power will sooner or later bring about the universal law of cause and effect which will re-balance itself through karma. Karma, in a sense, means that the fruits of our actions come back around to us. What we send out eventually returns to us in some form and often intensified. If bullies understood this, they might think twice before acting.

When considering power, it is valuable to consider the concept of reincarnation. Scholarly research estimates that reincarnation is believed in by at least 25% of the people in the world today. It is a basic tenant in numerous of the great religions of the world including Hinduism and a large segment of Buddhism. Many other religious groups throughout Central and South America, Asia, and the world believe in reincarnation. Sensitive intuitive people often spontaneously remember prior lives through dreams or when awake. Awareness of prior existences is woven into the fabric of human life. Since so many people in the world believe in reincarnation, it is a concept worth some serious attention.

The reason that I am mentioning reincarnation at this time is because sometimes it may appear that people who abuse power get away with it unscathed. I believe that isn't true. If someone has been abusive with power in a lifetime, at death that individual's soul will go through intensive retraining in the Spiritual realms. This is called purgatory in some religions. When that soul is reborn in a new physical body and new personality, the life purpose will probably include some experiences to facilitate learning harmlessness and humility. In future reincarnations the behavior is likely to be more respectful of other's rights. It really is an effective system for learning the Divine wisdoms. Earth is truly a school house for learning to embody the Divine Qualities of God

Our Soul Power is Enhanced by Believing in Our Selves

The more that each of us embodies noble qualities such as peace, pure love, harmony, clarity, truth, wisdom--the more innately powerful we become. Others recognize a noble person and know that they are in the presence of an extraordinary being who deserves respect. Truly we all deserve respect at all times. Respect is power; the two go hand in hand. Some people grow up in a family or cultural situation where they are taught to feel unworthy. The sense of feeling unworthy can become so all-consuming that the individual begins to abuse him or herself. That is not how the human experience is intended to be. I feel that life is meant to be a joyful process of learning and growing and embodying ever more fully the Divine Qualities of God. This is the noble human. The noble human is powerful in order to be able to act effectively to actualize his or her soul mission. No one has a right to interfere with that God given right.

It is very important that people who may be feeling unworthy seek out therapeutic support to help them heal. In addition, I encourage them to read my article "We Can Heal Childhood Wounds From Abuse," which can be accessed from the website accompanying this book. Also, numerous of the chapters in this book can be very helpful to them in their healing journey.

The Balance of Power Between Men and Women

Let's look at the balance of power between men and women. Men held the power in most cultures throughout much of history on planet Earth. Women were expected to be obedient to their father until they were married. Then they were expected to be obedient to their husband. If their husband died before they did, then they were expected to be obedient to their oldest son, if there was one. This was how it usually was, and it was not to be questioned or the woman would probably be shunned or worse. That was the reverse of power. That has been the general paternal tone of much of planet Earth for thousands of years. Here and there power has been shared semi-equally between men and women. Occasionally cultures appeared that were maternal where the women held the major power, but that has been the rare exception. Having power concentrated so strongly in the men has in many ways deprived the world of the true gifts and contributions of the women. This balance of power is improving now--but still has a long way to go.

Power is not only a matter of who is in charge; it is also a matter of who will be allowed to develop his or her fuller potentials. When power is concentrated in a certain group, that group is likely to try to limit the opportunities of the less powerful. Frequently a powerful elite tries to limit education for the less powerful. There have been many periods where it was against the law for certain groups to learn to read. It is easier to control illiterate people. In the Middle Ages in Europe very few people could read, and they were easily controlled as serfs. All that people were expected to do was to farm a tiny piece of land and raise a few animals to provide food for themselves. They usually had to give to the King or Governor a large part of what they managed to raise. Life was lived on a subsistence level. The serfs had very little or no power--and their innate capacities had minimal opportunity to flourish. The same or worse was true with slaves in the United States. The crucial point here is that power gives one the opportunity to truly develop oneself and one's talents and capacities. This is of extreme importance.

Let's Not Be Afraid of Change. Helpful Ideas Accessed From Higher Intuition Can Flower and Bring Forth Valuable Innovations to Help Heal Our Planet

It would be wonderful if people who are unusually creative and who have strong initiative were given room to try out their valuable ideas--and be encouraged in whatever ways possible. With some support, genius can flower and bring forth innovative new ways of accomplishing basic societal needs for housing, energy, healing, travel, food production, and communication. Don't be afraid of change! It can enhance the welfare of everyone in the human family.

If these ideas resonate with you, talk with people you know about the role of true power for everyone--not power for just the few. Believe in your power and exercise your constitutional right to speak out and communicate your ideas in whatever form is natural for you. We can communicate our ideas through email and social media, letters to the editor, public speaking at organizations, teaching adult education or child education, through the arts, in staff meetings, and by voting in elections. These are just the tip of the iceberg of ways in which we can exercise our true power for the good of all. We can start a community group to help address a community challenge. This is power in action. We can each be powerful in our own way. The ways are unlimited--there is room for everyone to express his or her true power. The vision can grow and expand and bless us all. Let it fill your heart and put wind in your sails. Hold the vision that we are one whole powerful human family standing up for the good of all.

There are so many who are walking around with a sense of emptiness or yearning in the heart and not sure why. Everything may appear to be more or less O.K. on the surface. Inside, though, there may be a sense of urgency to unravel what seems to be constrained within. May we all let it out--that is essential to our empowerment. That is our sense of destiny. We are all powerful when we are coming from our true selfhood--being our authentic self. We don't need to travel far away or spend a lot of money in order to be our authentic powerful self. It just means being true to ourselves and what we feel we were born to express. That is powerful. We can all be powerful because we are each unique. If we are each expressing our soul calling in whatever way possible in the moment, then we will each contribute a piece of the mosaic panorama for the healing of planet Earth and all its people. Take a breath and feel the majesty of it all. Each one of us can be our own powerful self in our own unique way contributing to the world and people around us. Blessings to all of us as we claim our rightful power.

Real Life Sharings Of Embodying Power For The Good Of All

A Lawyer Dedicating Legal Power to Serving the Public Interest
~ Anonymous

As a lawyer, I've tried to use the law to serve the interests of the public. I've done environmental protection work, as well as work on behalf of low income consumers and coal miners. It has taken a few different forms. Currently my focus is teaching and environmental protection.

Lawyers are taught to zealously advocate for their client's position no matter what, with a few exceptions. The other side does the same thing for their client. That is regardless of what their client's position is. Clients who have their own power and money are perceived by most lawyers as the work of most stature and reward. As you can imagine there is a lot of attention given to clients who have money. I've never seen it as fulfilling that way. A person only has a certain amount of time on earth, so why not do something that is going to be impactful for someone who can't get a good result on their own? I also feel "how much money do you really need to live?" For me it is not just about making money. There are other considerations, such as feeling good about what you are doing. Of course, lawyers have to make a living just like everybody else. You can't work for free all the time if you are going to take care of your family, have a home, eat, and pay for health insurance.

I teach at the law school of the university here. We have a clinic setting which takes on clients pro bono (free). The law students take on cases for the clients of the clinic. The students are supervised by licensed lawyers like myself who are experienced in the matters that they are working on. It is a really good situation for everybody. Virtually every law school has at least one legal clinic where their students can practice in that manner.

In addition to my work at the university, I take on a number of clients that I often don't get paid for. Lawyers have an ethical duty to render some pro-bono service. Sometimes, if I prevail in a case for the client, the other side is on the hook for the legal fees. Other times I've had fellowships and grants to cover my legal expenses. It's never easy doing public interest legal work. If it were, a lot of people would be doing it. But it is meaningful. There are plenty of good lawyers out there that are available for moneyed clients. I try to help people who can't afford legal service.

Learning To Live From My Heart
~ by Cindy Morton

When I was a teenager, I volunteered at an agency. I was hired on at eighteen fresh out of school. By the age of twenty, I was supervising a group. I loved my job, and my main focus was to please my bosses. I was a stern task master and had a lot of power in my position. I felt important, respected and powerful--but never happy or fulfilled. After I retired from that same job nearly thirty years later, I no longer had that identity. I then realized that I had lived my whole life thus far striving to please others and that I had no idea who I really was.

One day I attended a church service when the minister was talking about experiencing life from inside out. She was talking about experiencing life from the heart. I know there was a big question mark above my head, because I wasn't sure what it meant to live life from the heart. Before the service was over a huge light bulb shone brightly above my head, and my life changed dramatically in that moment.

When people who knew me in the past see me now--they say, "What in the world happened to you?" I am a totally different person now. Back then I was super-controlling and intolerant. Currently I don't have any power over others; I don't want any power over others. I don't want to think for a moment that I have power over anyone. As far as situations go, I think that God puts us where we are supposed to be. We run into issues or problems because we need the lessons. They will just keep popping up until we learn them. What I now feel is true is often the opposite of what I used to believe. Everything that I ever believed, I now step back from and reexamine.

I now feel that I don't need to impress or control anyone. I held on to that need tightly for so long like a locked box in my heart. Finally I said I'm going to have to let go of this. When I opened and released that box and let go of that need, it's like all of a sudden there was a sense of lightness that I'd never experienced before. When we muster up the courage, the faith, the belief - - then we don't need to hang on and hide behind that need to impress or control. When we let go of that weight, then we'll have more of what we really wanted in life than we ever dreamed possible. It's amazing. That is how I feel about living from inside out "from my heart." Now I feel I'm free. Now my power comes from being in touch with my heart and Spirituality, not from trying to control or please others. As the Unity Prayer of Protection says, "The Light of God Surrounds Me."

Experiencing Power as a Wilderness Naturalist
~ by Darrel Joy

Our roots as humanity came from living in the forests. We are dependent on our relationship to nature. We empower ourselves by preserving and protecting nature, not by destroying it. I feel that understanding life in the woods and forests and being able to survive there with minimal equipment is powerful. When we are in the woods, power comes from our ability to pay attention, pick up information, and knowing what to do with that information.

When you are out walking in the woods or a forest, it is important to know what direction you are going so you don't keep walking in circles and possibly get lost. When you see moss on one side of a tree, that side of the tree is likely to be north because it gets less sun. You can also watch how the sun is moving. Of course, the sun rises in the east and sets in the west. If you wish to move steadily in a particular direction, choose a very tall tree in the distance or some other high land mark and keep moving toward that.

If you need clean water when out in nature and available water seems muddy or undependable, you can cut a grape vine and good drinkable water will drip from that. You can also cut a twig of a water maple tree (also called silver maple) or a sugar maple tree and they will drip sufficient good drinkable water. A twig one fourth inch or less can work fine. We can readily learn what plants are edible and which are medicinal. There are excellent field guide hand books on that.

You can create a very small lean-to hut called a debris hut using branches, lots of leaves, and other natural debris from the woods. This can help keep a person warm and dry overnight if out in the forest without protection from the weather. One time I had constructed a debris hut and then a storm was due. I stayed in a tent that night and got washed out. In the morning I found that the debris hut was bone dry inside.

Take a long pole (limb of a tree with branches removed) and lean it against a low fork in a tree. Then take individual smaller branches and lean them against the pole limb. This way you are basically making a small A frame structure. The whole thing is long enough so that you could lay underneath it with your toes pointing up without touching anything. Once all those angled sticks/branches are in place, weave some more sticks horizontally on top of the A frame. Then just cover it all with leaves, get as many leaves as possible. Don't leave any holes where cold air can get in. Take a shirt and fill it with leaves. That can serve to plug the entrance after you enter. Your body heat will warm up the interior, the leaves keep the heat from dispersing, and you can be quite comfortable. For really cold weather, the thickness of leaves needs to be three feet. That will keep you warm inside the debris hut, and can keep you from freezing to death in an emergency.

Those are just a few suggestions for empowerment in nature. I like knowing that I can feel at home and can take care of myself out in a forest, and that I can help others. (See Resources Page)

Sports And Sportsmanship As An Expression Of Power
~ by A.L.H., Dunlap, Tennessee

I am the Head Coach of the cross country running team for boys and girls at the local county high school. This year will be my ninth season, and over fifty students signed up for cross country; that is 10% of the whole school. I work with them in an ongoing self-selecting process. I don't get mad at the kids. I don't punish them for their performance. I think of all of them as varsity. The seven boys and seven girls with the best clocked racing times in the previous meet get to represent the school at the next one (or race). I brought the team to the state championship which had never happened before.

I love running. I've been doing it for twenty two years. Running is hard work, but it is fun. It is a great weight management tool. I run in the mornings--3.1 miles. I don't listen to music; I keep proper form and pay attention to my breathing. I'm a competitor, and this is a safe way to do that. I like to have the distinction of placing in my age group; I've been able to do that for nine years now.

I have a much better day when I run than when I don't. I am calmer, and I am less reactive to negative stimulation. The effect on me is similar to when I meditate. It takes me "out of myself," and I'm more in tune with the Universe. When I get back and cleaned up I feel refreshed, emotionally stable, my mind is clear, and I have more energy. I really feel more in my body, grounded, and prepared to go on with my day. Over the years running has helped me get through some emotionally challenging times. I love what running does for me. I've raised three sons who are excellent runners.

Note from Joyce: Before beginning any form of exercise that is new for you, it is very important to check with your health care provider first. Brisk walking is also an excellent form of exercise, with almost as excellent benefits as running. It's just a little gentler.

Unlocking Your True Power
~ by Paul Graber

Everyone wants power. Many think they are powerless. There are countless opinions as to what it means to be powerful. Sadly, most seek power outside themselves. Any power found there is often not what they wanted and is always temporary. The power that made the Universe and us is incredible and limitless. It is all around us and within us. It has been scientifically proven that we humans are made up of the same cosmic material as the stars shining in the sky. Another name for power is energy. It has also been proven that literally everything we perceive to be physically real, is merely energy vibrating at different frequencies. This is the exact same energy or power that made the Universe and us. It has been further proven that this energy is sentient and responds to our thoughts.

Lao Tzu teaches us that, "mastering yourself is true power." Given our new knowledge concerning the true nature of power and energy, this simple lesson gives us access to incredible power. The simplest path to mastering yourself is meditation. Meditation begins with learning to control your breath. If you remember that breath is actually energy, you see that you are actually learning to control your energy. This energy is your true self. Once you master yourself in this manner, you will have all the power you will ever need. If you use it wisely and with love, you will find happiness and accomplish great things. (See Resources Page)

Effective and Heart-Centered Store Manager
~ by Brent

I'm a manager at an electronics store. I really enjoy it. I try not to be like a boss. I act in a friendly way so everyone feels I'm just like everybody else--except that I just have more duties and responsibilities. That way we all get along, and everyone sort of feels on the same level. If someone isn't working as well as needed, we give them a few tries. We try to teach them ways to improve their performance. If coaching doesn't help, then we have to let them go. We definitely try to enable them to stay. We give everyone at least three chances.

Managers in our stores will bend all the rules to make sure that the customer is satisfied at the end of the day. It's all about the customer. In order to meet customer's needs, it is important that managers ask what their customers want.

I feel that the national minimum wage should be raised. My store pays more than minimum wage to entry level employees. That can help keep a more even playing field between people's salaries. Tons of people work forty hours and still can't make ends meet, so they work sixty hours and can still barely survive. It is almost necessary for them to live with someone else in order to share expenses.

Concerning businesses in general, even though I am a manager at a national chain store, I wish that there were a lot more small independent businesses. They can be unique and fun to shop at.

We Can Harness Power, But We Can't Control It
~ by Becky G.

How do people perceive power? In today's society I feel many people think of power as control. They feel that a powerful person has control over others as in a business or in regard to creating a product.

I personally think of power as how a person can channel power. Everything is energy. It's not a matter of my being powerful or not powerful. Those are just terms. We can harness and channel power by our thoughts. We tend to forget how powerful our thoughts really are. If we change our way of thinking, then we will change the outcome of whatever we are doing. Power is not something we can control, it is something that flows. It's not innately destructive, even though it can become destructive. Storms are a form of power. They can indeed become so vast and so forceful that they level the earth. The news media study and report closely on storms, but they have no control over them. They can say, "It's going be a big one, you probably ought to get out of the way." I feel that storms are the earth moving energy to order to clear or free itself.

We have the ability to utilize and harness power to help us make our lives better. Energy healing is releasing the stuck places in us so that we can allow power to flow through us more readily. We can channel that energy so everybody benefits. We can tap into that power, without trying to stop it or hinder it or change it. We can stand in awe of it. We can sense the flow of power and allow ourselves to harmonize with it and be with the power as it flows. Chi Gong is a discipline of body movements coordinated with a person's in breath and out breath. This practice helps me to enhance the flow of energy (chi, prana) throughout my body. Chi Gong helps me to feel powerful.

Four Women Express Power in the World
Original Art by Joyce J.C. Gerrish

WORKBOOK: Enrichment Experiences For Enhancing Divine Power In Your Life

Enjoy the adventure of exploring these enrichment experiences on your own--or gather a few friends to share the journey with you. Be inspired by the audio meditation and soul song for this chapter. Reflect on some of the stimulating ideas and questions.

Questions For Reflection And Discussion

Reflection, discussion, journal writing, expressing your feelings in drawings or other creative ways can all be very valuable to help you delve into these questions in truly meaningful and relevant ways. Before focusing on the questions, you may wish to meditate with the twelve minute audio or transcribed meditation for power--and/or listen to the soul song "True Power is to Stand in the Light."

1. When do you feel powerful, and how do you feel about that? Do you like the experience of power in that way? Do you keep strongly in mind how to help empower others at the same time?

2. When do you not feel powerful? How is that experience for you? Do you like yourself better when you feel powerful or not powerful? Is there some way you can enhance your sense of positive power when you don't feel powerful, such as speaking out more, or volunteering to lead something, or taking on a little more responsibility?

3. What are your feelings about people in your life who you sense use power in a positive way for the good of all? How would you compare this with people you know who seem to use power to control and hold down others? Explore thinking about specific people in your life and how they use power. Also, explore thinking about some people in your life and how they may not claim their full share of power.

Action Suggestions For Enhancing Power In Your Life

1. Choose some aspect of your life and decide on a project for practicing your enhanced positive power. It can be a smallish project to start, if you like. What is something you've wanted to do and have perhaps been afraid to attempt? Maybe you didn't want to seem pushy. Decide on an assertive act that would be helpful for not only you but for everyone else involved. If you wish, ask someone else to do it with you or lend moral support in some way. An example of a project for practicing enhanced positive power might be suggesting and working to support a change or special project you feel would be beneficial for a group or organization to which you belong or are affiliated.

2. Visit and perhaps join a group that seems to epitomize powerful positive action in a field of special interest to you. For example, someone who loves to create art or a craft might choose to join a co-operative gallery. Someone who likes to sing or play a musical instrument might seek to join (or start) a musical group that performs locally. Become active in a local organization supporting a valuable cause about which you have strong feelings. Help organize a festival in your town to help build community spirit. When one feels empowered and reaches out confidently, possibilities and opportunities often manifest in surprising places and ways. It helps to think outside the conventional approach.

3. How can you use your positive power to support someone who doesn't seem to really appreciate how wonderful they are? Can you help them take their next step in positive empowerment?

Audio: "Meditation To Enhance Your Experience Of The Divine Qualities," with Focus On Power

Pray to the Divine to bless your meditation and enhance Divine Power in your life. With this audio you will be guided to sense yourself immersed in the clear centered strong feeling of positive power. Choose one or more of the following affirmations (or something similar) that feels particularly helpful to you for affirming during the meditation.

◆ I am created in God's image. I am powerful.
◆ Following my life purpose as I sense it in my heart and soul IS my path of power.
◆ I am powerful as I truly believe in myself.
◆ I know that true power is responsible stewardship--not privilege.

Helpful color to visualize when meditating on Divine Power: Blue

I encourage you to enjoy this meditation when you wish to support and enhance the quality of power in your life. Connect to SecretsofWisdom.net where you can listen to the twelve-minute audio "Meditation to Enhance Your Experience of the Divine Qualities," with focus on Power.

(Also, see transcribed version of this meditation at end of this chapter.)

Uplifting Audio Soul Song: "True Power is to Stand in the Light"

~ By Joyce

Consider it a prayer in song for enhancing your sense of benevolent power. The words are:

True power, True power. True power, my friend.

Is to stand in the light. Is to walk in the light.

Is to serve in the light of God.

As you sing it or listen to it, sense yourself beginning to feel enhanced confident strength. Close your eyes and allow it to help bring you into a centered clear feeling of positive power. Connect to SercretsOfWisdom. net where you can listen to: "True Power is to Stand in the Light."

Transcribed Version of Meditation To Enhance Divine Power

If possible, listen to some relaxing nonverbal music. Say a short prayer calling on the Divine to bless your meditation and enhance Divine Power in your life.

Visualize yourself in a ball of light to help strengthen your energy field.

Become aware of and follow your breath as it gently flows in and out at its own pace.

Imagine yourself as a large tree sending powerful roots deep into the earth to help you feel grounded and prevent possibly feeling spacey.

As you breathe in through your nose, imagine you are breathing up the strength of the earth into your body.

For a few minutes listen to the relaxing music.

As you breathe in through your nose, imagine you are breathing in light into your being.

Next visualize blue light.

Periodically as you breathe in through your nose, imagine that you are breathing blue light into your whole being.

Silently pray to the Divine that your life be uplifted and blessed with Divine Power.

Next breathe in thorough your nose and out your mouth for about a minute VERY GENTLY.

Now, very gently breathe in through your mouth and out your nose for about a minute.

Then extra gently breathe in and out your mouth for a minute or so.

Now return to breathing in and out your nose.

As you breathe in through your nose, imagine you are breathing in blue light into your whole being.

As you breathe out through your nose, periodically silently say one or more of the following affirmations (or something similar) that feels helpful to affirm during the meditation.

◆ I am created in God's image. I am powerful.

◆ Following my life purpose as I sense it in my heart and soul IS my path of power.

◆ I am powerful as I truly believe in myself.

◆ I know that true power is responsible stewardship--not privilege.

Pray for support in helping you expand your positive power for the good.

Continue in that manner for a few minutes or as long as you choose.

Conclude by thanking the Divine and sending down roots to Mother Earth for stability and grounding.

Enjoy this meditation when you wish to enhance your sense of Divine Power.

Peace.

Devoted Mother Reads to Child
Original art by Joyce J.C. Gerrish

Chapter Nine

DEVOTED HEARTS ALIVE WITH PASSION

Enhancing Divine Devotion in Your Life

Enjoy listening to or sing along with this uplifting Soul Song I've composed and sung: "*Devoted Hearts.*" Connect to SecretsofWisdom.net to hear "*Devoted Hearts*" and gaze at the full color design, "Devoted Mother Reads to Child."

Devotion Helps Keep One's Heart and Consciousness Lifted and Open to Receive and Share Divine Love and Peace!

In this chapter we're looking at Devotion as both a very personal Spiritual experience--and as devoted service to the people and world around us. Devoted service is the natural outgrowth and expression of our Devotion to the Divine. Indeed, one of the fastest ways to Spiritual growth is through loving devoted service.

Devotion to the Divine is a precious gift. It can sustain us in powerful ways. Devotion helps us be thankful and appreciative for the good that is in our life. Thankfulness is healing because it encourages us to focus on what is positive in our life, and helps us reintegrate ourselves at the close of each day before going to sleep. It is so easy to feel depressed when things don't go exactly as we wish. It can feel as though all of our efforts are futile. It is beneficial to focus on what **IS** going well in our life.

Life tends to move along in cycles and stages, as we probably all know--right? Things may be going along well for quite awhile. Then off and on there may seem to be a stalemate where development feels somewhat blocked or slowed down. There may be times when serious disappointments or traumas come along. Life simply does sometimes flow in unpredictable ways. It is valuable to be patient with ourselves, others, and life flow--and focus on being thankful for what we do have and what is going well. That is the time to pray and meditate and lift our consciousness perhaps even more than usual. Maybe we simply need to keep going as well as possible until the situation opens up again more fully. But also, it may be time for a small or larger adjustment, for refocusing, or for expansion of our vision. Maybe in times of change our life is about to shift and reflect the Divine vision more fully--and move into an even better period. In times of uncertainty, may we lift our hearts even closer to the Divine--to God!

The simple prayer, "Thank you, God," silently repeated over and over as a mantra (silently repeated phrase or word) can be calming and uplifting. One's own mantra can surely be some other phrase that may feel meaningful. "Divine Peace is blessing my life" would be a good mantra. Of course, one could use the same phrase and exchange the word peace with another of the Divine Qualities such as "Divine Love is blessing my life." It's helpful to focus in one's heart center (in the center of the chest) and silently chant the mantra while feeling love and appreciation for the Divine. This can be very stabilizing, nurturing, and uplifting in times of challenge--and any time!

Spiritual Devotion Can Be One's Constant Support and Bulwark

Spiritual Devotion can be a powerful act of courage that can hold a person steady no matter what may be going on. It can be a person's constant support and bulwark that holds him or her up from possibly stumbling. When a person allows stress, worry, fear, or trauma to engulf his or her consciousness--it can create a heavy matted layer of static energy all around the person's aura energy field and mind. Once that heaviness sets in it can be harder to be open to receive helpful insights and to be receptive to encouragement and help that comes one's way. When one is feeling down, helpful opportunities that may be available and offered may not even be noticed or the person may not feel worthy to try to step into them. Thankful devotion can help keep one calm and alert in times of potential stress or problems. It can help access Divine blessings to grace one's path. It can also be joyful in one's most treasured times. Devotion and thankfulness can be one's ongoing response to life and all it brings.

Valuable practices for daily devotion can include reading Spiritual books and periodicals that inspire you, lighting a candle, praying, meditating, listening to or creating Spiritual music, taking a contemplative walk in nature, ecstatic dance, meditative art, and many other uplifting approaches. There are so many ways to express our devotion! People who truly maintain an attitude of Spiritual Devotion often have a glow about them that is undeniable. Their facial expression may seem gently blissful for no apparent reason. Every act of the day can become an act of devotion when accompanied with a prayer and with thankfulness. This can be valuable and surprisingly transformative for all of us!

Everyone Sings From Their Hearts and the Joy Is Contagious. I Get High on God's Love!

~ Sharing from Larry

The church I attend almost every Sunday morning is a sanctuary of prayer, praise, and song. Everyone sings from their hearts and the joy is contagious. There's no way to feel self conscious even if you feel like your singing sounds like a frog croaking--like I do! It feels good to sing anyway, and nobody notices or judges! A lot of the members like to clap and sway. Pretty soon everyone is praising the Lord and singing out even if they came in sort of sad. The Pastor's sermons seem to have a healing soothing effect on me, and he often says just what I am needing to hear. God's love opens all of our hearts and by the end of the service there is a smile on just about every face. I'd rather get high on God's love than on alcohol like some of my buddies want me to do with them. There have been times when I've felt like my whole body is kind of tingling in a pleasant way, and I feel really light--it's hard to describe. Other members say they feel that way sometimes, too. After the service everyone likes to hug each other. I'm so grateful to have this support in my life. My girlfriend has started coming with me from time to time and seems to enjoy it. My faith in God and the support of my church and loved ones help keep me going. I teach junior high math. Even though I love it, there can be hard days. When a problem comes along I do the best I can, and then I pray and put it in God's hands. (End of Sharing. Name changed to preserve privacy.)

Devoted Service Means Expressing One's Soul in Joyful Heart-Centered Action!

When one is devoted to the Divine, then it is very important that in some manner one expresses devotion in joyful service to others. Service is an important way that one can demonstrate devotion to the Divine. Service can be an act of devotion in and of itself. Think of Mother Theresa and her great work in India. Devoted service is truly courageous action undertaken by courageous people. When one is devoted, in the true sense of the word, it means that one is standing on one's principles and beliefs, and is devoting oneself to active service in forwarding that cause. What a powerful statement! It means that a person not only believes in a cause, but is doing what he or she can to support it. The word devotee means to dedicate one's time and energy and one's heart.

What are you devoted to? Some people are devoted to their job. They spend long hours fulfilling their responsibilities very carefully and completely. They may volunteer for extra assignments, and put themselves out in whatever way they can to do an excellent job. Other people are devoted to their country, and they may join the military to serve their country in that brave powerful way. Excellent teachers are devoted to their students. When a person is devoted, his or her work is fueled with sustained passion.

Today we are all greatly needed to feel devotion for a worthy cause. There are so many worthy causes desperately in need of dedicated workers and supporters. This is very active, not passive. It is exceedingly important to state our beliefs and stand by them. Sometimes people who don't give service in some way to a worthy cause may ridicule those who do. Ridicule is sad and self-defeating. Let's all try to make it a point to really support each other in our devoted service to worthwhile causes.

One Woman's Creative Way of Showing Devoted Attention to Her Elderly Grandfather

Rosalyn (not her real name) shared: I try to visit my ninety-two year old grandfather once a week if only for a little while. He lives in an assisted living facility here in town. He means a lot to me. I've always been Grandpa's girl. I'd been concerned about him recently because he was getting quieter. He doesn't see or hear well anymore, and that seems to be causing him to withdraw more. He's always been quite jovial and sociable. I'd heard about creating an audio life memoir with an older person, and I thought, "He might enjoy that, why not?" When I told him of my idea, he at first seemed hesitant. He said his life hadn't been all that unusual. I told him, "It's your life, and I really want to hear all about it---and so do your children, other grandchildren, great grandchildren, and the rest of the family!" I told him I'd make audios of most of what I record. I said, "Come on Grandpa, we'll have fun doing it!" So he agreed and we started at my next visit.

Every time I visited, I got him to tell me a story. We sort of started when he was quite young and gradually moved through the years. I got to hear about fascinating things I'd never heard before. Sometimes I asked questions to keep him telling his tales. Sometimes he really got into dramatizing the events. I loved it! Often we laughed. There were times when we cried. Usually we didn't record for more than about thirty minutes.

After we'd been doing this a couple months, one time when I arrived I found him in the lounge happily telling a story to some of the other residents. I quietly sat down and listened, too. He seemed more like my Grandpa I'd always known and loved. Recording the memories had benefits beyond the recorded life tales. I did create audios for our close relatives and gave them as presents in Grandpa's name. One of my brothers is creating a family tree website, and is really grateful for the information about our ancestors to augment the website information. It's been a wonderful experience for all of us, and so simple. A nice off-shoot is that one of Grandpa's friends at the facility said he'd like to create an audio memoir. So sometimes the three of us get together for a little while and record a story for his friend. That can perhaps grow more gradually. It's all good. (End of sharing.)

It's Very Important To Pour Our Precious Life Energy Into a Purpose That Is Worthy of Our Devotion

Sometimes people get devoted to something that takes their time and energy and doesn't really help them or anyone else. That behavior might more appropriately be called a habit or obsession than devotion. There is a continuum between helpful devotion to a worthy cause--and obsession to something meaningless or even destructive such as substance abuse or some other addiction. It is very important to pour your precious life energy and time into a purpose that is worthy of your devotion. Vast numbers of people spend endless amounts of time watching T.V. or playing computer games or doing something similar. Certainly some of this is valuable for relaxation and entertainment. Some programs on T.V. are educational or informative, wholesome entertainment, relaxing, or artistic. But moderation is essential. We are all needed to share some time to help our neighbors, and help heal our communities, cities, countries, and planet.

The opportunities are endless and exist in every walk of life. If we haven't already, maybe it is time for all of us to really look around more than ever before and open our hearts as wide as possible. May we consider responding to a piece of the world with which we somehow feel a bond. Maybe it is something that directly affects us or a loved one as Roslyn described above. Maybe it is a part of life that we know almost nothing about but would like to know more. There is something calling for our loving attention. For people who don't have children, participating in a "Big Sister" or "Big Brother" program or something similar can be rewarding. How about volunteering to tutor students in public schools?

Giving Devoted Service to a Cause That Warms and Opens Our Hearts Is Healing for Ourselves, Too

I've had many people tell me how much deep, meaningful pleasure they get from volunteering to assist with really worthy causes. One person said, "It helps put life in perspective to see the smiling grateful faces of those who were tangibly benefited in needed ways." It can change our lives as well as the lives of those we touch. Pursuing a pastime that doesn't make a positive difference for some part of our world can begin to be boring or seem meaningless. We may begin to wonder, "what is life all about?" We may begin to ask, "Why am I here?" We may begin to feel a little barren or flat inside. Devoted service can help set our life aflame with new possibilities and opportunities. It can awaken us to new dimensions of our being.

I'll tell you about a fun project that I did with great devotion, with people I adored. As I mentioned earlier, awhile back I was helping to lead arts and crafts, drama, and singing at a day center for people with developmental disabilities. The idea occurred to me to put on a musical drama "extravaganza." We had already put on about four short dramas in the previous year or so. I wrote an adaptation of an old musical comedy set in the nineteenth century that was out of copyright. For months we all practiced the songs and "by George" got pretty good. Everyone interested received a part and they all got inspired practicing their roles. They blossomed into convincing actors and actresses. I read the script as a narrator, and they acted it all out. They put their hearts into it. We all sang the songs together at the appropriate places. One of the staff created some attractive costumes by starting with clothes that the participants already had. She added special ruffles, drapes, hats, and so forth. Energy was building! I was going non-stop preparing for the special evening performance. We all helped make lively scenery that gave a festive feeling and supported the drama. Invitations went out. Families and friends arrived the evening of the performance. The actors and actresses performed magnificently. That was a joyful evening none of us are likely to forget!

Each of Us Is Unique! It's Important to Never Compare Ourselves With Anyone Else

Each of us is unique. It is very important to never compare ourselves with anyone else. Sometimes what someone else is doing may appear to be so much more than what we are doing. On the other hand, what another person is doing may look insignificant to someone else. It may, though, be serving a profound need for a group of individuals who might be floundering without that important assistance.

A student in one of my meditation classes named Nat (not his real name) was concerned about his fourteen year old son being so shy. Nat told me he had decided that some days after work he would go out with his son to a nearby park to play basketball for awhile. Nat periodically let me know how things were going with him and his son. A few other teens about the son's age also tended to sometimes be there playing casually, including another father. They all had a good time playing together--and agreed to try to meet up there at the court for about an hour on Tuesdays and Thursdays at 6:00 pm. One day the other father suggested that they all go hiking together at a nearby state park on an upcoming Saturday afternoon. The group enthusiastically agreed. On the agreed upon day a group of the boys and the two fathers met at the basketball court and drove in two cars to the state park. They had a good time hiking, and Nat was delighted to see his son clearly enjoying the company of his new friends. Over the summer and autumn the group continued to get together to play basketball informally and periodically took outings together to hike or fish. Through the basketball games and the outings, Nat's son had found a group of good friends. He became particularly close with two of the boys and tended to eat lunch with them at school, walk home together, and sometimes hang out or study for awhile. Nat told me with a smile, "You know, my son and I seem to have a closer bond now, too. --And besides, I've enjoyed the exercise and getting out in the fresh air!"

If We Keep a Healthy Balance In Our Lives, We May Find That We Have the Energy to Share More Fully In Service To Others

Many of us feel tired after a day's work or a day's responsibilities. This is understandable. We need to listen to our body, for sure. Along this line, it is valuable to know that sometimes what can revive us most is a change of pace to help create more balance in our lives. If we have been at a desk all day, then it is highly possible that what our body may crave is to do something active for a little while. We may wish to try a dancercise class or exercising at a local fitness center. This can help relax tight muscles and help deliver oxygen more amply around

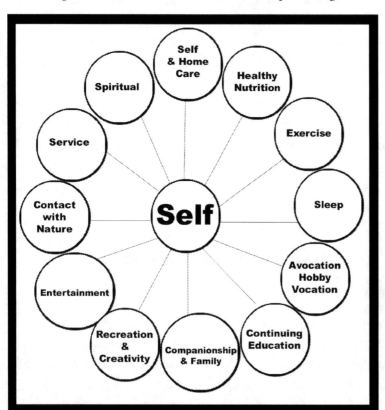

the body to help us feel revived. If we have been working hard physically much of the day, then we may need something physically soothing. This may be a sauna or soaking in the tub for awhile, taking a nap, or reading a book with our feet propped up. We have different aspects of our life that are important to maintain in some kind of balance. These might include: vocation (or avocation/hobby), exercise, Spiritual, sleep, companionship and family, service, healthy nourishment, relaxation & entertainment, self care & home care. If we keep a healthy balance in our lives, we may find that we have the energy to share more fully in service to others.

There is a place in one's being that craves to make a difference in the lives of others. If one has a large family, that need may be largely met in tending to their needs. It is so important that it be quality attention that is given to those people in one's life. Do they need someone to whom to tell their hopes and dreams and fears? Do the young ones need someone to help them with their homework? Do they need someone to accompany them to stimulating events and places that will expand their life horizons? Sometimes one can combine attention for family with service to others. There are family groups that on some holidays go as a group to help provide a special meal at a center for homeless or needy people. Getting involved in that way can be very heart warming.

Devotion Adds Color to One's Life, and Can Help One Feel Happy and Fulfilled

A wonderful thing about devotion is the sense of joy that one feels in the process. Devotion is not a rigid cut and dried thing. Devotion warms one's heart and nourishes one's Soul in a loving way. Devotion adds color to one's life, and can help one feel happy and fulfilled. When filled with a sense of devotion, the giver often gets as much out of the sharing as does as the receiver. This is well known! A truly devoted action is complete in itself; it is not particularly looking for return. (Of course, one needs to earn a living.) There is great joy in the giving. But such joyful selfless loving service naturally does bring a return of good through the Universal Law of the Circle known as Karma. What one sends out tends to return to one from some source, and often multiplied.

This period of the twenty-first century can potentially be a time of magnificent growth and transformation for the better. Major innovations in energy technology, health care, communication, and every aspect of life are occurring at breathtaking speed. Adjusting to these may not be completely easy because change can be challenging, but the opportunities for exciting creative innovation exist everywhere. It can be the birth of a new and wondrous era for ourselves and everyone. Imagine the courage of a baby chick pecking its way out of its egg. The chick has no idea what it will find outside the egg, and it has to work very hard to crack through. We need that courage to work through to the new expanded reality for ourselves and our planet. It is something to feel passionate about; it can inspire our devotion. There are endless examples of how we can support this transition. Opportunities exist within every walk of life to help and inspire those around us to wake up to their true potential. Each of us is created in God's image. The spark of the Divine is within us. We are each awesome. If we truly acknowledge this, nothing can stop us from together creating a better world for everyone. The knowledge and creativity are there, the technology is there, the human network of caring is there. What is needed is all of our devoted service to help actualize our new reality.

Perhaps we have all seen the difference between one person walking his or her life path in resignation or apathy--and another person treading perhaps a similar life path but filled with the flame of devotion to the life around. It can be as different as night and day. Each of us can make that leap of faith to help make a difference. It is totally possible, and it can help bring our beloved planet Earth and all its inhabitants up a turn of the spiral to what could truly be experienced as a new more wondrous reality. It is possible; it is a goal worth striving for. May we invoke the Divine to fill each of us with the courage, energy, wisdom, creativity, and devotion to help create an ever more peaceful, joyous, compassionate world full of awesome potentials!

Real Life Sharings of Different Forms of Meaningful Devotion

Devoted Service as an Assistant Minister
~Rev. Valerie Mansfield, Louisville, Kentucky

For me, being Devoted Spiritually is a sense of wanting to give back to the Universe everything that I've been given. The church has given me so much love and peace. I have received a tremendous amount of guidance for positive living and an awakening of my own Spiritual growth. I am an ordained Unity Minister now. For many years, I have been giving to the church members, the community, and to the whole world some of the good that has been given to me throughout my life. As a church we do service programs where we go out and serve the greater community. Part of being a Spiritual person is to serve others. Service is something that I feel very strongly about--not only within our church community, but outside our community.(See Resources Page)

Devotion as a Yoga Instructor and President of a Major Yoga School

~by Laura Spaulding

Yoga consists of body postures called asanas which are profoundly helpful for physical health, emotional peace, and Spiritual upliftment. Yoga helps to relax and strengthen the muscles and bring fresh blood to all parts of one's body. It helps to support optimum functioning in all one's organs, body systems, and skeletal structural alignment. It also vitalizes one's aura energy. There are numerous different styles of yoga. Gentle Hatha Yoga can be a good place to start.

I first heard of yoga when I was very young, and I knew then that I wanted to learn it. I've been studying and practicing yoga since 1967. I've met and studied with great teachers. All of that I feel has been due to grace. I found myself in the right place at the right time where I could learn what I needed to learn. I've spent a great deal of time studying in India.

Spiritual Devotion is a big part of my yoga practice. It is very helpful in yoga, even though it is not a religion. Most people who practice yoga, including me, feel that this is a deeply Spiritual practice. Devotion helps the yoga practice by giving it a lot of juice. That helps me get up every morning and do my practice. I don't think of it as a workout, far from it. For me it is a Spiritual offering that I make to the Divine out of my gratitude for what I have received from this path.

It nourishes me in a million ways. It brings me a lot of joy. There is so much bliss there in the practice. Although the positions can be challenging sometimes, it doesn't feel that way. It just feels blissful. I feel very fortunate to have all the things that make this practice possible. Yoga East has always been there to support me in my practice. It provides a great community. Three of us took over running this yoga center in 1994. I have had a very blessed life due to yoga.

Note from Joyce: Laura has over 10,000 hours of yoga teaching experience and has trained well over 100 yoga teachers. It is interesting to know that she had previously earned a law degree from Georgetown University. (See Resources Page)

My Devotion To My Husband as He Journeys Through Alzheimer's

~ by Linda Cassidy Lee, Louisville, Kentucky

In sickness and in health. This sacred marriage vow that Ed and I exchanged thirty one years ago is now being tested. Ed is in a nursing home with Alzheimer's, and I pledge my Devotion to him by comforting Ed as much as I can as he journeys through the trials and tribulations of the disease. Presently there is still laughter and love between Ed and me, but the day will come that Ed will not recognize me as his wife anymore. I will continue to show my Devotion to Ed until his soul enters the Divine Eternity.

Devoted Mother and Grandmother

~ Anonymous

It's a gift to have such wonderful children that I've felt so connected with and have loved so much. I pretty much tried to build my life around them, particularly when they were young. It went too fast. What I felt with my children was that there was always a Spiritual hand that guided them and helped them find their direction and their talents. We're lucky that we are entrusted with these children. When painful disappointment came up for them I would sometimes say, "You know, it may just mean that there is another direction for you that may be even better in the long run." It is very hard as a parent to reassure your child that even though something is devastating, maybe there is something better.

I feel that sometimes there is a karmic soul connection between a parent and child, and there's a reason that we are together. They may help us as much as we help them. We try to find that balance, and hopefully be joyful about it. As parents, we hope to say the right thing and do the right thing.

Being a grandmother is lovely. What I'm seeing with my children is what good parents they are. How loving they are. Maybe they're better parents than I was. All of them do have the advantage that they are in good marriages and have supportive partners. It is beautiful to watch your children be loving parents. It's an adjustment to be there without being intrusive and without offering advice. I try to just be there when they need me. My children have all grown up and have become independent. They have wanted to be on their own. They are spread out now in different states and cities. One is in the same city where I live. Once you're a parent, you are always a parent. It doesn't ever go away. It changes, and maybe it's not so much in your face, but it is always there like a night light--even though time changes things. I feel that their guardian angels go with them, and my guardian angel stays with me. That's comforting.

I Feel Closest To God When I'm In Nature, And When I Pray And Meditate
~ Anonymous

My faith is what keeps my life fairly even and steady. My grandfather was a protestant minister and my father is a deacon and very involved at his church. My mother often played hymns on the piano when I was growing up. Some of my happiest memories are of singing hymns with my mother. Another special thing about my mother was that she used to once a week light a candle at home, sing a hymn or two, read some scriptures, and say prayers for the members of our family and close relatives. It was sort of a nice family ritual. Dad and I often joined her. Since she passed away from cancer a few years ago, I've continued her tradition. It helps me feel a connection to her and my family and to God. I enjoy going to church sometimes, Dad appreciates that. I love him very much. To tell you the truth, I feel close to God wherever I am when I close my eyes and pray and meditate. This is particularly true when I'm out in nature. My wife and I often go for a hike on Sunday morning. It feeds my soul. She says she feels the same way. We usually feel really peaceful and renewed when we get back. I try to meditate for a while each evening. It helps set an even tone for my work as a customer service rep the next day. I really try to help all those people. From time to time I pause a moment or two and imagine that I'm in the woods by a stream, and I pretend that I'm breathing in that peace.

Devoted Service To Animals
~ by K.C.

I have deep love and compassion for animals. I hate to see them suffer. I have three dogs of my own that bring me much joy and comfort. I live in a fairly rural area. They help me feel safe. I volunteer at our town's animal shelter. It's hard work cleaning so many cages, but someone needs to do it. We try to find homes for as many dogs and cats as possible, but you can imagine it's not easy. We walk them and try to spend at least some time with each of them. Animals that are used to living with people get depressed if left alone in small spaces. We do what we can. I'm devoted to trying to help give them a new chance for a good life.

Woman With Star of Inspiration
Original art by Joyce J.C. Gerrish

WORKBOOK: Enrichment Experiences For Enhancing Devotion In Your Life

Enjoy the adventure of exploring these enrichment experiences on your own--or gather a few friends to share the journey with you. Be inspired by the audio meditation and soul song for this chapter. Reflect on some of the stimulating ideas and questions.

Questions For Reflection And Discussion

Reflection, discussion, journal writing, expressing your feelings in drawings or other creative ways can all be very valuable to help you delve into these questions in truly meaningful and relevant ways. Before focusing on the questions, you may wish to meditate with the twelve minute audio or transcribed meditation --and/or listen to the soul song "Devoted Hearts."

1. What warms your heart? What opens your compassionate love and draws you to it irresistibly with the desire to assist or somehow be a part of the situation? Is it a religion and a warm supportive congregation? Is it children? Is it healing in a holistic or medical setting? What opens your passion to be of service?

2. Have you ever seriously thought about what is your deepest source of joy? Some people feel that entertainment is their strong source of joy. That does have its place for most of us. For many people, though, there is a much more profound source of joy which comes from devoted service to a cause that glows in their heart. Have you experienced that profound joy from helping and being of service to others in some manner? This may be service to people, or animals, or plants,

or some other aspect of Mother Earth. That deep joy of service can sometimes be its own reward in a way that is at times hard for others to understand.

3. How do you feel about being of service to a worthy cause? Is this something that your family members embrace and practice? Service to a worthy cause can be built into one's vocation, or it can be pursued separately as a volunteer. For some people, their whole life is an act of devoted service in many ways. What are your forms of service and how do you feel about them? Are you considering changing or rethinking your forms of service in any way? Are you thinking of continuing or expanding your service?

Action Suggestions For Enhancing Devotion In Your Life

1. Talk to a trusted friend about what inspires devotion in your heart. Ask what inspires devotion in his or her life. Talk to your friend regarding how you feel about being of service to one or more worthy causes. This may open deeper understanding between you. Maybe there is some kind of service project which you would enjoy participating in together.

2. You've probably heard the phrase "Share a random act of kindness today." How do you feel about that? Do you enjoy sharing random acts of kindness as you move through your day? If you like, try increasing your random acts of kindness for a few days for the joy of it. If you feel good about it, try continuing at that level. It warms the heart, and what goes around--comes back around.

3. One of the fastest ways to Spiritual growth is through loving devoted service. This is not always fully understood. The reason for this is an excellent seed thought for meditation. Try talking to a number of people you respect highly and discuss the relationship between heartfelt devoted service and Spiritual growth.

Audio: "Meditation To Enhance Your Experience of The Divine Qualities," With Focus on Divine Devotion

Pray to the Divine to bless your meditation and enhance peaceful Divine Devotion in your life. With this audio you will be guided to sense yourself immersed in the profound feeling of Devotion. Choose one or more of the following affirmations (or something similar) that feels particularly helpful for affirming during the meditation.

◆ Thank you, God. Thank you, Divine.

◆ My Spiritual Devotion blesses and steadies me.

◆ I share "random acts of kindness" everyday.

◆ My devoted service opens and warms my heart.

◆ I give joyful devoted service to life around me.

Helpful color to visualize when meditating on Devotion: Ruby Gold (Ruby with flecks of Gold).

I encourage you to enjoy this meditation when you wish to help support devotion in your life. Connect to SecretsofWisdom.net to listen to the twelve-minute audio "Meditation to Enhance Your Experience of the Divine Qualities," with focus on Devotion.

(Also, see transcribed version of this meditation at the end of this chapter.)

Uplifting Audio Soul Song: *"Devoted Hearts"*

By Joyce.

Consider it a prayer in song for enhancing warm loving Devotion within yourself. The words are:

Devoted hearts, serving our human (earthly) family.

Helping our brothers and sisters, in service to the Lord.

Devoted hearts--sing praises, sing praise, sing praises to the Lord.

As you chant it or listen to it, just feel yourself beginning to lift into the experience of Divine Devotion. Connect to SecretsofWisdom.net where you can listen to "Devoted Hearts," which was composed and sung by Joyce.

Transcribed Version of Meditation To Enhance Your Experience Of Divine Devotion

If possible, listen to some relaxing nonverbal music. Say a short prayer calling to the Divine to bless your meditation and enhance peaceful Devotion in your life.

Visualize yourself in a ball of light to help strengthen your energy field.

Become aware of and follow your breath as it gently flows in and out your nose at its own relaxed pace.

Throughout this meditation you don't need to breathe extra-deeply or hold your breath extra-long. Just be aware of your breath as it flows gently in and out.

To help yourself feel grounded and prevent possibly feeling spacey, imagine yourself as a tree sending powerful roots deep into the earth from the base of your feet or the base of your spine.

Then as you breathe in your nose, imagine you are breathing the strength of the earth up into your body.

For a couple minutes listen to the relaxing music.

As you breathe in your nose imagine you are breathing in light into your being.

Next visualize ruby gold (the color of ruby red with flecks of gold in it).

As you breathe in your nose, periodically imagine that you are breathing glowing ruby gold light into your whole being.

As you breathe out your nose, silently say one of the following or similar affirmations that you feel would be helpful to affirm during the meditation.

◆ Thank you, God. Thank you, Divine.

◆ My Spiritual Devotion blesses and steadies me.

◆ I share "random acts of kindness" everyday.

◆ My devoted service opens and warms my heart.

◆ I give joyful devoted service to life around me.

Continue in that manner for a few minutes or as long as you wish.

Conclude by thanking the Divine.

Then once again send down roots for grounding.

I encourage you to enjoy this meditation as often as you wish to enhance Divine Devotion in your life.

Peace.

Man Feels New Growth and Expansion
Original art by Joyce J.C. Gerrish

Chapter Ten

ACTIVATING THE ENERGIES OF YOUR AURA
Enhancing Divine Illumination in Your Life

Enjoy listening to or singing along with this peaceful soul song "*Oh, Holy Light.*" Consider it a prayer in song. Connect to the website to hear the audio "*Oh, Holy Light.*" *There* you can also view the full-color design, "Woman With Luminous Bird."

What is Illumination and How Can It Help Us?

Illumination is the activation of our aura with more and more luminous energy and the gradual clearing away of old energy blockages that may limit our joy and our radiance. Gradually embodying the Divine Qualities in our lives is a big part of the path to illumination. Illumination and Spiritual growth tend to develop hand in hand. I feel this is the most exciting journey and magnificent adventure in existence. It can enhance our physical health, emotional peace, mental clarity, Spiritual upliftment, and bliss. Each of us has amazing potential. In terms of Spiritual illumination, we are each like an incredibly beautiful flower waiting to more fully open its petals. Some are like flowers in the stage of a barely opened bud brimming with potential new life. What will bring the bud into the fuller expression of its splendor of illumination? Let's explore some of this potential that is within each of us, and some ways that it can be developed more fully.

We and Everything on Planet Earth Exist Within a Sea of Energy

Energy Vibrations and Frequencies

Spiritual Level
Vibrational Frequency of Energy

〜〜〜〜〜〜〜〜〜〜〜〜〜

Shorter Electromagnetic
Wave Length

Physical Body
Vibrational Frequency of Energy

〜〜〜〜〜〜〜〜

Longer Electromagnetic
Wave Length

Note: The above chart is not drawn to scale and is not meant to give specific wavelengths. It is simply diagrammatical to give a general idea for the layman of what is intended when the word *vibration* is utilized in these writings. The electromagnetic spectrum consists of the entire range of wavelengths or frequencies of electro-magnetic radiation extending from infinitesimally tiny gamma rays through x-rays, ultra-violet rays, visible light, infrared, to the longest radio waves measured in feet.

Our sun radiates powerful light to illumine and energize our planet and the other planets of our solar system. All people, animals, plants, and minerals have an energy field within and around them which is experienced intuitively as light. Everything in creation is energy. Einstein's theory of relativity said that matter is energy/light that has slowed its rate of vibration. Indeed, the body of each of us is energy that has slowed its rate of vibration. Every atom in our body is like a tiny solar system with electrons whirling around the nucleus. Every atom has the potential power of an atomic bomb. Awesome, right?

Divine Illumination is a major goal of Spiritual growth. The human energy field, which is called the aura, can gradually be purified and illumined with Divine light and activated to its fuller potentials. This requires humility, healing old traumas within oneself, opening to higher meditation, faithfully pursuing Spiritual practices, and service to life around one. This eventually can lead to achieving oneness with the Divine and with the higher levels of one's consciousness--and finally total enlightenment. One can gradually become an ever more wondrous glowing light and blessing unto the world.

How Sunlight Helps and Sustains Us

Let's take a brief look at the sun's energy in relation to life on Earth. The sun's radiation is a powerful source of energy to sustain us. Photosynthesis is the scientific explanation of how plants transmute sunlight into chlorophyll to grow and sustain themselves. Through photosynthesis sunlight, along with water, air and nutrients from the earth, becomes the body of the plants. Now that is a miracle! Sometimes we don't notice the miracles that are constantly taking place all around us in the world. When we eat fresh fruits and vegetables created through photosynthesis, we are only one step away from being sustained by light. One way to gradually purify our body and increase its capacity to absorb light energy is to eat more fresh, raw, organically grown vegetables and fruits. (Any significant change in nutritional intake needs to be undertaken a little at a time and under the supervision a health care provider.) Drinking lots of pure water is also very helpful to hydrate our body and flush out toxins. Then our body can absorb more energy directly from the sunlight.

We also can increase our absorption of sun energy and Divine Spiritual Light by consciously breathing in light into our being. Periodically as we breathe in our nose--we can visualize/imagine that we are breathing in sunlight and Spiritual Light. This can be particularly effective when we are outdoors, but it is also helpful if we are indoors. There have been some humans who have been able to gradually cleanse and develop their aura and energy system and physical body so greatly that they could absorb all or almost all of their sustenance from the sunlight, Divine Spiritual energies, water, and air. I'm not expecting the reader to necessarily believe this, but to perhaps consider it as an interesting possibility.

How We Can Keep Our Aura Energy Flowing Freely

Aura energy is also referred to as prana, chi, qi, life energy, or universal life force (and other terms) in various cultures and languages. This energy is ideally constantly flowing freely in definite pathways throughout our body to maintain our vitality. When there is a strong healthy energy flow, it supports our physical health. When a person is ill, injured, seriously stressed, not sleeping well or not eating well, his or her energy field may weaken. The flow may slow down or get partially blocked here and there.

Energy blocks could be compared to a traffic jam in a complex expressway intersection. You know what it is like to be caught in a traffic jam. All the vehicles are blocked and stuck and can't get where they need to go. People can't get to important appointments and responsibilities. Valuable cargo on trucks may be greatly needed at their destination--and there they sit unable to get through the congestion on the highway. The flow of our energy field/aura can get sufficiently blocked and congested so that our aura is hampered from allowing adequate intake or circulation of fresh clear life energy to truly sustain us optimally well. Our consciousness may feel foggy and unclear. Our body may ache and feel somewhat weak.

We have numerous ways that we can help get the energy/light in our aura energized and flowing more freely again after being sick, injured, or depleted. The following methods and tools are some of the ways we can help bring ourselves back into harmony with the natural rhythms of life and enhance our illumination and health.

- ◆ Regular time out in the sunlight and fresh air.
- ◆ Healthy living habits such as nutritious food, pure water, sufficient sleep, regular exercise, positive loving thoughts, and nurturing relationships.
- ◆ Energy Healing such as Reiki, Healing Touch, Polarity, and Quantum Touch.
- ◆ Yoga, Tai Chi, Qigong, and other holistic movement disciplines.
- ◆ Meditation is an extremely important way to renew our being.

Meditation Can Help Enhance Our Energy

When people think about meditation, they often think about a seated person peacefully relaxing his or her mind and body--and focusing on the breath. A highly Spiritual person may additionally think about meditation as communion with the Divine and with one's Higher Self (higher levels of one's consciousness). That person may or may not think about meditation as a way to enhance life energy and Spiritual Light in his or her aura. In truth, that is an exceedingly important part of the meditation experience. The more that one meditates and lives a wholesome healthy lifestyle, the better the aura can stay energized/illumined with Divine Light and life energy. What a gift from the Divine!

As one's energy field replenishes, one can begin to feel enhanced well-being physically, emotionally, mentally, and Spiritually. That is good motivation to meditate regularly, isn't it? The tricky part is that not all meditations are equally as effective in accessing Divine Light and life energy to activate the aura. Also, some people catch on more easily than others as to how to enhance this absorption of light energy into one's aura. Yet with a little patience, it can be learned by all.

There may be people who think this whole idea of absorbing Divine Light and life energy is simply symbolic language. The truth is that science is now routinely photographing people's auras with Kirlian photography and other means. It is a fact. Many people can feel and perceive this energy very easily and clearly.

Others may require some practice and sensitizing. This is the same energy with which holistic healing modalities work. These modalities include acupuncture, acupressure, reflexology, and energy healing work.

Activating Our Chakra Energy Centers

Seven major chakra energy centers are located along a person's spine from the coccyx at the base of the spine up to the neck and on up to the top of the head. There are other energy centers located throughout the body such as in the palms of the hands and in the bottoms of the feet. When a person does Spiritual practices such as meditation, prayer, yoga, and chanting--these energy centers can gradually open and cleanse of old stuck energies. Once the energy centers are cleansed, the higher clearer energies can begin to be accessed more freely. As higher Spiritual energies begin flowing into one's aura, one is likely to begin feeling more and more uplifted, relaxed, and at peace. A pleasant tingling sensation may be experienced or some other sensations such as slight warmth or gentle joy.

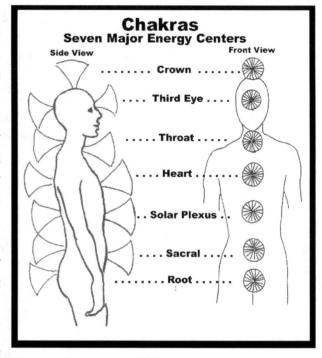

This chart shows the seven major energy centers/ chakras. The word chakra means wheel in Sanskrit. The chakras are referred to as wheels because as each energy center becomes activated, it begins to open and spin gently like a wheel. This can be a superb vitalizing feeling. The spin is ideally clockwise as viewed by someone looking at the person.

The next chart shows the names and locations of the seven major chakras, as well as colors which are helpful to visualize when meditating on them. Different systems of teaching associate slightly different colors with the chakras. Either indigo or violet are sometimes correlated with the third eye, and either white or violet with the crown. It is O.K. either way. Basically the colors associated with the chakras correspond with the colors of the visible spectrum as sunlight shines through a prism: red (root), orange (sacral), yellow (solar plexus), green (heart), blue (throat), indigo (medulla oblongata), violet (third eye), white (crown). Pink is widely associated with pure love, hence it is often associated with the heart chakra as an alternative to green. The medulla oblongata is not one of the seven major chakras, though it is important. The colors discussed above and shown in the chart are not necessarily the colors that a clairvoyant would see looking at that chakra or that the chakra should be. These are colors that are helpful for the chakras when visualized during meditation, worn as clothing, utilized as room décor, or seen in nature.

About Chakras			
Chakra Name	**Location**	**Helpful Color**	**Main Issue**
Crown Center	Top of Head	White or Violet	Spirituality
Third Eye Center	Between Eyebrows and slightly up	Violet or Indigo	Intuition, Wisdom
Throat Center	Throat	Blue	Communication & Creativity
Heart Center	Center of Chest	Green or Pink	Compassionate Universal Love
Solar Plexus Center	Just above Navel	Yellow	Personal Power
Sacral Center	Center of Abdomen	Orange	Personal Emotions, Sex
Root Center	Base of Spine in Back	Red	Physical Needs & Survival

As the energy centers/chakras begin to activate, the following gradually begins to occur:

1. The Sacral, Solar Plexus, Heart, Throat, and Third Eye centers each open out like a flower to both the front of one's body and to the back of one's body from their location along the spine.

2. The root center points out back (and not to the front) from the base of the spine, also like a flower.

3. The crown center gradually points straight up from the top of the head like a flower.

As each of these energy centers begins to activate, it can help support health in the area of the physical body where it is located. Each chakra has an endocrine gland and an organ or body system that is associated with and nourished by it. As the chakra opens it can also enhance the behavioral aspect and main issues of one's life that are related to that chakra. See table "About Chakras" regarding the main life issues and related behavioral aspects associated with each chakra. See following table "Chakras In Relation to Organs and Endocrine Glands" regarding which organs or body systems and which endocrine glands are benefited as the chakras are gradually cleansed, activated and developed.

Chakras in Relation to Organs and Endocrine Glands		
Chakra	**Supports Organ or Body System**	**Supports Endocrine Gland**
Crown	Brain (Cerebral Cortex) and more	Pineal (Master Gland) supports whole body
Third Eye	Eyes and more	Pituitary (Master Gland) supports whole body
Throat	Throat, Nose, Teeth, Ears, Neck, Mouth	Thyroid, Parathyroid: supports rate of metabolism
Heart	Heart, Lungs, Chest, Circulation	Thymus supports immunity
Solar Plexus	Digestive Organs	Pancreas: supports normal blood sugar levels
Sacral	Sex Organs, Bladder, Prostate, Womb	Testes / Ovaries: supports reproduction
Root	Skeletal Structure, Bones	Adrenals: activate body reserves in response to emergencies & stress

The endocrine glands secrete very small amounts of powerful substances directly into the blood circulation. These secretions have a significant impact on healthy body functioning. Keeping the chakras cleansed, opened, and balanced helps to support healthy functioning of the organs and endocrine glands. That supports enhanced body health and well-being.

An excellent way to gently open and cleanse the chakras is to briefly meditate on each of them fairly regularly. As you breathe in your nose, imagine you are breathing in glowing light into a chakra. As you breathe out your nose, imagine you are breathing out any stress or stuck heavy energy or limiting emotions from that chakra. I encourage you to meditate with my audio "Meditation to Enhance Spiritual Awakening and Illumination" (34 minutes) which you can access from SecretsofWisdom.net. If you feel that you don't have time to listen to all of it, consider meditating with part of it. A major focus of that audio is activating and illuminating your chakras and aura.

Balancing the Chakras/ Energy Centers

It is important for the seven major chakras to gradually open at relatively the same rate, rather than one being a great deal more open than the others. A good way to help keep your chakras in balance with each other is as follows. Please hold these hand positions very lightly with no pressure at all.

1. Very gently hold one hand behind your neck and one hand at the base of your abdomen in the front (at the pubic bone). Relax and be aware of your breath for a minute.
2. Very gently hold one hand in the center of your abdomen and the other hand on your forehead. Relax and be aware of your breath for a minute.
3. Very gently hold one hand slightly above your navel and one hand on the front of your neck. Relax and be aware of your breath for a minute.
4. Hold both your hands gently side by side at the center of your chest. Relax and be aware of your breath for a minute.

Our Awesome Aura

There are numerous different levels or planes to a person's aura. Most of these are like concentric interpenetrating ovals. All levels of the aura interpenetrate to the core center of an individual.

Starting from the physical body, each level of the aura tends to be larger and of more refined (less dense) energy. There is the etheric body which is like an energy double of the physical body except a little larger. Next there is the emotional/astral level of the aura where feelings and emotions are experienced and to a certain extent stored. The next larger and more refined level of the aura is the mental body where thoughts are experienced and also to a certain extent stored. Then there are the progressively more Spiritual levels of the aura and consciousness which are the buddhic, atmic, monadic, and adi. As a person grows Spiritually, he/she gradually becomes more intuitive and conscious on these higher more subtle levels of consciousness. This is discussed more fully in later chapters.

A person's aura is changing all the time depending on his or her mood and what the person is experiencing physically, emotionally, mentally, and Spiritually. The size of the different levels of the aura and which level of the aura is relatively larger will vary from person to person depending on his or her life experience and personality. This is all quite variable. Some groups utilize different terminology and may describe the levels of the aura slightly differently. If all this is fairly new to you, just get a general feeling for it--and don't worry about the details.

Strong emotions and habitual thoughts get "recorded" in these layers of the aura, somewhat similar to a digital recording device. What is "recorded" can have an ongoing positive or limiting influence on us as subliminal messages. These are often called thought forms. Positive thought forms may be peaceful and loving and supportive such as "I'm a good person" or "people appreciate me." They may help us feel good about ourselves and life. Limiting thought forms may be angry, jealous, depressed, bored, fearful, or other emotions. They may sometimes feel like static or a slight heaviness in the mind and/or body--and may make us feel down on ourselves, others, and life. They may reflect feelings such as "I'm no good" or "people don't like me."

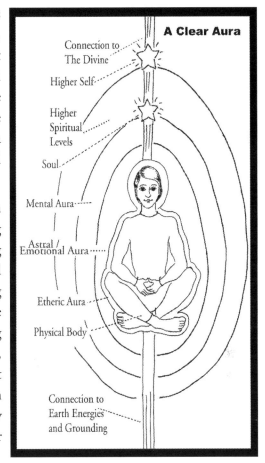

Most people have a certain amount of those self-limiting thought forms. Healing our emotional wounds is a part of the Spiritual growth process. In truth, it is part of every life fully lived. We can learn through challenging difficult experiences. Nothing is wasted as long as we learn wisdom through it--and then heal it and let it go. Positive thinking about ourselves and life is so very important for our well-being and our enjoyment of life.

It sometimes requires a Spiritual warrior to hold steady through the occasionally challenging periods of the Spiritual growth process. Perhaps the most challenging stage of the journey is to truly face one's own "shadow self." The "shadow self" is the parts of oneself which one repressed, or from which one tries to hide. Some may think that repressing certain emotions is the right thing to do. The truth is, though, that constant repression can act as an inhibiting straightjacket on one's being. It can cause constriction where there is ideally spontaneous joy and creative free expression. That which is within oneself can be lovingly faced, healed, and transmuted along the Spiritual path. There is no place to hide in the presence of God. God knows everything in one's heart and loves one anyway. As one opens to the Divine and prays for light and love and grace, one can be gradually blessed with more and more peace and illumination and joyous freedom.

As you meditate regularly, old repressed emotions and stuck energies will naturally start to gradually release now and then. This is good, but it is important to not be worried if you feel some old emotions surface that you haven't felt in a long time. It is only coming up BRIEFLY TO BE RELEASED--NOT TO STAY. ALL YOU NEED TO DO IS TO BREATHE INTO IT AND LET IT GO. Know that it is past and over. You may wish to give yourself some way to express it such as journal writing, drawing a picture with colored markers, or talking to a trusted friend. If feelings are intense, it could be helpful to see a counselor or energy healer. Just remember that you are letting go of old repressed feelings and limitations, and you are freeing yourself to move ahead. It is a wondrously liberating process.

Spiral Energy Clearing Meditative Exercise

The following can be very helpful to clear out the old blocked energies that are described above. First meditate with the twelve minute Audio "Meditation to Enhance Your Experience of the Divine Qualities" (with Focus on Illumination) or the transcribed version of it. Then visualize a spiral of light energy coming from above your head and spiraling through your body. Visualize that spiral moving out any old shadowy stuck energies that are ready to move and clear. Then "see" that spiral going on out beneath your feet and taking with it whatever is ready and needs to be released. Just let it all go. You may wish to repeat that twice, if you wish. (Visualize the spiral going clockwise as if viewed from above your head.) Pray that the disqualified energy be dissolved into the light. Then spend a few minutes breathing in light and energy. As you breathe in your nose, imagine you are breathing light into your whole being. You may wish to then do the following "Energy Field Activator Exercise" to help realign your aura and help you feel balanced and calm.

Energy Field Activator Exercise

This is helpful before meditation to calm the body, emotions, and mind. It can also be helpful after the "Spiral Energy Clearing Exercise" (or anytime) for the same reasons of calming, centering, and balancing oneself. There is an energy pathway that rotates around the body from head to toe in all directions and forms a shape like an apple--with the individual in the center like the core of the apple. See the "Energy Field Activator" chart.

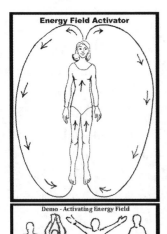

While you listen to relaxing nonverbal music, hold your hands together in prayer position at your waist for sixty seconds. During that minute focus on gently breathing in and out your nose. Then as you breathe in, raise your hands upward together. As you breathe out, bring your hands out and around in a big circle as shown in the chart. Smoothly bring your hands back into prayer position at your waist. Then as you breathe in, once again raise your hands upwards together. As you breathe out bring your hands around again in a big circle. Repeat that for six times or as many times as feels good. I think that you will really enjoy the feeling. It is stabilizing and soothing. This process helps activate the energy flows as shown in the chart.

The illumination of our aura is a gradual process. It is very beautiful to see the levels of the aura gradually clear, activate, and illumine. The light can eventually wash out any cloudy or darker energy or static that may have collected from past trauma or stress or illness. There often is a sense of relief and greater clarity and peace as heavier energies move out and are displaced by the light energy/prana. We can just let the old heavy energies go. As we meditate regularly and focus on breathing in light with each breath, the layers of the aura can begin to be clear of those stressful and limiting thought forms--and fill with light, peace, joy, and love.

Accessing Energy Through the Star Center

In addition to Divine Light entering through the major chakras and through the aura in general, a significant entrance can be through the "star center" above the head. To facilitate this, first meditate on each of the seven major centers up the spine. (As in the audio "Meditation to Enhance Spiritual Awakening and Illumination.") The star center is usually located six to twelve inches above your head, directly above the crown chakra. Sense what feels right for you. There are more star centers that can be worked with, but one is plenty for now.

As you focus in the star center, pray to God that Divine Illumination and Divine Blessings flow into your aura. Visualize Divine Light flowing in through the star center luxuriously. Keep praying to God for Divine Light to bless you. It is real, not figurative. With practice, Divine Light can gradually totally fill your aura. Though total Spiritual Illumination may be a long-term journey, there are many stages of illumination along the way. It is an unbelievably wonderful journey that need not be hurried.

An integral part of the path to illumination entails embodying as well as we can the Divine Qualities of God. The Divine Qualities of God include the ones that we are exploring in this book such as Divine Wisdom, Love, Truth, Devotion, Forgiveness, Freedom, Clarity, Harmony, Balance, Peace, Purpose, Joy, and more. How to enhance the Divine qualities in our life is the primary purpose of this book. What an adventure!

During the journey to Divine Illumination and Enlightenment there are numerous energy pathways in a person's aura that need to be activated and filled with light energy/prana. We have already discussed the chakras and the levels of the aura. There are other energy pathways in a person's aura which ideally eventually become filled with light and free flowing energy. In chapter eleven, we will explore the energy pathways of Zone Therapy and the energy dynamics of hand and foot reflexology. In future writings on the website, I will delve into numerous other energy pathways in the human aura such as the meridians of acupuncture and acupressure, the microcosmic orbit, the powerful hara energy, and more.

Our Aura as an Energy Generator

The human energy field is in a sense like an energy generator which can gradually be increasingly activated so that the individual can be a light for greater and greater good in the world. This is not symbolic language. This is referring to the capacity to emanate powerful energies that can have the effect of helping to awaken the consciousness and aura of other people. That awakening happens through resonance. As one person holds the energy of a certain level of consciousness, it makes it easier for other people interacting closely with him or her to hold that level of consciousness. This upliftment through resonance can be experienced and can be particularly helpful during a guided meditation or during energy healing. All this opening of energy pathways, aura energy activation, and illumination can be greatly facilitated by working with natural healing techniques and/or working with energy healers and holistic therapists.

The more that we grow in the Light, the more well-grounded we need to stay. There needs to be at least some degree of balance between our solid stable grounding to Mother Earth and our heavenly orientation. Feeling spacey isn't helpful for effective living.

When a person's energy field is sufficiently developed, the kundalini energy which is coiled at the base of the spine begins to rise. Ideally the kundalini energy gently rises up the spine on its own. It is important that this occur naturally at its own pace. There are numerous stages of the kundalini rising. May we enjoy each stage patiently without being in any hurry. The chakras and aura need to be sufficiently developed and ready to ensure a comfortable safe assent of the kundalini energy.

Our chakra system could be compared to a prism separating sunlight into the different colors of the visible spectrum. When the kundalini fully rises, it brings a reintegration of all the different chakra energies/colors back into brilliant pure white light in a powerful way at a higher turn of the spiral. All these activations take place slowly over time. Illumination is a gradual magnificent journey, not a single event. A person's consciousness needs to adjust to each stage.

The earth needs as many enlightened people as possible to help heal the planet. One enlightened person can help uplift a whole town. As one grows Spiritually, one's aura and the higher levels of one's consciousness can expand greatly over vast distances. Hence a whole town can be within the aura of one enlightened person - - and uplifted thereby. The more the crown chakra opens, the more a person feels oneness with all people, all creation, and the Divine. The more the heart chakra opens, the more a person feels Divine love for all people, all creation, and one's soul. A person can feel oneness with one's soul and the Divine by focusing in the heart chakra or in the higher levels of one's consciousness.

Illumined ones feel very close to the Divine and have experiences and visions of the Spiritual levels of reality. They may "hear" the Divine communicate encouragement or information to them. This is generally an inner awareness, not a physical voice. People on all stages of the journey of illumination may experience clairvoyance (ability to "see" intuitively on the inner Spiritual levels), clairaudience (ability to "hear" intuitively on the inner levels), and clairsentience (the ability to sense very subtle energies intuitively). People on the Spiritual path may have a profound gift of healing. They may have a gift of speech that can help lift and reassure those around them who walk the path of Life with all its joys and challenges. Different people may have several of these Spiritual gifts depending on the needs of their line of service to their fellow humanity.

The goal is total union with the Divine and with one's Higher Consciousness. What more noble goal can there be? This is the path of saints and prophets. This is also the path each one of us can follow eventually. Some will take longer than others. There are those who are already bridging the world as we know it today and wondrous new possibilities. Today we are each being called to be all that we can be in order to help uplift ourselves, each other, and all the people of this beautiful planet. An important part of illumination is the burning desire to help one's fellow humanity and the planet.

Let us lift our hearts and aspirations and take the high road. Then all will be well. Heaven is blessing and supporting us on our journey to step into our true magnificent destiny as blessed people and faithful stewards of our beloved planet. May we believe in ourselves! We are created in the image of God and the Spark of the Divine is within us!

Some Experiences With Illumination Along My Path

As a young child fidgeting in the sanctuary pew every Sunday during the hour church service, I gazed at the stained glass windows that told Biblical stories. My favorite stained glass window showed the story of Jacob's ladder. Jacob was sleeping outside on the grass with a stone for a pillow. Many angels stood along a glowing golden ladder all the way up to Heaven. The angels were beckoning him to climb. That was emblazoned on my young mind. I grew to love it.

When I went away to college, I had a burning desire to come to an understanding for myself as to the nature of the Divine Realms. I knew that there was something extremely important here, and I needed to clarify it for myself personally. I was searching-searching-searching to grasp more fully the nature of existence. Something deep within me had already experienced glimpses, but I had to "KNOW" more. I searched in the Bible, and in the great literature of the world. I searched at the ancient pyramids of Yucatan Mexico, in the magnificent cathedrals of Europe, and in studies of the symbolism of the ancient cultures from around the world. I searched in symphonic music, in Greek and Shakespearean theater, in opera and ballet, and in the visual arts. There were glimpses of profound truth and unfathomable mysteries in all of these and more. But I felt that there was something very important that I hadn't grasped yet--and I felt an intense desire to experience it. I poured my passion into painting large inspirational mandala canvases.

I had been doing a form of deep relaxation for years when I decided to take it to the next step as focused meditation. One day after an hour of inspiring conversation with a friend who taught meditation, a curtain opened in my consciousness and Light shone through me with a brilliance that changed my life forever. There happened to be a beautiful cathedral nearby that was open. I went into the peaceful huge sanctuary--it was lit only by sunlight shining through the glowing colors of the stained glass windows. Tears of joy poured down my cheeks for over an hour. I felt filled to overflowing with brilliant Light and energy--and total incomprehensible boundless peace. That afternoon transformed my life. FINALLY I HAD FOUND WHAT I WAS SEARCHING FOR! I knew that it was the opening of a greater part of my consciousness that had been latent and waiting for me to remember who I was. Since then I've been steadily aware on more and more levels of my consciousness and levels of reality. Life has opened for me in ways I wouldn't have known were possible.

Possible Support For Your Path of Illumination

There are many Spiritual groups, philosophies, schools, churches, and approaches that can possibly support a person's Spiritual path of illumination. It is of great importance to choose with care, and to be very aware of how you feel with a particular group. It can be desirable to have positive recommendations from people you know and greatly respect.

I have meditated and been active with a wide variety of meditation and Spiritual growth groups and disciplines in the many years since my awakening in this life in 1970. It has always been the essence of the Spiritual energy within a group and the heart-centered caring among group members that interested me more than complicated doctrine or rules. There are many good approaches to try, and they can be beneficial in different ways. I encourage you to find one that feels right to you, if you don't already have that. It can be good to stay with one path your whole life if that feels helpful, or it can be fine to experience numerous approaches over time. A traditional church may be just right for you. Everybody is different. I'll share with you some groups and approaches that have been helpful for me along the way.

Reiki Energy Healing. Reiki (pronounced Ray-key) truly is profoundly Spiritual, even though it isn't a religion. It can enhance whatever one's Spiritual path or religion may be. It has three levels of training and energy/consciousness expansion activations, plus a fourth level where one learns to teach Reiki. These trainings can be extremely beneficial even if one only wishes to use it for benefiting oneself and one's friends and family. Reiki is received fully clothed with the practitioner's hands lightly touching or slightly away from one's body. The practitioner prays to be a channel of Divine universal healing energy to flow to the receiver. Reiki can gradually truly illumine one's energy field and consciousness. There are Reiki Share groups in many parts of the country that get together free of charge on a regular basis to share giving and receiving energy healing. You might wish to take Reiki I training and share in such a group. It is truly an excellent support for one's health, peace of mind, and Spiritual upliftment. I am a Reiki Master (teacher) and there are thousands of others around the United States and world.

The Tibetan Five Rites of Rejuvenation. These are a group of movements/exercises created long ago in Tibet to activate the energy centers (chakras) and the energy field. I have been doing them for fifteen minutes almost every morning for about twenty years. They help me start my day out feeling vibrant and recharged. There are books and websites that show how to do them. It is crucial to get your health practitioner's O.K. before embarking on this, or on any discipline of physical movement.

The Theosophical Society. They have centers around the United States (and other countries) that offer excellent classes and group support for meditation, natural healing, and Spiritual growth. I enjoyed being a resident staff at one of their centers for a period of time.

Churches, Synagogues, and Temples. There is magnificent Spiritual work done within churches, synagogues, and temples in the United States and around the world. Each person is an individual and may feel Spiritually uplifted and inspired in their own way--and may be drawn to different Spiritual groups and teachings. Churches that have been helpful to me during different parts of my life have been Unity, Unitarian, Presbyterian and others. I feel it is of tremendous importance that churches, synagogues and temples respect each other as paths to the Divine Source.

Traditional Native American Spirituality & Healing. I pursued this path enthusiastically for three or four years (thirty years ago) in the mountains of northern Vermont and elsewhere. There was much traditional Native American dancing and chanting as well as ecstatic spontaneous dancing to flutes and drums. There was intense training in sensitivity to a wide variety of subtle energies, and profound meditations. There were sweat lodges and vision quests out on the land.

Independent Healing Exchanges. Many years ago I shared healing once a week for two hours with a friend who was also a therapist and energy healer. We each received for an hour. This was incredibly helpful during that period, and I would recommend it for anyone. We pursued that faithfully for three or four years. Energy healing can be a very important part of opening to illumination.

Mysticism. Mysticism can be a beautiful path. One can pursue this on one's own or with a group. I was active for a number of years with a Christian church led by a family of ministers of Afro-American descent. They are very mystical in their approach. There was lovely heart-centered energy and caring in that church and wonderful Spiritual experiences. Jewish mysticism can be equally powerful. There is a mystical heart to most major religions.

Oneness Blessing. Oneness Blessing was founded by Sri Amma Bhavagan. It is excellent for meditation and energy healing training. It involves meditation techniques, chanting, energy healing, and awakening experiences.

Treading the Spiritual Path to Illumination Independently. For decades I read so voraciously about many phases of Spirituality that it felt like indispensable food that I couldn't eat fast enough. Then eventually I knew that it was time to begin writing, and that has been a significant part of my path for more than thirty years. I have been steadily teaching meditation and Spiritual growth and providing natural healing and therapy during those same years. Of course, singing and art have been important to me in this journey. Meditating on my own has been my most significant source for Spiritual growth and insight. My connection to the Divine inspires and guides me onward. It is a mystical journey beyond compare.

Opening Lotus
Original art by Joyce J.C. Gerrish

WORKBOOK: Enrichment Experiences For Enhancing Illumination In Your Life

Enjoy the adventure of exploring these enrichment experiences on your own, or gather a few friends to share the journey with you. Be inspired by the audio meditation and soul song for this chapter. Reflect on some of the stimulating ideas and questions.

Questions For Reflection And Discussion

Reflection, discussion, journal writing, expressing your feelings in drawings or other creative ways can all be very valuable to help you delve into these questions in truly meaningful and relevant ways. Before focusing on the questions, you may wish to meditate with the twelve minute audio or transcribed meditation for illumination--and/or listen to the soul song *"Oh, Holy Light."*

1. How do you feel about meditation? Meditation is intended to be a peaceful uplifting experience. Do you enjoy it? Can you feel a sense of greater peace and clarity afterward? Can you sense the lightness when you meditate? What helps you have an uplifting meditation?

2. Have you had one or more Spiritual experiences that felt transformative to you--when you felt you were filled with Divine Light or a sense of profound Spiritual upliftment? Describe it and how it affected your life thereafter.

3. Do you ever get a "gut feeling" when you enter a room where people are or where they have been recently gathered? This gut feeling is independent of anything you might see. That is a form of intuition. How would you describe the difference in the feeling of the "vibes" between a library, a cathedral or church, a gym, a bar, a sleeping baby's nursery room, or your home? Try being attentive when you go places as to how it feels if you close your eyes a moment or two. This is one way to help develop your intuitive sense of energies.

Action Suggestion For Enhancing Illumination In Your Life

1. Meditation is truly the essence of illuminating your energy field/aura. During effective meditation you are accessing Divine Light and life energy/prana. After meditating can you sense the energy

helping you feel more uplifted and lighter? This sense will be enhanced over time as you sincerely pursue it. Enjoy it. Blessings to you. (See Meditation Audio section.)

2. A meditation class series or a meditation group can be helpful. There are many approaches to meditation. If you are interested in such a group, look for one that feels comfortable and uplifting to you. Some groups represent a specific religion. Others are independent of any specific religion. Some have a long period of silent meditation. Some chant quite a bit, and may include some moving meditation such as yoga or tai chi. Some include a period for discussion of the philosophy of meditation and for sharing of insights.

3. Are you ready and interested in choosing a specific time each day for the uplifting support of a regular meditation practice? Perhaps you already have that. A regular time each day is valuable to help you establish a meditation habit that will enhance your life. Even twelve minutes a day can be very valuable. The beginning of each day is ideal, before you start your busy responsibilities. When you get home in the evening can be good, also. Just before bedtime it may become difficult to stay awake and focused. My audio "Meditation to Enhance Your Experience of the Divine Qualities" is about twelve-minutes long. Each day you could choose the Divine Quality that you wish to focus on enhancing in your life at that time. Perhaps you have another meditation with which you are familiar and that you enjoy--that is good, too. That daily period could also certainly be some other form of Spiritual practice, if preferred.

4. Have you visited a holistic energy therapist for a session? Such a session is usually exceedingly peaceful, and can be very valuable to support your health. Energy healing is done with the receiver fully clothed. I encourage you to consider finding a friend to refer you to an excellent energy healer, or consult staff at a natural foods store. Reiki Energy Healing, Healing Touch, Polarity Energy Therapy, and Quantum Touch are very good techniques. Reflexology is also helpful for enhancing energy flow and clearing energy blocks, as are Acupressure and Acupuncture.

Meditation Audios

1. Audio "Meditation to Enhance Spiritual Awakening and Illumination." This special 34-minute audio is very helpful for enhancing aura and chakra activation and illumination, and Spiritual awakening. I encourage you to take time to meditate with this audio at least once a week to help enhance your chakras and aura---and expand your Spiritual focus. Find this audio at SecretsOfWisdom.net.

2. Audio "Meditation for Enhancing Your Experience of the Divine Qualities," with Focus on Illumination. With this 12-minute audio you will be guided to sense yourself immersed in this wonderful uplifting feeling of Divine Illumination. The first six minutes help you relax your body, emotions, and mind. The second six minutes help enhance your experience of Divine Illumination.

Choose one or two of the following affirmations that you feel would be particularly helpful for you to affirm while meditating. Write down the affirmation(s) you choose. Later, place it where you will see it and be reminded to affirm it for a minute or two several times a day.

◆ I breathe in Divine Light with each breath.
◆ I am filled with Divine Light and I shine it out to those around me.
◆ I am blessed with God's Divine Light and Peace.

Helpful color to visualize when meditating on Illumination: White

I encourage you to enjoy these meditations when you wish to support this quality of Illumination in your life. Connect to the SecretsOfWisdom.net to listen to these meditations.

(Also, at end of chapter see transcribed form of second meditation described above.)

Uplifting Audio Soul Song: *"Oh, Holy Light"*
~ by Joyce

Consider it a prayer in song for enhancing your sense of peaceful illumination of your being. The words are:

Oh Holy Light, illumine me.

Shine in my Heart, and set me free.

E – e – e, E – e – e. Ah – a – a, Ah – a – a. Oh – h – h, Oh – h – h.

As you chant or listen to it, feel yourself relax and begin to flow with it. Close your eyes and really sense the song helping to bring you into an inspired sense of upliftment. Connect to SecretsofWisdom.net to listen to *"Oh, Holy Light."*

Transcribed Version of Meditation To Enhance Your Experience of Divine Illumination

If possible, listen to some relaxing nonverbal music. Say a short prayer calling on the Divine to bless your meditation and enhance Divine Illumination in your life.

Visualize yourself in a ball of light to help strengthen your energy field.

Become aware of and follow your breath as it gently flows in and out at its own pace.

Imagine yourself as a large tree sending powerful roots deep into the earth to help you feel grounded and prevent possibly feeling spacey.

As you breathe in your nose, imagine you are breathing up the strength of the earth into your body.

For a couple minutes listen to the relaxing music as you follow your breath.

Next visualize pure white light. Periodically as you breathe in your nose, imagine that you are breathing glowing white light into your whole being.

Silently pray to the Divine that your life be uplifted and blessed with Divine Illumination.

Next breathe in your nose and out your mouth for about a minute VERY GENTLY.

Now, very gently breathe in your mouth and out your nose for about a minute.

Then extra gently breathe in and out your mouth for a minute or so.

Now return to breathing in and out your nose. As you breathe in your nose, imagine you are breathing in pure white light into your whole being.

As you breathe out your nose, periodically say one or two of the following affirmations (or something similar).

◆ I breathe in Divine Light with each breath.

◆ I am filled with Divine Light and I shine it out to those around me.

◆ I open to receive God's Divine Light and Peace.

Pray to the Divine that you truly be blessed with Divine Illumination.

When you are ready to conclude your meditation, thank the Divine and then send down roots to Mother Earth for stability and grounding.

Enjoy this meditation whenever you wish. Write down the affirmation(s) and put it somewhere you will see it several times a day and be reminded to affirm it for a minute or two.

Peace.

NOTE: Printable versions of the charts and tables in this chapter are available at SecretsofWisdom.net.

Woman Feels Healing Renewal in Garden
Original art b Joyce J.C. Gerrish

Chapter Eleven

WALKING THE PATH OF WELLNESS
Enhancing Divine Healing In Your Life

Enjoy listening to, or singing along with, this soul song: "*Dear Divine, Heal Me.*" Connect to <u>SecretsofWisdom.</u> <u>net</u> to hear it and also gaze at the full color design "Woman Feels Healing Renewal in Garden."

These Natural Healing Techniques and Information Are of Priceless Benefit For You and Your Family

In the first part of this chapter I'm sharing how to actually do Zone Therapy, and the therapy of Hand and Foot Reflexology. Both of these can be exceedingly helpful for you and for your friends and family. They are surprisingly easy to get started doing in a way that can actually help support your health and well-being. In the second part of the chapter, I will be focusing on how you can additionally enhance your health in major ways with natural foods and other very valuable approaches. This information is priceless. I can't tell you how important these techniques and this information have been in my life and in the lives of my students and clients and countless others.

The essence of life is to learn and grow and evolve. It is exciting to develop new potentials within ourselves. We are never bored with life in this way. Life is always ideally in transition. It is in a constant renewal cycle. When life ceases to evolve, it becomes stagnant. So it is normal and good to be in a period of transition. Healing is basically a process of letting go of the old outgrown parts of ourselves and opening to new growth. Looking at life from this perspective, then healing is a natural part of the process of developing and expanding ourselves.

If we just keep doing the same things over and over in the same way, we begin to be sort of half asleep. There aren't interesting challenges to solve. Things become overly habitual. The ritual of life can become more important than the inner meaning. Judging others can set in. When we are constantly in a process of growth and renewal, then we are too busy moving into our next step to be judging others. There is no one right way to do things, as long as we are respectful and harmless to others. There are as many approaches to life as there are people. The crucial thing is that we honor each other and treat everyone as we would wish to be treated.

Health Is Being In Harmony With The Flow of Life and Nature

Health is the state of vibrant openness to the flow of life. Life is always surprising us. It keeps us guessing. The important thing is to not fight life, but to flow with it and explore the opportunities it presents. Of course, we can't explore every opportunity life presents. We can choose the ones with which we resonate--those which inspire us. This is a state of consciousness where life energy flows through us freely. When we are open to the life flow, our body is relaxed and enthusiastic. We naturally embrace the cycles of the day. We wake up to greet the morning eagerly, walk in the sunlight, apply ourselves to our work and projects, love those around us, and sleep soundly at night. We are in harmony with the flow of life and nature.

When this natural cycle is disrupted--that is when healing may be particularly needed. When we feel out of rhythm with life, we may start feeling stressed or depressed. Our muscles may start to contract and breathing may become shallow or somewhat irregular. Life may cease to feel like an adventure and may seem more like a burden. Clouds of static energy may start forming in our energy field. When the aura gets progressively more congested and blocked, the fresh renewing life energy can't flow through as freely. Our body may start to gradually slow down and even age prematurely. We may begin to feel sluggish and wonder why.

Doing healing sessions with a holistic therapist can be exceedingly beneficial. Taking classes in natural healing can also be very helpful for learning how to keep your own energies clear and flowing well. There are numerous excellent forms of natural healing you can receive and/or learn. Reflexology and acupressure are two popular time honored methods. Zone Therapy is another related technique. It is less well known yet quite effective and easy to do. These all involve fingertip pressure to help stimulate the aura energy flow. In all these forms of natural healing, the receiver normally stays fully clothed. It is important to remember that for any medical issues, consult and stay in touch with your health care provider.

How To Do Zone Therapy to Help Yourself or Someone Else

Quick Start Summary

There are streams of energy that flow/circulate around and around your body from head to toes, and out your arms to your fingers. To beneficially enhance these energy flows--start by gently massaging one of your hands and then the other. Next, focus on gently massaging each of your fingers one at a time. After you massage each finger, then gently hold it and give a VERY SLIGHT outward pull for about thirty seconds. It would be helpful to play some relaxing music while you do all that. Also, as you are massaging and stimulating each of your fingers one at a time, be aware of your breath flowing in and out your nose at a relaxed pace. If you have ever injured or broken a bone in a finger, it would be good to skip that finger. Once you have completed what is described above, congratulate yourself! You have just given yourself a beginning zone therapy experience. Consider giving your feet and toes a similar treat (if it is comfortable to reach them for at least ten or fifteen minutes). Everyone knows how good a foot massage can feel. You may wish to share this with a friend, and do it for each other.

Explanation of Zone Therapy

Look ahead and see the zone therapy chart with all the stripes going from head to toe and out to the fingers. Energy is constantly flowing like a conveyor belt or river around and around the body in the zones. There are five zones on each side of the body which correspond to the five fingers and five toes. The thumbs and big toes are Zone 1. The index finger and "index" toe are Zone 2. The middle finger and middle toe are Zone 3. The ring finger and "ring" toe are Zone 4. The little finger and little toe are Zone 5. Each zone carries a different quality of energy--all good, just different. Each zone is like an ever flowing river circulating around a person's body in the manner shown in the chart. If these flows slow down or get disarrayed because of fatigue, illness, injury, depression, poor nutrition, or other reasons--the

Zone	Chakra	Therapeutic Color	Life Expression	Element
1	Throat	Blue	Spirituality	Ether
2	Heart	Green	Intuition	Air
3	Solar Plexus	Yellow	Mind	Fire
4	Sacral	Orange	Emotions	Water
5	Root	Red	Physical Body	Earth

Zone Correspondences

zone therapy technique described above can help reactivate and normalize them. If you are doing zone therapy for someone else, you may wish to imagine you are sending Light (energy) or love into each toe or finger as you manipulate it. Do this in a very relaxed gentle way. Another variation while you are doing zone therapy is to visualize the corresponding color for the toe or finger you are working on (see Zone Therapy Chart). Imagine you are sending the corresponding color into each zone. With practice, you will actually be channeling Light and love and colors along with your zone therapy. Visualization and intention can be quite effective. If you do one hand or foot it is important to do the other hand or foot in order to stay balanced.

It is helpful to start and end any healing energy therapy session for yourself or someone else by visualizing yourself in a ball of light and sending down roots for grounding. Say a brief prayer asking for the highest good, and acknowledging that the Divine is the true healer, not yourself. After doing a healing session for someone else, visualize yourself in your ball of light and also visualize the other person in his or her own ball of light separate from you. Then rinse your hands under running water to clear any energy you may have picked up from the other person. If water is not available, then shake your hands a few times as though you are flicking off water. Everything described in this paragraph prevents taking on stressful energy from the receiver. It is desirable to drink a glass of water after receiving or giving energy healing therapy--to help wash out of the body any toxins released.

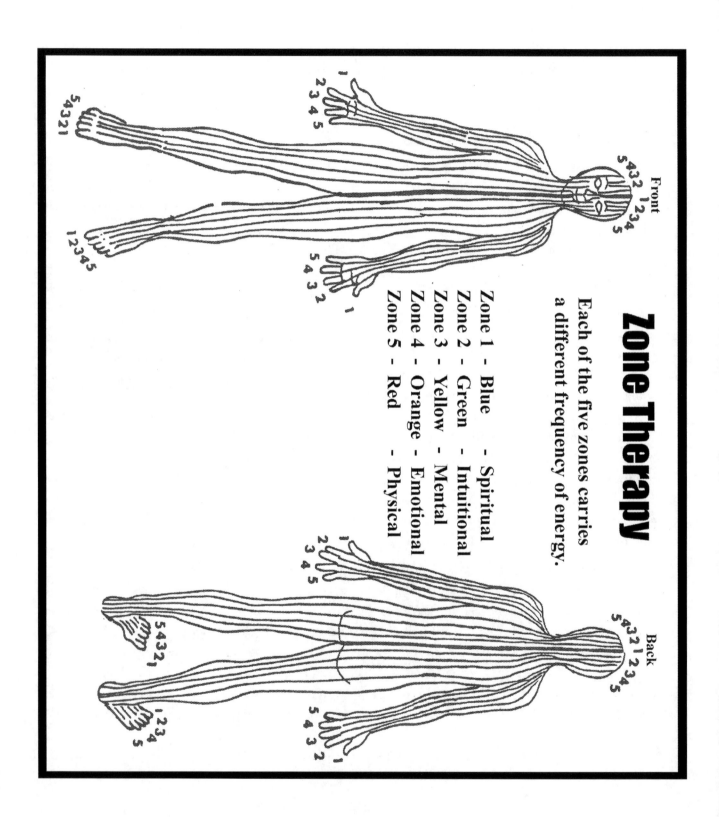

Zone Therapy

Each of the five zones carries
a different frequency of energy.

Zone 1	-	Blue	-	Spiritual
Zone 2	-	Green	-	Intuitional
Zone 3	-	Yellow	-	Mental
Zone 4	-	Orange	-	Emotional
Zone 5	-	Red	-	Physical

Front

Back

How To Do Basic Reflexology Therapy For Yourself Or Someone Else

Hand Reflexology

Reflexology works on the same principles as zone therapy, but is more specific. By massaging or applying firm pressure on particular pressure points in the appropriate area of the palms of the hands (or the soles of the feet) you can beneficially affect a specific organ or part of the body.

Take a moment to look at the Hand Reflexology Chart ahead. You will notice that on the palms of the hands there is a point for almost every organ and aspect of the body. By massaging these various points somewhat firmly (<u>not</u> hard pressure), you can stimulate an increased flow of vital life energy to the corresponding areas of the body. This aids the relaxing or healing of these areas. Any point you work on one hand should be repeated on the other hand to keep the energy flows on the two sides of the body balanced. The right hand corresponds to everything on the right side of the body, and the left hand corresponds to everything on the left side of the body.

To get an idea of where the pressure points are located, imagine superimposing a chart of the human head and torso over a chart of the palms and fingers of the hands. Pressure points for the head are on the thumbs and fingers. Moving down the palm toward the wrists, you will find the same progression of pressure point locations as the actual organ locations occur in the body. Reflex points in the middle of the palm (half way between the fingers and wrist) correspond to the waist area of a person. Points for the bottom of the torso are located in the lower half of the palms (near the wrists). Knowing these general location guidelines, you can use your intuition to locate pressure points. Notice how the reflex points for the spine go from the outside edge of the upper thumb (neck) all the way down the side of the hand almost to the wrist (base of the spine).

If you massage both palms and all ten fingers completely, you will have benefited the entire body. Where there is tenderness (unless it is caused by direct injury to the hand), that spot may benefit from extra massaging to loosen stagnant or blocked energy in the area of the body corresponding to that reflex point on the hand. Press the thumb with moderate (NOT HARD) pressure on a point which needs extra attention. A guide for the length of time to stimulate a particular pressure point is:

◆ Endocrine glands (pituitary, pineal, thyroid, thymus, sexual glands, adrenals, pancreas): A few seconds.

◆ Organs: One minute.

◆ Spine and other bones: Up to a five minutes.

As indicated, the amount of time to stimulate an endocrine gland is shorter than for the other points. This is because they secrete minute amounts of powerful substances directly into the blood circulation to help maintain proper functioning of the body. They perform major roles in regulating total body functioning. (Note: Part of the pancreas functions as an endocrine gland and is secreting insulin. The remainder of the pancreas functions as an organ. I suggest limiting stimulation of the pancreas reflex point to only a few seconds.)

Different ways to stimulate a reflex point:

1. Place your thumb on the reflex point and make very small circles without lifting your thumb. You are basically gently moving the skin and underlying tissues slightly, not sliding your thumb across the skin.
2. Place your thumb on the reflex point and move your thumb back and forth slightly without lifting your thumb. Once again, you are gently moving the skin and underlying tissues slightly, not sliding your thumb across the skin.
3. Place your thumb on the reflex point and apply moderate (definitely not hard) pressure without moving your thumb. Never hurt yourself or someone else.
4. Inch worm technique. Place your thumb on the reflex point and let your thumb sort of "inch" its way along like a tiny inch worm (one-eighth inch at a time).

Experiment and sense what feels right for you. Professional reflexologists apply quite firm pressure, but I feel that it is very important to start out gently. In passing I'll mention that I used the word massage a few times in the description because it is a word with which everyone is familiar. Reflexology is not a form of massage, though it is sometimes included in therapeutic massage, and it does involve touching.

It is also important to mention that reflexology charts from different sources will often be a little different. Don't be surprised! Every human body is at least somewhat different. The way to know if you have the correct reflex point for a particular part of the body (such as the stomach) is to look at the chart, and then gently work around the general area of the palm indicated until you possibly find a tender spot. There is a good chance that if you find a tender spot, it may be the reflex point to support the health issue in question (unless that spot on the hand was injured in some other way). Work that tender reflex point in one of the ways described above. If you don't find a tender spot in the area of the hand indicated for the part of the body you are seeking to help, then work all around the whole palms and fingers. You may find another spot that is tender, and that may be a reflex point that will be helpful for the situation in question, or for the body as a whole. Go easy, and let it be a relaxing gentle experience. To close your session, please read again the last paragraph of the zone therapy section. Those directions also apply to closing a reflexology session.

Foot Reflexology

Foot reflexology works in exactly the same manner as hand reflexology. Familiarize yourself with the Foot Reflexology Chart. The choice between hand reflexology and foot reflexology is up to you. For some people, the main advantage of the foot is that it is larger than the hand--and the reflex points are a little further apart and perhaps easier to differentiate. Other people find it somewhat uncomfortable to try to work on their own feet. Some people like to do both the hands and feet. It can be beneficial to simultaneously hold the pressure points for the same organ (or body part) on both the right foot and right hand--- then repeat with the left hand and left foot. For people who may find it difficult to reach their own feet, you may wish to purchase a "wooden foot roller reflexology massager." You can google on-line and purchase one very inexpensively. That can be very helpful.

Treat yourself to relaxing and healing hand and/or foot reflexology often. It is very good for supporting health in a preventative way, even if one is already feeling excellent. It stimulates natural energy flow throughout the body. One to three times a week is probably plenty for a thirty to sixty minute session. Any type of therapeutic body work may tiger a release of toxins from the body. This is good, and is a natural part of the healing process. Drink extra water to help wash out toxins possibly released during a session. Also, you may wish to consider taking a brief rest afterward if you feel tired. You are doing yourself a lot of good.

It is important to mention that reflexology and zone therapy can be combined effectively to reinforce each other. These introductions can get you started with the wonderful benefits of reflexology and zone therapy.

Super Quick Pick-Me-Up Technique

This is a reflexology technique that involves stimulating for three to five seconds the points for the major endocrine glands. Do this for each hand or for each foot. The whole technique only requires two or three minutes. See the chart "Endocrine Glands and Their Reflexology Points." This chart focuses on the feet. For the points to stimulate on the hands for the major endocrine glands--look at the "Hand Reflexology Chart."

Notice that for the thyroid gland you work all the way around the fleshy area below the thumb or below the big toe. Sort of gently work your fingertips (or finger nails) slightly into the fold of the skin there. The adrenal points are exactly in the middle of the foot or hand. For the thymus point, move directly up from the adrenal point until your thumb reaches the base of the fleshy pads directly beneath the fingers or toes. The points for the sexual glands are exactly in the middle of the area between your ankles and the back of your heals (for the points for the hands see the charts). For all the reflexology points in general, don't get overly worried about whether you have exactly the right point location. Just be gentle at first. As previously mentioned, the endocrine glands have important regulating effects for the whole body functioning. They release powerful hormone secretions directly into the blood which immediately get circulated around the body to provide support.

You may wish to enjoy this energy pickup technique up to three times a week.

Hand Reflexology

ENDOCRINE GLANDS- Stimulate only a few seconds per session;
ORGANS and all else -- Stimulate one minute per session;
SPINE Stimulate up to 5 minutes

Legend - Right Hand

1 thru 4 = Sinuses
5 = Ears
6 = Nerves and Ear
7 & 8 = Nerves
9 & 10 = Ears
11 & 12 = Eyes
13 = Pituitary
14 = Pineal
15 = Stomach
16 = Colon
17 = Intestines
18 = Throat
19 = Thyroid
20 = Bladder
21 = Shoulder
22 = Liver
23 = Gall Bladder
24 = Pancreas
25 = Appendix
26 = Hip
27 = Testes / Ovaries
28 = Prostate,
    Uterus, Penis
29 = Hemorrhoids
30 = Spine
31 = Lungs
32 = Thymus
33 = Adrenal
34 = Kidney
35 = Head
36 = Neck

Legend - Left Hand

1 thru 4 = Sinuses
5 = Ears
6 = Nerves and Ear
7 & 8 = Nerves
9 & 10 = Ears
11 & 12 = Eyes
13 = Pituitary
14 = Pineal
15 = Stomach
16 = Colon
17 = Intestines
18 = Throat
19 = Thyroid
20 = Bladder
21 = Shoulder
22 = Heart
23 = Spleen
24 = Pancreas
25 = None
26 = Hip
27 = Testes / Ovaries
28 = Prostate,
    Uterus, Penis
29 = Hemorrhoids
30 = Spine
31 = Lungs
32 = Thymus
33 = Adrenal
34 = Kidney
35 = Head
36 = Neck

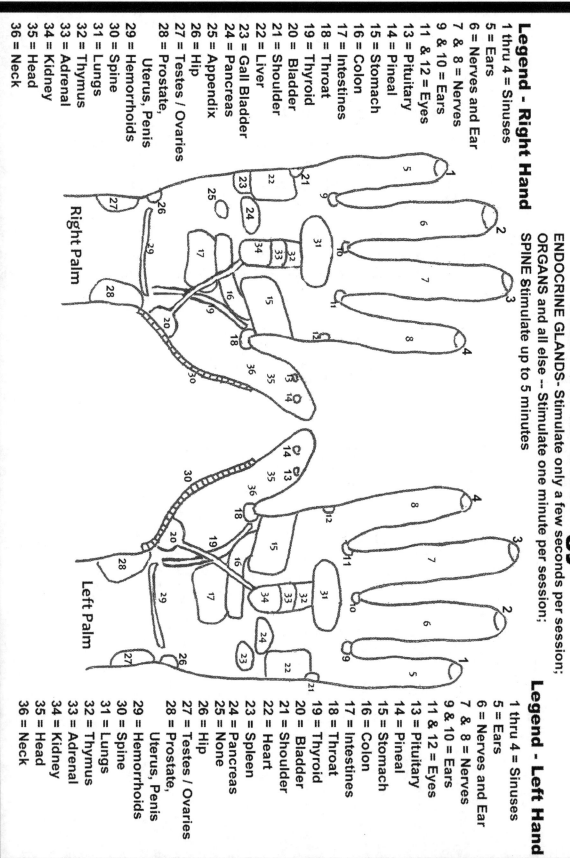

Right Palm

Left Palm

Foot Reflexology

Right Foot

1 - 5 Sinuses
6 - Pineal*
7 - Pituitary*
8 - Eyes
9 - Ears
10 - Neck
11 - Throat
12 - Lung
13 - Thyroid*
14 - Solar Plexus
15 - Thymus*
16 - Pancreas*
17 - Stomach
18 - Adrenals*
19 - Kidney
20 - Liver
21 - Gall Bladder
22 - (none)
23 - Urethra Tube
24 - Transverse Colon
25 - Colon
26 - Small Intestine
27 - Sciatic Nerve
28 - Spinal Vertebrae
29 - Bladder
30 - Appendix

Left Foot

1 - 5 Sinuses
6 - Pineal*
7 - Pituitary*
8 - Eyes
9 - Ears
10 - Neck
11 - Throat
12 - Lung
13 - Thyroid*
14 - Solar Plexus
15 - Thymus*
16 - Pancreas*
17 - Stomach
18 - Adrenals*
19 - Kidney
20 - Heart
21 - (none)
22 - Spleen
23 - Urethra Tube
24 - Transverse Colon
25 - Colon
26 - Small Intestine
27 - Sciatic Nerve
28 - Spinal Vertebrae
29 - Bladder
30 - (none)

- ENDOCRINE GLANDS* - Stimulate only a few seconds per session
- ORGANS and all else -- Stimulate one minute per session
- SPINE - Stimulate up to 5 minutes per session

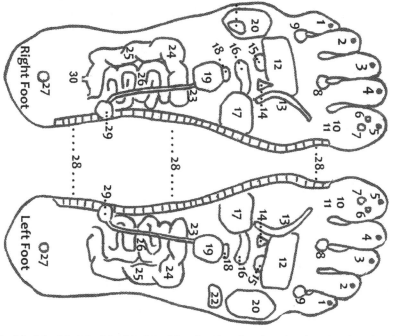

151

Endocrine Glands and Their Reflexology Points

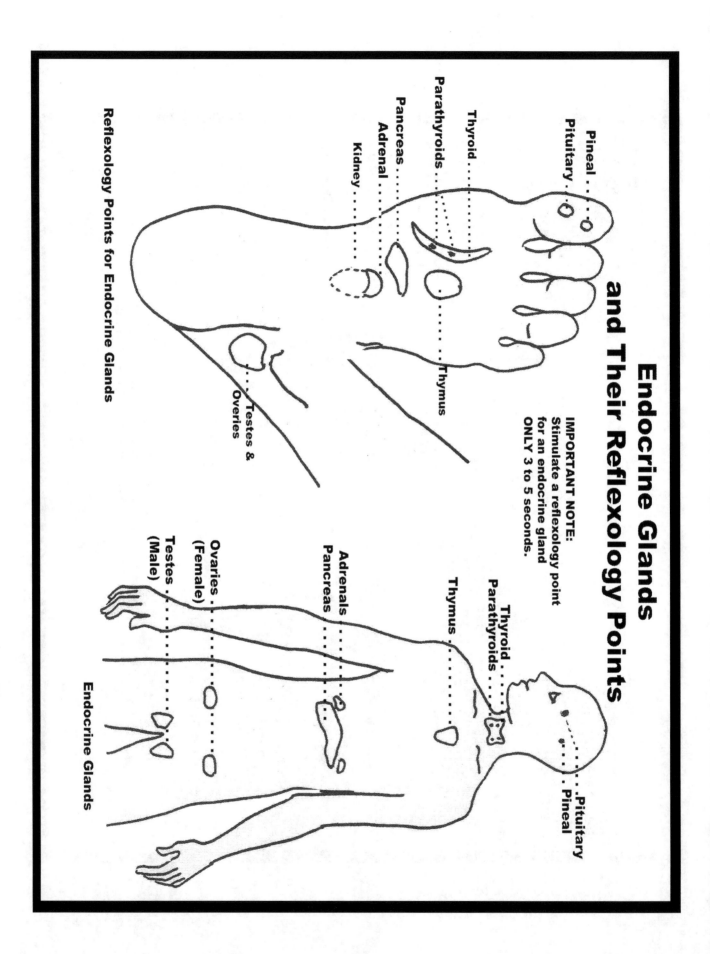

IMPORTANT NOTE:
Stimulate a reflexology point for an endocrine gland ONLY 3 to 5 seconds.

Reflexology Points for Endocrine Glands

Pineal
Pituitary

Thyroid
Parathyroids

Pancreas
Adrenal

Kidney

Thymus

Testes & Overies

Thymus

Thyroid
Parathyroids

Pituitary
Pineal

Adrenals
Pancreas

Ovaries (Female)

Testes (Male)

Endocrine Glands

152

Little Understood Food Facts That Have The Potential To Change Your Life And Health For The Better In Major Ways!

There are reasons America has an epidemic of increased diabetes, obesity, cancer, heart disease, stroke, asthma, childhood hyperactivity, and many other diseases and health problems. One reason is high stress, another is insufficient exercise. An additional unbelievably huge reason (the elephant in the room) is unnatural processed food that is often sky high with sodium/salt, fat, sweeteners, additives, and other less than desirable substances. This can be turned around, it really is possible! Truly healthy natural food is extraordinarily powerful preventative and restorative medicine--particularly if it is prepared at home from fresh vegetables, fruits, whole grains, beans, fish, low fat dairy products, modest amounts of lean meat, and other nutritious foods. But many people don't usually eat at home. If they do they don't necessarily prepare fresh vegetables and fruits and other truly natural foods. The next best thing is to get to know the facts about the prepared or processed food you are buying and eating. Please don't take it for granted that it is health supporting for you just because it is for sale in a grocery store or at a restaurant or take-out shop.

Prepared Soup
Nutrition Facts

Serving Size 1 cup (228g)
Servings Per Container 2

Amount Per Serving

Calories 250   Calories from Fat 110

	% Daily Value*
Total Fat 12g	18%
Saturated Fat 3g	15%
Cholesterol 30mg	10%
Sodium 470mg	20%
Total Carbohydrate 31g	10%
Dietary Fiber 0g	0%
Sugars 5g	
Protein 5g	

Vitamin A	4%
Vitamin C	2%
Calcium	20%
Iron	4%

* Percent Daily Values are based on a 2,000 calorie diet. Your Daily Values may be higher or lower depending on your calorie needs:

	Calories:	2,000	2,500
Total Fat	Less than	65g	80g
Sat Fat	Less than	20g	25g
Cholesterol	Less than	300mg	300mg
Sodium	Less than	2,400mg	2,400mg
Total Carbohydrate		300g	375g
Dietary Fiber		25g	30g

Be informed and choose wisely! Study the "Nutrition Facts" label on packaged foods that you buy. To understand it more fully, you may wish to read my article "Understanding The Nutrition Facts Information Label on Food Packaging" (see SecretsofWisdom.net/articles). Another very valuable source of information is that most restaurants, fast food chains, and food producers have websites that give nutritional information on the foods and products that they offer. That information is your protection for choosing as wisely as possible.

Most people who like to eat out probably have some favorite dishes that they tend to order. Also there are definitely food products that people buy regularly at grocery stores. One needs to check the nutritional information on one's favorite dishes and products to make sure that they are health sustaining. Due to the fact that manufacturers periodically change their ingredients in a specific product, it may be wise to occasionally re-read labels. An additional word to the wise, "natural" on a label can be misleading. Just because a package may say "natural" doesn't mean it is healthy, the sodium or fat or calorie content may be excessive. It may have some fairly healthy natural ingredients, but also some that aren't in one's best interests such as excess high fructose corn syrup or sugar, food coloring, MSG, and other artificial additives and ingredients.

Andrea Regained Health By Empowering Herself As A Food Detective

~ Case History from Joyce's Files

Andrea (not her real name) came into my office because she had been feeling low energy for about six months. She said, "My friends have been asking me if I'm O.K. I just don't feel as good as usual, and it seems like I'm sort of looking older. I think that I take pretty good care of myself. I saw my doctor recently, and she didn't find anything particularly wrong. She ran some blood tests. I try to get some protein and vegetable or fruit three meals a day. I'm careful to not eat too many sweets--I prefer chips. I don't touch coffee, alcohol, or cigarettes. I don't even pick up the salt shaker. I'm careful about salt, I really am. I faithfully workout at the gym three times a week. I've always considered working out kind of fun--but more recently I've been sort of dragging, if you know what I mean. My job keeps me on the go. So-o-o-o I eat out more than I wish. I love all kinds of different foods, it's an adventure for me--life should be an adventure. When there's no time to eat a real meal, I try to choose a nutritious sandwich like turkey or chicken---and vegetable soup if it is available."

Andrea continued, "When I'm at home, I really intend to fix home cooked meals for myself. I know that is best--like mother did, right? But who has the time with deadlines like I have? So I reach in the freezer and out comes dinner all set to microwave and eat. --Can't beat that! There it is in the plastic platter - - meat, potatoes, and carrots or green beans. That has all the bases covered, right? Other times I heat up some packaged or bottled foods that look pretty healthy to me--like a sauce, soup, or stew where the directions just say to add water, stir, and simmer for ten minutes. And I may fix quick rice or pasta to go with those. That I do. I keep the shelves well stocked with packaged food. It isn't fun to cook for one person, anyway. I do like salads, they're quick. When I'm at the grocery store I make a point to buy lettuce, tomatoes and salad fixings--and fresh fruit which I adore. Other fresh vegetables just might go to waste. I hate to see food wasted."

So Andrea and I settled down to talk. I explained, "For the average person, about 2000 mg. of sodium (salt is sodium chloride) is considered O.K. The range could be between 1,500 mg to 2,500 mg for people a good bit smaller or larger than average. Continually eating a high sodium intake tends to cause one's body to hold excess fluid, which puts stress on the kidneys, heart, and blood vessels, and can set the stage for high blood pressure. Excess sodium contributes to an acidic condition in the body which can adversely affect crucial enzymatic reactions in the body. This can make one vulnerable to many serious health problems, general fatigue, and not feeling well. **I can't emphasize enough that the sodium level can be extremely high in processed foods and in restaurant food without one realizing it. The food may not even taste particularly salty, but the sodium can be extremely high even if one doesn't pick up the salt shaker**. Some very popular upscale national restaurant chains have entrees with 2000 or 3000 or even 4000 or more milligrams of sodium which is way out of line with the 2000 mg limit for sodium for the whole day!"

I told Andrea a story from my life. "At one time about twenty years ago I started snacking on bags of salted popcorn as I drove my daily long commute to and from work assignments. After awhile my fingers started periodically turning white as a sheet if they got at all cold. This was terrifying. Each time I wondered if they would warm up and turn normal color again! Even opening the freezer compartments at a grocery store became a concern. Going for a walk in the snow became out of the question. My legs were sort of painful to the touch of clothing. People were telling me I didn't look as good as usual, they were concerned."

I continued, "It turned out that my body chemistry had become overly acidic from the excess sodium. When I quit over doing salty popcorn and refocused on a healthier diet--THE WHITE FINGERS COMPLETELY STOPPED within a few months! Other symptoms also phased out. It was magic! Unbelievable! In a lot of ways the body is a self healing organism when it is given the optimum conditions. It is worth taking good care of oneself, right?

So Andrea and I talked about the sodium content in some of the salads, soups, entrees, and other dishes that she tends to eat at some of her favorite restaurants. I explained that this information is easily available online. Google the name of the restaurant or food manufacturer followed by the words 'nutritional facts.' I mentioned to her that this very valuable information is also available in apps and in books. We looked online together at information about some of her favorite foods and here is what we found:

- **Chef's Chicken Salad** at a very popular moderate priced franchised restaurant Andrea liked, **l,255 mg sodium**, 38 grams fat, 670 calories. That is more than half the whole day's quota of sodium and 3/5 a day's quota of fat--just in a chef's chicken salad. That excess sodium and fat are in the dressing, toppings, and additives. (Some people may be fooled into thinking it is good nutrition because it is fairly low in calories.) As an alternative, a large garden salad could be ordered. You can request vegetable oil (hopefully olive oil) and vinegar on the side for you to add on your own. Then different additional foods can be selected that are lower in sodium and fat, such as plain baked fish (with a lemon slice squeezed on it) and a plain baked potatoe with one pad of real butter and a modest sprinkling of salt.
- **Turkey, Cheese, and Vegetables Wrap**, 1280 mg. sodium, 20 grams fat, calories 650. That is almost two thirds a day's quota of sodium and more than a third of a day's quota of fat in one dish.
- **Burrito** with black beans, rice, green tomatillo salsa. 1,350 mg. sodium, 36 grams fat, 750 calories at Andrea's favorite Mexican restaurant. That is more than two-thirds of a whole day's quota of sodium and fat in one dish, and one-third of the day's quota of calories. Wow! (The beans and rice in their natural state are very low in sodium and fat, it is all that is added to them in the preparation that makes them a problem. They can be prepared at home with low numbers.)
- **Vegetable Soup Bowl**, 1 ½ cups, 1100 mg. sodium, 4 grams fat, 135 calories at one of the restaurants Andrea likes. This is half a day's sodium quota. This shocked her because she had been counting on the vegetable soup to help her stay healthy. That sodium level or much more is not unusual for restaurant or canned soup unless it is labeled low sodium. Even then, what is labeled low sodium may not be more than a **little** lower. Be sure to read the actual numbers and/or percent of the daily quota. Homemade vegetable soup can be made delicious with plenty of herbs and spices, leaving out excess sodium!
- **Roast Beef Sandwich**, varied between 600 to 1,200 (or higher) mg. sodium at some of Andrea's favorite places to eat. It tended to have about 500 calories and 10 grams fat.

I added up some of those figures and said, "Let's imagine that you have a roast beef sandwich and soup for lunch, and the chef's chicken salad described above for dinner--then the total sodium for the day just counting only those items might be a scary 3500 mg. sodium. Add in some sodium for breakfast and snacks, and it's at least double the O.K. amount for a day. Replacing the roast beef sandwich with a burrito, spaghetti with sauce, pizza, or packaged processed food at home is likely to add up similarly. That is all without lifting a salt shaker and possibly not even noticing a salty taste." Andrea looked at her hands, and quietly said "Oh -h-h - h - h."

I continued, "The moral of this story is to look up the nutritional facts on the foods you like to eat. Be a 'food detective.' There is an unbelievably huge range of sodium and fat and calorie content of foods at popular restaurants and in processed food at grocery stores. The low sodium and low fat and low calorie foods are there, you just need to look for them. Be sure to read the actual numbers, don't just trust the words low sodium or low fat, etc. on the label. Who is going to watch out for you if you don't? An even more important moral to this story is to buy fresh produce and cook at home whenever possible. Food preparation can be fun and easy. Fresh salads can be very nutritious, delicious, quick to prepare, and easy on your waistline--just use olive oil and apple cider vinegar for your dressing. Sprinkle on a few herbs and maybe some delicious pumpkin seeds or bits of cheese. You can do it! Also, it just takes a few minutes to put a baking potato, half an acorn squash, and chicken legs into the oven. Take a nap and/or get some exercise while they are in the oven."

I continued, "As previously mentioned, packaged foods have the Nutrient Facts label on the package. Be sure to check it. The Nutrition Facts label on packaged foods is worth its weight in gold. All the information is given in terms of what the package states is a serving size. If a bottle of spaghetti sauce says that a serving is ¼ cup, and you eat 3/4 cup of spaghetti sauce on your pasta--there is a little multiplication to be done. Let's say the bottle label says that there are 300 mg. sodium in a serving. In that case, eating ¾ cup of the sauce on pasta is a whopping 900 mg. of sodium (almost half a day's quota in one food item). If you don't like to deal in milligrams (mg) or grams, then use the percentages on the right side of the label. That means the percentage of the day's allowance of that nutrient. If you or someone eats what the package calls two servings of something, than multiply the percentage on the right by two. Be sure to also check the fat and calorie levels. Be your own best friend. There is additional valuable information there, too." Andrea quietly said, "O.K., I learned something here today. I've got a lot of food detective work to do. I'll get back to you." I encouraged her to give me a quick call or an email at least twice a week and to let me know how it was going. She made an appointment for two weeks ahead.

Andrea did start checking out online about her favorite dishes at restaurants. She also got serious about checking the "Nutrition Facts" label on products she liked to buy from the grocery store. It didn't take long for her to make it pretty much a habit to check sodium levels and the fat and calories levels. It almost became a game for her to be a 'secret agent food detective.' There were some minor back slides along the way, but progress was made. Also, she made a bargain with herself that every time she prepared a home-cooked meal with fresh ingredients, she gave herself a star on her kitchen bulletin board. Ten stars--and she rewarded herself with a massage at her workout center. She loved getting massages. Within about three months, Andrea was feeling and looking much better. Her friends were now saying, "You look really good, Andrea, what's up? --Got a new guy?" She was telling me about her favorite recipes for crock-pot soups and stews. Good for you, Andrea! (End of Case History)

NOTE: It is worth keeping in mind that there are some restaurants which specialize in "Whole Natural Foods." You may wish to Google "Restaurants serving whole natural fresh foods" in your area.

Fresh Foods Still Have Vibrant Life Energy--Some Processed Packaged Foods Have Almost None

We need to consider that not all food is equal in its capacity to sustain health. Food has its source in energy as it grows in the rays of the sun. Every living plant has its aura and energy field, just as do animals and humans and minerals. Some food when we eat it is still vibrant with life energy and some is almost void of it. This is an extremely important and little understood subject. If we pick some vegetables in the backyard and go inside to wash and eat them raw, those vegetables are still full of life sustaining energy and nutrients and enzymes. Everything that happens to vegetables from the point of being picked until they are eaten affects the degree to which they can sustain vibrant health. It is a continuum. This is not to say that people don't survive when they eat food that has been picked a long time ago and that has been processed, it just doesn't support health as well. Nutritious food can also become unhealthy when laced with additives and pesticides and cooked inappropriately.

To some people, processed food may even sometimes seem to taste better than meals prepared at home from whole natural foods. Many people's taste buds have become accustomed to very high levels of fat, salt, sweeteners, and various artificial ingredients. Two-thirds of the adults in the United States are now overweight. One-half of those who are overweight are seriously obese. This strongly contributes to the development of diabetes, heart disease, stroke, and much more. Many people don't understand the effect of what they are putting in their bodies. These days most people are not eating the natural foods that humans have been eating for thousands of years.

Having the food capable of being stored a long time before it is sold is often an important consideration for manufacturers of packaged food. This is to provide for extended warehouse time, shipping time, shelf life at the store, and then time on the shelf in someone's home. The longer that food is stored, the more it loses its true nutritional value to sustain health. Exceptions to that are natural whole beans, whole lentils, whole grains, and nuts in the shell. They can be stored for up to a year in a cool dry place, in a jar with a lid, because they are, in fact, seeds. As long as they are not irradiated or processed in any way, the germ of new life is held in a seed until it is planted in the ground or placed in water for a new cycle of growth, or cooked and eaten.

For preparation, natural organic whole grains can be rinsed and then simmered until soft and delicious. Natural organic whole beans and lentils can likewise be rinsed and simmered until soft and tasty. The larger beans do well to be soaked overnight to shorten the cooking time. To avoid getting intestinal gas from beans, after ten minutes simmering pour off cooking water and add fresh water. A crock-pot is very helpful for cooking dried beans and lentils, and rice cookers are helpful for cooking grains. Using those devices a person doesn't need to keep stirring and checking the pot. It is very important for people to take cooking their food back into their own hands. Food preparation is too crucial for one's health to trust it to others who often have commercial interests foremost in mind.

I want to clearly and unequivocally give tribute and much credit to those farmers and food business people who work very hard to provide truly high quality fresh and packaged nutritious foods. I particularly want to give deep appreciation and honor to the farmers and food packaging companies that provide organically grown food. To receive the right to label food as organically grown is a very rigorous process. It means that no pesticides were used, no GMO (genetically modified organisms), no irradiation, no artificial colors, no wax, no harmful preservatives, and many other precautions. Some farmers and food companies are in a transitional stage where they are working toward fulfilling the requirement to be labeled organically grown. Much well deserved appreciation needs to be extended to them. Their fresh produce is sometimes labeled transitional.

Some of the largest supermarket chains in this country (as of this writing) are greatly expanding the amount of organically grown fresh produce and packaged products they carry. This is extremely encouraging! What I seem to hear from some of the supermarkets in this city is that if customers continue to actively buy organically grown foods and products, the stores will keep expanding that section. Of course, in many cities there are also a few stores that actually specialize in selling organically grown foods. It is a growing trend, and greatly needed! As expansion into conventional grocery stores continues, we need to support organic growers' associations in upholding rigorous standards.

Appreciating the Delicious Taste of Fresh Foods

We can reclaim our ability to truly enjoy and appreciate the delicious tastes of fresh natural foods as we receive them straight from Mother Earth. In addition to the natural taste of foods, it's valuable to keep in mind that herbs and spices can add variety and interest to your food preparation--without excess sodium, fat, or sweeteners! A good idea for getting to know an herb or spice that is somewhat new to you is to add only one at a time so you can actually taste it and enjoy its aroma without too many flavors and aromas intermingling. Experiment and have fun! Organically grown herbs and spices tend to have healthful benefits in addition to lending delicious taste and enticing aroma to food. A few are listed as follows:

Basil – beneficial for indigestion

Cayenne – aids circulation, antiseptic, helps sore throats

Cinnamon – helpful for colds, diarrhea, digestive upset

Garlic – supports immune system

Ginger – lessens intestinal gas, helpful for sore throats, anti-inflammatory, stimulates digestion

Oregano – helpful for infections

Peppermint – aids indigestion, fever, headaches

Rosemary – calms nervous system

Sage – helpful for sore throats, intestinal gas

Thyme – aids respiratory tract infections and urinary tract infections

Turmeric – anti-inflammatory, aids indigestion

There are easy ways to prepare natural foods which don't take long at all. It is our health. Let's reclaim our food preparation if we have given away responsibility for it. Food preparation is a sacred trust. The food we eat becomes our body. This cannot be stated strongly enough. Mother Nature provides us our food. She is generous with her gifts! We need to keep our food pure and natural until it enters our body. Please let's all think about this. Food is not entertainment. As the saying goes, "Let's eat to live, not live to eat."

This is extremely important information. There is a desperate need for people to understand what is going on nutritionally. Let's talk with our friends and acquaintances about this. There is a groundswell movement underway to return to natural and organically grown food, but it is still only beginning in many parts of the country. We are all needed to help actualize this renewal for the health of American people. It needs to happen now before the epidemic of degenerative diseases gets worse. Because of unnatural foods and lack of sufficient exercise, even children are succumbing to obesity, hyperactivity, diabetes, and other serious diseases in record breaking numbers. We can reverse it. We can all do it together. What is going on today isn't normal.

The Magic of Pure Olive Oil and Flax Oil--High Quality Oils are Very Important in the Diet

We need high quality oils like olive oil and flax oil. Fried foods, excess animal fats, and many processed foods can gradually build up blockages and plaque in one's arteries and veins. This can eventually contribute to high blood pressure and the possibility of some of the related serious health problems such as heart disease and stroke. **Uncooked organic extra virgin olive oil can help prevent or lessen such plaque or blockage build ups.** Olive oil really is a superstar when it comes to fats. A good guideline is to eat a tablespoon of olive oil with two meals a day--on a salad or on any food. It is best to add it **after** the food is cooked. Cooking with olive oil at a moderate to high heat can, to a large degree, destroy its healthful benefits. A tablespoon of flax oil with the third meal would be very helpful. Even more so than olive oil, it is crucial to add flax oil **after** the food is cooked or add it to a breakfast smoothie. It is important to mention that at least a small amount of good quality saturated fat (such as real butter, coconut oil, or fairly lean meat) is beneficial for the body. Everything in moderation.

Real Life Sharings for Using Nutrition to Regain or Enhance Vibrant Health

Roger Solved His Weight Gain Problem
~ A client case history from Joyce's files

Roger (name changed to preserve privacy) came into my office concerned about his weight gain. "I feel that I HAVE to have sweet snacks or soft drinks just to keep me going throughout the day. My job keeps me physically on the go and I can't stop and rest. Sweets have always given me that quick boost to do the next job. I pride myself on being fast. But look at me, I'm gaining weight. I've had to buy bigger clothes twice. My wife's concerned. During the recent year I'm finding that a candy bar doesn't hold me up as long as it used to. I seem to crash faster. Sometimes after one snack, I feel like I'm just counting minutes until the next one. Occasionally when my schedule is really tight, to save time I just grab a large cup of coffee or even a bottle of fruit juice and keep going. I figure that might help me lose weight--but then I pretty soon just have to stop and pick up a couple quick donuts or soda or something else sweet. What can I do?"

I explained to Roger, "We need a somewhat steady blood sugar level to have steady sustained energy and feel good. Sweets spike our energy way up and then drop it low again before long. It can be a vicious cycle trying to jack your energy up with sweets and then before long feeling serious craving for another pick up. It's no fun. Your pancreas provides the insulin to allow your body to utilize the sweets for energy and not store them away as fat. With too many wide swings of high and low blood sugar--the pancreas can get overworked, confused, and eventually malfunction. Then the sweets may get mostly stored as fat and not as much available for energy. That can be a serious cause of weight gain and can eventually contribute to the development of diabetes. Complex carbs like whole grains and beans can help keep your energy steady all day. Solid protein like meat, fish, or tofu is important to support your energy levels, too. Maybe an apple and water rather than fruit juice which is high concentrated fructose (a form of sugar). Protein foods, complex carbs, vegetables, and raw fruit don't cause the yo-yo effect of your energy level going up and down and making you crave that next sweet snack "pick-me-up." Foods that are high in fiber (like the raw apple and other fresh fruit, vegetables, and the complex carbs) help to slow down the digestion of the food and keep it from being absorbed as quickly. You don't need to starve yourself, just make the choices that won't turn around and crash you."

Over time Roger started having a solid breakfast of 100% whole grain cereal with 2% cow's milk or soy milk and a whole piece of fresh fruit. He took almonds and a couple apples or other nutritious foods for snacks. He took a lunch box (with an ice pack) along for the day with a good sized sandwich of 100% whole wheat bread and meat saved from the last night's dinner or low fat cheese plus lettuce and a big slice of tomato. It was a gradual process with a little back sliding here and there, but he and his wife encouraged each other along the way. They started including more fresh vegetables with their dinners, and avoiding fried foods. They were both delighted that they were gradually losing weight. They would text back and forth during the day for mutual support. At a later check-in session Roger said that he just didn't need all those sugar snacks any more. His energy held strong fairly steadily. Now when he did feel tired during work he took time to stretch and breath deeper for a few minutes. Then he sat down and relaxed for a few more minutes and ate an apple and some almonds (or another nutritious snack). Then he was fine for several hours until the next meal. (People doing sedentary work might want to walk a few minutes on their break.)

Note: The Glycemic Index (GI) relates to how much a food raises a person's blood sugar level after eating it. A GI of seventy is high and a GI in the twenties is low.

Hidden Food Allergies: How I Discovered Mine & Feel Much Better

~ by **Chris and Allison Singler**

When I first heard about this plan (toquietinflammation.com), I felt like no way! Give up bread, wine, popcorn, pizza? What?! Life is too busy to prepare whole foods! My husband's older brother, who is a doctor, suggested this plan to us as a way to discover our food sensitivities and lose weight. Their younger brother lowered his cholesterol without taking prescription medication. My husband and I felt that this was the window we had been looking for to stop the weight gain, body aches and indigestion we had both been experiencing--yet we had been looking the other way as so many of us do. To make such a major change in our diet sometimes seems incomprehensible. But, we made it through the six weeks! It was challenging, but it was easier than I thought it would be. It was more preparation time in the kitchen, but I got it down to a science. My husband lost twenty-three pounds and so far I am maintaining my eight pound loss. I no longer have irritable bowel or indigestion. My skin looks better to boot.

The theory of this plan is to initially (for three weeks) cleanse your body of artificial ingredients in order to establish a base line for your system. This involves excluding common allergens such as peanuts, dried corn products (like corn chips), dairy, gluten (wheat contains gluten), sugar and sugar substitutes, alcohol, GMO (genetically modified organisms) products. GMO products include most vegetable oils other than organic olive oil, and a great many processed foods (other than those organically grown). At the same time we added more fresh fruit and vegetables to our diet.

After three weeks cleansing as described above, you can start to add back the common allergens one at a time for a week to sense how they do in your body system. (You may know right away that one kind of food isn't good for you, and one day is enough for that food.) I was amazed to discover that artificial ingredients and GMO products cause my digestive problems. This plan helps eliminate common inflammation associated with diabetes, auto-immune diseases, arthritis, and weight gain.

The rule is to eat two-thirds of each meal as vegetables or fruits--and one-third of each meal as protein and/or grain. Fresh vegetables and fresh fruits are more alkaline in the body than animal proteins. Excess protein creates uric acid in the body which can contribute to gout and kidney stones.

I learned about kale chips, which actually taste better than popcorn. Tear, wash, and thoroughly dry kale before tossing in olive oil with a little salt. Bake for twenty minutes at 275 degrees. I also learned to make fabulous muffins with rice flour and garbanzo flour, and ingredients such as sweet potatoes, squash, and figs. I have to say that I feel so much better now on this food plan. (See Resource Page)

Note from Joyce: Consult your health care practitioner before embarking on any significant nutritional change.

Using Natural Supplementation to Heal Chronic Uncomfortable Moods

~ Dr. Lynda J. Wells, Certified Nutrition Specialist, NS,

I've been working in natural health care for twenty years, primarily with nutrition and herbs, and I'd like to share with you about using targeted supplementation.

There are many unpleasant mood states that may be caused by our genetic biochemistry or by a poor diet. They may also be caused by stress, being an abuse survivor, the lower light conditions of winter, not getting enough exercise, and more. Three common mood states are:

1. a dark hopeless depression
2. a bored, apathetic, blah depression
3. various anxiety states

Often pharmaceuticals are prescribed for these conditions. These medications may have serious side effects such as disturbed sleep, feeling emotionally flat, weight gain, low libido, no orgasm, and even breast cancer.

I would encourage you to consider trying natural supplements first and see if they can help you. Everyone's needs are somewhat different. Natural supplements nourish the nerve cells rather than flog them as many of the drugs do. These supplements are the amino acids: (1) tryptophan, (2) tyrosine and (3) GABA, respectively. Along with the help of a diet with enough protein (about 60 grams per day for most people) and 4- 5 cups of vegetables per day, these supplements will be converted (in the nerve cells themselves) to the highly specialized and potent mood molecules that keep your brain cheerfully firing away and helping to transmit positive thoughts and feelings. Some herbal supplements and other natural substances may also be necessary for some people along with the amino acids.

There are questionnaires and also lab tests (paid for by most insurances) that help decide which supplements are best for you. Since this short article is not designed to contain complete instructions, it is important to work with a nutritionist or naturopath who has experience with this method for mood healing. As always, it is important to stay in touch with your health care provider. (See Resources Page)

Acid / Akaline Balance and Its Extraordinarily Important Role in Health

~by Joyce

This is of urgent importance in maintaining and rebuilding health. In order for a person to be healthy, the pH of his or her body chemistry needs to be slightly alkaline. What we eat or drink or ingest affects the pH of our body fluids. Some other factors that can adversely affect our acid-alkaline balance are emotional stress and environmental toxins. Let's look at the influence of nutrition.

Some foods are alkaline forming in the body, and some are acid forming in the body. Some foods that are acidic before they are eaten such as lemon can have an alkaline effect on the body chemistry once they are eaten. Some healthy foods have an alkaline effect on the body when eaten, and some healthy foods (such as numerous whole grains) have a slightly acidic effect on the body when eaten. The crucial thing is to have a BALANCE of more foods that have an alkaline effect in the body. Fresh vegetables and fruits are almost all alkaline forming in the body. Substances that have a seriously acidic affect in the body chemistry include sugar, corn syrup, artificial sweeteners, and soft drinks. Coffee, black tea, and alcohol have an acidic effect in the body. Excess salt (sodium) has a very acidic effect. Stevia sweetener is totally natural and is alkalizing, as are herbal teas and herbs and spices. To learn more search for "acid and alkaline balance" online. Let's enjoy eating lots of delicious fresh vegetables, fruits, and natural whole unprocessed foods to help strengthen our health!

Lowering Hyperactivity in Children with Nutrition

~ by J.M.W.

When my son was five or six years old, I began to think he might be hyperactive. He was a very active kid, as were other children in the neighborhood--but he had difficulty falling asleep at night. While reading a bedtime story to him, I would find myself drifting to sleep and he would still be wide awake. I found a wonderful book by Ben F. Feingold, MD addressing the role food additives play in children's behavior. I began to closely monitor my son's food intake. I cut back on sugar and checked the ingredients on all packaged food items. Breakfast cereal became a real problem due to the high sugar content and artificial ingredients of some brands! For breakfast we mostly settled on cream of wheat, oatmeal, or eggs. As all parents are aware, there are a number of "teasers" for children at each grocery check-out stand. I was constantly saying, "No."

After following Dr. Feingold's advice and cooking natural foods, limiting processed foods and sugar, over the next two weeks I noticed a marked improvement both in his hyperactivity and his ability to fall asleep. The big problem when he was young was children's birthday parties. I did not wish to limit his time with friends; however, I could see that the addition of cake, artificial red/grape punch, etc. would wind him up. Monitoring his food intake while he was at school was difficult, but when I noticed behavior changes I would ask what he had eaten. It is extremely difficult for parents to always monitor their child's food intake when they are away from home; however, we can begin to gradually teach them how food plays a vital role in their health, behavior and nutrition. This worked out well for my son as he grew up. (See Resources Page)

Hyperactivity and High Stress In Children or Adults

Note from Joyce: If you have a young child or an adult in your life who seems hyperactive or highly stressed, it would be valuable to really focus on improving the nutritional intake before seriously considering drugs which can have serious potential side effects. Please study the nutritional information in this book and elsewhere. See the sharing earlier in this chapter about hidden food allergies, and see the "Roger" case history about dependence on sweets. Consider your intake of pure water. Some people actually drink a lot of pop or artificial drinks instead of water. Can you imagine putting those drinks instead of water into a fish bowl where a fish is swimming? What would happen? Help children and adults embrace pure filtered or spring water. An idea for transitioning to pure water is to add about one eight cup of fruit juice as flavoring to a cup of water. That creates a very refreshing light drink.

Grain Motif in Circle
Original art by Joyce J.C. Gerrish

WORKBOOK: Enrichment Experiences For Enhancing Healing In Your Life

This can be an excellent opportunity to help you move ahead on your life path, and enhance your health. Enjoy the adventure of exploring these enrichment experiences on your own, or gather a few friends to share the journey with you. Be inspired by the audio meditation and soul song for this chapter. Reflect on some of the stimulating ideas and questions.

Questions For Reflection And Discussion

Reflection, discussion, journal writing, expressing your feelings in drawings or other creative ways can all be very valuable to help you delve into these questions in truly meaningful and relevant ways. Before focusing on the questions, you may wish to meditate with the twelve minute audio or transcribed meditation--and/or listen to the soul song "Thy Healing Light."

1. How would you evaluate your health? Do you feel that you are presently living your life in a way that enhances your health? Were your health habits in the past different than they are today? Do you feel that you are making progress toward creating or maintaining better health for yourself? (Accidents and hereditary disease can, of course, affect our health.)

2. Are you aware that you can choose foods and drinks that are delicious as well as nutritious? Name at least ten of your very favorite things to eat or drink that are also healthy and good for you. How do you feel about the idea that if you crave to eat something you know isn't good for you --that you can substitute one of these healthy foods or drinks that you love?

3. Do you have a way of exercising that you enjoy regularly? Is there a form of movement that is a pleasure for you? Walking? Social Dancing? Ballroom Dancing? Square Dancing? Swimming? Tennis or golf? Yoga? Other? How do you feel about exercising?

4. Stress directly affects your health. What helps you maintain your inner peace? What is the stress level in your life? How do you release stress on a regular basis? Do you need help in this area? Does meditation, tai chi, yoga, or taking a relaxing walk help?

5. How do you feel about alternative natural healing therapies? Have you tried receiving acupressure, reflexology, therapeutic massage, energy healing, homeopathy, acupuncture, or other natural

alternative therapies? Was that helpful for you, if you did? Have you read about any of these therapies or talked to people who have tried them? Describe your experiences in any of these areas.

Action Suggestions for Enhancing Healing In Your Life

You can do it! Take a step now!

1. What is one improvement that you feel ready to make for your nutrition? Less caffeine? Fewer sweets? More vegetables? More water? More fresh fruit?

2. If exercise isn't already a priority in your life, are you ready to give yourself that life-preserving gift? See Journal Writing Suggestion #3 above. Choose some form of movement and allow it to be fun. Find a friend to take walks with you. Dog friends can also help keep you active, too. Try joining a movement class/group or joining a YMCA. It is important to check with your health care provider before making a significant change in your exercise pursuits.

3. Consider making an appointment with a natural healing therapist. Talk to your friends and let them recommend someone to you. One good way to learn about different forms of natural healing is to attend a holistic health expo or fair. There you can talk to various practitioners and perhaps experience a mini session for a small fee. This is not to replace medical care, but to perhaps complement and enhance it.

4. Consider learning to do some natural healing techniques for yourself. That way you can support your own health at a time convenient for you in your own home for free. Now there's a bargain! Reiki energy healing is an excellent technique to learn. The beginning course can be taken in one or two days and for a reasonable fee. You can check at local natural foods stores for fliers about classes, or inquire in adult education programs. Hand and foot reflexology (see beginning instructions in this chapter) is also a superb place to start.

5. How can we best keep the energies within our body and consciousness as clear as possible? The number one thing is to start. We have free will, so it is valuable to pray and ask for Divine assistance. In order to more fully let in God's peace and Divine Light, it is important to "delete" some of the static of old stress. Higher Spiritual energies can flow more freely and effectively in a renewed and fairly clear energy field and consciousness. It is very valuable to practice using some of the techniques presented in this chapter and book as a whole.

Audio: "Meditation to Enhance Your Experience of The Divine Qualities," with focus on Healing

Pray to the Divine to bless your meditation and enhance Divine Healing in your life. With this audio you'll be guided to sense yourself immersed in this nurturing feeling of healing. Choose one or more of the following healing affirmations (or something similar) that feels particularly helpful to you to affirm during the meditation. Before transferring to the website to listen to the meditation, write down the affirmation(s) you choose and the helpful color green. Later, place the affirmation(s) where you'll see it often and be reminded to affirm it for a minute or two several times a day.

- ◆ I am completely well.
- ◆ I choose to enjoy _____regularly. (i.e. My favorite form of exercising that I want to do more of.)

◆ I choose to eat natural fresh foods.

◆ I open to receive healing energies, and I release old stuck emotions.

◆ I often pause to breathe deeper and relax.

I encourage you to enjoy this meditation when you wish to enhance healing in your life. Connect to the website SecretsofWisdom.net to listen to the audio "Meditation to Enhance Your Experience of the Divine Qualities," with focus on Healing.

Helpful color to visualize when meditating on Healing: Green

(Also see transcribed version of this meditation at the end of this chapter.)

Uplifting Audio Soul Song *"Dear Divine, Heal Me"*
Composed and sung by Joyce

Consider it a prayer in song for enhancing nurturing healing in your life. The words are:

First verse: Dear Divine heal me, hold me, in Thy healing Light. Dear Divine heal me, hold me. I know I'm precious in Thy sight.

Chorus: Come healing Light, come Holy Light. Come healing Light, come Holy Light. Oh, I'm filled with Light. Yes, I'm filled with Light. Oh, I'm filled with Light, I am whole. I thank Thee, Lord. I am whole.

Second verse: Dear Divine teach me, show me. Oh, Thy healing ways. Dear Divine, Teach me, show me - - To live in peace throughout my days.

Repeat Chorus.

As you chant and/or listen, feel yourself relax and begin to flow with the music and the peaceful feelings the song creates for you. Close your eyes and really sense it helping to bring you into an uplifted clear sense of well-being. You can hear *"Dear Divine, Heal Me"* at SecretsofWisdom.net.

Transcribed Version of Meditation to Enhance Divine Healing

If possible, listen to some relaxing nonverbal music. Say a short prayer calling on the Divine to bless your meditation and enhance Divine Healing in your life.

Visualize yourself in a ball of Light to help strengthen your energy field.

Become aware of and follow your breath as it gently flows in and out at its own relaxed pace.

Imagine yourself as a large tree sending powerful roots deep into the earth to help you feel grounded and prevent possibly feeling spacey.

As you breathe in your nose, imagine you are breathing up the strength of the earth into your body.

For a few minutes listen to the relaxing music.

As you breathe in your nose imagine you are breathing in Light into your being.

Next visualize green light like a glowing emerald.

Periodically as you breathe in your nose, imagine that you are breathing glowing emerald green light into your whole being.

Silently pray to the Divine that your life be uplifted and blessed with Divine Healing.

Next breathe in your nose and out your mouth VERY GENTLY for about a minute.

Now, very gently breathe in your mouth and out your nose for about a minute.

Then extra-gently breathe in and out your mouth for a minute or so.

Now return to breathing in and out your nose. As you breathe in your nose, once again imagine you are breathing emerald green light into your whole being.

As you breathe out your nose, periodically say one or two of the following affirmations (or something similar) that you feel will be helpful to affirm during your meditation.

- ◆ I am completely well.
- ◆ I choose to enjoy _____ often. i.e. My favorite form of exercising that I choose to do more of.
- ◆ I choose to eat more fresh vegetables.
- ◆ I open to receive healing energies, and I release old stuck emotions.
- ◆ I often pause to breathe deeper and relax.

Pray for support in helping you to move forward with your healing goals.

Continue in that manner for a few minutes or as long as you wish.

Conclude by thanking the Divine and sending down roots to Mother Earth for stability and grounding.

Enjoy this meditation when you wish to enhance Divine Healing in your life. Write down the affirmation(s) you choose and place it where you'll see it several times a day and be reminded to affirm it for a minute or two.

Peace.

NOTE: A printable version of Natural Healing charts and tables presented in this chapter are available at: SecretsofWisdom.net.

Wise Woman Considers Both Sides Of An Issue
Original art by Joyce J.C. Gerrish

Chapter Twelve

LET WISDOM GUIDE YOUR LIFE
Enhancing Divine Wisdom in Your Life

Enjoy listening to, or singing along with, this soul song: "*Wisdom's Pearl.*" Connect to SecretsofWisdom.net to hear "*Wisdom's Pearl*" and also gaze at the full color design "Woman Under Tree Contemplates Life."

A Secret of Wisdom is Knowing How to Recognize Opportunities

How can we travel along our life path as wisely as possible? Life offers us endless opportunities from which to choose. Sometimes it may seem as though our options are limited, but in truth they are many. The secret is in knowing how to recognize our opportunities. They may come in many ways--they may come in disguise. Opportunities may even come in the form of an emergency, our own emergency or someone else's. In learning how to deal with our own or someone else's emergency we may draw on strengths and capabilities that we didn't realize we had. We may realize that there is a need in our community for a skill we possess. Wisdom could be said to be the art of understanding and recognizing truth.

We Each View the World Through Our Own "Colored Eye Glasses"

Most people are constantly viewing their world through "eye glasses" colored by their preferences and prejudices. The world that one person sees is not the same world that someone else sees, even if they are looking at the same slice of the world. If there are numerous people visiting the same beach, each is likely to experience it somewhat differently. A little girl and her parents are happily playing ball. One person feels that it is much too dull because there aren't snack bars, loud music, and lots of people to hang out with. Another person has a headache and feels it's too noisy even if it's fairly quiet. Two friends are happily splashing about in the shallow water as the waves come in. A fourth person is busy with his metal detector looking for valuable items people lost. The lifeguard is bored. Another person comes to the beach and falls asleep for a few hours under a beach umbrella dreaming about being promoted to vice president of his company. A couple comes who are angry at each other and spend their time arguing. Another person is disappointed because he had heard that there was a "nude beach somewhere around here." Then there is a peaceful older person who finds a quiet area of the beach and enjoys observing the sky and the waves, listening to the seagulls, feeling the breeze, and daydreaming about younger years. What is the truth of the situation? It is the same lovely beach on a beautiful day, yet everyone experiences it through his or her own viewpoint. It is safe to say that none of the people really experience the whole reality of the beach. Wisdom is the art of being able to understand the nuances of life beneath the surface reactions of oneself or other people.

It is a special person who is clear enough to recognize truth in its essence. It is important to be very aware of how enmeshed humans are in the world of illusions. The way most people experience the world is filled with illusions in many ways. The levels of reality within which we exist are the physical, emotional, mental, and then increasingly Spiritual levels of reality. It is valuable to understand that the way most people experience life physically and emotionally and mentally has elements of illusion. We can make a point of being alert to this. Being aware of these distortions is the job of wisdom. Let's not be fooled.

If we are watching an advertisement on T.V., it could be that what is being presented is only partially true. It might be that sometimes part of an ad's purpose is to mislead through half- truths. Life itself is more like that than we might think. There is an old saying "Don't believe anything that you hear and only half of what you see." That may be extreme, but it makes the point to be cautious of making easy assumptions. A lot of people we meet are attempting to sell us something. They may be trying to sell us on their super importance, special beauty, or unusual capabilities. They may be trying to convince us that they are weak and need us to take care of them in some way. Many people come to us with some kind of agenda to prove. It is wisdom that can help us see through appearances to the reality within--to not be fooled by appearances. Appearances can be like a costume donned to make an impression in a particular way. It may have little to do with the reality of the situation. Wisdom can help us see through all this.

How can we discern through the cloudy lens of appearances to the reality within? We can stay very calm and centered. This will allow us to be as clear as possible in the moment--and for the emotions, mind, and aura energy to be quiescent. Life is viewed through the aura energy. If the aura is turbulent with upset emotions, then we are going to experience and see everything through the lens of those emotions. If our mind is stuck, it can distort everything we perceive. If we are determined that something must occur in a particular way, no other options are likely to be perceived in an unbiased way.

A Guided Experience in Seeing Through Illusions

Here is an exercise you may wish to try to help sensitize yourself to seeing through illusions. Choose a situation in your life concerning which you would like wise insight. Become aware of your breath comfortably flowing in and out. Just sort of relax with your breath for awhile. As much as possible, feel neutral to the outcome of the situation. This gives the possibility of being more objective. It can be an interesting experience to try temporarily letting go of preconceived expectations. Then allow yourself to be an observer of every detail and nuance of the situation. In this state of calm attention, you may find yourself aware of more levels of vested interests from others than had previously been apparent. When you are feeling calm and relatively detached, it may be easier to not get hooked by other's illusions and emotions. You may find that it is easier to get a clear view between the expected or habitual responses. Here are some questions to ask yourself:

◆ What are the benefits of the situation to you?
◆ Are there one or more people with vested interests in the situation who are exerting influence on you in one way or another?
◆ What are the disadvantages of the situation for you?
◆ Where is your growth in the situation?
◆ What option in the situation gives you a sense of inner peace and encouragement and joy?

It may come as a surprise to realize that the situation doesn't seem to be what it had originally appeared to be. By temporarily detaching and observing calmly any aspect of your life, you can find valuable insights.

If we wish to enhance our wisdom, it is helpful to meditate on a regular basis. Meditation is the art of quieting the chatter of the mind and finding that peaceful place within. It could be called the art of coming home to ourselves. During meditation we learn to be aware of what the mind is doing--and how it frequently jumps around and perhaps obsesses on something. This is the perfect opportunity for learning to relax the overly anxious mind and allowing the consciousness to expand into peace. We learn that we are not our busy thoughts. Our thoughts can seem all consuming sometimes, but in meditation we can remember that we are not our worries or fears. We are the peace of our oneness with the Divine. From that place of peace everything can be understood better for what it truly is. Solutions for some of our life issues may clarify. We don't have to solve a particular problem the same way that a certain relative or friend did, maybe there is a different approach that would work better for us.

Wisdom Comes From Reading Between the Lines

Wisdom comes from "reading between the lines" and not taking life at face value. Listen to the silence between the words and the events. It is the silent pauses in music that create the rhythm and expressiveness. Listen for the unsaid words. Look for the symbolic meaning within an action. You, I, or anyone else may act in a certain way as a symbolic expression of something that doesn't seem easy to say. If you sense that someone is exhibiting symbolic gestures or actions, hold the behavior in your mind and ask yourself what message is being conveyed here. A person quietly humming a particular tune could unconsciously (or consciously) be expressing something in a symbolic way. A friend giving you a ride somewhere may take an unusual route and drive by a place that may have emotional symbolic overtones for one or both of you. A person may wear a particular style of clothing or a particular piece of jewelry that has symbolic meaning. I encourage you to always be alert to the possible multiple layers of meaning in an interaction. For some people life is like an ongoing poker game where they keep their "cards" carefully out of view. Consider it an interesting challenge to observe, listen carefully, and seek to understand the nuances. All this can be helpful. We all probably know people who have difficulty expressing their feelings. Our being alert to symbolic expression and "reading between the lines" can help enhance communication and clarity.

The Divine Qualities Help Us Move Through Illusions

There is so much more to life than striving predominately for prestige, beauty, fashion, exciting entertainment, and wealth--though those have their valid place. To lift us out of the world of illusions and into greater clarity and wisdom--it is valuable to observe life through the perspectives of the Divine Qualities. We have been exploring these Divine Qualities throughout this book. They are like the facets or aspects of the sparkling jewel of true life. Each of these aspects of the jewel is capable of reflecting the radiance of the Divine in a unique way when gradually understood and embodied more fully. They hold the secrets for bringing the jewel of life into its rightful radiance.

It is important to develop the different Divine Qualities within ourselves in a balanced way--not focusing on just one or two. This supports a more wholesome well-rounded joyful life. Divine Wisdom holds the broad vision of the beneficial role of each of the Divine Qualities. There have been times in Earth's history when one or another of the Divine Qualities gained dominance over the other qualities. This is not the intention. They need to develop together and hold each other in balance. Power is very important, but it needs to be guided with wisdom and softened with Divine Love and compassion. Devotion to a cause is very noble, but it needs to be balanced with clarity. During some periods of time and with certain people there is admiration for spontaneous behavior free of serious planning. During other periods of time and with other people there may be intense almost rigid planning. The pendulum tends to swing back and forth. The truth is that balance in-between is wisest.

As you have been reading this book, I hope that you have been sensing the immense power and radiance of each of these Divine Qualities and aspects of God. Tremendous potential energy, light, and healing can be unleashed as you focus on these Divine Qualities and seek to embody them in your life. There are numerous additional Divine Qualities as well--such as Divine Renewal, Divine Courage, Divine Hope, and Divine Creativity which are equally as valuable.

We Can Enhance the Wisdom of Our Decisions Through Inspiration From Our Higher Consciousness and the Divine

Wisdom has a timeless feel to it of ancient history and carvings on marble monuments. It may bring to mind misty-eyed poets and prophets. In truth, wisdom is extremely relevant and up to date in the action of the moment. What good is action if people are rushing at top speed in the wrong direction? Choosing the ideal life path is of massive importance. Many people try very hard to achieve something that they feel passionate about. Then when they get there, they may discover it wasn't what they really wanted anyway. They may have been striving for social status, significant recognition, or great wealth--and then found along the way that they felt sort of empty inside. People need to take the time to stay in touch with their heart and soul.

Doing what we feel we are "supposed to do" according to other people can be a dead end. Living by trial and error can be discouraging and exhausting. Certainly the adventure of trying something new is exhilarating.

By all means let's experiment, explore, and blaze new trails. But first, may we go to wisdom's source to connect to the Divine and to the truth of our being as soul and Higher Self.

Staying in touch with our soul and Higher Self is not as impractical an idea as it may sound. We each exist as a physical embodiment of our soul and Spirit. The higher mind is a part of the soul. The brain is the physical expression of the mind. We often think of our brain and our mind as the same, but they aren't the same. The mind has unlimited potential, whereas the brain is very much a physical organ in the head.

Our brain can be responsive to what is going on around us in the physical world, and it can also be responsive to subtle intuitive insights from within. Certainly we can be aware of both. It is important that we remember that we have our Spiritual source within. Some people aren't particularly aware that there is a source of Spiritual guidance within. Our soul/Higher Self and the Divine can be accessed there if we will take quiet time to attune within through prayer and meditation. This guidance may come in the form of a valuable insight or a knowing. It may come later through a dream that we remember at least part of in the morning. It may come through our feeling drawn to check some things out on the internet and then finding by "luck" a really helpful website.

The more that we stay responsive to the inspiration of the Higher Self and the Divine, the more we will be exactly where needed at the right time to create a fulfilling life. Staying responsive to our Higher Self and the Divine really facilitates doing something significant with our life and being helpful to the world around us. That is wisdom. Wisdom is not about honoring something that happened in the distant past. It is very much rooted in the present moment, and being alert and aware of our larger vision or purpose. Wisdom is meant to be the compass for our life direction.

To be alert and awake to the larger vision of our life requires taking quiet time on a regular basis. If we are so busy dealing with the details of life that we lose sight of the larger vision, we may find our self off track. Wisdom can help give us the needed perspective and "the big picture." Periodically it is helpful to take out a piece of paper and write down what is truly important in our life. This can be a fascinating eye-opening process. It is valuable to allow ourselves to feel this deeply.

Meditate on the following questions. "What is truly important in your life at this time? What are your goals? Are you moving in that direction?" A good approach is to meditate for a while first. You can meditate on your own or with a guided meditation audio. Then you can pose those seed questions to yourself. There are no right answers except to be honest with yourself. Different times that you do this, the answers may be somewhat different, but there will be a basic pattern. I personally find this quite useful periodically.

Journal writing can be very helpful for staying in touch with your inner feelings and truth. Try journal writing about the questions at the end of this chapter. Journal the questions at the end of the other chapters, too, as you read them or review them. I think that you'll find it a quite enlightening and valuable journey. It may help you get to know your true self and your life path better.

Intuitive Awareness Expands As We Grow Spiritually

Nearly all of us are aware that things are changing quickly all around us in today's fast paced world. Probably lots of us feel real change going on within us. This is likely to continue for the foreseeable future. We all need as much clarity of wisdom as possible to handle this rapid development well. Many people are becoming more aware and awake to life. Lots of us will be discovering capacities within ourselves that we did not know were possible. There is already a widespread interest and openness to intuitional knowing. Intuitive awareness expands naturally as we grow Spiritually and as our energy intensifies. Now as this begins to manifest for more and more of us, it is very important that we use our new developing gifts well. Whenever an important decision is to be made, it's best to give ourselves time to meditate on it and think about it for awhile. It is a good idea to "sleep on it." That gives time for us to receive valuable insights from our Higher Consciousness and the Divine. Let's not permit the enthusiasm of the moment to drown out the voice of reason and conscience.

Intuitive Technique #1 for Accessing Helpful Insight on a Question

If there is something about which you would like to gain intuitive insight, take time to center yourself and feel very peaceful. Visualize yourself in a ball of light. It is valuable to meditate for a while to clear and raise your consciousness. Then ask yourself a question about the issue of concern or interest. Then meditate quietly for awhile longer and sense if a helpful insight occurs to you. It can come as an image or a word or simply a "knowing." The insight might come right then or it might come later in the day or the next day. It might come through a dream, through something you notice in a book or elsewhere, or through something someone says that makes a strong impression on you. It is very important to use common sense in evaluating intuitive insights and to check it out with whatever objective sources are available. Close your intuitive session by thanking the Divine and grounding.

Intuitive Technique #2 for Accessing Helpful Insights on Your Relationships With Others

This technique can help you better understand and enhance your relationship with other people. Meditate for a while to help clear and raise your consciousness. Then focus your attention at your third eye chakra between your eyebrows and up a little. Visualize a blank screen just in front of your third eye. Then bring to your mind the relationship into which you would like to gain insight. On the screen visualize the two of you in a very simple way standing fairly close to each other (it could be like stick figures or cartoonish figures). Ask yourself a question such as "what are the dynamics between us?" Then simply be aware of what you sense about the two figures in your image. Do they seem comfortable standing together? Do they seem to want to move further apart? Is there a peaceful feeling or a frantic feeling or other feeling? Does one have his or her head bent down as if depressed or overburdened? Is one shaking fists as if angry? Is one dancing around as if happy? Is one busy doing something? Is there something else being expressed? When you are ready you may wish to ask, "what is helpful for me to understand about this relationship?" Just be aware of what insights may come to you then or later. Close by sending love or goodwill to the person and the relationship. Thank the Divine and send down roots to the earth to help ground yourself. This may help you understand the people in your life better and improve those relationships. This same technique can be used to help understand the dynamics between two people other than yourself.

Ethics of Intuition

There are ethics to intuition, particularly for people for whom the intuitive insights are quite clear, fairly accurate, and dependable. Please know that even for excellent intuitives or psychics, the insights can be colored by the intuitive person's own feelings. No intuitive person is 100% correct. Any predictions being offered are possibilities or probabilities--not fate. The individual for whom the "reading" is being offered has free will, and it is up to him or her to make choices as to how the life path is to develop. Each of us is in charge of our life and makes our own choices. The valuable thing about a good intuitive "reading" is that it may possibly offer helpful insights. It may help us be a little more aware of things we need to be alert to handling well and making wise decisions concerning. It may point out some valuable options available to us.

Awareness is power, and it is a responsibility. When tuning in to another person intuitively, one is entering that person's private space. It is actually not considered appropriate to tune into someone unless the person asks one to do so, or one needs information in order to make an important decision for one's own life. Sometimes intuitive insights come strong and clear on their own without the intuitive person intentionally "tuning in." Then it would be desirable to treat it as confidential as though you accidentally overhead a private conversation. An intuitive person needs to be respectful and gentle and not even say anything about what he or she senses unless asked. If you intuitively sense that a person needs help in some way and they haven't asked you for help, the best idea might be to simply gently say something like, "How are you doing? Tell me how your day is going." In talking with someone regarding your intuitive insights if they ask you, don't give a person more information than they can handle constructively. Any insights a person may pick up intuitively would ideally be used to gently encourage an individual in a direction that would be helpful for him or her.

Intuition to Support Our Service Work or Career

Some of the great scientists got their breakthroughs for their inventions from intuitive flashes of insights and dreams. Intuition is powerful and can put us in touch with higher levels of consciousness where valuable information can be available for all fields of service and work to help humanity. Intuitive insight and information can be best received by someone who already has experience and skills in the area of knowledge involved. We wouldn't expect a sculptor to receive information for a symphony. We wouldn't expect a poet to receive information for a scientific invention. This is because the person needs to place the intuitive information into a useable frame of reference and with usable technical language, comprehension, and abilities. We can solve a lot of our societal, planetary, and environmental problems by opening to higher intuition. Any information gained by intuitive insight from higher Spiritual levels of consciousness must, of course, be used harmlessly for the highest good of all. Otherwise the well is likely to dry up.

Intuition and Spirituality in Prehistory and Moving Into Today

I encourage you to consider what is presented in the following paragraphs and in some other parts of this book as interesting ideas for you to think about. If some of the concepts are new to you, don't feel that you need to immediately accept or reject them. Just perhaps allow them to be interesting ideas to reflect on. Everyone doesn't have to believe the same thing. It is important that your core beliefs grow gradually from within your heart and soul. At the same time it is valuable to keep in mind that sometimes beliefs may expand or transform somewhat due to life experiences and personal growth. Sometimes there may be ideas that can help you feel and live freer, and may help explain some of what you've perhaps been beginning to feel inside.

Humanity developed higher intuition to a very great degree in previous periods of planetary history. There were periods of very high advanced culture long before what is currently considered recorded history. The Atlantis civilization was very real. It lasted for thousands of years and was far more advanced scientifically in some ways than our present civilization. There was great good accomplished by many during the times of

Atlantis, but there was great abuse of power by others. Leaders must be good stewards and caretakers of this precious planet and its people. It cannot just be about lust for power and wealth. So about 10,000 B.C. the continent of Atlantis sank into the Atlantic Ocean through a series of massive earth quakes. Small parts of the original Atlantis still protrude above the Atlantic Ocean here and there, but the original advanced culture was lost. Some of the information was preserved and is resurfacing.

Now is a period of decision for planet Earth and its people. Many people are opening to unusually rapid Spiritual growth. Very high Spiritual energies are flooding the planet. People can partake of this gift through meditation, yoga and tai chi practices, churches and synagogues and temples, Spiritual development groups of all kinds, prayer, reading Spiritual books, listening to Spiritually uplifting music, and spending time peacefully out in nature. Additionally, there are certainly other valid approaches that can support Spiritual growth, such as energy healing. All of these approaches are greatly needed and valid at this time to help lift humanity.

The more that we live our lives in harmony with the Divine Qualities and are good stewards of our planet, the more that we can be blessed by the Divine with the gifts of higher Spiritual development. These Spiritual gifts or capacities might be in the form of powerful inspiration for expression in any and all of the creative arts. They might manifest in the field of highly effective natural healing. A person may find that his or her capacity to be an effective helpful leader Spiritually, politically, or in business expands significantly. An individual may become aware on higher and higher levels of consciousness and feel great blissful oneness with the Divine. The possible gifts of higher Spiritual development are as varied as the individuals themselves who seek this growth. Spiritual capacities and power tend to develop a little at a time for specific purposes and to the extent that we use them with wisdom and for the highest good of all. We are all needed to share our Spiritual gifts for the good of our whole human family and our beloved planet. I wish you a fascinating exhilarating adventure of growing wisdom. As you explore this path further, it will bring you ever more into the company of other people who treasure truth and wisdom and the Divine.

Real Life Sharings Regarding The Power Of Wisdom In One's Life

We Can Move Beyond Suffering
~ by William Evans, M.D.

I've been a psychiatrist for thirty-five years, and I have been deeply involved in meditation and Spiritual growth for thirty-eight years. What I'm finding fascinating right now is non-dualistic metaphysics--and what it offers us for clarification of Spiritual truth and for amazing healing. Non-dualistic metaphysics isn't new; it has been handed down through the ages. I feel that it profoundly contributes to our understanding of true forgiveness, Spiritual enlightenment, waking up, and overcoming suffering. We've always been taught by the Spiritual teachers and the different religions that during Spiritual growth something "dies and we are born again," or something is "overcome," or that there is something we need to be "saved" from. It is steadily becoming more clear to me that what we really need to "die to" or be "saved from" is this deeply held, mostly repressed and unconscious, core belief that we are separate from God. That belief, and the consequences of that belief, of being separate from God is the actual cause of all suffering. I am every day more and more accepting the truth that it is impossible to have truly accomplished separation from God--except in our illusions or what we could call our dream of separation from God.

The following is an updated modern story of the parable of the prodigal son (derived from my understanding of the metaphysics of <u>A Course of Miracles</u>). The prodigal son didn't leave home [Oneness with God], but the prodigal son had a thought of "what would it be like to be separate from God?" That thought became real and had seemingly real consequences. The prodigal son fell into a sleep and had a dream that the separation from God, eating of the "tree of good and evil," and the "fruits of duality" actually happened. In the Bible it says that Adam fell asleep and there is no point in the Bible where it says he woke up!

But the prodigal son can and will wake up from the dream and realize that what is not the Will of God could not be true or at least could not have real or eternal effects. We will wake up and realize, because of our Oneness with God, that our will and His Will are shared in Oneness: that is truly the nature of our free Will. That is what the totally Spiritually enlightened individuals in the world wake up to. That is why they experience peace and why they are peace. They have the realization like <u>A Course In Miracles</u> states, "Nothing real can be threatened. Nothing unreal exists." In other words, GOD IS and nothing else is. Spiritual enlightenment occurs with just releasing, dissolving, turning away from and transcending this false "separation consciousness"/ false belief/ limited and imprisoning mind set.

We have this screen in our mind that we project all this seeming reality of "separation consciousness" upon. Our history [his-story] is the story of "Adam's" separation from God--or duality, good and bad, the tree of "good and evil." It is the duality illusion that GOD IS and I am very separate from God as an ego-body-identity. The only True Divine reality is in our Oneness with God as unchanging, eternal, immortal, invulnerable, and all the other Divine qualities. We are afraid of what we think we have done and are literally afraid to go within and "BE SILENT AND KNOW THAT I AM GOD" because if we did so the lower ego identity would dissolve. Ultimately, and in reality, this false separation we have made is impossible and the impossible couldn't have happened except in illusions.

At a woman's prison where I provide some psychiatric services we developed a wellness program in which we have people for whom we are providing extra mental health programming. I was asked to run one of the groups. Most of the women in our prison setting have some history of alcohol abuse and drug abuse. This is often in the context of their history of other abuse. They probably ideally will need ongoing involvement in recovery programs upon release from prison, and the Higher Power is a very important concept within the most successful traditional recovery programs. I made a decision that I would help them have a better understanding of the Higher Power and its great importance in those recovery programs. We discuss what the great Spiritual teachers have said and continue to say about the Higher Power and Higher Self--and that the "perennial Spiritual philosophies" contain the concept of the Higher Self or Higher Power.

I talk to the women about how one's unconscious guilt sets one up for an unconscious pattern of self-sabotaging and self-punishing behavior. Psychology teaches that unconscious guilt demands punishment. Sure enough these women have set themselves up to be punished. They punish themselves with having the wrong people in their lives, by harming themselves with drugs and alcohol, and with being sentenced to prison. In prison they continue to be punished and feel punished. So I help them understand the unconscious problem of guilt that is setting them up for unconsciously sabotaging their lives and therefore unconsciously punishing themselves for unconscious guilt. I help them understand that unconscious guilt can be healed. There are ways of healing the problems in our unconscious mind so that we can break these recurring patterns of self destructiveness and suffering.

Beads On One String

~ Rev. Alta Burnett, Ph.D., Louisville, Kentucky

In January 2009 fifty pilgrims (strangers for the most part) from several different countries traveled together to various sacred sites (Hindu, Buddhist, Muslim, Jain, etc.) in India. Although the journey itself was incredibly arduous and challenging in many ways, by its end we pilgrims realized that we had shared an incredible experience of feeling our oneness with each other, with others we saw, and with all religious traditions, irrespective of our own individual religious faiths. We understood that all life is one, that all religions are one, that the basic message—and messenger—of all religions is one—in short, that the Source of all is One. Within a few months a new international, non-profit organization—Beads On One String—was created.

Beads On One String is "dedicated to the exploration of the unity of all life." Its "abiding interest is in humanity's common endeavor to understand, experience and creatively express the Oneness that lies at the heart of all." This search for unity "is independent of existing traditions yet actively appreciates and connects people from all religions, backgrounds and cultures, sacred and secular." "Through education, pilgrimage, film and media, arts, sciences and companionship," its intention is "to invite opportunities to explore and experience this unity." (Quotes are a full expression of the vision/mission statement for Beads On One String found in "Neti Neti," *International Meher Baba Newsletter* No. 193, Jan. 2012, p. 6.)

Several offerings have been provided since 2009 including a 61-minute documentary DVD of the 2009 pilgrimage; seminars in Germany and Spain; two additional pilgrimages in India; an afternoon pilgrimage to various religious centers in Louisville, Kentucky, USA, and a heartland pilgrimage in the United States. (See Resources Page)

Insightful Ways to Help Heal Adult Learning Blockages (Children, too)

~ by David

What I say to people in my classes is "When you come in this door there is no guilt. This is a guilt free zone. Nothing that happened before today matters. All that matters is that you are here, we're working together, and we're going to understand things in a new way. You can set aside whatever trauma there is out there, and let that get quiet. We're going to understand things together." I get to experience that with people sometimes one-on-one and sometimes in a group. Every time it is just amazing. It is different every single time.

I teach adult education math mostly. What I'm sharing can apply to other fields of study also. One of the things that I've discovered is helpful for my classes is moving the furniture around and putting the people face-to-face instead of having their backs to each other like in a traditional classroom setting. It completely changes the dynamics of things. People automatically start opening up and trusting each other. There is something about when people are at the same level height-wise and facing each other. It's O.K.--it's not confrontational --it's good!! It's what I think has to happen to learn. You have to open up to learn, you have to trust other people, and that's a vehicle for helping it happen. You open up in a different way even if you're a quiet person who ordinarily doesn't trust other people. You've maybe been hurt in some way by other people. Everybody that I have worked with has opened up. People who previously didn't respond very well, or just didn't pay attention--those people shift, too. In this kind of setting they participate more, they are part of a group.

I teach math, and so many people have horrible memories about math. There's so much fear. Many times when I get into certain aspects of math, I see some people just blank out. They'll just totally zone out. If I can talk with them one-on-one, I explore with them what they are afraid of. It can be just gut wrenching horrible things that happened to them regarding math. Often they don't recognize--they don't even know what is going on inside when they freeze. All they know is that they just can't do it--at least that is what they say. When I talk with them a little bit they realize that when they were in third grade this thing happened, or when they were in fifth grade. Sometime in the past something happened, they were doing great until then-- but all of a sudden it was slam! It's like their brain shut down! I feel like I'm pretty good at slowing down and taking a different perspective or a different way when someone doesn't understand something. I show or model something in different way.

There are some times when no matter how many ways I explain something, I'm just not getting through. I think that it's because there is a "wall" of emotional trauma or panic. In panic the rational and intuitive parts of the brain shut down, and the more primitive parts of the brain take over. All of us get into a panic now and then about even little things. My thing is finding my car keys. I have to go somewhere and I may go into a panic because I can't find my keys. We can't mentally understand things clearly when we're in survival panic mode. The mind is racing and the body feels like it's struggling to survive. Everything else goes out the window. No math problems or anything linear or logical can survive as long as we're in a panic. We have to relax and get to that calm place. When we do get to that calm place, then we can think more clearly and learn more easily.

One good way of getting to that calm place is the Emotional Freedom Technique (E.F.T.) where you tap gently on different acupressure points on your head, shoulders, and hands. This can help you balance in peace and enhance clarity for learning. (See Resources Page.)

Note from Joyce: Simply being aware of your breath and focusing in your heart center can be very calming, too. Parts or all of David's ideas can also be very helpful with children who struggle to learn.

A Young Man Shares His Wisdom

~ Anonymous

When I was younger, I felt that I was unnoticeable. I wasn't liked or hated. When someone hates you, they have to notice you to hate you. When I was fifteen I discovered Buddhism. Then I realized I was selfish. Before I wanted the people around me to think the way I think and like what I liked. I was trying to get my friends to talk with me about science, history, and things like that. They just wanted to talk about cars and sports, and I wasn't really a big fan of those. Now I hang around with people who like to talk with me about things I'm interested in--like different belief systems, science, and history. Since I've found people with whom I can share who I really am, I'm happier. I feel that I've made some soul growth.

Woman Reaches To Highest Good
Original art by Joyce J.C. Gerrish

WORKBOOK: Enrichment Experiences For Enhancing Wisdom In Your Life

Enjoy the adventure of exploring these enrichment experiences on your own--or gather a few friends to share the journey with you. Be inspired by the audio meditation and soul song for this chapter. Reflect on some of the stimulating ideas and questions.

Questions For Reflection and Discussion

Reflection, discussion, journal writing, expressing your feelings in drawings or other creative ways can all be very valuable to help you delve into these questions in truly meaningful and relevant ways. Before focusing on the questions, you may wish to meditate with the twelve minute audio or transcribed meditation--and/or listen to the soul song "Wisdom's Pearl."

1. What have you learned in this lifetime so far that you consider guiding wisdom for your life?

2. What do you consider one of the wisest decisions that you made in this life? What influenced you to make that decision?

3. When you need to make an important decision, how do you approach it? Do you make the decision based on your emotional response? Do you think it through carefully and do research on it? Do you talk to people you trust and who you feel are particularly knowledgeable on the issues involved? What seems to work best for you?

Action Suggestions To Enhance Wisdom In Your Life

1. Who do you consider the wisest person you know? Who is someone who seems to move through life making decisions that work out well--and finding life fulfilling? Would you like to spend time with that person hearing about his or her philosophy of life and approaches to decision making? This might entail meeting for lunch, taking a walk together, or taking a class with the person-- depending on your relationship.

2. What would you like to contribute to your community that would support rational and wise behavior? This could be as simple as volunteering at the local library in some way. It could be tutoring students. It could be helping on election days. It takes all of us together to foster wise behavior.

3. Are you doing something in your life that you feel is not really wise for your highest good or in your best interest? How do you feel about that? Do you feel ready to change that? It is not always easy to change, but sometimes taking the first step can start you on the healing journey to restoring balance. Would it help to find a group such as a Twelve Step Program or a church or a support group of some sort to help you?

Audio "Meditation To Enhance Your Experience of The Divine Qualities," With Focus on Wisdom

Pray to the Divine to bless your meditation and enhance Divine Wisdom in your life. With this audio you'll be guided to sense yourself immersed in the uplifting clear energy of Divine Wisdom. Choose one or more of the following affirmations (or something similar) that feels particularly helpful for affirming during the meditation. Before transferring to the website to listen to the meditation, write down the wisdom affirmation(s) you choose and the helpful color yellow. Later, put the affirmation(s) someplace where you'll see it daily and be reminded to affirm it for a minute or two several times a day.

◆ I stay calm and centered so I can act wisely.

◆ In meditation I access the wisdom of the higher levels of my consciousness.

◆ I choose to recognize and stay clear of illusions.

◆ In quiet moments I am more aware of my intuitive insights.

Helpful color to visualize when meditating on Wisdom: Yellow

I encourage you to enjoy this meditation when you wish to support wisdom in your life. Connect to SecretsofWisdom.net to listen to the twelve-minute audio "Meditation to Enhance Your Experience of the Divine Qualities," with focus on Wisdom.

(Also, see transcribed version of this meditation at end of this chapter.)

Uplifting Audio Soul Song: "Wisdom's Pearl"

Consider it a prayer in song for enhancing Divine Wisdom within yourself. The words are:

Wisdom is the precious pearl in the sea of life.

I swim the cresting waves in my search for truth.

Dive deep, dive deep my soul in the sea of life.

Dive deep, dive deep, my soul

For the precious wisdom's pearl,

For the precious wisdom's pearl.

You may wish to visit SecretsofWisdom.net where you can listen to the audio: "Wisdom's Pearl." As you sing or listen to it, just feel yourself beginning to let go of distractions and relax into the clear, uplifting experience of Divine Wisdom. Close your eyes and really sense it helping to bring you into a calm, peaceful alert feeling.

Transcribed Version of Meditation To Enhance Your Experience of Divine Wisdom

If possible, listen to some relaxing nonverbal music. Say a short prayer calling on the Divine to bless your meditation and enhance wisdom in your life.

Visualize yourself in a ball of light to help strengthen your energy field.

Become aware of and follow your breath as it gently flows in and out at its own pace.

To help yourself feel grounded and prevent possibly feeling spacey, imagine yourself as a large tree sending powerful roots deep into the earth.

As you breathe in through your nose, imagine you are breathing up the strength of the earth into your body.

For a couple of minutes listen to the relaxing music as you breathe in light into your being.

Next visualize glowing yellow light like sunshine or a yellow flower.

Periodically as you breathe in through your nose, imagine that you are breathing in glowing yellow light.

Next breathe in through your nose and out your mouth for about a minute VERY GENTLY.

Now, very gently breathe in through your mouth and out your nose for about a minute.

Then extra gently breathe in and out through your mouth for a minute or so.

Now return to breathing in and out your nose.

As you breathe in through your nose, visualize you are breathing in yellow light into your whole being.

As you breathe out your nose, periodically say one or two of the following (or similar) affirmations silently.

◆ I stay calm and centered so I can act wisely.

◆ In meditation, I access the wisdom of the higher levels of my consciousness.

◆ I choose to recognize and stay clear of illusions.

◆ In quiet moments I am more aware of my intuitive insights.

Pray for support in helping you to grow in wisdom.

Continue in that manner for a few minutes or as long as you wish.

Conclude by thanking the Divine and sending down roots to Mother Earth for stability and grounding.

Enjoy this meditation when you wish to enhance Wisdom in your life. Write the affirmation(s) you choose and put it someplace where you'll see it several times a day and be reminded to affirm it for a minute or two.

Peace.

Tree of Life
Original art by Joyce J.C. Gerrish

Chapter Thirteen

THE BLESSINGS OF HARMONY
Enhancing Divine Harmony In Your Life

Enjoy listening to or singing along with this harmonious soul song I've composed and sung "*Hope Flows.*" Please visit SecretsofWisdom.net to hear "*Hope Flows,*" while viewing the full color design "Man and Woman Dance in Harmony with Nature and Luminous Bird."

Harmony With Nature
~ Sharing from K.C.

The land is alive and is filled with living creatures. I feel good when I'm close to nature, it gives me peace. Living in harmony with the land and with nature is Spiritually uplifting to me. I love animals a great deal. It is important to me to encourage my grandchildren to love and respect animals, nature, and the Earth. We're dependent on the harmony between all of us.

With all these weather extremes, I think Mother Earth is trying to show us that we need to live more in harmony with her and all the other species on the Earth. We've created imbalances in our climate with the "greenhouse effect" and the warming trend melting the ice caps of the North and South Poles. We're polluting our waters with pesticides. We're polluting the air with smokestack releases from factories. Mother Earth is hurting and needs to re-balance herself.

For me it is important to live by water. I live by a beautiful small river. Walking my dogs along the river every day is a very nice part of my life--such a pleasure. When my husband and I bought our home, it wasn't the house itself that attracted us; it was the land and the river running by it. It's a truly beautiful little river with its boulders and rocks of all sizes--the water flows and cascades around the rocks. It feeds my soul. I love large rivers, too. When I visit a river, it's like visiting a friend. The Earth also nourishes me as I walk--as do the plants, animals, earth, gentle winds, and the sun. (End of sharing from K.C.)

Harmony Between Humanity and Animals, Plants, and the Earth

Harmony on earth involves not only harmony between people, but also harmony between humanity and the plant kingdom, the animal kingdom, and the mineral kingdom. It includes honoring the earth, the water, the fire, and the air. Some people seem to feel that it is O.K. to treat the planet anyway they choose. Humans are causing disruption on the planet. This is very sad. To some extent this may be caused by some people not being truly conscious of the long range or even short range effect of what they are doing. God created this awesome planet Earth in all its tremendous natural diversity and complex ecological interdependence. All aspects of creation have a right to thrive in harmony together. The deep forests and woodlands, meadows, hills and mountains, streams and rivers are priceless treasures and need to be preserved and restored. I feel that part of humanity's role now and in the future is to somehow rethink and heal its relationship with the different kingdoms of nature. We are family.

If we could possibly comprehend the dedicated devotion, purity and love of the plant kingdom in its profound service to planet Earth and humanity, we would be overwhelmed with appreciation and awe. Think of the extraordinary beauty and gifts of the flowers and all the lovely plants. The vegetables, fruits, grains, and beans give us delicious food. Even many of the plants we consider weeds are medicinal--such as dandelion.

We Are Dependent on The Trees For Every Breath We Take--Trees Transform the Carbon Dioxide We Exhale Into the Oxygen We Inhale

The trees are our precious allies. It is extremely important that we be grateful for the extraordinary number of crucial gifts the trees provide for humanity and for the planet. They take the carbon dioxide we exhale with our breath and transform it into oxygen for us to breathe in. What a miraculous gift! They create shade to cool us in the summer. They give us wood to create homes to protect us from the rain, cold weather, and from harm. They hold the soil from eroding and washing away. They give us nuts and fruits. Their majestic beauty is an extraordinary blessing. The trees are of great importance to our survival as a species, yet the forests and jungles around the planet keep being destroyed at an alarming rate.

Ideally the trees are given time to reseed and replace themselves after they are cut down. It doesn't work to cut down trees at a faster pace than they can reseed and replenish. Also, it is crucial to not cut down all the trees (clear cut) in any area. Common sense needs to be practiced here. When I lived surrounded by woods for many years, I and friends used to enjoy hiking all around. It was so sad and unnecessary to find acres of beautiful woods suddenly barren and the small animals traumatized because of having lost their homes. The trees can be harvested through thinning the woods by selectively cutting down some trees but not all. This can leave the balance of nature and the plant life and animal habitat more intact. Wise thinning can actually enhance the growth of the remaining trees by giving them more space to spread their limbs. We thank the awesome trees and all the plants.

Likewise, when we really pause to consider the massive gifts to us from the animal kingdom--we are certainly flooded with deepest appreciation for the mammals, birds, fish, and reptiles, amphibians, and all. Even the insects have their absolutely essential roles to perform, such as the bees pollinating the blossoms and the worms aerating the soil. Some of these animals we love as pets, some give us milk and wool, some help us do our work, and some give of their lives for our food. Some inspire our awe and respect as they live their natural lives in the wilds, and some contribute to our lives and the welfare of the planet in ways we don't yet understand, or only understand partially. Our complex relationship with animals is discussed in more depth shortly.

All Species of Animals and Plants Exist for a Reason

All the kingdoms of nature and all the species are there for a reason and have different important purposes and energies. They support each other and the balance of the whole. People can easily distort that delicate balance with technology. What is harmful to the balance of nature is when one species, such as humanity, overtakes the boundaries of another and leaves it devastated and unable to meet its needs to thrive as a species. Humility is desperately needed on the part of humanity in regard to the rest of the family of planet Earth. Respect and harmony within the family of Earth have been eroded and need to be restored.

The Native Americans, when they were still living in their natural state before they were sent into reservations, lived in harmony with Mother Nature and all aspects of creation. They prayed to the Great Spirit/ Creator and gave thanks for every part of creation with which they interacted. They used only what they truly needed and lived simply. Every act was taken with an awareness of how it would affect seven generations to come and how it would affect all the aspects of creation. This is a totally different approach than is pursued today by a high percentage of people in developed nations. Many live with no real thought for the Sacred natural balance of God's creation or for the welfare of generations to come. Often the only thought is for the desire of the moment.

On farms we don't need to poison our earth in order to keep the insects in check and grow abundant food. The organic farmers are demonstrating this in stunning ways. Heavy use of chemical pesticides has happened increasingly since the 1950s. But now people are gradually becoming aware of what has been happening to their food sources. More and more people are realizing the great importance of organically grown foods and are buying it. As more and more people are buying it, the prices are coming down through mass marketing. Even some huge conventional supermarkets are carrying large amounts of organically grown foods now. This is very heartening. This is healthier for us-- it is better for the soil to not have all those pesticides in it, and it is better for water that runs off the fields into streams and then into lakes and into our drinking water. It is healthier for the farm workers to not be immersed in all those pesticides.

Change is gradually taking place. More awakened people are beginning to move back into power here and there. I pray that stewardship will be taken more seriously again. May we each do our part to help rebuild the Sacred balance of creation on our planet. I believe that the blessings of God are pouring in to support the healing process as we rebuild harmony and balance within our family of Earth.

The Harmony Enhancing Native American Ceremony of the "Medicine Wheel"

The Native Americans have an inspiring ceremony called the Medicine Wheel. A group creates, on the ground, a circle which symbolizes Earth and the surrounding Heavens. This circle can be as large as thirty feet or more, or it can be fairly small. In the center is placed a special stone to symbolize Great Spirit/ Creator. One at a time the participants say a prayer and place a stone within the circle to symbolize some aspect of creation and its harmony within the whole. These would include the directions of the North, South, East, and West. Stones would be placed for humanity, different animal and plant species, and many more. There are heartfelt chants, prayers, and stylized dances throughout the ceremony. I love the Medicine Wheel ceremony. Placing stones for all of these within the Sacred circle is a powerful direct experience of the oneness and harmony of all creation. It is a very Sacred and special ceremony that creates beautiful uplifting energy. If you have the opportunity to attend one of these, I believe that you will find it a very beneficial experience.

It is extraordinarily important for people to spend time in nature. I feel that the need is embedded in our DNA to be out embraced by the natural landscape. It is crucial for us to feel the sun and the breeze, to sit by bodies of water, and to experience deeply our relationship with the trees and plants and animals. We are all the family of planet Earth.

The following valuable ideas and techniques will truly help anyone to have a fascinating experience observing and listening to birds and small animals up close in nature. When we have nurturing personal experiences with nature, it enhances our desire to protect all this treasure.

How to Observe Animals and Birds Up Close in the Woods

~ by Darrel Joy

To truly experience and enjoy nature, being quiet makes all the difference in the world. People who are talking scare the birds and animals away. The conversation gets picked up by the birds, and they immediately send out alarm sounds to cause the other birds and animals to move away or hide. Secondly, to enjoy seeing animals and birds, it helps to be still. There are various gradations of being still. You may wish to sit on a log somewhere away from all the people trails. Animals don't expect you when you are quiet and still.

The third thing is to be in a meditative state of mind. There is something about the thoughts and conversations that you may have within yourself--they put out a signal that the animals can detect. They may not know what it means, but they sense "something" is coming from that direction. They look over and there you are and they will evade you. If you are keeping your mind quiet, that doesn't happen. My way of silencing my internal dialogue is to turn into a sensory sponge and constantly absorb everything I see and hear--soaking in everything going on around me and not sending anything out.

Eye contact will make any animal, such as deer, pretty nervous. It is better to observe through your side wide angle vision and not look directly at the animals--and squint slightly to hide the whites of your eyes. Smiling with your teeth showing can make animals in nature nervous because they think you want to eat them.

When I go out into the woods, I wear earth tone colors to not attract attention to myself. I take a little gift like almonds or trail mix to attract the animals and birds. I may put a nut on a log maybe ten feet ahead of where I am sitting. These suggestions can enhance your contact and enjoyment observing birds and animals in nature. If you want to help protect animals and nature, you may wish to contact nature preservation groups.

(See Resources Page for websites concerning nature preservation, bird watching, and wilderness groups. - - End of sharing by Darrel Joy.)

Note from Joyce: Some of these ideas can be helpful even in your own yard.

Intuitive Communication With Animals

A lot of us are fairly intuitive or have friends who are. It is a normal human capacity which I feel will be developing for more and more people over time. Many animal species are quite intelligent and intuitive, as we all know. Most of us have probably known a dog or cat or other animal who amazed us with displays of intelligence and their capacity to communicate. Animals in the forests and in the ocean are intelligent, too. It is important not to assume they don't know, in their own way, what is going on.

I had a wonderful experience of oneness with the animal kingdom when I went on a "whale watch" boat ride off the coast of Massachusetts. I found the whales very communicative. We had been out to sea only a short time when whales came around. I understand that on many whale watches people are happy if they see one or two whales at a far distance. Several whales circled around our boat happily. Because I am very intuitive I could easily "hear" them telepathically communicating hello and inviting us to come in and swim with them. Over and over they jumped very high up out of the water as if dancing. I communicated friendly greetings. It felt very loving all around. They stayed for over forty-five minutes. They were so close I could smell their breath, and we got liberally sprayed by their splashing water. Two men in a small sailboat eagerly came close even through their boat was smaller than any of the whales. No one was afraid; we were filled with joy and wonder!

When I watch Seeing Eye dogs and other dogs that help humans with "special needs," it always touches my heart deeply. I love to observe their gentle patient obviously intelligent compassionate ways. I took care of a cockatiel bird for a year that belonged to a relative that was out of the country at the time. When I sang and played the guitar, the bird used to tap enthusiastically on the kitchen table very much in time with the rhythm. We often sang and "talked" back and forth at length. Watching films of elephant families gently living together in the wild is tender beyond belief. You could probably tell me many amazing and heartwarming animal stories.

Humane Treatment is Crucial for Animals Raised for Human Consumption

Harmony between the humans, animals, birds, and other creatures is clearly a complicated matter. I've been either completely vegan or close to it for about thirty-five years. Being a vegetarian or vegan needs to be a very personal decision. The truth is that many animals eat each other in nature; I can't pretend that animals are mostly gentle with each other. Some are, some aren't. Apparently checks and balances are needed to keep some species of animals from over populating their hunting and feeding territories. What is important is that animals in the wild have a natural fairly good life while they are alive. They can move and run in ways that feel good to them. They can create dens and nests and homes that please them. They can find food that their bodies can digest well. The chickens can flap their wings and find worms and other delicious morsels as they peck in the earth. The turkeys can scurry around in the woods with their friends. They can look up and see the sky and breathe fresh air.

What is tragic is when animals that are intended for human consumption are kept in extremely limited cramped spaces, abused, and live a life of suffering. To save money, many "farm factories" that raise the animals often feed them inexpensive subsidized foods that are totally inappropriate for the animals' digestive systems. In the past on small farms cattle, pigs, and chickens tended to have a fairly content natural life until the ones that were intended to be eaten were butchered. There are humane farms today from which meat and poultry can be purchased. If you wish, check with your local grocery store or natural food store and see if they carry humanely raised beef, pork, and poultry that weren't fed hormones or antibiotics and were allowed to be out on the land somewhat naturally. This is becoming available now even in some large conventional supermarkets. It's valuable to look for it and inquire about it.

Enjoying Some Delicious Vegetarian Meals Each Week Can be a Delightful Adventure!

It is worth exploring delicious vegetarian alternatives to meat and poultry. A lot of people decide to eat less animal protein and then enjoy vegetarian dishes some of the time. It can be a journey of discovering new taste treats! There are many countries around the world, such as Greece and India, that have delicious vegetarian cuisine that one can sample. Good plant sources of protein include combining beans with whole grains or seeds--in all their multitude of variations. There are endless ways these can be prepared. Dairy products are, of course, available if one isn't lactose intolerant. It requires at least seven times as much plant food to feed cattle until they are fully grown and then consumed by humans as meat--compared to people eating protein-rich plant food to begin with. People eating less meat and more plant foods can mean that there is much more food to go around for everyone--and it depletes the soil less. It is a win-win situation! If one is making dietary changes, it is important to be somewhat gradual and to first consult one's health care practitioner.

Harmonious Relations Between Humans

Let's now shift our exploration to a focus on harmonious relations between humans. It's not always easy to achieve that harmony, but I believe that is the goal. There are so many personality dynamics that can seem to interfere with smooth mutually beneficial interactions.

Each aspect of creation has its own blueprint and plan, to use inadequate words to describe something so profound. With the guidance of Divine ones, each human soul chooses a mission before being born into a life. Once in the physical body he or she very often loses touch with the specifics (or even generalities) of the soul plan for that life. This is where guardian angels come in. The guardian angels do what they can to influence an individual to follow the soul plan. That can be a challenge when a person is busy with the responsibilities and diversions of life on earth. It is only when one is in a very clear state of consciousness such as during higher meditation, prayer, or when feeling very peaceful and uplifted that he or she can hopefully be impressed with needed guidance and inspiration. Sometimes dreams can be helpful in that respect.

If every person and every aspect of creation follows the Divine Plan or soul mission, then all creation will blend in perfect harmony. That is the essence of harmony--following the Divine Plan or soul mission as closely as possible. The Divine Plan for everyone and everything is held in Heaven in what is called the Akashic Records, along with information on everything else. It is like Divine memory. This is Sacred information that is held in the subtle planes of reality in a manner perhaps slightly similar to computer memory (except this has nothing to do with computers). Information can be accessed from the Akashic Records by highly developed intuitives. Readings with excellent intuitives can sometimes be helpful for insights regarding life purpose. Any readings need to be very carefully evaluated in light of what one senses in one's own heart and soul. One should put foremost trust in what one senses within one's own inner knowing, and what feels helpful and meaningful in one's own life.

In regard to pursuing the soul mission/life purpose, people on earth are often greatly subjected to emotional (astral) illusions. These illusions can be confusing or misleading when people are really caught up in them. It is difficult for the soul purpose or life in general to be understood in its true reality when people are in that state. The problem is that a great many people are caught up in astral illusions. That is a major problem regarding creating true harmony on planet Earth at this time.

Given the reality that much of Earth does not currently exist in a state of harmony, how can you enhance harmony as much as possible in your life? It is very important to give yourself quiet time to be still and connect to the higher Sacred levels of your consciousness and the Divine. This can help you have a clearer perception of the true nature of reality and your life purpose. Please remember that you have very special capacities which are your precious gift to enjoy and share with the people and life about you.

The People Around You in Your Life are There for A Reason

In regard to experiencing harmony with others, the people around you in your life are there for a reason. You have probably agreed as souls before you were born to help and support each other in your life journeys. This is a Sacred trust and is important to honor it in some way, if possible. But if someone close to you or related to you has gotten off the path and is not behaving appropriately, you may need to help them through tough love. In that case you can pray for them and set an example of upright responsible living. It is crucial to not allow anyone to pull you down no matter how much you love them. You can't help your loved ones unless you keep yourself strong and Spiritually uplifted through prayer or meditation and balanced wholesome living. That is particularly important to keep in mind at this time of unusually rapid change and transformation for many.

A good degree of clarity is needed before we can achieve true awareness of our soul mission and step into it fully. To achieve that clarity, we may need to do some healing of old emotional traumas and aura blockages. That process was described in the chapters "Healing Your Heart With Forgiveness," "Activating the Energies of Your Aura," and "Walking the Path of Wellness." As we proceed with that healing, we can walk our soul path more and more effectively and compassionately. It is as each of us is walking our soul mission that all together we can bring to greater fruition the upliftment and healing of our own life, our communities and cities, and planet Earth. This is a noble purpose beyond belief. As we heal our planet, we heal ourselves; as we heal ourselves, we also heal our planet. The connection between humans and the planet is symbiotic.

The Road Ahead to Greater Harmony

No longer do violence and greed need to reign on our planet. It is time that those backward behaviors are over. The clock is ticking and has moved on. The Spiritual realms are holding the template of Spiritualization for planet Earth and all its people. I feel that unprecedented assistance is being extended to each of us to lift up out of limitation and to embrace Spiritual wholeness. This is a period of great joy and celebration because this opportunity of moving forward to the next step of our higher good is here for all of us. That doesn't make it easy, but the rewards of success are tremendous for everyone. We are each being called to do our part to create a better, more just, loving, and equitable life for everyone. Our sense of accomplishment needs to come from seeing everyone's needs met, not just our own. Our delight needs to come from seeing everyone developing and expressing their talents, wisdom, and skills to contribute to the whole. We are all in this together to step into the fuller potentials for ourselves and all life around us. May we daily pray to God to bless ourselves and everyone with enhanced Divine Harmony, Divine Peace, Divine Love, Divine Healing, Divine Illumination, and all the Divine Qualities.

Harmony Through Living Close to the Land

~ by Marjorie Morningstar

Now that I have raised my three sons, I have more time to enjoy living very much in harmony with nature. I'm very connected to the seasons and Mother Nature. In the spring I start planting. I plant flowers and vegetables. I watch my goats give birth in the spring. The baby goats have such joy of life. It gives me joy being with them. Our cattle give birth throughout the year. We have chickens that lay eggs.

The summer is the time of the hot sun. I tend my gardens. I get in my lake and swim in the water. I enjoy the harvest from what was planted in the spring. In the fall--that is the time when I really start bringing in foods grown. I particularly love tomatoes, zucchini and corn. The harvest lasts a long time. Some of it I freeze.

In the winter I go out and feed my animals hay. Then I contemplate about life and the cosmos and where everyone fits in with this--and where I fit in. Every day is a very Spiritual day, and depending on what season it is--it is a different type of Spirituality for me.

I have a Medicine Wheel on the hill of my land. It is a circle of stones about twenty feet across with eight spokes. It has special crystals and stones from my travels and from the land here. My horses like to graze there; they keep everything nicely trimmed and manicured for the Medicine Wheel. I consider them the "guardians" of the Medicine Wheel. We're very connected.

We have milk, eggs, and meat from the land. We have all the vegetables that we grow, and fruit trees and berries. Our spring water comes down from the hill and goes into a holding tank where it is pumped up to the house for our drinking water. The rest of the water goes out to the lake. There are turtles and fish in the lake. Geese and ducks come during the winter. Cranes come in the summer.

It gives me joy to peacefully take care of and enjoy all this. I feel like I live in the Garden of Eden. I also enjoy my job working as a naturalist at a state park--which ties together teaching people about nature and sustainability. (End of sharing by Marjorie Morningstar)

Holding Hands Around the World
Original art by Joyce J.C. Gerrish

WORKBOOK: Enrichment Experiences For Enhancing Harmony In Your Life

Enjoy the adventure of exploring these enrichment experiences on your own--or gather a few friends to share the journey with you. Be inspired by the audio meditation and soul song for this chapter. Reflect on some of the stimulating ideas and questions.

Questions For Reflection And Discussion

Reflection, discussion, journal writing, expressing your feelings in drawings or other creative ways can all be very valuable to help you delve into these questions in truly meaningful and relevant ways. Before focusing on the questions, you may wish to meditate with the twelve-minute audio or transcribed meditation for harmony--and/or listen to the soul song *"Hope Flows."*

1. What is a situation in your life where you may be experiencing some lack of harmony? What are the dynamics of the situation and how would you like to see them resolved? What do you realistically feel would be helpful to bring greater harmony? (After you do some real reflection, discussion or journal writing, see Action suggestion #1.)

2. Do you feel that you help support harmony in group situations, or do you feel that you perhaps sometimes contribute to lack of harmony? What are your insights on the reasons that you contribute to group harmony or group lack of harmony?

3. There are times when speaking out for what one senses is important truth may appear to be causing lack of harmony because some group members may seem to have vested interests in the status-quo--even though current group needs aren't being met very well. How do you feel about

that dichotomy of the importance of maintaining harmony--and the need to help a group move forward in a positive way and stay relevant? How do you feel that can be bridged?

4. Do you regularly spend time outdoors enjoying and appreciating nature? What are some of your favorite memories of being out immersed in nature? Being in nature is not only fun and wholesome, it helps build and maintain a strong desire to protect it.

5. What are your feelings about living in harmony with the earth? How do you feel about avoiding pesticides in the soil and in your food by buying or growing organically grown food? How do you feel about buying recycled paper products (or paper made from materials such as sugar cane husks) to help avoid cutting down so many trees? How do you feel about other steps to support the ecological movement?

Action Suggestions For Enhancing Divine Harmony In Your Life

1. What would you feel ready to do to help bring harmony into the situation you may have described in Journal Writing Suggestion #1 above? It's O.K. to begin with a small step and allow it to heal gradually. You may wish to begin by sending the feeling of love to the person or persons on a regular basis. Visualize or look at a picture of the person and send the feeling (and energy) of love from your heart center. People will sense that goodwill on a subconscious or Spiritual level and may be more responsive to harmonious relations. If it doesn't soften the attitudes of the other person or persons, it will probably help you relax somewhat about the situation. This could start a thawing of the situation into a more harmonious flow.

2. What do you feel ready to do to enhance your expression of harmony with the Earth? Maybe you already do a lot, and that is wonderful whatever that may be. The Earth is your wonderful home and needs your help. Every species of plants and animals are Sacred and created by God. What is something specific you can do to protect them and their habitat? This might be as simple as voting for politicians who support environmental protection. What else comes to your mind? Volunteer at a nature center? Whatever love you extend to nature will return to you multiplied greatly.

3. Is there a group situation of which you are a part where there is disharmony? How can you be an influence for enhancing harmony in the group? Sometimes this can be done very quietly without anyone particularly even noticing. It may be that talking gently with some of the key people and helping them to release steam and to consider alternative ideas even a little--can really help. Opening a group discussion where members can listen to each other quietly can help. Having someone as the moderator to oversee that only one person speaks at a time is valuable. The Native Americans often used a talking stick which was passed around. Only the person holding the stick could speak.

Audio "Meditation to Enhance Your Experience of The Divine Qualities," With Focus on Harmony

Pray to the Divine to bless your meditation and enhance Divine Harmony in your life. Choose one or more of the following affirmations (or something similar) that feels particularly helpful to you for affirming during the meditation. Before transferring to the website to listen to the meditation, write down the affirmation(s) you choose and the color magenta. Later, place the affirmation(s) where you'll see it daily and be reminded to affirm it for a minute or two several times a day.

◆ I treat the earth, water, air, animals, and plants with great respect.

◆ I choose to live in harmony with those around me.

◆ In every action I consider the welfare of seven generations to come.

◆ I choose to be a good steward of Mother Earth.

I encourage you to enjoy this meditation when you wish to support harmony in your life. Connect to SecretsofWisdom.net to listen to the twelve-minute audio "Meditation to Enhance Your Experience of the Divine Qualities," with focus on Harmony.

(Also, see transcribed version of that meditation at the end of this chapter.)

Uplifting Audio Soul Song: *"Hope Flows"*

~ by Joyce

Consider it a prayer in song for enhancing Harmony within yourself, with the people around you, and with all life. The words are:

Hope flows, Hope flows from heart to heart.

I open my heart, hope flows. I open my heart, hope flows.

Let someone know how much you care.

Let someone know how much you care.

As you chant it or listen to it, feel yourself relax and begin to flow with it. Close your eyes and really sense it helping to bring you into a warm uplifted feeling of peaceful Harmony. Connect to the website SecretsofWisdom.net to listen to "Hope Flows."

Transcribed Version of Meditation To Enhance Your Experience of Divine Harmony

If possible, listen to some relaxing nonverbal music. Say a short prayer asking the Divine to bless your meditation and enhance Divine Harmony in your life.

Visualize yourself in a ball of Light to help strengthen your energy field.

Lift your consciousness and feel yourself one with the higher levels of your consciousness (your Higher Self).

Become aware of and follow your breath as it gently flows in and out your nose at its own relaxed pace.

Imagine sending down roots deep into the earth to help you feel grounded and prevent possibly feeling spacey.

As you breathe in through your nose, imagine you are breathing the strength of the earth up into your body. For a few minutes listen to the relaxing music.

Visualize magenta, like a pinkish purple.

As you breathe in your nose, imagine that you are breathing glowing magenta light into your whole being.

Silently pray to the Divine that your life be uplifted and blessed with Divine Harmony.

191

Next breathe in your nose and out your mouth for about a minute VERY GENTLY.

Now, very gently breathe in your mouth and out your nose for about a minute.

Then extra gently breathe in and out your mouth for a minute or so.

Now return to breathing in and out your nose.

As you breathe in through your nose, imagine you are breathing in glowing magenta into your whole being.

As you breathe out your nose, periodically say one or two of the following affirmations (or something similar) silently.

- ◆ I treat the earth, water, air, animals, and plants with great respect.
- ◆ I choose to live in harmony with those around me.
- ◆ In every action I consider the welfare of seven generations to come.
- ◆ I choose to be a good steward of Mother Earth.

Continue in that manner for a few minutes or as long as you wish.

Conclude by thanking the Divine and sending down roots to Mother Earth for stability and grounding.

Write down the affirmation(s) you choose and place it where you'll see it several times a day and be reminded to affirm it for a minute or two.

Enjoy this meditation anytime you wish to support Divine Harmony in your life.

Peace

Angel Flies Free
Original art by Joyce J.C. Gerrish

Chapter Fourteen

FREEDOM TO EXPLORE
YOUR MAGNIFICENCE

Enhancing Divine Freedom in Your Life

Enjoy listening to or sing along with this uplifting soul song I've composed and sung, "*My Spirit Flies Free*." You may wish to visit SecretsofWisdom.net where you can listen to the soul song audio and simultaneously gaze at the full color design, "Galloping Horse Symbolizes Freedom."

Freedom Supports Each of Us to Be Who We Truly Are! The Great Adventure!

Freedom is a precious gift beyond compare. It is crucial that we not let anyone try to take away our freedom. We each have our natural style of how we wish to live our life. Frequently during the past and now in the present people in many countries are controlled and do not have the freedom to live their lives in the manner of their choice. What is freedom? Freedom is the respect we hold for each other to not interfere in another person's natural wholesome development as long as it isn't harming others or breaking a law. Each of us is like a melody. This melody needs to be nurtured and given space. If it is seriously tampered with it can become flat and off key. Only each of us can sense for ourself how our melody is meant to develop. How tragic if the melody is cut off and distorted and not allowed to evolve naturally in its own beauty and power. No one else can sing our unique melody; if they tried it would not ring true for them. Freedom supports each of us to be who we truly are.

In a melody there are periods of rest and periods of active moving forward. The periods of pause are as important as the active soundings. The pauses in music could be compared to meditation and realignment to the higher levels of our consciousness and to the Divine. Meditation or contemplative prayer or similar reflective time is crucial in order to refill our being with higher Spiritual energies and clarity and insight for our next step.

Living free is a skill that sometimes needs to be actively developed. Frequently people take the path of least resistance or of least effort. To live free requires a consciousness that is wide awake and very aware of choices. Sometimes people feel that being lethargic is living in a free manner because they aren't particularly doing what someone else wants them to do. That is an illusion. They are opting out of dynamically creating their reality in a manner that expresses their inner melody. Living in that manner is losing out on the precious opportunity to create something wonderful and unique with life.

There are people who are controlled by another person or by an organization which tries to tell them how to think and behave. Where there isn't a strong desire for self expression, others will always be eager to step in and control to whatever extent they are allowed. Even if people live within a fairly free government, they still have to be constantly vigilant to not allow others to impinge on their individuality. Nice people are sometimes seen as an open invitation for someone else to mold according to their convenience. This is not to discourage people from being nice, it is to encourage everyone to be so clear on their inner melody that they instantly sense if someone has an agenda in their mind for them.

What Dream Do You Hold In Your Heart? What Helps You Feel Free?

Having your livelihood involve doing something you truly enjoy is a blessing and helps one feel free. If that is true for you, how wonderful! May your inspired melody soar! May others be led by your example to also find the work that makes their heart sing. It can take real focus, clarity, and good fortune to achieve this. If a person has a job they don't really care for, in today's tight economy it might be wise to stay with it for awhile--unless there is another job waiting.

Sometimes it is possible to make some creative changes in how one perceives, approaches, and performs the job one has now. This can sometimes help one feel more fulfilled with one's current job. One can also follow the call of one's soul in whatever way possible in the time one has available outside the job. Opportunities may well come along later to make a shift seamlessly to a job that is closer to one's heart, if that seems important.

Real Life Sharing of Freedom to Choose

~ Sybil's Story

During the late 1980's, I worked in a bank in the Real Estate Collections Department. Yep--when mortgage interest rates were at 10 to 19 %. It was the beginning of Adjustable Rate Mortgages. Payments fluctuated (usually raised) every quarter when the Fed raised the interest rates. This was also a time of very high unemployment—over 20% in the county where I lived—and I was a single parent. So I felt like keeping this job was imperative for my survival.

After about five years of feeling guilty because I was starting the foreclosure process on people's homes, I began to get really ill. I hated the job and didn't much care for most people I worked with. The department manager seemed to do everything she could to intentionally increase the stress as much as possible. I felt like a part of me died a little each day I was there. Because I was so ill from the stress and began missing a lot of work, I became worried that I would lose my job. I was barely functioning.

One day I had an inspired thought that I could choose to stay "stuck" where I was, or I could choose to move on, or I could change the way I viewed the job and make it a better place for me. The choice was totally up to me. What choice was I going to make? After some thought, prayer and meditation, inspiration came like turning on a light bulb. I was in charge of how I viewed any situation. If that was true, then I could change my whole situation at work. But how?

I had an inspirational thought: I could become an open channel through which healing energy flowed. From that thought, I made a life-changing decision to serve however and wherever I could and offered a prayer: "I'm here, and I'm willing to serve where I am, right here, right now. Show me opportunities where I may serve the Light in this place."

From that inspiration, I took on the attitude at work that I had a dual responsibility. These responsibilities were to protect the bottom line of the bank, and to keep people in their homes, if there was any way possible to do that. The payments were past due, that was why I was calling people. They were possibly going to lose their homes if someone did not help them find a way to work through whatever current crises they were experiencing. I was that someone. If I could talk to people, I could help them make decisions that would turn out to be for their highest good—whether they kept their home, or let it go.

Shortly after that decision, the bank did something completely unprecedented – they gave me the authority to offer 18 month payment arrangements, without any additional approval. Prior to that, payment extensions beyond 60 days required signatures of the department manager and a VP, and approval was rare.

"Ask and ye shall receive!"

The ways and opportunities began to show up, and I did whatever felt right in the moment, even if it meant pushing the "rules of engagement" to the very edge and beyond of "OK" by company policy. Miracles, both small and large, were the result. Every day I was able to help people stay in their homes, or guide them to places where they could get additional assistance if their needs were greater than just spreading a couple of payments over a longer period of time. That worked because I stopped hating the job and began to ask how I could be of service right where I was.

Three months later, I went from being very ill and barely hanging onto the job, and my life--to being the top producer. The cases I worked didn't go to foreclosure if the homeowner truly wanted to keep the property. For as long as I remained in the position, I only had one arrangement fall through. I had a feeling that it would not work when I set it up, however the extended time to catch up gave the homeowner time to make other living arrangements before being evicted by foreclosure process.

I worked there for another five years, until the time arrived for me to move on to the next phase of my life. During that time, the number of loans that actually went to foreclosure from my desk was lower than anyone in the department, and those few were because the owner didn't care whether or not they stayed in the home—usually because the home had decreased in value so much that they could never sell the property for what was owed.

The lesson I learned: I always have choices, and they are mine to make. When I show up, God always puts up and comes through. Know your reasons for being where you are. Know your reasons to move on to another place. Either way, the choice is really up to you to be happy, healthy and free wherever you are. Choose consciously. (Conclusion of Sybil's story)

As Sybil did in the story above, sometimes by changing how we view a situation, and making changes within, we can transform a job to become more what we would like it to be. We can step into our freedom to choose. Sometimes the same position can take on a whole new quality with creative ideas and with wise coordination with co-workers and related professionals and management. Transformation from within can happen, in fact that is the only way transformation can truly happen. Visualize it, work toward it, pray for it--if that is what you desire.

What dream do you hold in your heart? Is there something that you would really like to manifest that has set your heart aflame in the past and that you perhaps set aside because you were distracted with other responsibilities? Maybe you tried to pursue that dream years ago and it didn't seem to work out and you sort of gave up on it and more or less forgot about it. Maybe that dream resurfaces in your consciousness now and then like a gentle song refrain that you can't quite totally get out of your mind.

There are times when one gets the impulse to follow a vision and go after it wholeheartedly for a while. Then one may be confronted with a roadblock and may figure that path is too difficult or not meant to be. This happens over and over for many people. Dreams get dashed and the individual may have a sad place in the heart that holds a monument to that lost dream. A person can consider approaching that vision in a different way. Perhaps someone who wanted to be a professional actor may enjoy being active in a community theater or writing and directing plays for children. Every idea can have multiple levels of possibilities and endless ways to apply it. It can be helpful to consider working with a coach in order to help bring one's dreams to life. Sometimes it is valid to replace an old dream with a new vision that would serve at a higher level.

Expressing Ourselves Creatively is Part of Being Human, and is Part of Our Freedom!

Let's take creativity back into our own hands and into our own lives. Let's forget about the critics. We're not expressing ourselves for their judgment or to win a contest. Expressing ourselves creatively is part of our humanity. Through creativity we each claim our freedom. What a marvelous vision! Expressing ourselves freely is as important as eating, drinking, or sleeping. This is missing right now to a large extent for vast numbers of people. This is a hole in many people's lives and they don't realize it, they just sense that something isn't complete and they often try to fill that vacuum with excessive food or excessive shopping or something else. Our inner psyche needs to be given the opportunity to express itself freely in some manner whether it is in art, music, dance, writing, woodworking, gardening, or in other creative ways. This is programmed into our DNA, we each have an intrinsic need to express our inner psyche creatively. Creativity isn't something reserved for the museums and mass media. We don't need to put it on YouTube, though that is fine. It is like breathing when we allow ourselves to express freely. It may or may not be beautiful to others; the important thing is that we feel the joy of expressing our inner being. It is crucial that self expression be an integral part of our flow of life. This is very different from feeling numb inside, or feeling like life is happening outside of ourselves somewhere.

Some prehistoric people painted on cave walls, perhaps celebrating or praying for success in their hunting. People in earlier periods often decorated everything that they made for themselves and for their families to use. Creativity was a natural part of their lives. For many people back then it would have seemed strange to make objects for their use without personalizing and decorating the objects in some way to express themselves. Some earlier people felt that they put part of their Soul into their creations. Maybe you can identify with that feeling.

When we feel something deeply in our heart and soul, there is often a desire to express it somehow to immortalize that feeling. That feeling may come from deep in our psyche and be very personal and sacred to us. It's good to have that level of respect for creativity. When a person is truly creating from his or her heart, it is sacred to that person. Sometimes when we are creating in paint, sculpture, writing, or other media--it feels like giving birth. It may seem to have an ongoing life and a Spirit of its own. I personally have often felt that way about my paintings, songs, and writings. Comparison to what someone else does is totally irrelevant. What we create deserves respect when we have poured our essence into it.

To Live Free--Trust Yourself! You Are Worthy!

To live free, one needs to trust oneself. Many people feel that anything of value will have to come from someone else. A person with this mindset may copy what someone else creates or does. The very act of copying tends to shut down one's sense of confidence in oneself and one's sense of worthiness. It is saying that whoever made what one is copying is more worthy than oneself.

You are worthy! What you have to say and communicate is of value and importance. As you express what is in your heart and in your mind, it clarifies your perceptions for yourself. Sometimes you may not know precisely how you feel until you attempt to express it. Can you imagine the truth of that? Have you ever tried to express your opinion on something, and found that when you put it in words or gave it form in some way--it became much clearer for you or even came out somewhat differently then you expected? This is important to be aware of.

Expressing Yourself Creatively in an Honest Heart-felt Way is Healing

The very act of expressing oneself freely from the heart is healing. This is the basis of some forms of therapy. It helps prevent someone from going rigid and freezing at a stagnant stage of development. If a person goes rigid, he or she may just keep repeating the same formulas of behavior and belief systems over and over without evolving and growing. This happens more than one would wish to believe. This is not freedom. This person is in a cage of his or her own making.

To be alive and free we need to keep evolving--which involves a certain amount of courage. This is not intended to be scary, it is meant to be liberating. We don't have to be exactly the same person for the remainder of our lives. Isn't that an exciting possibility? Who will we be five years from now? That doesn't sound boring, does it? It sounds downright liberating to me. The sky is the limit. We can all give each other permission to evolve. It is tempting to expect the people to whom we are close to stay pretty much the same. It feels safe and dependable. We sort of know what to expect from them. But is it possible that it may become a little boring to always know what to expect? What if a loved one surprised us with some new interest, or an extension of a familiar interest? Now that is going to bring some fresh air into the relationship. Now there are different ideas circulating between us. We are being stimulated to think about these new concepts, and to respond. How do these concepts resonant in our lives? Maybe our pursuits will be somewhat colored by them. This may stimulate new growth for us. This is how relationships can ideally support the people involved. We can serve as catalysts for each other. That doesn't mean that everything a friend or family member gets involved in should be incorporated in our lives, but it may mean that we pay attention to it all and learn something from it. All this interaction can serve as fertilizer to enrich our own lives.

Let's Not Go to Sleep on Life

The crucial thing to enhance freedom is to not go to sleep on life or go stagnant. Too many people are walking around half asleep and they don't know it. The main clue that people are half asleep may be that they are bored. Boredom is a huge subject and needs to be understood for what it is. It is one's consciousness shutting down somewhat, the consciousness feels it isn't needed for what is going on. Boredom is a massive waste of human capacity and it is poison to one's inner growth and awakening.

Education is Ideally More About Exploring Subjects than Memorization

Rote learning is certainly valuable for some important aspects of a person's education. In general, though, rote learning is not as effective for awakening the consciousness as other possible creative approaches. A person needs to awaken his or her consciousness and mind, not fill it. That is an extremely important concept. It was previously thought that teachers had to fill the student's mind with all the necessary information for an educated person. A great deal of memorization was involved. This developed a lot of people who thought somewhat alike. Memorization is like data entry into a computer. It puts in some facts that can be shifted around for certain practical purposes, but it doesn't teach a student how to use the mind. People aren't robots that need to be programmed. We humans have vast potential waiting to be awakened in order for us to live more fully and to express our magnificence.

What is important in education is to teach young people how to explore a subject that is of intrinsic interest to them. Students should ideally be exposed to some stimulating environments. This might be through field trips to interesting locations where people are pursuing their work such as scientists, artists of various kinds, medical and holistic wellness facilities, research institutions, fishermen, animal shelters, ecological nature preservation projects, organic farms, police departments, community theaters, or other professions or businesses or trades where people are actually working their jobs in real-life situations. Open the eyes of young people to what is really going on in the world, and then have them do research projects on what inspires their curiosity. Have them interview people working in the field about which they wish to learn more, read about it, write papers, create plans that they feel would be beneficial for solving some of the issues facing people in the situation they are exploring. The students could come together after doing research on a topic and have a group debate or discussion or brainstorming on the issues. Get the students involved and thinking. It is important to realize that every aspect of life on planet earth is in evolution and development and has endless questions needing solutions and innovative approaches to meet the needs of humanity. Life is very alive and stimulating--not boring at all!

Innovative Solutions Can Come From People Who Claim the Freedom to Passionately Question and Attempt to Understand Life

As more and more of the jobs in business, industry, government services, health care, and technology are being relegated to computerized equipment--many humans are being freed up from routine work. We need people who can think and find new solutions to the massive problems facing humanity. These new innovative solutions can't readily come from people who learned by rote and memorization. Innovative solutions can only come from people who are passionately questioning and trying to understand life. These solutions will come from people who are not afraid to think outside the norm. Trying to keep doing things the way they have been done, except faster and with more sophisticated electronic equipment won't bring real progress. It would just keep moving us faster and faster in directions that clearly aren't working. That would be tragic!

A large percentage of the food available to us is becoming more and more processed and unhealthy. Pollution is continuing largely unabated with pesticides and toxic chemicals. A large proportion of people are generally exercising less and are getting more obese and less healthy. Violence is still rampant. Masses of children and adults are heavily immersed to an unprecedented extent with electronic devices of all sorts to socialize, play games, and be entertained. Creative new solutions are needed to help us all find a more balanced active and healthy lifestyle.

The world is changing rapidly and our psyches need to evolve and grow to keep pace. We can't solve today's challenges with yesterday's mind set. We are moving into a higher turn of the spiral for our world as we know it. We need to each lift our consciousness to become aware of broader and more inspired vistas. As we each rise up to meet the opportunities of the day, we can together create a beautiful creative tomorrow. May we all together open ever more fully to our magnificence so that we may learn to live more and more truly free.

Real Life Sharings Of Claiming The Freedom To Be Our True Authentic Self

Freedom Is Being The Truth Of Who You Are

~ by G. B.

I've grown to love that line from *Me and Bobbie McGee*, "Freedom's just another word for nothin' left to lose." When I first encountered it all I heard was pessimism. I missed the wisdom. As life unfolded I realized Kristofferson was singing about the ultimate freedom, the freedom from the bondage of any and all attachments.

I am not always free--I can still be a hostage to old ideas, old concerns, such as "I'm not doing it right" or "How could anybody love me?" I am sometimes trapped by fears of what other people think or even what I think they think. The list is pretty endless. So as I reflect on writing a piece on freedom, I feel as I did when I was single and never in a relationship--doing couples counseling.

How free are you? Really?

If you were to stop for a minute during a day and ask yourself, "Am I doing this because I choose to or because I have to? Is my primary motivation fear of the consequences or am I doing this out of love, caring, and compassion?"

Too often I will come to the awareness that I have been sleepwalking. I've been in "robot mode." I've been in a fugue of unawareness, doing most of the tasks life was assigning to me, but never really being conscious or present.

Sleepwalking through life sucks a lot of energy from the soul, even if we are not aware of it. It is Spiritually exhausting, and it drains energy from all aspects of life.

Let us examine a day in our life, or even a part of that day. All of us probably follow a well established routine. Nothing wrong with that, but how conscious are we?

I'm going to suggest that it is only when we are conscious, when we are aware, that we are truly free. Showing up at work, did you want to be here? Did you want to dress up? Have there been times when you have been sitting there bored to death or thinking to yourself—I could be playing golf?

That internal dialogue could be applied to any area of our life.

So how free are we?

Freedom and non-attachment go hand in hand. I am only free when I am aware, when I am choosing to acknowledge my freedom, and I am only truly aware when I am unattached and in the present moment.

Simply put, as long as there is attachment, old baggage, or expectations, we will not be free: we will be living in fear and 'stuckness.'

There is nothing left to lose because there never was anything to lose.

You already have it All, but you have to be present to win, you have to be aware to claim the prize that is already here. And what is the prize you might ask? Simple, the Truth of Who You Are.

(See Resources Page)

How I Came To Be A Free Spirit

~ by Alisse Weston Fisher, CA

I became comfortable with being a free spirit and willing to go off and do things spontaneously by myself when I was thirteen years old and had a pony. I was living with my family in Pennsylvania in a farm community. I was the only one in the area who had a pony. In the spring and summer the crops were taking up the majority of the land around where I lived. I would go riding up in the mountains in the woods with the hickory groves and blueberry brambles. In the winter time the crops would go fallow so the fields were open. Then I could ride almost anywhere unimpeded. I would go off for hours on end riding my pony anywhere. I didn't use a saddle. It was pretty empowering for me to be able to take off when I wanted and be away all day alone out in nature. I felt safe even though I was in situations with some potential risk. It was fun. It gave me a feeling of great freedom. I enjoyed galloping; I was always good at that. I still love speed.

Yes, I was freed by having a pony that I could ride across fallow fields and mountain forests. That sense of freedom and control of myself at an early age allowed me to take risks as I grew older. Backpacking in the Sierra and local Los Padres Mountains, rock climbing and canyoneering after that, rappelling down hundreds of feet of canyons were off shoots of the independence gained early in life. Some of the most fun canyons were the first descents. When no one else had done them and we had to figure out how to get down. Being a free spirit can mean taking risks, and taking risks makes me feel alive. When I look over a cliff ledge of 100, 200, and the biggest at 650 feet down, I pause and then plunge smiling. It is good to let go of the daily grind and let yourself go where ever. Experiencing yourself in nature and just letting go is wonderful, but it does take trust. Trust.

Dancing Helps Me Feel Free

~ by Ann

When I'm dancing I feel as if I can fly like the wind and move like spirit. Spirit flows through me. It is so exhilarating! Dancing has become a symbolic way of communicating for me. I remember when I was in a difficult situation with my first husband. We talked of divorce but when we danced together we could bridge the words that separated us. We could move through a difficult situation to the love that brought us together. We did divorce, but we left as friends. I continued to work on myself. Later when I was working with a therapist to heal the torment of child abuse, I remember that the therapist suggested that I dance. At the time I thought, how can I move when I'm so depressed and in so much pain? It took years before my spirit could soar again in dancing, but eventually I could once again love my body in movement. These days I have been finding myself in Zumba dancing. I love its joyous expression. This is what dancing is to me. It is freedom, and I love dancing. But now I am once again waiting for complete healing--this time physical--so I can once again return more fully to the joy and freedom of dancing. Meantime, I enjoy square dancing. Tai Chi and Qi Gong are my physical meditations. (Resources Page)

Feeling Free With Music

~ by Joyce

When I was a child, my family had a wonderful cocker spaniel pet dog. He taught me and my sisters about the joy of spontaneous singing. He liked to howl now and then, and we had fun howling and "singing" with him. It was marvelously freeing. I've never been afraid to sing since then. To me it is as natural as talking. If I have a feeling, I sing about it because it feels good. When I'm singing I'm happy and feel free. Everything seems O.K. and more manageable when I sing about it. I used to live surrounded by woods. Neighbors and I had picnics sometimes in the evenings, and then had campfires afterward. We would sing to the stars and the moon until they seemed to glow brighter and brighter. I know we felt glowing and free. The trees seemed to surround us with love.

Over the years I have periodically searched and searched for just the right songs to express my inner world. Finally I decided I wanted to create my own songs to express my love of life and of the Divine. Somehow through my love and devotion, the words and the melodies seemed to flow. The freedom and joy I have experienced from expressing my own feelings and visions in melody is indescribable. Feeling free to express who one really is and what one really believes is incredibly freeing--in whatever form one may choose to express it!

How I Experience Freedom

~ by Becky G.

For me, freedom is having (and expanding) choices. Freedom is a Spiritual and emotional feeling. It conjures up visions of magic, of flying, of beautiful art, or listening to powerful music. Freedom is exploration and an unlimited expanse of space and time. It is a feeling of flexibility and adaptability. It is the capability of feeling unbound. So how can I (we) have that feeling when we live in this physical world that feels limited, constricted, and bound by the constraints of time and space. I can practice gratitude for the now and affirm that the past does not imprison me. I can know that feeling limited is a cooperative event, that the more I feel limited--the universe sends me more experiences of feeling limited. I have the freedom to change that limiting belief--or not. Freedom is remembering my real self and acting accordingly. Love and blessings.

Letting Go of Expectations and Opening to Freedom

~ by Ann

Until we let go of our mental images of who we are or who we should be, our vision remains clouded by expectation. But when we let go of everything, open ourselves to any truth, and see the world without fear and judgment, then we are finally able to begin the process of peeling off the shell of false identity that prevents our true self from growing and shining in the world. It starts with nothing, and it leads to freedom. (See Resources Page)

Galloping Horse Symbolizes Freedom
Original art by Joyce J.C. Gerrish

WORKBOOK: Enrichment Experiences For Enhancing Freedom in Your Life

Enjoy the adventure of exploring these enrichment experiences on your own--or gather a few friends to share the journey with you. Be inspired by the audio meditation and soul song for this chapter. Reflect on some of the stimulating ideas and questions.

Questions For Reflection And Discussion

Reflection, discussion, journal writing, expressing your feelings in drawings or other creative ways can all be very valuable to help you delve into these questions in truly meaningful and relevant ways. Before focusing on the questions, you may wish to meditate with the twelve-minute audio or transcribed meditation for freedom--and/or listen to the soul song *My Spirit Flies Free,* on the website.

1. When do you generally feel the most free in your life? When do you feel the most free to be yourself and express yourself? Being out in nature? Dancing? Running? Exploring new places? Creating something? Sharing stimulating conversation? Achieving success or a breakthrough in your work? Describe how that feeling of freedom feels in your body and in your consciousness. How does that carry over into the rest of your life (if it does)?

2. What was an event that was one of the most freeing experiences in your life? What made it so special for you? How did it affect your life after that?

3. How can you support some of the people in your life to enjoy more fully exploring their freedom to be who they truly are?

Action Suggestions For Enhancing Freedom In Your Life

You can do it! Take a step now towards your freedom!

1. How can you enhance your favorite way of expressing your freedom? How often do you give yourself the opportunity to enjoy it? Are you craving more time to pursue it, or is it in a fairly good balance in your life now? Plan a time to enjoy your freedom enhancing pursuit in the next few days or soon (if it wasn't already on your schedule).

2. Have you ever been made to feel that you weren't skilled enough to participate in something that you enjoyed? That can be a devastating feeling. We all have a right to express ourselves harmlessly in the manners that we choose. We don't have to prove that we are good enough in someone else's estimation. Is there something that you like to do that you were made to feel ashamed of doing? Try it on your own just for fun! Consider taking an adult education class designed for people who never tried it before or who would appreciate encouragement.

3. Are you a teacher or leader in some form or a parent? Try designing a learning experience specifically to encourage your prospective or current students or your child to try something they would probably enjoy but might shy away from for fear of being judged. Some type of guided relaxation beforehand can be helpful for many people. Gentle stretching movements with or without music can be good preparation, also.

Audio "Meditation To Enhance Your Experience Of The Divine Qualities," with Focus On Freedom

Pray to the Divine to bless your meditation and enhance Divine Freedom in your life. Choose one or more of the following affirmations (or something similar) that feels particularly helpful to you for affirming during this meditation. Before transferring to the website to listen to the meditation, write down affirmation(s) you choose and the helpful color violet. Later, place affirmation(s) where you'll see it daily and be reminded to affirm it for a minute or two several times a day

- ◆ I am free to pursue my highest good.
- ◆ I am free to be my unique expressive self.
- ◆ I am free to be who I truly am.

Helpful color to visualize while meditating on Freedom is Violet.

I encourage you to enjoy this meditation when you wish to enhance the feeling of freedom in your life. Connect to SecretsofWisdom.net where you can listen to the twelve-minute audio "Meditation to Enhance Your Experience of the Divine Qualities," with focus on Freedom.

(See transcribed form of this meditation at the end of this chapter.)

Uplifting Audio Soul Song: *"My Spirit Flies Free"*

~ By Joyce.

Consider it a prayer in song for enhancing Divine Freedom within yourself. As you chant or listen to the song, just feel yourself beginning to lift into the experience of Divine Freedom. Close your eyes and imagine that you are a magnificent white dove with wings spread soaring free. Really sense the words helping to bring you into an uplifted feeling of freedom. Connect to SecretsofWisdom.net to listen to "*My Spirit Flies Free.*" The words are:

> My Spirit flies free round this world I love.
>
> I fly so free like a pure white dove.
>
> I fly so free, on wings so bright.
>
> My Spirit flies free in the Light.

Transcribed Form of Meditation To Enhance Divine Freedom

If possible and if it feels helpful, listen to some relaxing nonverbal music. Say a short prayer calling on the Divine to bless your meditation and enhance Divine Freedom in your life.

Visualize yourself in a ball of light to help strengthen your energy field.

Imagine your consciousness expanding into the Heavens.

Become aware of and follow your breath as it gently flows in and out at its own relaxed pace.

Imagine yourself a tree sending powerful roots deep into the earth to help you feel grounded and prevent possibly feeling spacey.

As you breathe in through your nose, imagine you are breathing up the strength of the earth into your body.

Now be aware of your breath as it flows gently in and out your nose for about a minute.

Next, very gently breathe in your nose and out your mouth for about a minute.

Now, very gently breathe in your mouth and out your nose.

Next, very very gently breathe in and out your mouth for about a minute.

Then - - return to breathing comfortably in and out your nose.

As you breathe in through your nose imagine you are breathing in light into your being.

Next visualize violet light.

As you breathe in through your nose, imagine that you are breathing glowing violet light into your whole being.

As you breathe out, silently pray to the Divine to enhance liberating, uplifting freedom in your life.

Continue in that manner for a few minutes or as long as you wish.

Periodically silently affirm one of the following affirmations:

◆ I am free to pursue my highest good.

◆ I am free to be my unique expressive self.

◆ I am free to be who I truly am.

Conclude by thanking the Divine for blessings in your life.

Send down roots again to help you feel well grounded and stable.

Meditate on Divine Freedom when you wish to help enhance freedom in your life. Write the affirmation(s) you choose and place it where you'll see it several times a day and be reminded to affirm it for a minute or two.

Peace.

The Rising Of the Phoenix Bird Transformed.
Original art by Joyce J.C. Gerrish

Chapter Fifteen

THE ADVENTURE OF TRANSFORMATION

Enhancing Divine Transformation in Your Life

Enjoy listening to the soul song audio "I Awaken to My Magnificence" that I composed and sang for supporting Divine Transformation in your life." I invite you to visit SecretsofWisdom.net where you can listen to the soul song audio and also gaze at the full color design: "The Rising of the Phoenix Bird Transformed."

Life as Ongoing Transformation

My whole life has been a journey of transformation. One thing I've learned for sure is that life can be an incredible process! It's crucial that we stay wide awake so as to embrace as much as possible of what the universe is offering. We're each on our own unique journey. We'll each respond to different road signs along the way. If we ever feel that we missed turning at an important fork in the road, we can stay alert and open to discovering and creating intriguing possibilities where we are or else find another route to our vision.

Life has a way of moving in cycles. My life has moved (and continues to move) in numerous cycles. Each cycle has been a highly valuable learning and growing experience. Some sections of my journey have opened up almost spontaneously to foster my creativity, joy, and service. Occasionally other periods have at first made me wonder why I chose that piece of the journey. My experience has been, though, that sometimes the less smooth patches of the road can truly bring out one's inner resources, power, and resilience if one stays open to the potential therein. These experiences can be diamonds in the rough as one allows the Divine to shine through.

I have off-and-on mused to myself, "Can life really keep becoming more and more of an amazing adventure?" And life has seemed to keep answering "Yes, it can, if you are willing to stay fully engaged and alive to it--keep questing how you can contribute to the greater good in your own way as you feel drawn from your heart."

Sometimes astounding opportunities are hidden in the least likely places waiting to be discovered and manifested. In fact, it is when we are willing to serve the highest good in unexpected places that sometimes the most wonderful magic can happen. Spiritual blessings can light the way. That is the gift of Divine Transformation.

I have shared parts of my life tales in chapters of this book. Each is about how a different slice of my life gave me the opportunity to open more fully to one or another of the Divine Qualities of God. All together they helped me move forward on the adventure of my soul path--and created for me an altar on which to place my love, devotion, and creativity. Through all of this I have received boundless joy, blessings, and peace.

Life on Earth is Changing at a Breathtaking Speed!

Now is a time of great change on our planet. Look around and see it everywhere! Life is reinventing itself at an astounding speed. It's crucial that all this change moves in directions that are beneficial for everyone's highest good. I firmly believe that the Divine is watching over us and keeping this planetary drama within bounds. Perhaps part of what we are seeing and experiencing is the growth pains and the adjustments of old repressed traumas working up to the surface for healing. This can be true even in large populations as a whole. In the midst of all this transformation whirling around and within us, we humans do have free will. We aren't just passive participants, we are powerful. All together we are weaving the fabric of tomorrow for ourselves, our children, grandchildren, and great grandchildren. Because we are in physical bodies at this time on our planet--we have a huge stake in helping to create and guide what is going on.

Would you like to see our world more peaceful, equitable, and safe? Would you like to see people everywhere staying healthier and feeling more joyful? Would you like to see the natural beauty and ecological balance of the earth treasured and protected more fully? How about ever more fantastic arts, music, drama, and dance? This is all possible if clear-sighted people everywhere are willing to work together to actualize it. But it won't happen by wishing. We all need to be part of the solution that we want to see happen! This is not a time for rigidly hanging onto the same old status quo. This is the time to explore life's fuller potentials. This is the time to step into the exhilaration and joy of discovering new and/or forgotten wondrous possibilities for helping solve some of today's pressing issues!

We Are Needed to Be Who We Truly Are Within

We each have a soul mission which we chose as a soul before we were born. Each of us is here on earth for a very important reason. It is no accident that we are here at this time of change and transformation. We each have an important role to perform, and our piece of the planetary puzzle is absolutely crucial. We are each needed to be who we truly are within. There is a purpose glowing in each of our hearts that is waiting to be fanned and awakened and actualized ever more fully. The world is counting on us to play our part. We are counting on each other to be all that we can be. The opportunity is now for all of us to wake up to our higher potentialities. It truly is within our reach. Many wise observant people feel that much of what we experience as reality here on planet Earth seems to be reinventing itself and going through a metamorphosis. Altogether, let's lift ourselves and life as we know it into the next step of more glowing possibilities!

It is irresistible to use the often mentioned metaphor of the caterpillar evolving into a butterfly. It is such a perfect description which is why it is so frequently invoked. We are each at some stage of the transformation through the caterpillar stage and on up into the butterfly stage of human evolution. The caterpillar eats and eats of the leaves which represent life experiences. The caterpillar digests these life experiences and draws from them the essences needed to create the incredibly beautiful ethereal butterfly wings. We are each in this process of distilling from our life experiences those wisdoms and truths needed to create or further expand our Spiritual wings to help lift us higher. May we allow the courage and beauty of the butterfly to inspire us!

What Do You Hold in Your Heart that You Yearn to Explore?

Many of us are feeling heart stirrings calling us to move into fuller expression of who we are. It is important to get in touch with what we may have held in our hearts that we are yearning to explore. This is an ideal time to give that dream some room to grow. This is not to say to drop everything and move far away or to turn our lives inside out. What is being suggested is to simply allow ourselves to begin to explore whatever is held most deeply within our beings that seems to want to express. May we be our true authentic selves! When we move from the core of our beings we are drawing on the power of the Universe.

When we are out of touch with our soul mission, we may feel that something is missing no matter how powerful the world around may see us to be. There can be an inner knowing that something precious is seeking expression in our beings, and we may not yet know how to bring it into focus consciously. It can feel like a misty mirage or a yearning just beyond reach, or it may have surfaced sufficiently to become a passionate recurring longing.

Maybe you are already firmly walking the path that you sense is your life mission, if so that is terrific! Tread it joyfully and courageously. That is your path of power. Even if the world doesn't seem to recognize your work as you might wish, it is still worthy. Even if that isn't how you earn your money, that's O.K. If your heart passion is meaningful and helpful to you and contributes to the world around you in some way, that is what counts!

We Can All Be Visionaries for a Better Tomorrow. Let's Each Start Where We Are

What is your area of endeavor? What is your special area of life exploration? Think for a few moments about the directions in which you would like to see your work or your area of specialty evolve. You probably have some pretty strong feelings about that. When you have worked in an area of specialty for a while, you very quickly realize where the weak points are and what needs renovating or improving. That awareness is inevitable. Life is always trying to improve. Sometimes, unfortunately, situations backslide somewhat. It is sad when that happens. This is a time of great human need all over the planet. Some of the old ways are shifting. Even with all the problems, this is also a time of great opportunity with vast advances coming to the fore in technology, electronics, healing, ecology and so many other fields of development. The possibilities are exciting, right? It's an extraordinary time to be alive!

Let Your Visions Soar High for Your Field of Work or Dreams

Take out a piece of paper. Write down what you would like to see happen to open up the work you do to allow it to better meet the needs of the population you serve and to better inspire you. Be as imaginative as you like. Let your vision soar high! The sky is the limit. You can always pare down the ideas a little later. Just get your visions rolling right now. Please put these ideas in a place where you will see them on a regular basis and be inspired by them. Now you are a visionary! That is a very important status. Earth needs visionaries. How does it feel to be a visionary? Try it on for size.

Being a visionary doesn't mean that you have to be a revolutionary. You don't need to go storming up to your supervisor's office and bang on the door demanding changes. Sometimes demonstrations are helpful for certain purposes. In general, though, most important change occurs quietly from within. Usually authorities in an area of endeavor are more receptive to new ideas that come from their colleagues than from outsiders. You may have done a great deal of preparation work to be in the position where you are currently involved. This may have been in the form of academic studies and formal education. You may have one or more degrees or a certificate to prove your qualifications to perform the work you do. On the other hand, your qualifications may be more in the form of a great deal of experience. Your peers may respect you because they know that you know what you are talking about. They have seen the success of your work and respect it. All these forms of qualification are valuable. Your track record adds clout to what you say and do. People will listen to you, whereas someone walking in from nowhere will probably be mostly ignored.

The Right Word at the Right Time From Someone Experienced in A Field Can Help Jump-Start a Needed Innovation

A visionary doesn't need to be a loudmouth. A visionary can be discrete and polite and soft spoken. The right words said at the optimum time by someone with some degree of authority or responsibility can sometimes ring a bell in the supervisor's head that maybe a different approach should be tried. This can help allow needed improvements and changes to occur. It is easy for people working in an agency or institution to get in a rut and not see beyond continuing to do the work pretty much in the way it has been done even if it isn't working all that well. Leaps of insights for needed improvements are thankfully increasingly going on everywhere. If you are quite young or new in your field, you are also definitely important and valuable. Young people and those new to a field can help bring fresh ideas, innovative insights, and enthusiasm.

To return to our earlier metaphor, the whole planet is like a caterpillar that is turning into a butterfly--just like each person is potentially transforming. The planet is waking up; just as so many of us are waking up. Every person on planet Earth is part of the human family. In a sense, what happens to any of us happens to all of us because we are interconnected as a human family. We can all help each other grow. This is a very dynamic situation full of hope.

Green Inventions Can Often Do Tasks With Less or No Fuel, While Being Harmless to the Environment and Us

There are a massive number of green technology inventions ready to be introduced and made available to humanity through gifted inventors around the world. Green technologies, of course, are those which are harmless to the purity and integrity of our earth, air, and water. Green technologies respect and protect the soil, land and rock formations, the plants, and the health of people everywhere. They protect the habitats and biodiversity and health of the mammals, birds, reptiles, amphibians, fish, insects, and all creatures. These green inventions are often able to do tasks with very little or even no fuel. The technology is available to make life easier and more pleasant for even the poorest people. Humanity doesn't need to suffer.

The sun has energy, the earth has energy, the sea and ocean have energy, and the wind creates energy. All these types of energy can be harvested and much more. We have many surprises in store with crystals and how they can help us. Magnetism is another expanding area. When we become aware of a new green technology that relates to our field of endeavor and our interests--we may wish to study it, witness it in operation, and try it. Let's all pay attention and support those who come up with new ideas that can improve our lives and go easier on the earth. Let's give that inventor a chance to show that his or her device can be useful. This can quickly revolutionize how people accomplish their work and meet their needs.

Health care is another area where major innovations are becoming available. It is worth visiting holistic health expos to find out about new technology and new techniques which can support your health and the health of your family. This is not intended to replace your medical doctor, but rather to be helpful alongside of your health practitioner. All fields of endeavor are opening up and discovering new less expensive and more effective ways to accomplish what is needed. Approaches are being presented that at the same time are easier on the human body and gentler on the environment. Try what seems to be appropriate for your needs. What has been going on in many areas hasn't been working all that well. It is worth trying new ideas in order to find even better solutions.

Protecting Mother Earth is Protecting Ourselves

If we support green technology, it can take a large burden off of nature. Mother Earth needs to be given time to recover from every onslaught on her body. May we protect the trees, plants, and endangered animal species. May we protect the waterways, air, and soil. These are not meant to absorb endless pollution or abuse. The waterways and the oceans are Mother Earth's blood, the air is her lungs, the soil is her flesh, the plants are her beautiful skin, and the rock formations are her bones. We probably know this instinctively. It is time to be gentle with our Mother. In being gentle with our Mother, we are also protecting and being gentle with ourselves.

This can be a time of great hope. I believe that the Divine is blessing and inspiring us ever more profoundly to help meet the challenges of the times and help uplift humanity. There is a cleansing going on. Humanity as a whole is being given the opportunity to heal from many millennia of suffering from wars, violence, and abuse. Good people everywhere need to speak out and be strong to help lead and show the way. Many confused people have been weighed down with greed, excessive materialism, abusing drugs and alcohol, and accepting violence as normal behavior. As far as I have observed, violence is one of the most popular subjects for television programs, movies, and computer games. Everything in me feels that this is desensitizing people to the tragedy of violence. May we be examples of clarity for those who are numbed to the extent that the inner connection to the Divine has been weakened. Through our own lives, may we each help inspire others to remember the Sacred truth of their beings.

Let's Shine Ever More Fully and Shed Any Remnants of Shadows

Powerful Spiritual energies and blessings are flooding our planet and activating everybody's consciousness and energy field (aura). Old repressed or neglected emotional wounds of many of us may be stirred up and lifted to the surface for healing. We need to work through old traumas that may possibly surface, keep the wisdom we learned from the experiences, let go of the pain, and forgive ourselves and others. May we give it all to God, mobilize the strength to move on, and open our hearts to be blessed with ever increasing Divine Love and Peace. It's not always easy, but this deep healing is needed in order to find real lasting peace for ourselves individually--and collectively for all of us to eventually join together in greater harmony. May we all work together for a better tomorrow of equality and the highest good for all in harmony with Mother Earth and the Divine.

I encourage you to meditate daily, if only for a few minutes. Pray for and invoke the Divine to bless you and your loved ones. Explore and experience the techniques described in this book for amplifying in your life the different Divine Qualities of God.

I believe that at this time humanity is being given the opportunity of a great step forward on this spiral of Spiritual growth of the soul. May the Divine help each of us to move through our challenges to more positive solutions. May we all experience blessings and grace flowing abundantly through our lives and transforming us and our whole planet into greater peace and optimum well-being. May we all awaken ever more fully to our magnificence!

Real Life Sharings Of The Positive Power Of Transformation In One's Life

Big Ed's Courageous Transformation

~ by Ann

The first night I met Ed, he was sitting at the top of the stairs collecting money for the singles dance. He had on his Mexican sweater and I had on my Mexican coat. Before I left that night, he whispered in my ear "marry me and I will take you anywhere in the world." He worked for an airline and he really meant flying anywhere.

The second time I met him at the dance, I told him I was going to visit my daughter in another state and would be gone more than a week. He forgot, and the next time I saw him at the dance he wondered where I had been. It turned out that he was drinking heavily and forgot a lot. I naively thought that love would make a difference and he would drink less heavily. I found out that his first wife ended her life in an institution and the second wife was alcoholic and committed suicide. There had been a lot of pain in his life.

We did get married, but soon I was ready to leave because of the drinking. A counselor told me that Alanon could stabilize me. Alanon was supposed to by my support for leaving the marriage, but instead Ed attended AA and Alanon with me for twenty-five years. He turned around. He stopped drinking and smoking and finally lost weight. Big Ed became a loving husband for me, and a loving father and grandfather to my kids and grandkids.

P.S. I traveled the world. (See Resources Page)

My Journey To a Clear View of My Life

~ by Wanda

Things are going very much better now. I still have distortion in my right eye that I've had for years. Two years ago I had swelling in the left eye which left me legally blind. I was very anxious and concerned that I would have distortion in my left eye which would have left me with very low vision.

The techniques that were really helpful for me when I was facing possible blindness were better nutrition, meditation, and Reiki energy therapy. (Reiki means life energy in Japanese. Reiki is widely practiced by people in all walks of life including nurses.) I regularly meditated and did the Reiki Joyce taught me, and those allowed me to center myself. I gave my life to God. I changed my diet completely. I did a lot of research on super foods for the eyes. I eat a lot of raw spinach salads. I eat a lot of raw vegetables. I fix my lunch every day. I try to eat things that are more natural. I changed my life. I think that is one reason that I got my vision back. Inflammation caused the swelling in my eye. I had irritable bowel syndrome. I had a body full of inflammation. I gave myself to a Higher Power, I really did. I told myself that I would enjoy my life whatever it is. I got better. I truly believe that a person has to come together in body, mind, and Spirit. I think that everything fell into place. The swelling went without a lot of distortion--so my vision has gotten better. I went to see my doctor last week and it has improved from six months ago.

Out of the blue, there was a need for a health coordinator to work with the residents at a wonderful assisted living facility. They have a rehab on the second floor which I run, and I also lead two programs a day for the residents. I'm certified through Silver Sneakers Exercise Program for Elders, in Range of Movement, and in Yoga Stretch. So I was able to put together a really good program using some of my knowledge. I recently did something that I was terrified to do. I just finished training to lead water aquatics. I'm going to shortly receive my Certification in Water Aquatics from the American Arthritis Foundation.

I take every day one day at a time. I drink in sight. I can't tell you what it is like to lose one of your senses and then have it return at least partially so that you can live a normal type of life. The freedom that I feel--I'm so thankful.

Birthing My Dreams

~ By Ashley Barnes, Sellersburg, Indiana

Recently I dreamed that I was with a woman who was giving birth. I and the other women present were encouraging her as she worked when suddenly the thought came to me "just a head." Next, I looked at the birthing woman lying naked on her side, bearing down one last time as the baby crowned. With one final push, the baby's head emerged--and dropped to the floor. Silence befell the room. And there, in the stillness, a miracle occurred. The baby's body appeared united with its discontinuous head. Then I awoke.

I knew the dream was symbolic. I've been hearing a voice sometimes while dreaming that says "This is important! Remember this!" However, I don't usually wake up enough to write down my dreams and they're lost by morning. But this dream happened just before I woke for the day, and I knew instantly that it had deep meaning. I pondered it for about a week, analyzing the possible symbolism. What does birthing represent? What can a headless baby possibly mean? What about the body appearing?

I started thinking about my life for the past few years, especially this whirlwind year: my growth, my soul expansion, my dreams, my goals, my blocks. And suddenly it came to me. The birthing woman was ME, laboring to bring forth my own truth, my authentic existence to the world. And just when I get to the moment of truth, the final moment when my labor of love is born into the world, it's decapitated, lopped off by my fears, insecurities, distractions from the goal, feelings of unworthiness. Despite all my hard work, there my dream rolls around, lifeless on the floor. But in this dream, the body materialized and reconnects with its head. The dream is made whole again, the labor complete, the need for mourning averted. This is my message--the time is here for me to throw off fear, to reconnect my head to my body (which contains my heart), to go forth and do that which I am called to do. (See Resources Page)

The Moving Experience of Helping to Support a Person's Transformation Journey

~ by Joyce

I want to share with you the deep sense of wonder and Sacred privilege I feel when I work with individuals to help them awaken more fully to their higher Spiritual awareness, life purpose, and enhanced well-being physically and emotionally. Each person's consciousness, aura, and life are very unique--and I feel tremendous appreciation and compassion for the inherent beauty of his or her soul journey. I honor each person's courage to move forward in spite of sometimes real challenges. It is extraordinarily heartwarming to help guide individuals to heal and release possible old limiting thought patterns or stuck energy so they may open more freely to their life goals.

Watching energy blocks lighten, move, and dissolve--and be replaced by lively healthy energy flow is more awe inspiring to me than any drama could ever be. To watch and keenly sense the higher Spiritual energies flooding from on high into the person's crown chakra and whole aura is a Sacred joy. To hear people say that they feel much better and freer and see their faces light up is awesome.

As I do energy healing with a person I can intuitively "hear" some of the old (or current) thought patterns in his or her aura. That helps me know what questions to ask to help the person in his/her healing process. Old unresolved issues ideally need to be understood, wisdom extracted, forgiven, and healed free. Sometimes this can be accomplished without too many words. Usually it helps the healing process when the individual talks about what he or she is experiencing. Intuitively I often sense what might help a person move forward on his or her path. My job is to help people be aware of and evaluate options--but in no way to direct. To watch a person over time evolve into his or her next step of self-actualization of greater joy, life purpose, peace, wisdom, and power is truly inspiring. Such is the profound joy of being an Intuitive Spiritual Therapist!

Transformation in Retirement

~ K.C.

I am getting older now--in my seventies. I'm realizing that this is my opportunity to do whatever I want to do. Who knows how long I'll be able to do these things. I'm fortunate to have good health, a very modest steady income, and a place to live that is all paid. I've been a professional potter most of my life. I regularly volunteer many hours at the animal rescue shelter. I'm enjoying painting and not feeling stressed that I have to accomplish anything specific with it. Maybe that is freeing for me. I'm volunteering at archeological digs. This period of my life makes me realize how important family and friends are. It is wonderful to share my interests with my grandchildren. I treasure all this. I feel free to do whatever I'm capable of doing, and that's very enjoyable.

Woman Under A Tree Contemplates Life
Original art by Joyce J.C. Gerrish

WORKBOOK: Enrichment Experiences for Enhancing Positive Transformation in Your Life

Enjoy the adventure of exploring these enrichment experiences on your own--or gather a few friends to share the journey with you. Be inspired by the audio meditation and soul song for this chapter. Reflect on some of the stimulating ideas and questions.

Questions for Reflection and Discussion

Reflection, discussion, journal writing, expressing your feelings in drawings or other creative ways can all be very valuable to help you delve into these questions in truly meaningful and relevant ways. Before focusing on the questions, you may wish to meditate with the twelve minute audio or transcribed meditation for this chapter--and/or listen to the soul song *"I Awaken To My Magnificence."*

1. What would you really like to have happen where you work to make it possible to better serve your population/clients/customers and for you to feel more fulfilled? If you are self-employed, a volunteer, or a homemaker--the question is the same. What would you like to have shift to make it possible for you to even more effectively contribute your gifts for the world around you and for your own sense of fulfillment? Be as imaginative as you like. Let your vision soar high. The sky is the limit. You can always pare down the ideas a little later. Just get your vision rolling right now. Writing your ideas freely can be helpful. Then write a few of those ideas on a separate smaller piece of paper and tape it up somewhere in your home. That way you can see them on a regular basis and be inspired by them.

2. What is going on in your personal life? What do you feel emerging in your heart and soul? Do you feel something shifting and evolving? Do you feel exactly the same about life today as you did a year ago or five or more years ago? What direction do you feel your life is moving? Is that how you would like it to move? If not, how would you like it to transform?

3. How do you perceive of the Divine? Do you feel a personal connection to the Divine as you experience it? Do you feel love glowing in your heart when you pray? Do you feel something shifting, evolving, or deepening in your Spiritual life? There are many ways to experience one's Spirituality--there isn't one right way.

Action Suggestions for Enhancing Transformation in Your Life

1. Take one piece of your vision from your answers to Question #1 above (Questions for Reflection and Discussion). How about making a start at putting it into action? No matter how small a step it is, start the journey. See if you can find some friends or co-workers to accompany you in this adventure. Enjoy it!

2. Do you have a church or Spiritual group that helps you feel really supported in your Spiritual life? If not, would you like to explore and find one that feels right for you? There is a very wide variety of churches and Spiritual groups to meet almost every possible approach to Spirituality. Group support can be extremely helpful for soul growth and transformation to the next step of your soul path. You don't need to attend all the time, but knowing that you have a group that feels Spiritually supportive to you can be very reassuring and empowering.

3. Explore and learn about some of the new green environmentally friendly innovations available today. Would you like to try an environmentally friendly product or device that you haven't tried before? Perhaps a friend has one that you could try. Look up Green Technology on the internet. It is a fascinating and worthy adventure.

Audio "Meditation To Enhance Your Experience of The Divine Qualities," with Focus on Transformation

Pray to the Divine to bless your meditation and enhance Divine Transformation in your life. With this audio you'll be guided to sense yourself immersed in this feeling of expansion and growth.

Choose one or more of the following affirmations (or something similar) that feels particularly helpful to you for affirming during the meditation. Write down the affirmation(s) you choose and the helpful color opalescence. Later, place the affirmation(s) where you'll see it often and be reminded to affirm it for a minute or two several times a day.

◆ My life is transforming and opening in marvelous ways for my highest good.

◆ I am a catalyst for hope, positive change, and transformation wherever I go.

◆ I am ready to take the next step for opening to my life purpose/soul mission as I sense it in my heart.

Helpful color to visualize while meditating on transformation: Opalescence (like mother of pearl)

I encourage you to enjoy this meditation when you wish to support Transformation in your life. Connect to SecretsofWisdom.net to listen to the twelve-minute audio "Meditation to Enhance Your Experience of the Divine Qualities," with focus on Divine Transformation.

(Also, see transcribed version of this meditation at end of chapter.)

Uplifting Audio Soul Song: *"I Awaken To My Magnificence"*
~ by Joyce

Consider it a prayer in song for enhancing your sense of positive renewal and growth within your life. The words are:

> I awaken to my magnificence.
> God created me in his image.
> The Divine spark within me –
> transforms my being into light.
> Ou – u – u – u.

As you chant or listen to this soul song, feel yourself relax and begin to flow with it. Close your eyes and really sense it helping to bring you into an inspired sense of upliftment. You may wish to visit <u>SecretsofWisdom.net</u> where you can listen to the audio: "I Awaken To My Magnificence."

Transcribed Version of Meditation To Enhance Your Experience Of Divine Transformation

If possible, listen to some relaxing nonverbal music. Say a short prayer calling on the Divine to bless your meditation and enhance Divine Transformation in your life.

Visualize yourself in a ball of light to help strengthen your energy field.

Become aware of and follow your breath as it gently flows in and out at its own pace.

Imagine yourself as a large tree sending powerful roots deep into the earth to help you feel grounded and prevent possibly feeling spacey.

As you breathe in through your nose, imagine you are breathing up the strength of the earth into your body.

For a few minutes listen to the relaxing music.

As you breathe in through your nose imagine you are breathing in light into your being.

Next visualize opalescent light like glowing mother-of-pearl.

Periodically as you breathe in through your nose, imagine that you are breathing glowing opalescent light into your whole being.

Silently pray to the Divine that your life be uplifted and blessed with Divine Transformation.

Next breathe in through your nose and out your mouth for about a minute VERY GENTLY.

Now, very gently breathe in through your mouth and out your nose for about a minute.

Then extra gently breathe in and out your mouth for a minute or so.

Now return to breathing in and out your nose.

As you breathe in through your nose, imagine you are breathing in opalescent light into your whole being.

As you breathe out through your nose, periodically say one or two of the following (or similar) affirmations silently.

◆ My life is transforming and opening in new and promising ways for my highest good.

◆ I am a catalyst for hope, positive change, and transformation wherever I go.

◆ I am ready to take the next step for opening to my life purpose/soul mission as I sense it in my heart.

Pray for support in helping you to move forward with your goals.

Continue in that manner for a few minutes or as long as you wish.

Conclude by thanking the Divine and once again sending down roots to Mother Earth for stability and grounding.

Enjoy this meditation when you wish to enhance and support transformation in your life. Write down the affirmation(s) you choose. Place the affirmation(s) where you'll see it several times a day and be reminded to affirm it for a minute or two.

Peace.

Man, Woman and Angel
Original art by Joyce J.C. Gerrish

Chapter Sixteen

THE MIRACLE OF DIVINE GRACE

Enhancing Divine Grace in Your Life

I encourage you to listen to the soul song "Grace of God" that I've composed and sung for enhancing Divine Grace in your life. Connect to the SecretsofWisdom.net to hear "Grace of God" and simultaneously gaze at the design "Angel With Stars" in full color.

Different Ways of Experiencing Divine Grace

We can view Divine Grace as a way of recognizing Divine miracles in our everyday lives, and we can also understand it as Divine blessings coming to us from higher Spiritual levels. First let's look at the awareness that life in its true natural flow is a miracle of Divine Grace. Our planet and all life on it are created by God. If we take even a tiny fragment from a hologram picture, it still contains the whole image. As a comparison, even a tiny fragment of God's natural creation can reflect the Divine. The miraculous is present in our daily lives if we stay open and receptive to be aware of it. It is easy from time to time to take life for granted and feel that it is mostly drudgery. Sometimes we are distracted by difficult challenges that may confront us. Life is not always easy, as we all know. But it is important for us to remember the good that is in our lives. We do live on a beautiful planet, and we're created in God's image. May we stay present to the everyday grace in the world around and within us. May we see the heavens reflected in the eyes of our friends, family, and even strangers!

Divine Grace also comes to us directly from God and the non-physical Divine realms of angels, saints, and ascended ones. Knowledge of these Divine beings is presented in varying ways in most of the great religions of the world. This is true beyond any doubt to me through faith and through direct experience. This probably is true for a lot of us. At the same time I feel that it is important that each of us only accept what resonates in our own heart and soul. If some aspects of the information presented in this chapter and book are new to some people, I encourage those parts to be read as interesting theories to consider. We don't all need to have exactly the same beliefs. Sometimes we grow in significantly beneficial ways by keeping an open inquiring mind and thinking about insights over time.

Life on Our Beautiful Planet Earth is a Gift of Divine Grace

The miracle of the gift of life is Divine Grace. Every breath we breathe is a precious gift. The blood pulsing through our arteries and veins is a miracle. How can I begin to write about all this wonder? One time I was relaxing under a tree and without thinking about it I rested my fingers lightly on the side of my throat. I became aware of the steady gentle pulse of my body pumping blood and doing its faithful ministry minute by minute, hour by hour, day by day, and year by year. I hope that it doesn't sound melodramatic, but in that moment I was overwhelmed with love, awe, and thankfulness for my body. I realized what a miracle of Divine Grace it is to have this wonderful body in which to enjoy life on earth. I tremendously appreciate and choose to take conscientious care of this Divine gift.

If you will, pause a moment and gently place your fingers on the pulse beat at your neck or wrist, or place your hand on your chest and feel your heart beat. Just quietly be with your body for a little while. Allow yourself to feel how faithful and steady your body is in its ministry to you. I encourage you to feel love and appreciation for your fantastic body that works so hard for you day and night in innumerable ways. Let gratefulness for the miracle of life fill your whole being with peace. This is the ever so precious body that each of us has been given in order to have beautiful experiences and learn valuable wisdom in the "school house of planet Earth."

Being Near the Ocean or a Lake or River is Grace that Feeds my Soul

For several years I lived within walking distance of the Atlantic Ocean. My daily pilgrimage was to walk to the ocean to renew my soul. I silently absorbed the mystery and grace of the massive waters. My mind would be still as I gazed with awe and respect. Every form of natural waters has its unique gift. Watching a stream or a small river meander along its path cascading over rocks is nurturing. Plants often nestle gracefully on each bank of the flowing waters. I love sitting on a large rock in the middle of a stream with water bubbling and swishing by. Once I lived near a quiet stretch of a beautiful river that felt like a temple to me. As I frequently walked that serene river bank the heavens seemed to open wide and immerse me in peace and grace. What memories come to you of the wonder of water in your life?

Water quenches our thirst and flows throughout our bodies. A very high percentage of our body is water. No wonder it is so beloved! One time when I was attending a gathering, each participant was asked to bring something that he or she treasured. We were to show it and talk a few minutes. I thought about some of my special keepsakes. Then it was totally clear that I would take a glass of water--which I did joyfully with all my heart! Have you thought deeply about the miracle of the cleaning, renewing, sustaining power of water?

I feel so thankful for water. Water is a Sacred gift of Divine Grace. May we preserve the purity of our Sacred waters unpolluted.

Flowers as Divine Grace

When I take time to really gaze at the exquisite beauty of a flower, I feel drawn into the glow of its radiant colors. I love seeing the flowers exuberantly rising up from Mother Earth. They are like unbelievably lovely gems. How can they possibly be crafted in such exquisite perfection? The petals and other intricate parts of the flowers are often unbelievably intricate and lush, as with an iris. The amazing detail of its forms can be breathtaking. The creation of such beauty baffles my mind. I feel embraced by the rich perfumed fragrance and the lovely light-hearted peaceful energy they emanate. What more can I say? Gardening was my mother's form of meditation, so I grew up surrounded by lavish flowers. Flowers are surely Divine gifts to lift our Spirits and remind us of our eternal home in Heaven. Truly the flowers and the whole plant kingdom are gifts of Divine Grace. May we give thanks. The awesome vegetables grow in abundance to feed us generously. For this, I feel endless gratitude. The trees, bushes, and the whole vast variety of plants are our extraordinarily generous friends. Which plants do you particularly love? In what ways do you feel that they are a blessing to you? The presence of the plant kingdom in our lives is truly Divine Grace.

A Starry Night as an Expression of Grace (Real Life Anonymous Sharing)

When I was sixteen I went to a church conference in a rural area. On the last night we sat out on a hill and just gazed at the sky. It was a clear night out in the country and the stars just seemed to stretch out forever. The beauty of creation lifted and inspired me. While I was gazing at the sky I felt a real connectedness to everything and truly sensed that I was in the presence of something greater than myself. I felt deeply blessed. Another special memory is that I used to love to sometimes sit in a tree during the day. I would sit in the tree and look up at the sky. I felt that there was something I needed to remember, something that was beyond me. It felt like it was right there, and I felt a real peace. I felt God, yes, I felt God so closely. (End of Anonymous sharing.)

Have You Ever Felt the Presence of the Divine As You Gazed at the Sky?

Since I was a child I've loved to gaze up at the vast endless expanse of the blue sky above. It helps me feel close to Heaven. Once I had the privilege to see the Northern Lights (Aurora Borealis) with brilliant undulating colors filling the sky for hours. What a thrilling sight! Another time when watching an extraordinarily beautiful sunset reflected over the Atlantic Ocean, I and friends were in ecstasy when we looked behind us and the full moon had risen in all its majesty. Who would believe it?! With simultaneously an awesome sunset and a powerful full moon we were surrounded by glory and were filled with gratitude for such a gift!

What a blessing! Maybe you like to gaze up at the sky, too! What memories come to you of times when you sensed you were in the presence of the Divine when gazing at the sky? A starry night? Sunrises and sunsets? Shooting stars? Rainbows? Aurora Borealis? Fluffy white clouds peacefully floating so high above across the vast canopy? These wondrous expressions of the sky are reminders of the miracle of existence, and are gifts of Divine Grace.

As we move through each day with our eyes and hearts open there is so much for which to be thankful. No matter what is going on in our lives, appreciation for the good that we do have will help sustain us. Life is an expression of Divine Grace and we can observe the signs of it everywhere. The mineral kingdom rises majestically as towering mountains and shines as sparkling crystals. The animal kingdom blesses this planet with its tremendous array of awesome animals that never cease to amaze and fascinate us. We see grace in the smiles of our friends and loved ones. We sense it in the gentle breeze, the warmth of the sun, and in the rhythm of our breath.

Divine Grace and Non-physical Realities

Now let us consider Divine Grace as it comes to us from non-physical levels of reality. Life on planet Earth can be wonderful beyond belief. It can also be challenging for probably all of us now and then. There are times when we may wish for some help to get us through a difficult situation. Divine Grace can sometimes help support us when we may feel heavily burdened or discouraged.

For many there is a mystery to the idea of Divine Grace. It may have overtones of the supernatural, like a Divine hand reaching down and helping us out. In truth, Divine Grace is simply science at a higher turn of the spiral. There are many levels of reality in different dimensions. Each level or aspect of reality exists in a different energy frequency or vibration. We could consider this like different channels on a radio or television. We choose the channel to which we wish to listen or that we wish to watch. Physical life on planet Earth could be considered one channel. Heaven could be considered another channel. There are many gradations between Earth and Heaven and within Heaven itself. In the Bible it says in St. John 14:2, "In my Father's house there are many mansions."

A person can be busy living life within physical reality (as a physical human being) and not be aware of Spiritual beings existing within the higher (more subtle and less dense) realities. This doesn't mean that the nonphysical realities don't exist. To help clarify the terms dense and subtle, I will give an example. Ice is dense and hard. Melted ice becomes water which is less dense and is fluid. Heated water can become steam which is subtle and can mainly be felt as warmth and moisture. It can be quite transparent or just slightly visible. Yet ice and water and steam are all the same substance chemically. If we compare angels and humans, you might say that a human has a relatively more dense physical body. Angels have a fairly subtle non-physical body that is transparent to most human's eyes. Scientists who are looking for life on other planets might possibly do well to look for less dense life forms.

These higher (more subtle and less dense) levels of reality are what the Spiritual texts refer to as Heaven. As said, there are numerous levels of Heaven. Sometimes people dream about these levels and consider it just a beautiful dream, and perhaps dismiss it when they wake up. It is worthwhile writing down a few sentences about a dream that seems special, and then letting it be in the back of our minds during the day and sense if some valuable insight comes to us. Uplifting dreams can sometimes be an experience of attending "Soul School" while we sleep. Valuable lessons can be learned from "Soul School" dreams. These higher realities can be experienced by some very sensitive Spiritual people not only through dreams, but also during meditation. This type of awareness can even be part of some people's normal ongoing experience. It is for me.

If we are interested in having Spiritual dreams, it can be helpful to meditate or do something uplifting before going to sleep--and then pray for inspiring dreams. It is important to not watch a frightening or depressing movie or T.V. program or read a scary book before retiring for the night. That can put us in the lower astral (lower emotional) level of consciousness where frightening or undesirable dreams may manifest. Let's try nurturing ourselves gently in some way, instead.

Divine Grace Can Come in Many Forms

We can sometimes be instruments of Divine Grace for others in small or large ways. Someone who we know and love may be in need in some way through illness, accident, trauma, or some other reason. They may have called us for help or we may have heard of their need through a mutual friend or relative. We care deeply and want to be of service in some way so we reach out to them in whatever way seems possible and appropriate. We may take a warm nutritious meal over to our friend and their family. We may drive the individual to a doctor's appointment, or help them in some other loving way. We all know what a huge difference this can make when we are in need. This is one way of being "God's hands and feet on Earth."

As we align ourselves with Spiritual realities, it may enhance the likelihood of help coming to us from these higher levels. There may be times when we may be dealing with a tough challenge and we are surprised by a helpful event that we sense is more than ordinary reality. We may feel that something miraculous has happened and we may not have any explanation for it. Angels and Spiritual helpers from higher vibrational dimensions are aware of our experiences on physical plane Earth and may choose to help us in unexpected ways. They may help us move through a difficulty that would not have any redeeming features for our soul learning. This kind of situation might be called a "Divine intervention." It is a form of Divine Grace. This may seem miraculous, but it is more like a friend deciding to "lend a hand."

God has many helpers who are very busy helping humanity. These could be angels, they could be loved ones from this life who have died and are now in Heaven. They could be close soul friends we knew in previous reincarnations on planet Earth. Sometimes human strangers may appear and help us in moments of great need. They could be moved by the deep kindness in their own hearts, or they could be inspired by the Divine--even to the extent of going out of their way to arrive just where we may be needing help and at just the right moment. Then there are the additional cases of angels actually taking visible form to help provide miraculous assistance in great emergencies or at very special Spiritual moments. Situations like these are well documented in the Bible and in more recent times throughout the world. This is all part of the normal expanded reality.

We can pray to God and to the angels for ourselves and for our loved ones and for the whole planet. The Divine wants to help us where possible. We can help open these doors by praying to God for Divine Grace.

Sometimes There Are Experiences We Agreed to Before We Were Born

It is important to mention that sometimes there may be difficult experiences that we are going through now that we agreed to before we were born. We perhaps agreed to them as a soul because they would help us learn certain very valuable wisdoms. It may be that by going through some challenging experiences we can thereby be better able to help others who would be going through similar experiences in the future. There are times that our lives develop in a certain way because of something we did in a previous life that our soul lived on planet Earth. We may need to complete something that our soul left unfinished then. There are many reasons that can contribute to events unfolding the way they do in our lives. Sometimes heredity and genetics are major factors in certain health issues that may develop.

Certainly one's present life is also a reflection of one's decisions and actions in the current life so far. One may have created imbalances with people during this life that need to be addressed and worked through in some appropriate way. If this doesn't occur with the person with whom the original situation occurred, then a similar situation may present itself with another person. It is important to recognize when "old unfinished business" reoccurs in one's life--and to resolve it wisely (and set it to rest) if only in one's own mind and attitudes.

So there may be situations in our lives that Divine Grace can't take away for us. It doesn't mean that God doesn't love us. It is important that we don't feel cheated if Spiritual help doesn't seem to manifest in the way we wish. By praying for Divine Grace, God can help give us the strength and courage to grow through and learn from challenges that come our way. When eventually it is our time to leave our physical body--God, Heavenly Saints, and the angels can help us ascend to our "Heavenly Home" embraced in radiant Spiritual Light and Divine Love.

Earth is in a Period of Rapid Change and Development

Planet Earth, as you may realize, is in a period of rapid change and development. Divine Grace is active not only for positive growth and progress for human life, but for the advancement of our planet as a whole. This is exceedingly true in technology. Grace is active as gifts of inspired insights for new inventions. Every year important new inventions are revolutionizing our world with amazing new breakthroughs in all fields of technology. We carry computers in our pockets that used to be the size of a very large room in the 1970s. What seems impossible one day becomes commonplace reality almost the next day. It is awesome and breathtaking. What used to be shown in science fiction films is now for sale in our stores. Some of our astronauts are living in outer space. Paper communication is rapidly becoming a thing of the past. We are becoming used to rethinking what is possible on a regular basis. This astounding technological change is coming from a combination of Divine Grace and from a source within the consciousness of the scientists that is going through a profound transformation. This transformation is going on within each of us in our own way. Humanity can actualize a higher level of spectacular technology because we as a human race have a higher and higher level of spectacular consciousness. As we challenge and open our consciousness to new ideas and ways of thinking and functioning, we are actually changing and growing in subtle ways ourselves.

It is well known that every atom in our planet and within the body of each of us is like a miniature solar system. The electrons in each atom move around the nucleus of the atom (theories vary somewhat as to the details). Planets in our solar system orbit around the sun. The space between the electrons and the nucleus within an atom is vast. Every atom is mainly empty space, just like our solar system is mainly empty space. It is all in constant motion. Awesome, right? "As above--so below" is a Spiritual truism. Hence our physical body is not as solid as most of us may tend to feel. It appears clear that according to mainstream science our physical body is vibrational in essence.

People in the field of Spiritual intuitive science are of the opinion that the speed at which these atoms in our body are vibrating is increasing slightly and that the human body is very gradually becoming less dense. Albert Einstein and noted astronomers put forth that our Universe is expanding. Matter within the Universe such as galaxies are observed to be receding very gradually in all directions. It is considered that the Universe was at one time in a more compact compressed state. Hence, the Universe is evolving and changing. Apparently, nothing stays still or the same in this Universe, and likewise nothing stays still or the same in our body. To repeat "as above, so below."

Now let's bring our attention back to the physical world as it is more familiar to us. The relative speed of life change and transition could be compared to the process of traveling. Let's say we need to get from one place or reality to another. How do we choose to get there? In past centuries if people needed to travel they either walked, rode a horse, perhaps road in a wagon, or a ship. Travel was slow. Today we can, of course, fly in a jet to the other side of the earth while we have a relaxing snooze. Just as transportation has sped up, so has life change sped up. You may sense something new evolving and growing within you.

Spherical Time Makes Intuitional Awareness More Possible

We traditionally have experienced one moment following the next in a linear manner. The idea has been that a person can only truly experience one moment at a time. It is like pouring water in a glass which represents the present moment, and then pouring water in a separate new glass which represents the next moment. Today, we are more aware of time being a flow. As we experience the present moment, we can sometimes simultaneously be aware of the past and the possible future. This is spherical time. In spherical time we are not dwelling in the past or in the future. To a certain extent we experience the past and future as part of the present. Some people may call this "no time" or "all time." The past and the future interpenetrate in the present moment. This makes intuitional awareness more possible. More and more people today are finding that they have intuitional flashes of awareness. We probably all have intuitional flashes now and then (or often). Intuition is a normal part of human consciousness that is expanding. This fluidity of consciousness opens us to be more aware of the Spiritual dimensions. In the Spiritual dimension, atoms are vibrating at a higher turn of the spiral that moves from more dense to less dense.

We Can Open to Receive Divine Grace More Abundantly

This brings us back to our helpful "friends" in the Spiritual realms who can sometimes help us through Divine Grace. We can't count on Divine Grace for our every request for reasons mentioned previously, but invocation and prayer can definitely help. A person can be waiting outside a door a long time if he or she doesn't knock or ring the doorbell. This is where prayer and invocation come in. It helps to let the Divine know that we are ready and waiting for the next step of our life path. In this regard it is desirable to meditate first to raise our consciousness. It can be helpful to listen to my audio "Meditation to Enhance Your Experience of the Divine Qualities" (with focus on Grace). Then, a helpful prayer can be: Dear God, please bless me and my loved ones with enhanced Divine Grace. It can be beneficial to put the prayer in our own words and to include names of those for whom we wish to pray. Another approach is an affirmation such as, "I gratefully open to receive the blessings of Divine Grace. Thank you, God." An additional important value of such an affirmation is that it is communicating with our subconscious that we are worthy of this blessing and we are letting it into our life.

Another way to enhance our receiving Divine Grace more abundantly is to live the life that we are wishing to manifest through grace. Whatever it is that we wish to create in our life--it is helpful to live as though it is true now to whatever extent possible. This is showing the Universe that we are serious about creating this in our life. We may pray and invoke to the Divine that we wish to be a musician, but at the same time we need to practice our instrument daily. It would be important to study music theory and to listen to and attend performances of the type of music we wish to be able to play. This is common sense, but it is important to mention so that we don't feel that Divine Grace can do it for us without our participating.

If you are praying to the Divine for Grace to heal you, it is crucial for you as much as possible to actively live a healthy life style including your food, drink, exercise, peace of mind, and seeing your health care practitioner. You need to create the action and will power into which the energy of Grace can be poured. If mobilizing the needed will-power is part of the problem, then certainly pray to God to support you in that way.

Everything works together in synchronicity. Never doubt yourself and your capacity to accomplish your dreams. Take steps as you feel ready, believe in your goal, pray to God to bless you with Divine Grace, and keep working and applying yourself in that direction. Amazing things can be accomplished. Not all goals require money or even a great deal of time. Some goals mainly require confidence and persistence and luck. Luck is really Divine Grace in disguise. Know that you are not alone in your adventure of life. You are the visible partner. God, your Higher Self and Soul, the angels, and the Spiritual realms are the invisible partners. Allow Divine Grace to bless your life as you move ahead on your soul journey.

Enhancing Divine Grace Through Participating In Churches, Synagogues, Temples, and Spiritual Groups and Classes Everywhere

I feel that Divine Grace is always blessing us and our planet through churches, synagogues, temples, and through countless Spiritual organizations, groups, and classes everywhere. The important thing is to sense what Spiritual group truly helps lift our heart and soul and resonates with our inner being. Do we sense Divine Love, Peace, Joy, Grace, Truth, Wisdom, and other Divine Qualities in a particular group? We're all different and resonate with different Spiritual groups.

Real Life Sharings Of How Divine Grace Can Bless One's Life

I've Had Many Experiences Of Grace In My Life
~ by Rev. Valerie Mansfield, Louisville, Kentucky

I've had many experiences of Grace in my life, many experiences of Divine Spirit moving through myself, my family, and my church. I'm very open to the Spiritual. I live my life every day as I feel guided. When I make a decision in my daily life, I pray and meditate on it as to what is best in the situation for me and those involved. My prayers are answered for the best.

A group of us drove a distance to a funeral service for our friend, an assistant minister at our church. On the way back I pulled out of the church where the service was held, and I went a different direction than everyone else considered to be the right way. They all said, "You're going the wrong way, turn around." I said, "No, we need to go this way." So I drove along making turns this way and that way, and they talked and didn't pay attention. An hour later they looked at me and said, "You're lost," I said, "I'm not really lost, I'm finding my way to where I need to be." When we finally came to a visitor's center, I looked at the map there--and I knew how to get home. We were in the hills of Tennessee. We stopped at a little store right before we came to a tunnel that we needed to go through to get home. A woman at the store said that there had been a wreck on the other side of the tunnel that had stopped traffic for three hours. Traffic had just started moving again. Some people were stuck in the tunnel for all three hours. We were stunned because one of the girls who were with us had claustrophobia. Had we not gone a roundabout way, we might easily have been trapped in the tunnel and it would have been traumatic for her and everyone. So it worked out well. Spirit guides me. (See Resources Page)

My Whole Life Has Been Led By Divine Grace

~ by Sue R.

I feel my whole life has been led by Divine Grace. The first time I really felt it was when I left Florida. I had been in a really bad marriage. I was literally beaten and bruised from my head and shoulders to my knees. When I left I was just completely guided. I headed north, and I was able to go to my sister's home in New York where I received a lot of help. I had loving family. I never really doubted that everything was going to work out O.K. I met my wonderful second husband there.

Sometimes when issues have come up in my life, I have struggled to make something happen in a certain way. I always knew that once I stopped trying to make things happen in a way that wasn't working, everything would come together. It's kind of like when you try to put a puzzle piece in where it doesn't go. You try to force it and it doesn't work. When you find the right one, it just slides right in. It works. There's just no doubt in my mind. I don't have a belief in Divine Grace; I have a knowing about Divine Grace. I'm always guided. Every problem I've ever had was because I've chosen to do it on my own, and not listened to my inner knowing. Finally when I pay attention the situation resolves itself. I feel led by Grace. Sometimes I sense a word. I have "wow" moments. If I had a choice between having physical luxuries and having this inner peace, I would take this inner peace.

Miracle of Grace During and After a Fire

~ by Elsa Lichman, Waltham, Massachusetts

I had an extended stay in a small motel one winter while my house was under repair. The front desk staff was congenial; a light breakfast was set up daily in the lobby. Guests came from the U.S. and abroad, from all walks of life. I encountered a Haitian family from the inner city staying there. One morning they were being picked up to go off to school, and I commented to the older girl that it was too cold to go out without a coat. She turned out to be the mother of four and the aunt of one child! They had been burned out of their apartment, and were left with nothing. Her kindergartner had saved the three of them who were home at the time. The girl remembered her school visit from the fire department and their directive to: "Stop, drop, and roll." When the kids came back to the motel from school, the mother showed us their artwork and papers, all with excellent grades. In two motel rooms, she had them study hard and do their homework. I told her I was amazed, and she said, "In my culture, education is very important." I worked in public education, and knew many families with lovely homes and state of the art computers, whose children were unmotivated and doing poorly. Every night a tall, bearded, husky, Jewish teacher from their distant school arrived like Santa with a huge vat of home-cooked food for the family. I decided to call our city newspaper to have them write up this inspiring story. But just then an apartment was found for the family, right before Christmas. The basement of their school was overflowing with donated household furniture and goods for their new home. (See Resources Page)

During Dangerous Moments Driving My Car I Experienced Grace

~ by David

When I left home the road conditions weren't bad. When I got on the interstate it kept snowing faster and faster. Before long it was really coming down and the visibility was starting to get bad. I thought to myself, "The road is starting to look slippery out here, I better be careful!" Right about that time the back end of my car started doing a little fishtail. The car very quickly slid off the road. Within a fraction of a second the back end of my car completely lost control. The car went up an embankment and spun around. I kept thinking, "I hope that my car doesn't get hurt." It didn't occur to me that I might get hurt. It was so fast that there was nothing I could do, I couldn't hit the brakes. I couldn't steer out of it; I just had to hang on. By a miracle I landed back on the interstate heading the same direction as before. It felt like Grace. I hadn't hit a car, or a pole, or anything else. I was fine, the car was fine, and everything was fine. Since then, whenever I drive by that spot I think about what a miracle that really was. There are so many things sticking up in that area it seems almost impossible that I could do that and not hit something. I felt like I was tapped by an angel with a reminder that I need to slow down.

Miracle Rose

~ Elsa Lichman, Waltham, Massachusetts

I am with a friend who leads me to a steep hill during our walk by the water. She forgets my limitations and runs ahead, not remembering I may need help over the rough spot. Just as the slope becomes almost vertical, I look down. There, on the ground, with no house or garden in sight, is one perfect rose. When I had my mother, it was the exact variety she used to pick, only very rarely, when Dad was ill and could not get out to see the garden.

It is a soft orange, with velvety curled petals, and a particular, exquisite scent. The seven-inch stem is perfectly cut on an angle, ready to be displayed in a vase. It looks and smells so familiar, I say out loud, "Thanks, Mom." I know I can scramble safely up the last assent. I take it home with the stem wrapped in wet towels, and place it in a vase. Every time I see it, I stop whatever I am doing and stare at this reminder of mystery and magic, and of my mother's love. Now the petals and stem are dried, kept for those discouraging moments when the world seems too bleak or uncaring. (See Resources Page)

Four Angels Expressing Divine Grace
Original art by Joyce J.C. Gerrish

WORKBOOK: Enrichment Experiences For Enhancing Grace In Your Life

Enjoy the adventure of exploring these enrichment experiences on your own--or gather a few friends to share the journey with you. Be inspired by the audio meditation and soul song for this chapter. Reflect on some of the stimulating ideas and questions.

Questions for Reflection and Discussion

Reflection, discussion, journal writing, expressing your feelings in drawings or other creative ways can all be very valuable to help you delve into these questions in truly meaningful and relevant ways. Before focusing on the questions, you may wish to meditate with the twelve-minute audio or transcribed meditation for Divine Grace--and/or listen to the soul song "Grace of God."

1. Have you ever had an experience that you felt was Divine Grace occurring in your life or in the life of a loved one? Describe it and how you felt about it. What was the effect of the Divine Grace in your life and/or in the life of your loved one?

2. When you are facing a serious challenge in your life or in the life of someone to whom you are close, do you pray for Divine support and Grace? How do you feel about prayer? Is prayer important to you in your life? Do you pray on a regular basis?

3. How do you feel about the possibility of Spiritual Realms where humans reside after they leave the physical body at death? This is traditionally called Heaven. Do you believe that people go to Heaven when they leave their physical body at death, or do you believe that a person's consciousness simply ceases to exist at death? Do you believe in purgatory where some people

go to continue their Spiritual growth until they are ready for Heaven? How do you feel about the possibility that there are various levels in the Spiritual dimensions of more and more refined radiant luminous Spiritual realities of Holy Divine Angels and Ascended Saints?

Action Suggestions For Enhancing Divine Grace In Your Life

1. Try meditating with the audio "Meditation to Enhance Your Experience of the Divine Qualities," with focus on Grace. You can access it through SecretsofWisdom.net. Meditating for awhile before praying can enhance the prayer experience.

2. Try listening to the Grace soul song audio "Grace of God." Try singing along. Inspirational singing can be a form of prayer in song. Listen and sing with it several times, if you like. Once you feel immersed, that is an excellent time to pray to God that Divine Grace be enhanced in your life and in the lives of people you know who are in special need. "Grace of God" soul song can be accessed through the website.

3. One's whole life can really become a prayer and an expression of Divine Grace. As you align yourself with the Divine and with your Higher Self, you truly can become an expression of Divine Grace to the life around you. If you wish, try keeping a prayer or mantra in your mind periodically throughout the day. A mantra is a short Spiritual phrase or word that one says over and over silently (or out loud in private) to help keep one's consciousness uplifted and connected to the Divine. That connection allows Divine Light and blessings to flow more freely to you and to those around you.

4. Prayers of worship, adoration, and thankfulness are important and they are a valuable balance alongside prayers of invocation for Divine Grace. This is true when invoking all the Divine Qualities of God as described in this book. "I thank you, Divine. I thank you, God, for the blessings in my life. I love you, God. Thy Divine Love and Light and Grace lift my heart and Soul and hold me steady in the Spiritual Truth of my being." Feel free to pray in your own words.

5. If you are interested in having Spiritual dreams, it can be helpful to meditate or do something uplifting before going to sleep--and then pray for inspiring dreams. As previously mentioned, it is important to not watch a frightening or depressing movie or T.V. program or read a scary book before retiring for the night. In the morning when you first wake up, ask yourself "what did I dream about last night?" Whatever impression you recall no matter how small or faint it may be, jot it down in a journal or notebook that you keep ready by your bed. The act of writing down or telling someone else helps to bring the memory more solidly into your mind and brain--and may bring additional recall. Do this on a regular basis, and you may find that you begin to have more vivid and uplifting dreams. If you find that you sometimes have dreams of problems that need solving, you may wish to read the article "Dream Exploration" at SecretsofWisdom.net/articles and/or consult a counselor or therapist who works with dreams.

Audio "Meditation to Enhance Your Experience of The Divine Qualities," With Focus on Grace

Pray to the Divine to bless your meditation and enhance Divine Grace in your life. With this audio you'll be guided to sense yourself immersed in Peace, Light, and the balm of Divine Grace. Choose one or more of the following affirmations (or something similar) that feels particularly helpful for you to affirm during your meditation. Before transferring to the website to listen to the meditation, write down the affirmation(s) you choose and the helpful color Ruby Gold. Later, place it where you'll see it daily and be reminded to affirm it for a minute or two several times a day.

◆ I pray to God to bless my family and myself with Divine Grace.

◆ I thank the Divine for the continuing blessings and Divine Grace in my life.

◆ Divine Grace fills my being with Light and Love and Peace.

Helpful color for meditating on Divine Grace is Ruby Gold (ruby with gold flecks in it).

I encourage you to enjoy this meditation when you wish to support Divine Grace in your life. Connect to SecretsofWisdom.net where you can listen to the twelve-minute "Meditation to Enhance the Divine Qualities," with focus on Grace.

(Also see transcribed version of meditation to enhance Divine Grace" at end of this chapter.)

Uplifting Audio Soul Song: *"Grace of God"*

~ By Joyce

Consider it a prayer in song for enhancing your sense of opening to receive the blessings of Divine Grace. The words are:

Grace of God, wash me.

Wash away all fears and trials.

Waters of Grace, cleanse me anew.

As you chant or listen to this Soul Song, feel yourself relax and begin to flow with it. Close your eyes and really sense it helping to bring you into an inspired sense of openness to Divine Grace. Connect to SecretsofWisdom.net to listen to "Grace of God."

Transcribed version Of Meditation To Enhance Your Experience Of Divine Grace

If possible, listen to some relaxing nonverbal music. Say a short prayer calling on the Divine to bless your meditation and to bless your life with enhanced Divine Grace.

Visualize yourself in a ball of light to help strengthen your energy field.

Become aware of and follow your breath as it gently flows in and out your nose at its own pace.

Imagine yourself as a large tree sending powerful roots deep into the earth to help you feel grounded and prevent possibly feeling spacey.

As you breathe in through your nose, imagine you are breathing up the strength of the earth into your body.

For a few minutes, focus on listening to the relaxing music and being aware of your breath flowing in and out your nose.

As you breathe in through your nose, imagine you are breathing in light.

Next breathe in through your nose and out your mouth for about a minute VERY GENTLY.

Now, very gently breathe in through your mouth and out your nose for about a minute.

Then extra gently breathe in and out your mouth for a minute or so.

Now return to breathing in and out your nose.

Visualize ruby light with gold flecks in it.

As you breathe in through your nose, imagine you are breathing in ruby gold light into your whole being.

As you breathe out your nose, periodically silently say one or more of the following affirmations that you feel would be helpful to affirm during the meditation.

◆ I pray to God to bless myself and my family with Divine Grace.

◆ I thank the Divine for the continuing blessings and Divine Grace in my life.

◆ Divine Grace fills my being with Light and Love and Peace.

Pray for Divine Grace to bless you and your loved ones.

Continue in that manner for a few minutes or as long as you wish.

Conclude by thanking the Divine and once more sending down roots to Mother Earth for stability and grounding.

Write the affirmation(s) you choose and place it where you'll see it several times a day and be reminded to affirm it for a minute or two.

Enjoy this meditation when you wish to enhance Divine Grace in your life.

Peace.

Honoring Precious Water
Original art by Joyce J.C. Gerrish

Chapter Seventeen

ABUNDANCE WHILE LIVING LIGHTLY ON THE LAND

Enhancing Divine Abundance in Your Life

Music is one of the abundant blessings of life. We can all experience feelings of abundance through music. Connect to SecretsofWisdom.net to listen to the soul song "We Are Blessed," while gazing at the full color design "Man Honoring Nature."

Life Is Meant To Be Abundant And Joyful

I feel that God created humanity to enjoy being alive, not to suffer. God has unlimited potential, and we as humans are created in the image of God. Our capacity is immense. Too often people get into thinking about themselves as limited, which is very far from the truth. The whole human family can enjoy abundance if we each choose to truly use our vast creative ingenuity. There are plenty of resources on earth if we utilize them wisely without waste and if we all share fairly. It has been widely accepted that some people will inevitably have much more than other people. Today a few have staggering wealth, the vast majority is just getting by, and too many have almost nothing. This creates tragic suffering and unnecessary power struggles. I feel that God created earth and humanity with the intention that all would share--and there would be plenty of whatever is needed for everyone. (See section on Time Bank later in this chapter.)

The Native Americans lived in North America for a very long time before settlers arrived from elsewhere. The traditional Native Americans had a very natural life style on the land--they were very practical and had good common sense about life. They basically had everything they needed--they shared and no one was left out. Children were loved and watched over by the whole tribe or village. The elders were revered and respected for their wisdom, experience, and stories. There was a sense of group destiny together; everyone counted as being important to the whole. No one fell through the cracks. Cooking was considered sacred, and food was respected because it sustained the body in health. What went into the food was only what they knew from generation to generation would sustain health. Food came straight from Mother Nature to their meals. They lived naturally and were fairly healthy. If they did get sick, herbal remedies worked quite well. Life was basically good and met their needs.

Growing a Vegetable Garden Is an Excellent Way To Feel Abundant

How can this traditional approach to abundance help us today? Tending a vegetable garden is a really good way to feel plentiful as you work hand in hand with Mother Nature in growing your own food. If you have an available backyard, it is perhaps eagerly waiting to be a vegetable garden. People who live in apartments can find out about possible community garden plots which are available to people in many cities. Some small farms provide memberships for people who would like to pay in advance for a share of their organically grown produce. It can be even less expensive if one participates in gardening at the farm.

Vertical tower gardening utilizing hydroponics is an approach to gardening that may be just what a lot of city dwellers will love. For instance, in four square feet a person can grow fifty plus vegetable plants. Yikes! Now that is making excellent use of space! This approach to gardening involves growing plants without the use of a traditional soil medium. The plants grow in water that has rich nutrients added. You may wish to check out on line about vertical tower gardening and hydroponics. A friend of mine is thrilled with the vegetables she is growing with this approach.

The plant kingdom generously provides abundant food for humanity to eat. Plants grow bountifully for everyone who simply put seeds in the ground (or in water) and provides some care as needed. The plant kingdom has been providing delicious vegetables and fruits and nuts and seeds growing wild since before humanity appeared on planet Earth. The scene was set for people to have plenty of food to eat so that no one would ever need to go hungry. That was and is the intention. We owe deep appreciation to the plant kingdom.

Like Native Americans and indigenous peoples everywhere, we can grow foods naturally without chemicals and pesticides. We can stay healthier by living in harmony with planet Earth and eating fresh natural foods that aren't laden with pesticides. We can also support our wellness with organically grown herbs. These approaches, plus natural healing, can support our wellness and provide some preventive health benefits. Being naturally healthy can possibly save a lot on medical expenses and thereby help stretch the family budget.

Our Worth is Determined by Who We Are Inside--Not by What We Buy

I suggest that abundance is having good quality products that we truly need, and then taking exceedingly good care of them so they will last a long time. My car is over fourteen years old now and it is in excellent condition. It got a fine new coat of paint a few years ago and looks really good. The mechanics say it is ready to go for plenty of years to come. For those people who have the money to buy new cars, that is good--but many people can't afford it. The important thing is to not buy into the idea that what we purchase determines our worth. Our worth is determined by who we are inside. Please never forget that. We are here on earth to be supportive to each other, not to be in competition. We may even find that abundance is being content with a simpler but perhaps even more satisfying lifestyle.

Current consumer attitudes and behaviors in almost all developed countries are depleting our planet's precious resources at an alarming rate. We need to be respectful caretakers of our beloved planet and not deplete or disturb its resources at a faster rate than they can be renewed and restored. Our role as planetary caretakers is a profoundly crucial understanding to fully grasp. The good news is that it is possible for all of us to enjoy an abundant, joyful life totally in harmony with Mother Earth.

Some of what can help us find this ecological balance are time honored methods and wisdoms that have been pursued for thousands of years--such as composting food scraps and extensive recycling. Composting food scraps can be challenging for many city dwellers, but innovative designs for composting bins can assist there. Also very important for ecological balance are the extensive advances in green technologies such as solar innovations.

The Earth Is Our Abundant Mother. It's Our Honor and Responsibility To Protect and Preserve Her

Living lightly on the land is an art whose time is come. Living lightly on the land is an awareness that the Earth is a living organism. The Earth is not an inert huge revolving sphere. The Earth is a delicate ecological balance of untold numbers of species of plants, animals with their homes and food sources, and complex geological land formations. It is rich natural humus soil, the precious waters, and the air we breathe. All of this needs to be preserved and protected. The intended role of humans on this planet is as caretakers and stewards. How can we possibly let our Mother Earth down?

The Magic of Recycling Helps Preserve Our Natural Abundance

Full scale recycling on an individual and societal basis is a crucial and pivotal part of protecting Mother Earth and at the same time ensuring reasonable abundance or enough for all. Recycling and buying recycled products is still in a developing stage in much of the United States. With time and good intention, it can make a huge contribution to preserving our natural resources. It gives many of us a good feeling to collect all our used papers and recyclable things and take them to the recycling location or put them outside our home in a recycling bin to be picked up. I buy 100% recycled computer printer paper and writing paper, napkins, bathroom tissue, and facial tissue. Maybe you do, too. This all contributes to a healthy renewable cycle. It's valuable to know that paper products created from sugar cane husks and bamboo and other alternative sources are now available widely in addition to paper made from trees. If these aren't in your stores, it is worth asking for them. To grow a new tree for making paper products often takes about thirty-five years. Quick growing bamboo can regenerate in about six months. Sugarcane husks would normally be disposed of as a byproduct of sugar. Wow! That's a win-win situation! Theses papers made from alternative materials are not particularly more expensive than conventional paper products made from trees. Reasonable prices are extremely important for convincing large numbers of people to do something a little different.

Let's Look At Ways To Enhance Abundance If Our Housing Budget Is Tight

Is abundance having a really impressive home or apartment with a mortgage payment or a rent that is a massive strain to pay each month-- or having to work two jobs or overwhelming amounts of overtime in order to pay the bills? How large a home does a family or couple or individual need? At one time a family of four was very happy with a compact house or apartment. Their needs were met. They had comfortable places to sleep--perhaps several small bedrooms. There was often a bedroom for the parents and one for each of the two children. Maybe two children shared a bedroom, and that worked out O.K., too, if both were boys or both were girls. In the past there were often grandparents living with the family. It was simple, good, and adequate. They didn't bemoan that they didn't have a house twice as big. They had the whole outdoors to enjoy if they wanted big spaces. I had a happy childhood sharing a bedroom with two sisters. We had one bathroom in a house for six people. It sounds crowded perhaps, but we got along just fine and were contented and felt abundant. Feeling abundant can be dependent on one's outlook.

In the years leading up to when the housing bubble burst around 2008--I was very aware that more and more people were living in homes much bigger than they realistically needed. Homes were being built larger and larger during that period, even though there weren't necessarily more occupants. When the economy took a nose dive, many people started rethinking their life styles, their finances, and their priorities. Some family members moved in with each other to create multi-generational homes. Many young people lived in the family home longer or moved back in.

Elders living in a multi-generational home can possibly help with some cooking or child care while other family members are at a job. That help can perhaps ease worries for those family members who need to be away from home nine or more hours a day attending to work responsibilities and commuting. When an elder is getting to an age where living in an assisted care facility might be considered--living in a relative's home can possibly save massive amounts of money. These approaches are working really well for some people. It uses less energy resources and financial resources when people aren't heating and cooling large mostly empty homes.

Friends can share apartments or homes. Sharing can be very pleasant and interesting. I shared living in a house with friends for many years and enjoyed it. It can make for good companionship. It clearly takes a burden off the bank account and makes it possible to use the money saved in creative ways that may help one move forward toward one's life dreams. That certainly helped me finance my Master's Degree. It can feel reassuring to have options!

Participants in Intentional or Co-Operative Communities Support Each Other's Abundance

Are you familiar with intentional and co-operative communities? This is a growing phenomenon throughout the United States and in other countries. There are many different types of intentional or co-operative communities that are as different from each other as night and day. It can be as simple as an active neighborhood association that decides to co-operate together in really tangible ways. That sounds all-American like small town neighborliness, doesn't it? They may decide to meet for a shared potluck meal at someone's home once a month. The neighborhood association may decide to share tools so that everyone doesn't need to own every tool. They may decide to do child care exchanges. They could have a buying club to buy groceries and household products in bulk at great savings. The members of some intentional communities exchange their work skills with each other through bartering or a system called TimeBank. The sky is the limit as to the number of ways that they could decide to help each other to feel more supported and more abundant. Fantastic right? Likewise, a church can certainly function as an intentional community in all kinds of ways if they choose--along the lines of those just mentioned as well as other ways. An intentional community can be formed among people with a common interest such as visual artists or musicians. Some active retired people are creating special communities. Many different types of intentional communities are forming everywhere, reaching out hands to each other in friendship and mutual support. I've been active with some of these types of intentional communities and found them quite helpful and enjoyable.

Another type of intentional community is where a group of people with a common interest live somewhat away from a city in a semi-rural or rural area. They often will have a farm or large vegetable gardens that they take care of together. They might share meals daily and take turns cooking. They might offer workshops and classes in personal growth, organic gardening, creative arts, music, solar home construction, or other subjects. Visitors may arrive to learn and participate for a period. Some groups come together to share a strong interest in a specific religion. There is a wide variety of options.

Enjoying Abundance Through Pleasures Money Can't Buy!

Another part of my philosophy of abundance is that some of the most marvelous forms of entertainment are FREE! I love to take walks in the summer with the lush flowers, in autumn with the beautifully colored leaves, in the winter with the graceful lines of the bare tree limbs and branches silhouetted against the blue sky, and in the spring with the new delicate buds springing forth on all the plants and trees. What joy to observe the changes in nature day by day throughout the year. My body feels wonderfully alive as I walk, the air feels fresh as I breathe, and I am happy. It never gets boring for a moment. Riding a bicycle is another great way to have a good time and live lightly on the planet. There's no carbon footprint there. You can get your healthy exercise, have fun, and get to your destination at the same time. In a northern climate it is pleasurable and free to ice skate on a frozen pond, cross country ski, or to go sledding. In warm climates swimming and canoeing can be a lot of fun. I love how a canoe can glide almost silently through the water. Playing a musical instrument can be an unbelievable joy--once you get going a little. Ukuleles are popular now again and fairly easy to play. Bird watching is delightful. Try exchanging foot massages with a friend. Entertainment doesn't need to be expensive.

Life on Earth is here for us to enjoy, but not to abuse. Being abundant is not about abusing the planet by consuming more and more resources. This is a misconception that has grown up around the idea of abundance. Abundance is living joyfully in harmony with the planet and our fellow men and women. Abundance needs to always be perceived from the view point of the planet and all humanity, not only from one's own perspective. What is abundance? It may be that some people's idea of abundance needs to be adjusted. Maybe our life is abundant right now; maybe we just need to appreciate more fully what we have. May we develop our love of those gifts that are available to us free from God and from the Universe. These gifts include sharing love with our fellow humanity, breathing fresh air, enjoying a gentle breeze, waking up refreshed after a good night's sleep, drinking pure water, gazing at the stars on a clear night. We are abundantly blessed. May we do all that we can to protect these.

Insights For People Who Are Seriously Struggling Financially

I fully understand that some people are unable to find an appropriate job right now, and abundance may seem painfully out of the question for the time being. Large numbers of other people are only paid minimum wage or a low hourly rate for their hard work, or are only able to secure a part-time job. How can we feel abundant when our income is severely limited or on hold? We have certain basic physical necessities. Each of us definitely should have those needs met.

If the reader is seriously struggling financially, one or more of the following suggestions may be helpful. Have you checked for job retraining programs for low income people? Have you applied for the Supplemental Nutrition Assistance Program (formerly called Food Stamps) or other financial assistance programs? Is there any way that you can downsize your expenses such as by living in a smaller dwelling or sharing living arrangements with others? Are your interests really expensive to pursue--can you find a less expensive way to pursue them? Is there another individual who is pulling you down financially, to whom you need to say no? Are you addicted to some substance or behavior that is draining your finances? If so, it is imperative to seek the help of a rehabilitation program.

Prosperity Consciousness!

Whatever you do, do it with love. When you receive money, bless it and thank God for the prosperity. When you pay a bill or pay for something you need, bless the money or check or financial transaction. Give or send love and thankfulness along with it. As you circulate love and thankfulness along with your financial transactions, it helps keep the money flowing more freely full circle back to you.

Visualization is certainly a part of prosperity consciousness. Visualize what you want to bring into your life. Create a vision board, if you wish. Draw a simple picture of what you wish to manifest into your life. If you don't choose to draw, cut photos out of magazines and glue them onto a poster board or foam board. Have fun with it. The vision board can help focus your consciousness and mobilize your subconscious toward your goal. Try it! If you wish, include words to help describe your dream. For sure include the words "for my highest good." Sometimes what you have in mind might not really bring you the joy and peace that you hope. Sometimes God has something even better for you that is for your even higher good.

If the reader is wealthy, please look deep in your heart and donate very generously to help those in need. Wealth comes with some responsibility for the good of all.

Blessings to each and every one of you and to our whole planetary family for a naturally bountiful life living lightly on the land.

Real Life Sharings About Abundance In Everyday Life

Timebank--An Idea Whose Time Has Come! An Updated Improved Version Of Trade

~ by Joyce with Donna C. Phillips

TimeBank is a fantastic opportunity! It allows people to save money by providing valuable services for each other without exchanging money. The money saved can help stretch one's budget, or can be put toward a vacation or perhaps retirement. There are TimeBank groups in cities all around the United States and in thirty-six countries. The basic idea is that one lists in the group's computer data base the skills that one chooses to offer to others. These could be bookkeeping, gardening skills, moving something with a truck, cooking meals, repairing things, handyperson skills, art works, computer skills, pet sitting, babysitting, tutoring, sewing, counseling, violin lessons, car repair, or anything else useful. The other members also have listed the skills they would be interested in sharing. There are about 400 members currently in the Louisville group. Travel time and preparation time (if any) count toward the TimeBank hours you earn. Everyone's work is valued equally by time spent.

For each hour of work that one does for a member, one gets an hour of credit on the group's computer data base. That then gives one an hour credit to draw on the skills of someone else in the group--it doesn't need to be from the same person one helped. A member can always say "No, I'm too busy right now" when called about a service offered. To join, one needs to apply and have a background check done so that the members know that they are dealing with responsible people. The group shares a potluck meal once a month to get to know each other and find out what skills others are offering. I attended one of their meetings recently and was really impressed. They seem to be idealistic people with warm hearts and common sense. I feel that it is a fantastic way to support each other, save money, and have fun at the same time.

The following are insights of a friend of mine, Donna, who has been active with the group for a while. "One of the ways that I have provided services for other members is by helping to plan their gardens. (I have a background in master garden planning.) I also have earned work hours by taking extra food to the potlucks, and I'm helping the TimeBank administrators on projects for the group. I also have proof reading skills. A person can earn work hour credits by helping at the potlucks with setting up, cleaning up afterwards, and bringing extra food."

Donna continues, "As far as some of what I have received, a licensed electrician from TimeBank came over and put three ceiling fans up for me. I've had a leaky faucet in my bath tub for a while. I had called a plumbing company and they said that it would be $50 for the service run and $100 minimum for the first hour plus parts and other fees. So I just shelved it until I could get somebody from TimeBank. He was here for twenty minutes and showed me how to fix it. It was just a washer with a spring. He showed me how to get the old one out and the new one in. It took a heartbeat to get it done. Last week the same guy came over and got up on my roof and cleared out my gutters and then fixed the gutters where they were sagging in one place. Just as he was leaving it rained and we got to test it. Tomorrow six people are coming to put in my raised garden and mow the lawn. They are a wonderful group of people. They are amazing. Timebank members are what I think all people should be."(See Resources Page)

Bicycles For Transportation And Pleasure

~ by Cora, Louisville, Kentucky

For me biking is this relaxing thing I do that helps me get around. It helps me see scenery and different parts of the city. I grew up here, but I now know it much better than I did before because I need to think more carefully about my routes and how I'm getting places. Being on a bike gives me more time to notice plants around and the beauty of the different houses.

I don't have a car right now. I live with roommates who have cars, and they let me borrow one if I need it. Also, my parents have an extra car that they let me use sometimes. Whenever I have a car and drive around, I can't figure out why I'm doing it. Biking saves a lot of money. That was why I started. I was doing a volunteer year and I needed to keep my expenses way down. I wanted to live on my own and I wanted to be able to eat the way I chose. I stopped being a volunteer a year ago and I still haven't gotten around to buying a car because I've become used to the life style.

I have friends who also bike for their transportation. We all take this step together of being able to conserve oil and gas for the planet: we use our own energy to bike instead. Regarding safety, I generally feel very safe when I bike because I know the routes to take around town so I'm not on busy roads. I particularly choose my routes carefully at night. Weather, of course, is a real factor when using a bike for transportation.

One of my favorite things that I didn't anticipate when I started biking as much as I do now is that it causes me to focus on taking my time and really being aware when I travel from one place to another. I enjoy getting on my bike to get around.

Note from Joyce: Biking can, of course, be an enjoyable form of exercise on the weekends even if one has a car for regular transportation. Other ways to save money on transportation and to conserve fossil fuel are walking and riding public transportation. Those have provided excellent transportation for me during various extended periods of my life.

Community Garden Plots: Learning How To Grow Vegetables For Fun And To Enhance Abundance

~ by M.W., New Albany, IN

Gardening is fun. The more that you practice and try growing different plants, different varieties, and growing in different places--the more you learn. You can start really simply by planting a tomato plant in a large pot on your patio. There is so much joy in watching a seed that you planted grow, and seeing that develop into a flower, and then into a tomato. Then you see that ripen and you're able to eat it. A lot of the time it tastes so much better than what you would get at the supermarket. Besides, you can say, "I grew that." There is real pleasure in it. There are lots of reading materials to guide people through books, articles, and online. It also can be valuable to talk to other gardeners--people who know just a little more than you. It's helpful to hear what they tried, and what did and didn't do well in your area. It is also encouraging to see that here's another person like me. If they can do gardening, I can do it too. I think it is good to just dive in and try it. Try something new.

In the past I have planted a small garden in front of my apartment, but the city planted a tree in that space. So I thought that this is the perfect time to go over and get involved in the community garden plots. This community garden doesn't have running water. Hopefully we'll have plenty of rainfall. We're going to try to use rain barrels to collect water that runs off the roofs. It's a nice idea to use that runoff water and not waste it. We're going to have to use a lot of mulch around the plants to help hold in the moisture. Mulch is any substance put around the plant roots to protect them. Some community gardens have a water source and some don't. I'm planning to bring jugs of water with me. Concerning how much time is needed for watering and weeding a small garden plot, maybe half an hour a couple times on week days and maybe an hour or two on the weekend might be good.

It's becoming more and more common to have garden plots available to city residents. These are on land that is otherwise vacant or unused. Where water is available, there is probably a small fee for water usage. People want to get back to the land and grow some of their own food. Another benefit of the community gardens is the pleasure of doing things with other people. A lot of my special gardening memories are of having kids with me when I garden. They have so much joy in seeing things in a fresh way for perhaps for the first time. (For information on City Garden Plots, check your city's website or telephone information line.)

Mid-City Organic Gardening: Creative Critter and Insect Control, and the Magic Of Composting

~ Chris & Allison Singler

We don't need any pesticides, fungicides, or herbicides. We use companion planting as one means of pest control. Marigold flowers help to keep rabbits and squirrels and some insects away. We plant them around the perimeter of the garden. We grow basil and dill with tomatoes; they help keep away bugs that may harm the tomatoes. Apparently they don't like the odors. Native Americans traditionally planted corn, beans, and squash together. The beans are able to climb the corn stalks, and the squash have prickly leaves that help to keep away some pests.

I (Chris) had a dream of lots of rabbits driving colorful little convertible cars along the side of our house where there is a gate in the fence that encloses the back yard. In the morning I realized that the dream meant that the rabbits were getting into the back yard and garden through the small open places around the gate. I added pieces of screening to close up small open spots around the gate. Then there were no more rabbit troubles in the garden. For the squirrels, we put out water. When the squirrels go after tomatoes it isn't to eat them. They just bite them and suck out some juice because they are thirsty. The squirrels don't tend to eat the tomatoes. So when they have water to drink, they sort of leave the tomatoes alone. Also, when the fruit of the tomatoes start to come out, I buy some really cheap corn that I put out for squirrels. The squirrels love corn with a passion. I find the Rodale gardening book very helpful.

Composting transforms vegetable table scraps into wonderful free rich soil. We pretty much break a lot of the rules and it still works. You're not supposed to put any cooked food into the compost pile, but we do. We don't put any meat in the pile. In the kitchen we collect our vegetable scraps in a small bucket with a lid on it. It doesn't get smelly. We regularly dump the bucket out on the compost pile. We have a leaf pile (from the previous autumn leaf raking) next to our compost pile, and put some leaves on top of each deposit of vegetable scraps. You don't normally have to put water on the compost pile because the vegetable scraps have moisture in them, and so do the leaves that have been lying in the pile next to the compost bin. About every two weeks we put on some lime. Leaves are very acidic and the lime is very alkaline. If you have a lot of trees around, the soil is likely to be acidic. Lime kind of sterilizes the compost pile a little bit, and speeds up the decomposition process. We use a granular grey colored lime. It's derived from rock. You don't need much, you just sprinkle it on. We let the pile build up until it is several feet high.

Our compost bin is made out of chicken wire and is three feet square and four feet tall. Compost bins can be made out of other materials or they can be bought in different commercial designs. Our chicken wire one works fine. We can put a whole lot in there, and the stuff on the bottom is always compacting and decomposing. At a certain point, I dump the composting materials out to the side of the bin. What was on the bottom and in the middle of the bin is then like really good potting soil. What was on the top might not be so composted. The good compost I put on the garden. What wasn't yet well composted I put back on the bottom of the compost bin and start a new pile. Returning part of the compost pile is good because it has valuable microorganisms that help the composting process. The natural decomposition process of composting creates heat in the center of the pile near the bottom.

In the autumn I go out and get horse stable manure, lay it on the garden, and dig it in somewhat. It composts during the winter right on the garden. In the spring it is well composted and is totally safe for a vegetable garden. Sometimes adding a little sand to the soil is helpful for improving its texture. A soil testing kit is a very good idea to help you know your soil and what it may need. I highly recommend it.

Note from Joyce: When you are planning to grow plants for food in soil, it is important for numerous reasons to have the soil tested as Chris recommends. One reason is to make sure it isn't too high in any contaminants from cars or industry and such (it isn't all that likely, but it is good to check). If contaminants are too high, it is possible to create raised beds (these look somewhat like children's sandboxes), and fill them with good soil. Another option is to garden in containers such as large plant pots. With experience, a great deal of vegetables can be grown in an average sized back yard. That really is possible through placing the plants quite close to each other and perhaps using some innovative vertical gardening ideas. Some people, of course, can or freeze or dry some of their garden bounty. Inexpensive improvised "greenhouses" using heavy plastic sheeting can extend the growing season through much of the winter for some crops (depending on your geographical area). Also recall the description of hydroponic vertical tower gardening described earlier in this chapter.

Natural Abundance with a Solar Heated Home

~ by Ann

Building a passive solar, partially underground home was a dream that grew. When Alan and I got married, it was not our goal to build a home. Yet, the dream kept developing. He already had the land; both our parents had built their dream homes, so we began to plan. We went to workshops, bought the latest books, and were blessed with family who could guide us. I carved the front door from a beautiful slab of mahogany before we even had plans. We started buying used materials. We searched the newspaper for information on buildings being demolished. We got windows from an old building downtown. We found used 55 gallon drums that were eventually filled with water along with tons of rock to hold the heat. We decided on tile floors, again to hold the heat. Alan cut the ceramic tile where needed and I laid app. 2,000 sq. ft. of floor. Together we made drapes to insulate 10 x 25 feet of glass. We had two wood burning stoves. This kept the house warm economically.

An atrium filled with gravel became our garden room in the center of our home. The dome above the atrium was from the face of a huge clock on an old building. The garden was special, too. We had a pond with koi fish and a weeping cherry tree plus a dry creek bed (of ornamental stones) like I had seen in Japan. We were fearless. Alan had worked in construction as a young man, and I learned more about building than I ever believed I could. (See Resources Page)

My Energy Efficient Passive Solar Home in the Woods

By Joyce

Twenty one years ago I had a passive solar heated home built for me by builder friends. An important principle with passive solar heat is to have very large windows to the south and no windows to the north. Windows to the east and west are moderate size or fairly small. Window glass should be super efficient insulated to hold in the heat. It is very desirable to have insulated drapes to close after the sun goes down. Super insulation in the walls is also very important in conserving heat.

My passive solar home was three compact floor levels, about 2000 square feet total. It was heated by one gas area heater on the first floor near the stairs going to the upper floors. This small heater kept the whole house reasonably warm during frigid New England winters. We used an oil filled portable electric heater if we wanted a little more heat in a particular room. There was a wood stove in the living room that normally wasn't used except for pleasure now and then or during power outages. It could very easily heat the whole house on its own. When that wood stove really got going, the whole house could get overheated like a sauna.

That was truly an energy efficient house. I moved eleven years ago to a warmer climate, but I did love that passive solar home in the woods. In the summer it was cool without air conditioning or fans because of all the trees nearby on the north, east, and west. Awnings on the south windows in the summer did wonders.

Woman Honors Grain
Original art by Joyce J.C. Gerrish

WORKBOOK: Enrichment Experiences for Enhancing Abundance in Your Life

Enjoy the adventure of exploring these enrichment experiences on your own--or gather a few friends to share the journey with you. Be inspired by the audio meditation and soul song for this chapter. Reflect on some of the stimulating ideas and questions.

Questions for Reflection and Discussion

Reflection, discussion, journal writing, expressing your feelings in drawings or other creative ways can all be very valuable to help you delve into these questions in truly meaningful and relevant ways. Before focusing on the questions, you may wish to meditate with the twelve-minute audio or transcribed meditation focusing on abundance--and/or listen to the soul song "*We Are Blessed.*" Please give yourself time to feel these questions deeply in your heart. Habits can be very strong, and we may begin thinking that there is only one way to do things and still feel fulfilled.

1. What do I love to do that is more or less free? Maybe this is something I have sort of forgotten about or put on a back burner. What about picnics with friends or family? What about reading a fascinating book on a recliner in the back yard or in an easy chair? Libraries can be magical places. What about canoeing on a stream?

2. What do I really need in order to thrive, pursue my interests, and provide for my necessities? What is really essential to me, and what are some things that I maybe do or have because of other people's expectations? Do some things make me feel important? Peer pressure can be intense.

3. Do I own objects that I seldom use? Do I sometimes get excited about something and buy it, and then it just sort of sits there on the shelf? Do I sometimes replace a perfectly good object or tool simply because a newer interesting version exists? Are these possibly a strain on my budget?

4. Would I like to grow part of my food? A vegetable garden can save money. Growing food can be fun when done as part of a group; it doesn't need to be done alone. On the other hand, gardening alone can be very peaceful!

5. Do I take time to cook my meals from whole foods as they grow from the ground? This is a profoundly healthy way to eat, and it's economical. Do I frequently eat at restaurants, or buy takeout food, or eat frozen meals? These can be problematic for health and the budget. Some fast food and processed food may seem cheap at the moment, but can cost dearly in medical care up ahead.

6. Am I living in an area of the country where costs are reasonable? If I am living in an expensive city and my budget is limited, have I ever considered living in a smaller town or the countryside where the cost of living may be lower? Some areas have lower property taxes. Some jobs today are done on a computer and can be accomplished anywhere. Some companies have offices around the country, and transferring may be possible.

7. How large is my dwelling? Do I live alone or do I live with other people? If expenses are tight, it can be more economical to live with others and share expenses somehow. These might be family members or friends. What do I think of intentional communities (as described earlier) where people living nearby in a community create co-operative arrangements for mutual benefit-- such as sharing tools, exchanging child care, communal meals once or several times a week, and other helpful ways of sharing?

Action Suggestions for Enhancing Abundance in Our Lives

The possibilities for action in the area of enhancing abundance in our lives are endless. Let's consider a few as examples. Living simply is a crucial aspect of abundance for all. Living simply doesn't mean being uncomfortable at all. It simply means living with an awareness and respect for the needs of all.

1. What would you like to give away that you don't need and don't use? Does that sound like a strange action suggestion for enhancing abundance? Share the abundance. If you are wanting to create more clarity for your life direction, you may wish to clear away some of what you don't need or use. This may help you feel more clear on how you choose to live your life and enhance abundance. Some things such as old papers and magazines may simply need to be recycled. Some things could perhaps be sold on eBay or in a consignment shop or a yard sale. You may find that your dwelling and your life feel more spacious!

2. When you are talking with someone, consider telling them about your dreams and what you are seeking to manifest in your life. Find out their life dreams. See if you have some mutual interests where you can support each other. Mutual support and co-operation help to create abundance.

3. Check if you have a TimeBank group in your city. This can be a wonderful way to exchange skills.

4. Start a vegetable garden in season, if you aren't already a gardener.

5. Supportive coursework or training may be helpful if you are seeking to enhance your earning power in your current field of work, find a new job, or jump start your self-employment. This is an excellent way to keep your skills current and to keep you alert and prepared for new opportunities.

There may be aspects or areas of your field of interest of which you aren't fully aware and that could be fruitful for you. This course work could be online, through adult education programs, government sponsored training, through books, or other sources. Training can also occur through volunteer work in the area into which you would like to move.

Audio "Meditation to Enhance Your Experience of The Divine Qualities," with Focus on Abundance

Pray to the Divine to bless your meditation and enhance Divine Abundance in your life. Choose one or more of the following Abundance affirmations (or something similar) that feels particularly helpful to you for affirming during the meditation. Before transferring to the website to listen to the meditation, write down the affirmation(s) you choose. Later, place it where you'll see it daily and be reminded to affirm the affirmation(s) for a minute or two several times a day.

Helpful color to visualize when meditating on Abundance: Gold

◆ My worth and abundance is determined by who I am inside, not by what I buy.

◆ What I want to manifest into my life--I visualize clearly, believe in it with my whole heart, and work toward it earnestly.

◆ When I send love and thankfulness with my financial transactions, it helps keep abundance flowing more freely in return. What goes around comes back around.

◆ There is plenty for all of us if we utilize earth's resources wisely without waste, and share fairly.

◆ I am abundant in the gifts of God of sharing peace, love, joy, wisdom--and living in harmony with nature.

I encourage you to enjoy this meditation when you wish to support the quality of Abundance in your life. Connect to <u>SecretsofWisdom.net</u> to listen to the twelve-minute audio "Meditation to Enhance Your Experience of the Divine Qualities," with focus on Abundance.

(Also, see the transcribed version of this meditation at the end of this chapter.)

Uplifting Audio Soul Song: *"We Are Blessed"*

~ By Joyce

Consider it a prayer in song for enhancing our appreciation of the loving abundance of Mother Earth, and the importance of our role as caretakers to preserve and protect this precious planet. The words are:

Mother Earth is so loving and abundant for us.

The plants grow such bounty for our food.

The wood from the trees gives us warm safe homes.

The waters quench our thirst.

Shall we cherish our abundant Earth? (repeat)

And be wise stewards while we can. (repeat)

As you sing or listen to this soul song, feel yourself relax and begin to flow with it. Close your eyes and really sense it helping to bring you into an uplifted state of gratitude for our beloved planet. I invite you to visit the <u>SecretsofWisdom.net</u> where you can listen to *"We Are Blessed."*

Transcribed version of Meditation to Enhance Divine Abundance

If possible, listen to some relaxing nonverbal music. Say a short prayer calling on the Divine to bless you with enhanced Natural Abundance.

Visualize yourself in a ball of light to help strengthen your energy field.

Become aware of and follow your breath as it gently flows in and out at its own pace.

Send down roots deep into the earth to help yourself feel more grounded and prevent possibly feeling spacey.

As you breathe in through your nose, imagine you are breathing up the strength of the earth into your body.

For a few minutes listen to the relaxing music.

As you breathe in through your nose imagine you are breathing in light into your whole being.

Next visualize Gold light. Periodically as you breathe in your nose, imagine that you are breathing gold light into your whole being. Silently pray to the Divine that your life be uplifted and blessed with Divine Abundance.

Next breathe in your nose and out your mouth for about a minute VERY GENTLY.

Now, very gently breathe in your mouth and out your nose for about a minute.

Then extra gently breathe in and out your mouth for a minute or so.

Now return to breathing in and out through your nose.

As you breathe in through your nose, imagine you are breathing in gold light into your whole being.

As you breathe out your nose, periodically say one or more of the following affirmations (or something similar).

◆ My worth and abundance is determined by who I am inside, not by what I buy.

◆ What I want to manifest into my life--I visualize clearly, believe in it with my whole heart, and work toward it earnestly.

◆ When I send love and thankfulness with my financial transactions, it helps keep abundance flowing more freely in return. What goes around comes back around.

◆ There is plenty for all of us if we utilize Earth's resources wisely without waste, and share fairly.

◆ I am abundant in the gifts of God of sharing peace, love, joy, wisdom--and living in harmony with nature.

Sense yourself lifted into an expansive sense of abundant well-being.

Continue in that manner for a few minutes or as long as you wish.

Conclude by thanking the Divine and sending down roots to Mother Earth for stability and grounding.

Write down the affirmation(s) you choose. Place the affirmation(s) where you'll see it several times a day and be reminded to affirm it for a minute or two.

Peace

Woman Gazes at Vista and Contemplates Truth
Original art by Joyce J.C. Gerrish

Chapter Eighteen

TRUTH SHINING BRIGHT
Enhancing Divine Truth in Your Life

Music can help communicate important truths. I have composed and sung this soul song, "Truth Shining Bright" which you can listen to at <u>SecretsofWisdom.net</u>. There you can also gaze at the full color design "Angel Heralds Forth the Truth."

Sometimes Life Can Feel Like Sliding Mirrors and Rotating Doors

Truth is the real essence of a situation. Seeking to understand the truth of a situation can sometimes feel like we are dealing with sliding mirrors, distorted reflections, and rotating doors. We may frequently hear that truth is conditional, and that it depends on our perspective and other factors. After a while it may begin to seem as though there is no such thing as truth. Let's look at some essential truths that I feel are not subject to shifting variables.

How about the way we communicate with each other? To convey truth, we need to have the intention to be as direct and clear as possible. Often people try to package what they say in a manner that is intended to have a certain impression on the other person. Sometimes the speaker gets so involved in making an impression that the meaning gets distorted along the way. If there is something of significance to communicate, that needs to be stated as clearly and simply as possible without coating it with disguises to hide important aspects. May we allow truth to shine crystal-clear.

Sometimes people speak with the total intention to mislead. That, of course, is lying. Other times people speak with the intention to somewhat mislead. That is called half-truth. There may be something valid said, and then it may be glazed over with words to throw off the listener from comprehending the reality of the message. This distortion may be intentional or subconscious, or somewhere in-between. We often live in a world of half-truths or lies that politely masquerade as real communication. It's worth mentioning here that some lying may be based on good intentions--but on inaccurate information. It gets complicated! Oh, those sliding mirrors!

I once signed a legal document that was supposedly explained to me, and I thought I understood. It wasn't until later that I found out what it really meant. That discovery was a massive blow that required long intense legal work for a year to straighten out--but it was rectified. The truth had not been made clear at all, and it left me wondering about the whole phenomenon of truth.

What About White Lies?

Some people may not be ready to hear truth, and hence it may be kind to only share part of a truth with that person. That doesn't make what one says in that case true, it only makes it perhaps more appropriate information for that person. This type of decision needs to be made with great care and discernment--and not taken lightly.

This brings us into the whole realm of white lies. Are there times when a white lie helps, such as trying to cheer someone up by saying that they look good when they may not? What if a person lies about something bigger, such as saying they did something impressive that never happened? What about saying they were at one place and they were actually at another place? Does lying sometimes backfire because it can be hard to keep track of the details of fabrications if the need arises to repeat what was said? Ou-la-la!

Some people get so accustomed to telling "adjusted" truths that they begin to believe the "adjusted" truth themselves after a while. This is to be avoided at all costs. An individual needs to tell the truth to others and stay clear within him or herself as to the truth. There have been in the past and there still are cultures totally structured on distortions. These distortions may have been agreed upon by some people in power and then continued indefinitely. They perhaps are no longer questioned, but are simply followed. If anyone thought seriously about these distortions and said anything, the person was or is severely chastised or punished. Some examples may come to your mind.

The Two Sexes and the Different Races Are Equal

For a very long time, there was the myth that women were somehow inferior to men and shouldn't be educated or have legal rights. The fact that women are biologically capable of giving birth to children was given as a reason that they should not do anything beyond taking care of a home and children and perhaps helping with a small family farm or performing a minor role within a family business. These roles can be wonderful for those women who choose them. For long centuries these roles were enforced for women, and the women themselves began to believe it was inevitable. That was tragic. The human spirit can begin to wither when choice is limited. Choice is crucial.

Slavery is even more of a tragic lie of denying noble human beings their basic rights and causing unbelievable suffering. The abusers hurt themselves when they live such lies. People need to live the truth, or lie builds up on lie and the individual begins to lose touch with reality. Their hearts harden and they shut down inside to their higher potentials.

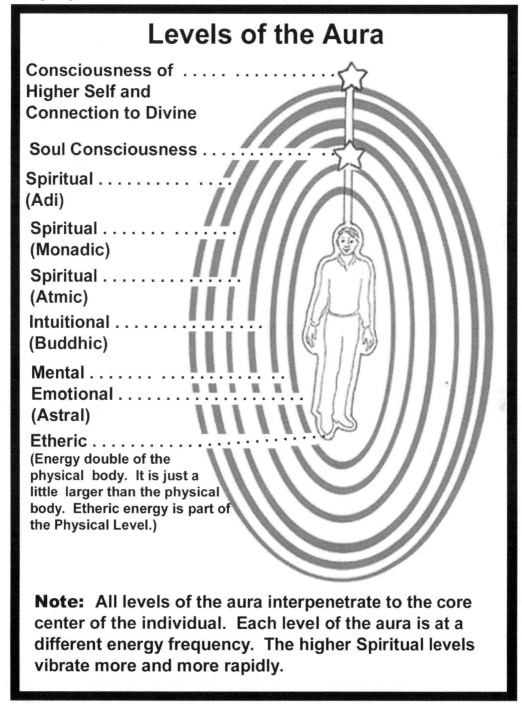

Levels of the Aura

Consciousness of . . . .
Higher Self and
Connection to Divine

Soul Consciousness . . . .

Spiritual . . . .
(Adi)

Spiritual . . . .
(Monadic)

Spiritual . . . .
(Atmic)

Intuitional . . . .
(Buddhic)

Mental . . . .
Emotional . . . .
(Astral)

Etheric . . . .
(Energy double of the
physical body. It is just a
little larger than the physical
body. Etheric energy is part of
the Physical Level.)

Note: All levels of the aura interpenetrate to the core center of the individual. Each level of the aura is at a different energy frequency. The higher Spiritual levels vibrate more and more rapidly.

The Truth of Our Soul Mission

Let's change our focus now as we continue our exploration of some of the truths that are not conditional. As mentioned in previous chapters, each person when born on planet Earth has a purpose or soul mission held deep in the heart. The most important thing about the person's life will be if he or she delves deep into the Sacred place in the heart and pays attention to this inner call. A person may become a multimillionaire tycoon in business, but if that is not his or her soul purpose with deep inner significance--it will likely leave the individual feeling somewhat empty inside and wondering why. Perhaps that person was intended to be a musician. For another person, being a very wealthy successful business professional could be the soul mission. An individual may find a deep place of inner connection to the Divine through dedicated service of offering a product of great value for humanity. That wealth could be channeled into programs to help lift fellow human beings. Wealth is good if it is utilized somehow for the betterment of not only oneself, but also for those in need and other worthy causes. Each person's soul mission is unique in some way. It can be seemingly very simple and humble, but that doesn't make it any less important and Sacred than a soul mission that may seem more grandiose.

Existence in Heaven

Pure Spirit is the core of reality. Physical appearances can be misleading. Trust the inner essence. Physical matter coalesces around the energy template. There is great power in pure Spirit. Pure Spirit is the "substance" on which all creation is molded. It is the Divine blueprint for all that is created. Around this Spirit template are formed layers of gradually more dense substance. At higher Spiritual levels the substance is pure Light. You may not be accustomed to thinking of Light as having substance, but there is a gradual continuum from Light to matter. There are Divine beings who exist as pure Light and have a reality of their own. This continuum of creation from Light to matter gradually proceeds from Spirit and the very high realms of Heaven where the ascended enlightened saints and archangels dwell. Then the continuum proceeds through the levels of Heaven where reside the angels and also the human souls who have completed the cycle of reincarnation on Earth. At this stage they are called Masters of Wisdom and are now being of service in many ways in Heaven and on Earth. These paths of service include guiding and helping reincarnating human souls between lives and also when those souls are actively living a life on Earth. While in Heaven, the reincarnating souls between lives meditate and contemplate on what they learned in the life that they just lived on planet Earth. Here the souls do not have a physical body, but they do have a subtle substance to their being that has the appearance of a human. Then the continuum proceeds through the astral plane (emotional level), part of which is sometimes referred to as purgatory. This is of denser substance than Heaven, but not as dense as matter on the physical plane of Earth. Human souls existing in this area of the astral plane are also learning important lessons about embodying the Divine wisdoms and truths. Sometimes this is remedial work for mistakes made in the previous lifetime. Next we come to the normal density of matter of humans on physical plane Earth. This description has been shared to clarify that pure Spirit is the essence of reality, and denser layers of matter gradually coalesce around this core of pure Spirit.

Each of these gradations of subtle higher Spiritual levels of consciousness permeates through the gradually denser levels all the way to the physical plane. For a human on earth, all the planes of consciousness are potentially available simultaneously. Each of the seven major planes has seven sub-planes as shown. As we learn/remember how to function on the higher planes of consciousness--we can still function effectively (even more so) physically, emotionally, and mentally by focusing on the higher sub-planes of the physical, astral, and mental planes. The higher sub-planes of these levels of consciousness could be described as feeling fairly clear and positive and open to the good in life.

The Human Soul is Potentially Immortal

Let us look at another eternal unconditional truth. The human soul is potentially immortal. A human being on planet Earth is an incarnation of the soul. Incarnation means having taken form in a physical body and personality. When a human dies, the higher more subtle (least physically focused) levels of the person's consciousness then leave the physical body and are usually guided up to Heaven by the angels. These higher essences of the person's mental and emotional/astral levels of personality and consciousness are drawn into his or her soul. The remainder of the person's mental and emotional consciousness simply dissipate into energy.

THE PLANES OF OUR CONSCIOUSNESS

Each of these gradations of higher Spiritual levels of consciousness permeates through the gradually denser levels all the way to the physical plane. For a human on earth, all the planes of consciousness are potentially available simultaneously. Each of the seven major planes has seven sub-planes as shown. As we learn / remember how to function on the higher planes/levels of consciousness -- we can still function effectively (even more so) physically, emotionally, and mentally

	ADI PLANE (Higher Spiritual)
	MONADIC PLANE (Higher Spiritual)
	ATMIC PLANE (Spiritual)
	BUDDHIC PLANE (Intuitional)
	MENTAL PLANE
	ASTRAL PLANE (Emotional)
	PHYSICAL PLANE (Includes Etheric)

The physical body is buried or cremated. If someone's emotional personality is backward and refuses to be drawn into his or her consciousness that ascends to Heaven, then it may hang around its original home or elsewhere for a while. It may occasionally be able to make itself seen or heard by embodied humans. This is what is generally called a ghost. It is to be pitied. It is not following the Divine Plan. The best thing to do if one is ever somehow aware of a ghost is to pray for an angel to come and guide the ghost to where it needs to be.

Once in Heaven, the personality consciousness is absorbed into the soul consciousness. The essence of the wisdom learned in that lifetime is meditated on and examined and analyzed with the Divine beings in Heaven. This is the most important time in the whole process of incarnation, when the wisdoms and truths learned are fully absorbed into the soul. That is the whole purpose of the soul incarnating on planet Earth, to learn and embody the eternal truths and wisdoms. The achievement of a truth learned is just as significant if a soul is the leader of a nation or is a farmer or a mother and homemaker. How impressive we may be in the eyes of those around us is not the crucial point. What is exceedingly important is how wise and kind and loving we are. After a period of time the soul normally reincarnates again to learn more soul wisdom on the physical plane Earth.

A soul incarnates many times as both feminine and masculine personalities, and usually seeks to have lives within as many different nationalities and races as possible. Sometimes a soul specializes in one or two types of work or endeavors during different life times, more typically a soul tries out many different types of work. All this supports better understanding of the total human experience. Each incarnation of a soul is a new personality, and is likely to look quite different. The essence of the soul is normally present in the heart and higher consciousness of the person, and retains the essence of all the wisdom gained in the lives it has lived so far and the memory of those lives. Sensitive intuitive people can be quite aware of their soul level consciousness. The soul holds the very important information of the soul mission for that life.

Soul growth is a gradual process of alternating between intense experiences during incarnations on Earth--and then time in Heaven meditating on the wisdoms learned in the life just lived. This continues until eventually all the Divine qualities of God are fully mastered and integrated within the soul. This ideally happens fairly simultaneously with the aura energy field gradually being totally illumined and activated by virtue of all the pure living, loving good thoughts, and prayer or meditation.

Some souls proceed very slowly through this process of gradually embodying the Divine Qualities and moving from incarnation to incarnation. Some souls move much more quickly and require far fewer incarnations. There is tremendous Spiritual Grace available at this time of history to support human souls in completing their path of enlightenment. Once a soul has achieved total enlightenment he or she becomes a Spiritual Master of Wisdom and resides permanently in Heaven doing God's work. That is a magnificent achievement. The Master of Wisdom may extend help for humans who are embodied on earth or who are between lives. There are many other service options which are possible for a Master of Wisdom. These might include helping guide the different species of animals or plants or minerals. They might become a Spirit healer to help wounded or ill humans. There are Masters of Wisdom who voluntarily choose to return to planet Earth in a physical body as a great Spiritual leader and teacher. They are called Bodhisattvas. The journey of the human soul is potentially ongoing to higher and higher spheres of Heavenly reality in service to the Divine.

There are Souls who become so identified with God that when they leave the physical body they are drawn into the consciousness of the Divine and become a part of the Divine. This is a form of God-Realization. Those Souls tend to no longer experience themselves as individuals separate from God at all. They are absorbed into the bliss of Oneness. Different individuals and groups may describe and name these states somewhat differently. Words are inadequate to describe such sublime states.

The Divine is in Charge and is Unfolding Before Our Very Eyes

Some people may try to divert God's creation from its natural purity, but the Divine is in charge and is unfolding before our very eyes. May we look within people's hearts to sense the truth of their beings. The surface is sometimes misleading. Let us look in their eyes and call them into remembrance of the truth of their beings within the Divine. This is the time for us to "remember" the Sacred trust that we each hold within our heart and higher consciousness. We each have a very important part to play in the "renaissance" that is going on right now for planet Earth.

Believe in yourself and in the unique piece of wisdom that resonates in your heart of hearts. Share your wisdom. Know that your unique qualities are needed to complete the Sacred mosaic of wondrous potential for planet Earth to the next step of its highest good. Don't be discouraged by abuse, degradation, or apathy you may see around you. Pray to God to lift the confused or waylaid people. Know that the spark of the Divine is deep in their hearts.

We are all being called to return to the Sacred truth that we are each created in the image of God. We can only wander for so long until we are called to remember the Sacred truths. May we each be a beacon of peace, purity, and wisdom. Together we can recreate the Sacred circle of respect for all life. This is the essence of true healing. We have looked at truth from many perspectives. Please take this into your heart and sense what resonates with you. Find your center and hold steady. Truth can stabilize you when life seems to be shifting around you. Let truth be your anchor in a complex world.

Real Life Sharings About Experiencing Divine Truth

The Afterlife

~ Dee Patterson

One of the hardest things for us to face here in the physical body is the loss of someone we love, including our pets. While this can seem unbearable at the time we are experiencing the loss, I have found that it is of great comfort to people to know that their loved one is being taken care of in the afterlife. As a medium who can talk to those who have departed, I can assure them that their loved one was met by those they loved and cared about who passed before them. This reunion takes place immediately upon their transition from this Earth. They are often surrounded by a beautiful, incredible light that is both healing and soothing. Reuniting with those who have gone before brings great joy, even while they may regret having to leave loved ones behind.

Once I have made contact, it is not unusual for them to show me that they return to visit and comfort their grieving family members and friends. Sometimes this is more obvious to the person still on the physical plane and at other times they seem to be unaware; although I have found that they are comforted just knowing that their loved one still cares. We will all make our transition from this Earth plane at some point and I hope it helps you to know that in the afterlife we are still loved by those who went before us.

(See Resources Page)

Reincarnation Insights

~ by Joyce

Some of the courageous, wise, loving qualities that we developed in past lives are still inherent within us in this life. When a soul reincarnates, he or she has a different appearance and personality, but some of the higher levels of the consciousness are intact. Various skills and inclinations that a soul developed in past lives will likely be carried over to at least some degree in a future life. For some people, learning how to do a particular skill is really more a matter of remembering what they already know from previous lives. Some children seem to come into life with wisdom or capacities beyond their years. An example of that is a child musical prodigy being able to almost spontaneously create beautiful music. One young man I knew, who had previously had no contact with the German language, was amazed to find that when he visited Germany he could almost spontaneously converse in the language. It is not unusual for a person to go to a place for the first time and "know for sure" that they have been there before. Many people meet someone new and "know" that they knew that person before. These are likely to be soul memories. Maybe you have had an experience along those lines. As described earlier in this book, the most important thing about reincarnation is the gradual soul growth and the embracing of the Divine ever more fully. For more insights about reincarnation, refer to SecretsofWisdom.com/Articles.

The Power Of Being True To Who You Are

~ by Joyce

There is great freedom in truth. Be true to the beat of your heart. Be true to the song flowing through you. Accept nothing less than recognition for who you are. Many will try to fit you into the image that they have for you. They may be nice to you as long as you dance to their song--their music. Find people who rejoice in welcoming the melody flowing through your heart. Don't try to force your melody to develop according to someone else's dictates. Breathe through your heart the healing balm of the true essence of who you are within.

How can anyone really know you and love you as you deserve to be loved--if they don't know who you are? They may just keep looking for reflections of their own desires and preconceived ideas of who they think you should be to fulfill their fantasies or expectations. Never be a chameleon! The days of being a chameleon are over, if they ever existed. Don't let anyone convince you to be their chameleon changing colors every time the colors of your surroundings change. Let your heart's melody create beautiful colors expressing the truth of you.

Treasure those people who sing their own song and welcome your unique song. Harmonize together and enjoy the interweaving complexities. Let the notes blend in melodious sounds. Keep your own melody - - otherwise the ever delightful surprising chords of rich intricate harmony are lost to an overbearing single sound. Let us each sing the truth of our being. All together we create the Sacred Harmony of Creation.

Celebration of Oneness

An original poem by Joyce C. Gerrish

One aspect of Spiritual awakening is when a person's crown chakra is very open and one feels profound oneness with the Creator and with all creation. I wrote this poem once while watching an extraordinarily beautiful sunset over a lake surrounded by the mountains of the western coast of Canada.

Golden light fills the far corners of the sky

Echoed by the vastness of eternal blue.

I stand here watching the gold and blue symphony of the sky.

The massive rocks beneath fill me with compassion,

Glued thus as they are to the bedrock of time,

My eyes wander over the wide expanse of rocks, sky, sea, and setting sun.

Hopes fly with the gulls in the gossamer air.

My visions and dreams vibrate with the meandering air currents,

And with the noble trees reaching for the sky.

The water is like my love and passion for life,

It rises, and falls with my heaving chest.

Yet when the waters meet the discipline of the solid rocks,

Graceful patterns radiate outward in ever larger circles - -

Carrying cleansing and renewal to all in its path.

My mind burns with the fire of the sun.

The intense light transforms any lingering shadows of fear or confusion into clarity.

The earth, the rocks--they are as my bones, my hold to the past.

The bulwark of stability, very slow to change,

Yet change they do, gradually yet perceptibly.

In the distance the rocks rise to meet the sky.

They lift high heroically, defying gravity for a time.

As I look at you, mountain rocks,

Your translucent blue hints of your true nature as dancing atoms - -

Dancing just a little slower than the sea,

Or the more rapidly vibrating air, or brother fire dancing with abandon.

So to which of you am I akin?

The answer is clear--it rings through the vast spaces,

Through the gold and blue reflections.

You are all within me, and I am within you.

All is one within the embrace of the Creator.

Now the quiet glow of the moon has settled.

Outlines begin to fade--forms blend into peace.

We are all one substance in Spirit--dancing together

Vibrating each to his own song.

In the morning the sun will rise again.

The new dawn will shine forth.

Each day is a miraculous breath in the life of Creation.

Woman With Two Birds
Original art by Joyce J.C. Gerrish

WORKBOOK: Enrichment Experiences For Enhancing Divine Truth In Your Life

Enjoy exploring these enrichment experiences on your own, or gather a few friends to share the journey with you. Be inspired by the audio meditation and soul song for this chapter. Reflect on some of the stimulating ideas and questions.

Questions for Reflection and Discussion

Reflection, discussion, journal writing, expressing your feelings in drawings or other creative ways can all be very valuable to help you delve into these questions in truly meaningful and relevant ways. Before focusing on the questions, you may wish to meditate with the twelve-minute audio or transcribed meditation for truth--and/or listen to the soul song "*Truth Shining Bright*." The audios are on the accompanying website.

1. What are one or more core truths that you hold dear in your life? What is something that is so true to you that nothing that someone else says or does could shake that knowing? An example of such a knowing might be to not judge people by their appearance no matter how impressive they look and act. Sense their inner character and kindness.

2. What do you do if someone in a position of authority starts talking half-truths to you? You know very well that they are twisting the truth to their advantage, or else they are misinformed. Simply being aware of untruth or half-truth is powerful, so that you can protect yourself better. Would you be ready to be a whistle blower? This, of course, can sometimes cause one to lose a job or position. On the other hand, sometimes it can open the way for real change for the good in the company or group. If the half-truth was caused by the speaker being misinformed, the speaker

might possibly welcome the truthful information and respect the person who politely offered it along with backup information.

3. How do you feel about lying a little to someone if it doesn't seem to hurt anyone and it helps you--or maybe even helps them? This might be called a white lie, if it is about something really minor. How do you feel about white lies? Are there times when you feel that a white lie helps? What if a person lies about something bigger? If you ever did any of these, how did you feel afterward? Does it sometimes backfire because it can be hard to keep track of details of fabrications if the need arises to repeat what was said?

4. How do feel when you sense people in your personal life are lying to you, but you can't prove it? What do you do about it, if anything? Does talking with the person about it help, or make things worse?

5. How do you feel about truth in advertising? Do you believe everything you hear or see in ads? How do you decide what to believe? How can you inform yourself about these products? "Consumer Reports" is one source of valid information, what are others? There is a great deal of valuable information available online.

Action Suggestions for Enhancing Divine Truth In Your Life

1. Try a "total truth day." This entails being truthful with yourself as well as with everyone else. Telling the truth about what you are feeling can sometimes deepen your relationship with people to whom you are close. A really crucial component to a "total truth day" is loving compassion. The old fashioned saying "if you can't say something nice, don't say anything at all" has at least a piece of wisdom. Is it possible that if the truth would offend or hurt someone that we could just not say anything? On the other hand, as previously mentioned, there is the courageous important example of a "whistle blower" who speaks up when there is something wrong going on in a company or a group situation.

2. Periodically throughout your day, ask yourself "what am I feeling now?" Sense your first awareness of what you are feeling now. Then ask yourself, "what am I really feeling now?" You may come to another level of your feelings. Knowledge and awareness are powerful. Being truthful with yourself is a major contribution to enhancing truly effective joyful living. Sometimes repressing what you feel can gradually cause you to numb out your true feelings, and cause you to feel less vitally interested in life. If you find some unexpected feelings coming up, give yourself a way to express those feelings constructively such as in journal writing or talking to a trusted friend. Sometimes talking with a counselor can be a really positive freeing experience. This is all good. Speaking your truth can be freeing.

3. Are people around us and on T.V., radio, or other media saying what they really feel or think? The clues for this and our awareness of them can be subtle or obvious. Either way it is extremely important. This is our protection and our guide as to how to relate or respond to these people. This awareness is part of what helps us be a good judge of character. It is crucial to surround ourselves with people who are telling the truth as much as possible. It is important for us to not be so thin-skinned that hearing someone else's honest opinion is shattering or even upsetting--even if it is different from our own opinion.

Audio "Meditation to Enhance Your Experience of The Divine Qualities," with Focus on Truth

Pray to the Divine to bless your meditation. With this audio you'll be guided to sense yourself immersed in the uplifting clarity of truth. Choose one or more of the following affirmations (or something similar) that feels particularly valuable to you for affirming during the meditation. Write down the affirmation(s) you choose and place it where you'll see it daily and be reminded to affirm the affirmation for a minute or two several times a day.

◆ I choose to stay in touch with my true feelings and thoughts.

◆ I understand that physical appearances can be misleading.

◆ I pay deep attention to the inner character or essence of a person.

◆ I choose to be clear and truthful with myself and others.

◆ I am created in God's image.

Helpful color to visualize when meditating on Truth: Green

I encourage you to enjoy this meditation when you wish to support this important quality of truth in your life. Connect to SecretsofWisdom.net to listen to the twelve-minute audio "Meditation to Enhance Your Experience of the Divine Qualities," with focus on Truth.

(Also, see transcribed version of this meditation at end of this chapter.)

Uplifting Audio Soul Song: "Truth Shining Bright"

~ By Joyce

Consider it a prayer in song for enhancing your sense of clarity and upliftment through Divine Truth. The words are:

Truth is like a beam of sunlight shining bright, Ou–Ou.

Truth illumines all on which it shines so bright. Ah–Ah.

Hold firm to the Truth, hold firm to the Truth.

Shadows vanish in the Light of Truth. Shadows vanish in the Light of Truth.

As you sing or listen to it, feel yourself relax and begin to flow with it. Connect to SecretsofWisdom. net to listen to "*Truth Shining Bright.*"

Transcribed version of Meditation to Enhance Your Experience of Divine Truth

If possible, listen to some relaxing nonverbal music. Say a short prayer calling on the Divine to bless your meditation.

Visualize yourself in a ball of light to help strengthen your energy field.

Become aware of and follow your breath as it gently flows in and out at its own relaxed pace.

Imagine yourself as a large tree sending powerful roots deep into the earth to help you feel grounded and prevent possibly feeling spacey.

As you breathe in through your nose, imagine you are breathing the strength of the earth up into your body.

For a few minutes listen to the relaxing music.

As you breathe in your nose, imagine you are breathing in light into your being.

Silently pray to the Divine to bless your meditation and to bless your whole life with the clarity and upliftment of Divine Truth.

Next breathe in through your nose and out your mouth for about a minute VERY GENTLY.

Now, very gently breathe in your mouth and out your nose for about a minute.

Then extra gently breathe in and out your mouth for a minute or so.

Now return to breathing in and out your nose.

As you breathe in through your nose, imagine you are breathing in emerald green light into your whole being.

As you breathe out your nose, periodically say one or more the following or similar affirmations silently.

- ◆ I choose to stay in touch with my true feelings and thoughts.
- ◆ I pay deep attention to the inner character or essence of a person.
- ◆ I understand that physical appearances can be misleading.
- ◆ I am created in God's image.
- ◆ I choose to be clear and truthful with myself and others.

Continue in that manner for a few minutes or as long as you wish.

Conclude by thanking the Divine and sending down roots to Mother Earth for stability and grounding.

Write down the affirmation(s) you choose and place it where you'll see it several times a day and be reminded to affirm it for a minute or two.

Peace.

Conclusion

EMBRACING THE DIVINE QUALITIES
IN ONE'S HEART, SOUL, AND LIFE
-- AND MOVING FORWARD!

Let Joy lift your heart,

and Love warm your soul.

May Forgiveness help you

release any entangled knots from the past,

and Healing dissolve

any remaining shadows of fear or doubt

that may be holding you back.

Let Clarity show the way forward,

and help you open to the Purpose burning in your heart.

Let true Power give you the strength to rise to your full stature

and claim your rightful place within the whole.

May Freedom inspire you to unfurl your wings and fly,

while Transformation gives you fearless courage to actualize your vision.

Allow Devotion to give you the steadfast desire

to serve and help lift the sons and daughters of God - -

and may Wisdom guide you always in the paths of righteousness.

Pray for Abundance to support your work

for the good of God's family of Earth,

and rejoice as the blessings of Harmony

help ease any trying moments along the way.

May the balm of Peace soothe your soul.

Praise God as Grace holds you steady on your way,

and thrill as Illumination floods your being with radiant Divine Light.

Welcome home to the ever more glowing beautiful Truth of your Being!

My love and prayers go out to each of you as you walk your path. Believe in yourself always! Be courageous! Daily nourish your soul with those practices that help keep you uplifted, strong, and joyful. My website SecretsofWisdom.net will be there for you with new inspirational and insightful writings, workshops and classes, individual telephone sessions, heart-warming songs, and uplifting art.

May Devine blessings surround you and guide you steadily to your highest good!

Joyce

About the Author

Joyce C. Gerrish, M.A. Is a highly experienced heart centered author, teacher, artist, musician, counselor, and energy therapist. For over thirty-five years she has been profoundly dedicated to supporting people in their personal and Spiritual growth. She believes that we are all magnificent; some of us simply need to be lovingly reminded of it. She feels that we all deserve to be encouraged in healing old self-doubts and moving on to ever more fully express the true miracle of who we are!

Joyce has always been an avid student of life in all its incredible beauty, challenges, and opportunities.

She is a graduate of the National Institute of Whole Health in Wellesley, Massachusetts, has a Master's Degree in Human Development from St. Mary's University in Winona, Minnesota, and has a Bachelor's Degree from the University of Louisville, Kentucky. She has certificates in numerous modalities such as Master Teacher of Reiki Energy Therapy, Polarity Therapy Energy Balancing, Nutritional Counseling, Guide for Higher Meditation, Public School Teacher Certificate, and more. For thirty years her writings have been published on topics of personal and Spiritual growth and natural wellness. Her teachings embrace the essence of all the major religions, and recognize the Divine as inherent in all Creation.

She teaches classes and workshops extensively. The soul songs that she composes she frequently shares with groups wherever she goes. She has recorded three collections of her soul songs. People find these songs, her voice, and her art uplifting and soothing. She felt strongly inspired to create this multi-media book on the wonderful topic of *Secrets Of Wisdom, Awakening to the Miracle of You*. It offers guidance and support for enhancing our lives physically, emotionally, and Spiritually. It helps us move into the next step of actualizing our dreams and life purpose. This book draws together in a powerful way the different aspects of Joyce's complex talents of inspired writing, soul songs, beautiful art, and peaceful uplifting guided meditations.

See SecretsofWisdom.net for the latest updated information about her services of counseling and energy therapy via telephone, classes and workshops, art, music, and much more.

Glossary

Akashic Records. The Divine Plan for everyone and everything is held in Heaven in what is called the Akashic Records, along with information on everything. It is like a Divine memory. This is Sacred information that is held in the subtle planes/levels of reality in a manner perhaps slightly similar to computer memory (except this has nothing to do with computers).

Asanas. Yoga consists of body postures called asanas which are exceedingly helpful for physical health, emotional peace, and Spiritual upliftment. These body positions are normally done slowly in a meditative manner, though some forms of yoga are performed vigorously.

Chakra energy centers. The chakra energy centers are located throughout the body. Seven major ones are located along the spine from the coccyx at the base of the spine up to the neck and on up to the top of the head. There are other energy centers located throughout the body such as in the palms of the hands and in the bottoms of the feet. When a person does Spiritual practices such as meditation, prayer, yoga, and chanting - - these energy centers tend to gradually activate and open like a flower and then higher energies can begin to be accessed more freely to enhance one's health, Spirituality, and general well-being. See the Chapter "Activating The Energies Of Your Aura."

Clairvoyance, Clairaudience, Clairsentience. People on all stages of the journey of illumination and Spiritual growth may experience clairvoyance (ability to "see" intuitively on the inner subtle levels), clairaudience (ability to "hear" intuitively on the inner levels), and clairsentience (the ability to sense very subtle energies intuitively). People may develop a profound gift of healing. They may have a gift of speech that can help lift and reassure those around them who walk the ups and downs on the path to God and on the path to ever more full Spiritual realization. Different people may have several of these gifts depending on the needs of their line of service to their fellow humanity.

Composting. Composting transforms vegetable table food scraps, tree leaves, yard and garden clippings and weeds, manure, other organic matter, and minerals such as lime into natural exceedingly rich soil for gardening. This transformation occurs over a period of months when these substances are mixed together in a pile or in a special container designed for composting. See Chapter "Abundance Through Living Lightly on the Land."

Divine Plan. The Divine Plan for everyone and everything is held in Heaven in what is called the Akashic Records, along with information on everything else. It is like Divine memory. Humans on Planet Earth have free will--which may complicate the unfolding of the Divine Plan. (See Akashic Records)

Enlightenment. Enlightenment involves actualizing within oneself the Divine Qualities. It entails activating and purifying one's energy field/aura and chakra energy centers. It involves steadfast service to God, one's fellowmen and women, and the planet. Finally, full Enlightenment occurs when the entire power of the kundalini energy reaches the crown chakra. This is all intended to be a slow, steady, gradual process of Spiritual endeavor.

Higher Self. This is a high level of an individual's consciousness. An individual's soul incarnates to the physical plane reality to learn to embody the Divine Qualities within a human personality. The Higher Self is that aspect of the consciousness that stays focused at Divine levels and is the individualized expression of Oneness with God. The wisdoms and key experiences of the soul are absorbed into the Higher Self of the individual.

Hologram. We are all familiar with flat hologram images that appear to be three dimensional. If one takes even a tiny fragment from a hologram picture, it still contains the whole image. Some scientists feel that every part of something contains information of the whole. Human genes are certainly an example of that. Interestingly enough, some scientists feel that our whole universe is a hologram.

Karma. Karma means that the fruits of our actions come back around to us. What we send out eventually returns to us in some form and often intensified.

Kirlian Photography. Scientists are now routinely photographing people's auras with Kirlian photography. Kirlian photography shows the colors and configurations of a person's aura at the time that the photograph is taken. A person's aura changes according to the person's mood, health, and state of consciousness.

Kundalini. The kundalini is a pathway of energy which lies along the spine. When a person's energy field is sufficiently developed, the kundalini energy begins to intensify and rise up the spine slowly and may eventually (with sufficient Spiritual practices and devotion) reach the crown chakra. It is important that this occur naturally and very gradually at its own pace. There are numerous stages of the kundalini rising. The subtle energy webs in the chakras need to be fully ready to ensure a comfortable safe assent of the kundalini energy. Full Enlightenment occurs when the entire power of the kundalini energy reaches the crown chakra--and the whole aura is illumined.

Mantra. A mantra is a repeated phrase or word included as a part of a meditation, as part of other devotional experiences, or during routine daily activities. A mantra can be recited silently or out loud. It can help keep the mind from wandering by giving the mind something on which to focus. Spiritual mantras can be very uplifting and can help bring in Spiritual blessings. A mantra can be as simple as the word "Peace" or can be a short prayer.

Planes of Consciousness means levels of consciousness. There are many planes of consciousness and planes of reality. With practice, devotion, and continuing Spiritual growth - - one can learn how to focus at higher planes (levels) of consciousness and reality at will. See Chapter "Truth Shining Bright."

Qi Gong (or Qigong) Qi Gong integrates physical postures, breathing techniques, and focused intention to improve health and support Spiritual growth. It originated in China.

Reincarnation. It is the belief that a human soul returns to Earth numerous times in order to grow Spiritually. It is believed that in each life the soul expresses itself as a different personality and looks different, but that it is the same soul and has some aspects of the self that are similar from life to life. Particularly, it is the higher consciousness that continues. (See Chapter "Truth Shining Bright")

Repressed Emotional Wounds. It is helpful for old repressed emotional wounds and stuck energy to gradually be allowed to rise to the surface of one's consciousness for healing. It's valuable to work through old traumas that may possibly surface, keep the wisdom learned from the experiences, let go of the pain, forgive oneself and others, give it all to God, and mobilize the strength to move on in life--stronger and wiser and freer.

Thought Forms. Strong emotions and habitual thoughts get "recorded" in the layers of a person's aura (consciousness) somewhat similar to a digital recording device. What is "recorded" can have an ongoing positive influence or limiting influence on a person in a manner similar to subliminal messages. These are often called thought forms. (See the definition for Repressed Emotional Wounds above.)

Vibrations. See chart "Energy Vibrations and Frequencies" in Chapter "Activating the Energies of Your Aura." Higher (more Spiritual) levels of consciousness and reality are at a higher vibration. Higher vibration correlates with shorter wave lengths of energy.

Yoga. See Asanas above.

Resources Page

Joyce Gerrish, M.A.

See SecretsofWisdom.net for information concerning arranging for or purchasing any of the following services and products.

1. Life Coach, Holistic Wellness Coach; Emotional Therapy/Counseling; Chakra and Aura Healing; Intuitive Readings (Relationships, Personal Growth, Spiritual Growth, Career, Past Life); and more. Available by telephone.
2. Classes and/or workshops.
3. Color Designs Reproductions, artist signed and colors approved, as shown on website. (E-book reading devices may distort the color of the designs or show them in shades of gray.) See the website for the most accurate renditions of the color designs. Additional color designs can be seen and are also available through the website.
4. One can listen to the soul songs and meditations that accompany this book at SecretsofWisdom. net for free. One can purchase a CD or mp3 download of these audios.

Editor / Webmaster

Editor for this book and Webmaster for accompanying website SecretsofWisdom.net.

Sybil Watts-Temple, sybil@yourwebmeister.com

Proof Reader

Judith Conley, missybell7@aol.com

1. THE MAGNIFICENT ADVENTURE BEGINS (no resource listing)

Most chapters in the book have some references to outside resources that you may be interested in learning more about. For your convenience in locating the references and the associated resources, I have listed each chapter with its associated resource references below.

2. LET JOY LIGHTEN YOUR DAY, Enhancing Divine Joy in Your Life
◆ Kesha M. Shahid, kshahid118@gmail.com
◆ Elsa Lichman, elsalichman@comcast.net, www.wickedlocalwaltham.com 'Nature in the City.'

3. LOVE NOURISHES AND HEALS. Enhancing Divine Love in Your Life
◆ Kenny Marine, www.Reverbnation.com/KennyMarine

4. HEALING YOUR HEART WITH FORGIVENESS. Enhancing Divine Forgiveness in Your Life (no resource listing)

5. TRUE CLARITY SUPPORTS BRILLIANCE, Enhancing Divine Clarity in Your Life

◆ Ashley Barnes, Sellersburg, Indiana. http://spiritledblog.wordpress.com

6. FOLLOWING YOUR HEART AND SOUL. Enhancing Divine Purpose in Your Life.

◆ Lisa Essenpreis, www.magiclanternstage.com.
◆ Dr. Renee Campbell, drcwesleyh@gmail.com
◆ Ashley Barnes, Sellersburg, Indiana, http://spiritledblog.wordpress.com
◆ Paul Graber, www.newpathfoundation.org
◆ Kimberly D. Withrow, kdowns3418@yahoo.com

7. CHOOSING PEACE GLORIOUS PEACE. Enhancing Divine Peace in Your Life

◆ Ann Hemdahl Owen, www.hypnotherapyempoweringyou.com
◆ Oxfam America, www.OxfamAmerica.org
◆ Emotional Freedom Technique, www.EMOFREE.com, Garry Craig
◆ Emotional Freedom Technique, EFT master. YouTube, www.BradYates.com

8. WE CAN ALL BE POWERFUL TOGETHER, Enhancing Divine Power In Your Life

◆ Darrel Joy: See resources listed under "The Blessings of Harmony" chapter
◆ Paul Graber, www.newpathfoundation.org

9. DEVOTED HEARTS ALIVE WITH PASSION, Enhancing Divine Devotion in Your Life

◆ Rev. Valerie Mansfield, Louisville, Kentucky, www.valeriemansfield.com
◆ Laura Spaulding, www.yogaeast.org

10. ACTIVATING YOUR AURA ENERGIES, Enhancing Divine Illumination in Your Life (No resource listings)

11. WALKING THE PATH OF WELLNESS, Enhancing Divine Healing in Your Life

◆ Dr. Lynda J. Wells, PhD, Licensed Nutritionist, Nationally Certified Nutrition Specialist, www.DrLyndaWells.com
◆ Hidden Food Allergies: www.toquietinflammation.com

12. LET WISDOM GUIDE YOUR LIFE, Enhancing Divine Wisdom in Your Life

- ◆ Rev. Alta Burnett, Ph.D., Louisville, Kentucky. www.beadsononestring.org
- ◆ Emotional Freedom Technique: See listing under "Choosing Peace Glorious Peace"
- ◆ The Wisdom of Bill Moyers, BillMoyers.com

13. THE BLESSINGS OF HARMONY, Enhancing Divine Harmony in Your Life

- ◆ Darrel Joy's suggested resources for harmony with nature:
- ◆ Tom Brown Jr.'s Tracker School http://www.trackerschool.com/
  - ○ Also read his books such as: The Tracker, Grandfather, The Search, The Vision, Guide to Wilderness Survival, and many more.
- ◆ Jon Young's Wilderness Awareness School (W.A.S.) http://store.wildernessawareness.org/
- ◆ Center for Biological Diversity http://www.biologicaldiversity.org/support/join/
- ◆ Organic Consumers Association (keep GMOs out of our food) http://www.organicconsumers.org/bytes/ob370.htm
- ◆ Defenders of Wildlife http://www.defenders.org/take-action/actions
- ◆ Sierra Club http://www.sierraclub.org/
- ◆ Greenpeace, www.greenpeace.org

14. THE FREEDOM TO EXPLORE OUR MAGNIFICENCE, Enhancing Divine Freedom in Your Life

- ◆ G.B, www.christintraining.com
- ◆ Ann, www.hypnotherapyempoweringyou.com

15. THE ADVENTURE OF TRANSFORMATION, Enhancing Transformation In Your Life

- ◆ Ashley Barnes, Sellersburg, Indiana. http://spiritledblog.wordpress.com

16. THE MIRACLE OF DIVINE GRACE, Enhancing Divine Grace in Your Life

- ◆ Elsa Lichman, elsalichman@comcast.net, www.wickedlocalwaltham.com 'Nature in the City.'
- ◆ Rev. Valerie Mansfield, Louisville, Kentucky, www.valeriemansfield.com

17. ABUNDANCE THROUGH LIVING LIGHTLY ON THE LAND, Enhancing Divine Abundance in Your Life

- ◆ www.timebanks.org
- ◆ Ann Hemdahl Owen, www.hypnotherapyempoweringyou.com

18. TRUTH SHINING BRIGHT, Enhancing Divine Truth In Your Life

- ◆ Dee Patterson, www.deepatterson.com

FROM ENDORSEMENTS PAGE

◆ Henry Lepler, Musician and Healing Sound Guide www.henrylepler.com

ARTICLES BY JOYCE

There are several articles that are referred to in book. These are listed below and can be accessed on the website in the Articles section. Much other valuable information and resources are also available on the website: SecretsofWisdom.net

"We Can Heal Childhood Wounds From Abuse"

"Reiki Therapy Training Description"

"Deeper Understanding of the 'Nutrition Facts' Label on Packaged Foods"

"Reincarnation Supplement"

"Dream Exploration, Understanding Dreams"

"Can We Lower the Cost of Higher Education?"